The Age of Dualization

International Policy Exchange Series

Published in collaboration with the
Center for International Policy Exchanges
University of Maryland

Series Editors

Douglas J. Besharov
Neil Gilbert

United in Diversity?
Comparing Social Models in Europe and America
Edited by Jens Alber and Neil Gilbert

The Korean State:
How South Korea Lifted Itself from Poverty and
Dictatorship to Affluence and Democracy
Stein Ringen, Huck-ju Kwon, Ilcheong Yi, Taekyoon Kim, and Jooha Lee

Child Protection Systems:
International Trends and Orientations
Edited by Neil Gilbert, Nigel Parton, and Marit Skivenes

The Age of Dualization:
The Changing Face of Inequality in Deindustrializing Societies
Edited by Patrick Emmenegger, Silja Häusermann, Bruno Palier,
and Martin Seeleib-Kaiser

 SCHOOL of
PUBLIC POLICY

The Age of Dualization

*The Changing Face of Inequality
in Deindustrializing Societies*

Edited by

PATRICK EMMENEGGER

SILJA HÄUSERMANN

BRUNO PALIER

MARTIN SEELEIB-KAISER

OXFORD
UNIVERSITY PRESS

OXFORD
UNIVERSITY PRESS

Oxford University Press, Inc., publishes works that further
Oxford University's objective of excellence
in research, scholarship, and education.

Oxford New York
Auckland Cape Town Dar es Salaam Hong Kong Karachi
Kuala Lumpur Madrid Melbourne Mexico City Nairobi
New Delhi Shanghai Taipei Toronto

With offices in
Argentina Austria Brazil Chile Czech Republic France Greece
Guatemala Hungary Italy Japan Poland Portugal Singapore
South Korea Switzerland Thailand Turkey Ukraine Vietnam

Published by Oxford University Press, Inc.
198 Madison Avenue, New York, New York 10016
www.oup.com

Library of Congress Cataloging-in-Publication Data

Library of Congress Cataloging-in-Publication Data
The age of dualization : the changing face of inequality in deindustrializing societies / edited by
Patrick Emmenegger ... [et al.].
   p. cm. — (International policy exchange series)
Includes bibliographical references and index.
ISBN 978-0-19-979789-9 (hardcover : alk. paper)
1. Social stratification.   2. Equality.   3. Labor market.   4. Deindustrialization.
I. Emmenegger, Patrick.
HM821.A346 2012
306.3'6—dc23
2011036988

9 8 7 6 5 4 3

Printed in the United States of America
on acid-free paper

CONTENTS

PART I   CONCEPTS AND MEASUREMENT

LIST OF FIGURES

LIST OF TABLES

CONTRIBUTORS

ROMANA CAREJA
Institute for Sociological Research
University of Cologne
Cologne, Germany

DANIEL CLEGG
School of Social and Political
    Science
University of Edinburgh
Edinburgh, United Kingdom

WERNER EICHHORST
Institute for the Study of Labor
Bonn, Germany

PATRICK EMMENEGGER
Center for Welfare State Research
University of Southern Denmark
Odense, Denmark

KARIN GOTTSCHALL
Center for Social Policy Research
University of Bremen
Bremen, Germany

SILJA HÄUSERMANN
Department of Politics and Public
    Administration
University of Konstanz
Konstanz, Germany

ALEXANDRA KAASCH
Center for Social Policy Research
University of Bremen
Bremen, Germany

DANIELA KROOS
GIB Gesellschaft für
Innovationsforschung
und Beratung
Berlin, Germany

JOHANNES LINDVALL
Department of Political Science
Lund University
Lund, Sweden

PAUL MARX
Institute for the Study of Labor
Bonn, Germany

MAREK NACZYK
Department of Politics and
    International Relations
University of Oxford
Oxford, United Kingdom

HERBERT OBINGER
Center for Social Policy Research
University of Bremen
Bremen, Germany

BRUNO PALIER
Centre d'études européennes
Sciences Po
Paris, France

ITO PENG
School of Public Policy & Governance
University of Toronto
Toronto, Canada

DAVID RUEDA
Department of Politics and
    International Relations
University of Oxford
Oxford, United Kingdom

ADAM SAUNDERS
Oxford Institute of Social Policy
University of Oxford
Oxford, United Kingdom

HANNA SCHWANDER
Political Science Department
University of Zurich
Zurich, Switzerland

MARTIN SEELEIB-KAISER
Oxford Institute of Social Policy
University of Oxford
Oxford, United Kingdom

PETER STARKE
Center for Social Policy Research
University of Bremen
Bremen, Germany

KATHLEEN THELEN
Department of Political Science
Massachusetts Institute of
    Technology
Cambridge, Massachusetts

MARK TOMLINSON
Oxford Institute of Social Policy
University of Oxford
Oxford, United Kingdom

ROBERT WALKER
Oxford Institute of Social Policy
University of Oxford
Oxford, United Kingdom

ACKNOWLEDGMENTS

This book is the product of years of collaborative work. First drafts of the chapters were intensively discussed in 2009 and 2010 at two workshops held at Green Templeton College, Oxford; presentations at international conferences and a number of meetings during the various integration weeks of the EU-sponsored network of excellence *Reconciling Work and Welfare* (RECWOWE) also proved very helpful in refining the conceptual framework, sharpening the analytical approaches and presenting the evidence. The editors are very grateful to the contributors for their original contributions and many revisions. Many more colleagues contributed to improving our work through their comments and suggestions at workshops, conferences, and meetings. To list them all would fill a number of pages. Hence, we refrain from listing them individually and thank them collectively. Furthermore, we thank the anonymous reviewers of the manuscript for their very helpful comments and suggestions, as well as Maura Roesner and Nicholas Liu from OUP, New York for their support. Last but not least, we greatly appreciate the financial and institutional support we received from the EU, the Friedrich Ebert Foundation (London Office), Green Templeton College, the John Fell OUP Research Fund, and the Oxford-Sciences Po Research Group. Without their support this project would not have been feasible.

Patrick Emmenegger, *Odense*
Silja Häusermann, *Konstanz*
Bruno Palier, *Paris*
Martin Seeleib-Kaiser, *Oxford*

This book has been published with the support of the European research project RECWOWE (Reconciling Work and Welfare in Europe), 2006–2011, co-funded by the European Commission, under the Sixth Framework Programme for Research—Socio-economic Sciences and Humanities (contract no. 028339-2) in the Directorate-General for Research.

The information and views set out in this book are those of the authors and do not necessarily reflect the official opinion of the European Union. Neither the European Union institutions and bodies nor any person acting on their behalf may be held responsible for the use which may be made of the information contained therein.

PART I

CONCEPTS AND MEASUREMENT

1

HOW WE GROW UNEQUAL

PATRICK EMMENEGGER, SILJA HÄUSERMANN, BRUNO PALIER, AND MARTIN SEELEIB-KAISER

Poverty, inequality, and social exclusion are back on the political agenda in many affluent democracies of Western Europe and North America, not only as a consequence of the Great Recession that has hit the global economy in 2008, but also as a consequence of a seemingly "secular" trend toward increased inequality, which began some time ago. In 2008, the Organisation for Economic Co-operation and Development (OECD) published a comprehensive report demonstrating that inequality has risen within this club of rich democracies since the mid-1970s (see Figures 1-1 and 1-2). At the launch event of the report, OECD Secretary-General Angel Gurría warned of the dangers posed by inequality and the need for governments to tackle it. He stated: "Growing inequality is divisive. It polarizes societies, it divides regions within countries, and it carves up the world between rich and poor. Greater income inequality stifles upward mobility between generations, making it harder for talented and hard-working people to get the rewards they deserve. Ignoring increasing inequality is not an option."[1]

Figures 1-1 and 1-2 document the increase in inequality. Figure 1-1 displays the trends in market and disposable income equality over the period from the mid-1980s to the mid-2000s for 15 OECD countries; Figure 1-2 shows the shares of pre-tax income of the richest 1 percent of the population over the period 1920 to 2004 for 13 OECD countries. Both figures document the increase in inequality in recent decades. In addition, Figure 1-2 shows that inequality reached the lowest value in the late 1970s and has increased since then.[2]

How can we explain this increase in inequality? Is it the result of structural change or, alternatively, have politics, as well as social and labor market policies, contributed to shaping the forms and extent of the new inequalities that challenge our societies? The OECD report itself highlights the fact that, although labor market developments have been a key driver, social policies have become less effective in reducing inequality and poverty during the past decade (OECD 2008).

Figure 1-1: Trends in market and disposable income inequality (Gini coefficients, mid-1980s = 1.0)

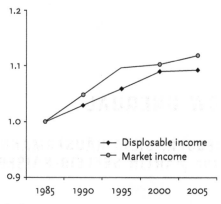

Source: OECD (2008: 34).

LABOR MARKET INEQUALITIES AND CHANGED LABOR MARKETS

The first and most visible labor market trend during the past decades was an increase in unemployment, and especially long-term unemployment, across the OECD. In many countries, there have been stepwise increases in unemployment rates during the past three decades. If unemployment were only of very short duration, one might argue that the exclusionary effect might not necessarily be troubling, as workers would (re-)enter the labor market after a brief period of time. In many countries of Continental Europe, unemployment has, however, become long-term (12 months or more) or even persistent for a substantial percentage of the unemployed. In most countries, the non-employment rate of people with low educational attainment is above 50 percent. In Belgium, Germany, and the United Kingdom, more than 15 percent of the population in households with a head of working age live in jobless households (OECD 2008: 88). While long-term unemployment affected 15 percent of the unemployed in 1975, the percentage of the long-term unemployed stood at above 40 percent every year from 1982 until 2007, only declining in the wake of the 2008 economic crisis, in the EU-15 countries (OECD Employment Database).[3] Even though labor market divides were not fully abolished during the *Trente Glorieuses* of welfare capitalism, the increase in long-term unemployment has created a deeper divide between those having a job and those persistently lacking one.

This development is, however, not uniform across rich OECD countries. In contrast to much of Continental Europe, we find low levels of long-term unemployment in Scandinavian countries and in the United States. Although not

Figure 1-2: Shares of pre-tax income of the richest 1 percent of population

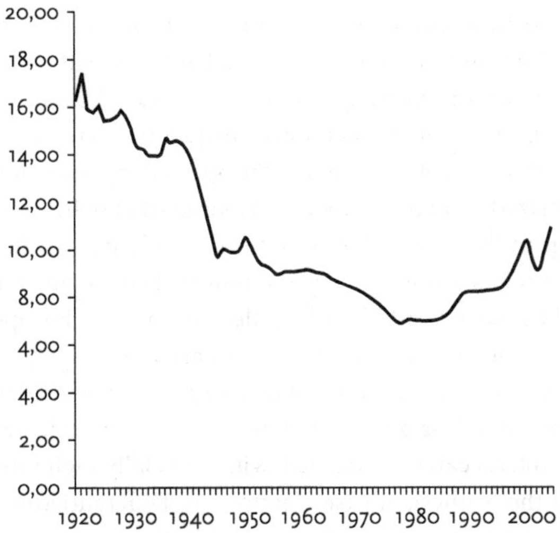

Sources: OECD (2008: 32) and Leigh (2007).

at the comparatively low levels of Scandinavia or the United States, long-term unemployment in the United Kingdom has also been below the EU-15 average since 1985. While it can be argued that the low levels of long-term unemployment in Scandinavia are at least partially the result of a strong commitment to active labor market policies, the relatively low levels of long-term unemployment in the United Kingdom and the United States seem not only to reflect the flexibility of the British and American labor markets, but also the very limited support for unemployed workers. However, long-term unemployment is only one indicator that may be used to measure the persistency of social exclusion. Taking income poverty as an indicator for exclusion, it tends to be most persistent in those countries with widespread poverty, such as the United States, while income mobility tends to be higher in countries with low poverty rates, such as Denmark (OECD 2008).

Labor markets in OECD countries have undergone significant transformations since the 1970s. Initially thought to be a development limited to the United States and the United Kingdom, wage inequality has also risen significantly in many Western European countries, as well as Korea and Japan; France and Belgium have for the most part resisted the trend. Although wage dispersion has increased in Scandinavia as well, it tends to be significantly lower than in the other OECD countries. Increasing wage inequality is largely said to be the result of the high-paid doing particularly well, not only relative to low earners, but also compared to middle earners. Nevertheless, in many countries the incidence of low pay has increased significantly, as well, not only in the United Kingdom and the United States, but also especially in Denmark and Germany, where it has historically been much lower (OECD 2010: 295). For some observers, the increasing levels of inequality in the United Kingdom and the United States might not seem surprising, given their market-liberal tradition. What seems surprising, however, is that wage inequalities have also increased in social market economies of Continental Europe and Japan during the 1990s—a period characterized by many changes in labor market policies.

A key change in this respect has been the deregulation and flexibilization of employment contracts. Consequently, the standard employment relationship, a core element of the post–World War II settlement in many European countries, seems on the retreat through the increase of atypical employment contracts, such as fixed-term contracts and (involuntary) part-time employment (cf. King and Rueda 2008; Standing 2009). Despite the overall trend, stark differences between the countries can be discerned, with especially high rates of part-time employment in the Netherlands (see Figure 1-3). Differentiating the incidence of part-time employment among socioeconomic groups, one has to emphasize the high levels of part-time employment among women, especially in some Conservative and Liberal welfare states (see Figure 1-3). In countries relying on the principle of earnings-related social insurance, part-time employment over a long period of time can have a substantial impact on the level of social protection.

Figure 1-3:   Part-time employment in 2009

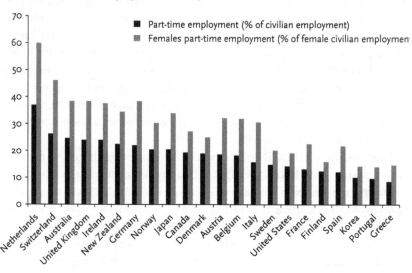

Source: OECD Employment Database. URL: http://www.oecd.org/document/34/0,3343,en_2649_33927_4 0917154_1_1_1,00.html (accessed December 14, 2010).

Next to women, young people are particularly affected by non-standard employment, as is demonstrated in the data for youth unemployment and the incidence of temporary employment (see Figure 1-4). Youth unemployment is high in a number of countries belonging to different welfare regimes, such as Britain, France, and Sweden. Temporary employment has also been on the increase, but again it is especially high among young people. To what extent this constitutes a social problem among the young largely depends on the institutional circumstances of the specific countries, as apprenticeships and training measures are also included in measuring the incidence of temporary employment.

THE DEMISE OF THE REDISTRIBUTIVE CAPACITIES OF SOCIAL POLICIES?

New inequalities, however, are not just a result of structural labor market changes, but they may also be a result of social policy developments. As social inequalities and poverty have increased, a key question must be addressed: To what extent has this trend been the result of policy changes? Indeed, social policy can either smoothen or amplify the divides resulting from labor market inequalities. Historically, market income inequalities and poverty have

Figure 1-4: Temporary employment and unemployment among young labor market participants in 2009 (15–24)

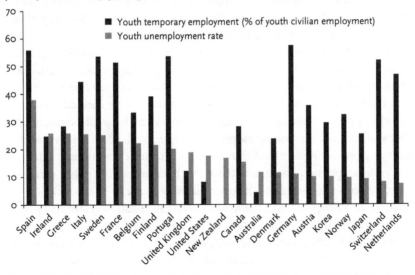

Source: OECD (2010) OECD Employment Outlook 2010. Paris: OECD, Tab. F. and OECD Employment Database. URL: http://www.oecd.org/document/34/0,3343,en_2649_33927_40917154_1_1_1_1,00.html (accessed December 14, 2010). No data on temporary employment for New Zealand. Data on temporary employment for Australia and the USA from 2006.

been moderated by redistributive social policies. Contrary to arguments about "frozen welfare state landscapes" (Esping-Andersen 1996: 24) and the stability bias of path dependence (Pierson 2001), social policies have indeed been extensively reformed in many countries and may have subsequently lost some of their redistributive capacities (Gilbert 2002): a trend toward means-testing, activation, and "privatization" of old-age security can be discerned in many countries. According to an analysis of social assistance programs in a relatively large number of OECD countries, the proportion of social assistance recipients among the population increased in many countries during the 1980s and early 1990s (Eardley et al. 1996). Yet, in most countries, social assistance benefit levels are insufficient to lift households close to or above the poverty threshold, as pointed out by Saraceno (2010).

Though in a number of countries the increase of the social assistance recipiency rate was the consequence of an increase in long-term unemployment and the subsequent *implicit disentitlement* of unemployed workers within earnings-related unemployment insurance, in a number of countries *explicit changes* in unemployment insurance programs have contributed to this development (Seeleib-Kaiser 1995). For instance, Britain has significantly cut the level of replacement rates and benefit duration, and France has extended the qualification period, making it harder for atypical workers to qualify (Scruggs 2004), while at the same time there have been processes toward activation in these countries. However, a job does not always protect from poverty; within the European Union (EU), 8 percent of workers live in households below the poverty threshold (Saraceno 2010). These reform trends are very likely to have contributed to the overall increase in inequality. Nevertheless, differences in social policy designs may partly explain differences in the extent to which inequalities and divides have expanded during the past decades.

While pension reforms across the OECD have not necessarily negatively impacted current pensioners, in many countries old age pension systems have witnessed important reforms that may contribute to an increase in inequality in future years. More specifically, many countries have enacted significant cutbacks in public pensions for future pensioners and have introduced multipillar systems in recent years (Bridgen and Meyer 2008). Furthermore, pension qualifying periods were extended in countries that have traditionally relied on a Beveridgean pension system and those that have introduced public earnings-related systems relatively late. The overwhelming majority of advanced OECD countries at the beginning of the new millennium require a qualifying period of 40 to 45 years, making it more difficult for workers with interrupted careers to qualify for a full state pension. Regarding benefits for current pensioners, the picture is quite mixed, and no clear trend can be discerned. For instance, the standard pension has declined since the 1990s in countries such as Belgium, France, Germany, Ireland, Japan, and Sweden, whereas in Austria and Italy the standard pension has almost continuously risen and was more or less at its highest level in the early 2000s. In Australia, Denmark, Finland, New Zealand, and the United States, there has been a decline in the level of the minimum pension, whereas pension minima have been bolstered in other countries such as Germany, the Netherlands, and Switzerland (Scruggs 2004; Häusermann 2010a).

DUALIZATION AS A POLITICAL PROCESS

How can we understand and explain these developments toward greater inequality? The literature has identified a number of structural drivers that have contributed to increased pressure on advanced democracies, most prominently among them deindustrialization and globalization. Deindustrialization has led to a significant decline of relatively well-paid jobs in manufacturing, even in those countries that still heavily rely on the manufacturing sector to generate wealth, such as Germany and the Scandinavian countries. Today, employment in the service sector outnumbers jobs in industry in all OECD countries. As Martin and Thelen (2007: 5) have argued: "In a context in which employment in manufacturing is declining, a competitive export sector (even with wage restraint) is no longer even remotely sufficient to generate the jobs needed to sustain full employment." Initially, deindustrialization has led to an expansion of welfare provision through early retirement schemes or similar schemes in many countries, especially in (Continental) Europe (Iversen and Cusack 2000; Ebbinghaus 2006). At the same time, there has been job growth in the service sector, which is traditionally less regulated and unionized. Combined with low levels of productivity growth in the service sector and an increasing return on skill investments, this trend is said to have accentuated wage pressure on low-skill employment (Iversen and Wren 1998; Baumol 1967). Moreover, it has been argued that there is a skill bifurcation between high and low general skills (Fleckenstein et al. 2011).

Closely associated with the process of deindustrialization is the feminization of employment. In recent years, women have increasingly entered the labor market. Female employment rates approach or even match male employment rates in many countries, especially in the English-speaking countries and Scandinavia (Oesch 2006). However, the feminization of the labor force has led to new challenges. Women suffer from discontinuous employment careers, because women are more likely to interrupt their working life in order to tend to family needs (Estevez-Abe 2005). Women work predominantly in the service sector and often in non-standard employment relationships (Oesch 2006). In parallel, the massive entry of women into paid labor has been accompanied by a destabilization of traditional family structures (Esping-Andersen 1999).

Globalization is identified in the literature as a further structural force, restricting the autonomy of the nation state (cf. Held et al. 1999). Competition from low-wage countries has intensified the pressure to constantly increase productivity and shed low-skilled jobs in the manufacturing sector within the advanced economies of the North (cf. Wood 1994). The inflow of low-skilled migrants with weak labor market attachment has placed further pressure on labor markets. The internationalization of capital markets is said to have reduced governments' autonomy to tax capital (Scharpf 1991; cf. Genschel 2002). Although much has been written on globalization and its effects on nation states, the causal relationship still seems to be inconclusive; moreover, domestic variables continue to be more important (Brady et al. 2005; Swank 2010).

In other words, structural pressures do not directly translate into policy change, as past policies, institutions, and politics are mediating factors in translating structural pressures into policy change. Governments have to decide how to react to structural pressures. Liberalization might be considered as one obvious political strategy for governments to pursue, especially if one takes into account the dominance of economic liberalism during the past decades. Liberalization is generally understood as a strategy of pushing back the state in the domains of economic and labor market regulation as well as in social policy. Furthermore, it is often associated with privatization. In the context of the changes witnessed in the German political economy, Streeck (2009) has argued that a political strategy of *liberalization* has been pursued. As a consequence more or less *all* economic actors are exposed to greater market risks.

We hypothesize, however, that we have been witnessing processes of *dualization*. Dualization implies that policies increasingly differentiate rights, entitlements, and services provided to different categories of recipients. Thereby, the position of insiders may remain more or less constant, while only the position of outsiders deteriorates. Alternatively, policies may lead to the creation of new categories of outsiders that were previously treated according to the same rules as insiders. Thus, dualization is a process that is characterized by the differential treatment of insiders and outsiders and that can take the form of newly created institutional dualisms or the deepening of existing institutional dualisms (*policy output*). At the *outcome* level, the process of dualization is very likely to lead to greater social divides, but this is not necessarily the case, as we can witness dualization at the policy output level without increasing divides at the individual outcome level, if, for instance, outsider policies are relatively generous. Hence, conceptually we differentiate between process (dualization), output (institutional dualism), and outcome (divide).[4]

Dualization can take three different forms: a deepening of existing institutional dualisms, that is, the differential treatment of insiders and outsiders becomes significantly more pronounced; a widening of existing institutional dualisms, that is, groups that have been previously treated like insiders are increasingly treated like outsiders; or, finally, it may be the product of new institutional dualisms, which we did not witness during the postwar era of economic growth. Even though dualization is first and foremost the result of political intervention, dualization is also possible in the absence of political intervention. If political actors *deliberately* refrain from adapting an institution in the face of external pressure—a process that Hacker (2002) refers to as "drift"—and accept the resulting widening, deepening, or the creation of institutional dualisms, then dualization can be the result of non-intervention. Finally, outsiderness in one societal realm is likely, but not necessarily, to trigger outsiderness in other areas because of feedback effects and vicious circles, thereby amplifying existing divides between insiders and outsiders. Figure 1-5 displays our conceptual framework graphically.

What distinguishes dualization from other concepts, such as polarization, segmentation, and marginalization? Most importantly, these other concepts largely focus on the *outcome* level and do not necessarily address the *politics* of change. For example, the concept of polarization is generally used in the literature to describe a pattern of employment growth that is characterized by the simultaneous creation of high-paid professional and managerial jobs and of low-paid personal service jobs, while no mid-skilled manual and clerical jobs are created (Wright and Dwyer 2003; Goos and Manning 2007; Autor et al. 2008). Segmentation refers to the division of labor markets into subgroups with very little mobility between these subgroups (Stinchcombe 1979; Berger and Piore 1980). Finally, marginalization describes the process of individuals being

Figure 1-5: Conceptual framework

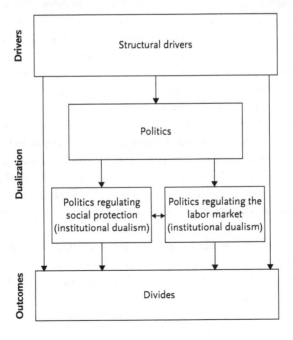

relegated to the margins of society (Mullaly 2006). Thus, all these concepts focus on the level of individuals. Political processes play a secondary role.

In contrast, dualization stresses political change and the politics of change. Dualization describes the widening, deepening, or creation of new institutional dualisms (*output*). Whether political change leads to new inequalities (*outcome*) is an empirical question, which has to be addressed separately. In general, we expect dualization processes to lead to greater divides (i.e., dualization may lead to the marginalization of outsiders or may lead to a polarization between insiders and outsiders), but we acknowledge that dualization without increasing divides is possible if outsider policies are generous. Thus, like concepts such as liberalization and privatization, dualization is located at the output level and not at the outcome level.

Our argument draws on four strands of literature: dual labor market theory; the insider-outsider theory of employment and unemployment; critical welfare state analyses; and the literature on welfare regimes and varieties of capitalism. The notion of dualism was initially developed in micro-sociological analyses investigating firms' behavior and labor market developments (Doeringer and Piore 1971; Stinchcombe 1979; Berger and Piore 1980). The work on *dual labor market theory* emphasized the distinction between primary and secondary labor markets. In this approach, the primary labor market is characterized by good working conditions, high wages, secure jobs, and promotion prospects, while jobs in the secondary labor market are poorly paid, unstable, and characterized by bad working conditions. According to Piore (1980: 24), dualism within the labor market arises when portions of the labor force tend to be insulated from uncertainty and variability in demand (primary labor market), while others have to weather the fluctuations in demand (secondary labor market) (for further analysis of this strand of literature, see Davidsson and Naczyk 2009; Tomlinson and Walker in Chapter 3 of this volume).

The allocation of workers in the primary and secondary labor market is not random, but rather a function of their economic, political, and social resources. Groups such as the young, women, or immigrants are more likely to find themselves in the secondary labor market. Research has shown that the inferior status of some labor market participants is persistent. Once trapped in the secondary labor market, chances of advancement to the primary labor market are slim, as social mobility between labor market segments is low (Stinchcombe 1979; Piore 1980). Thus, these inequalities might not simply vanish, once the economy starts to recover. Rather, they may have become institutionalized, as hypothesized by Palier and Thelen (2010).

Whether the inferior status of some labor market participants is longstanding, however, has long been an open question (Sengenberger 1981). Earlier research on poverty dynamics has demonstrated empirically that the overwhelming majority of the poor experience poverty only for time-limited periods. Esping-Andersen (1993b: 239) in research on the evolution of a "service proletariat" and an "outsider surplus population" concludes that "most of our new collective servants are not, as in the past, condemned to life-time servitude. Hence, the pessimists are wrong when they see a future of mass proletarization." Since much of this research, however, was conducted based on data from the 1980s, that is, prior to the recent rise of inequality, it is an empirical question whether outsiderness continues to be a transitory phase in the life courses of individuals, whether it affects them permanently, or whether we actually find different types of outsiderness in contemporary societies.

There is reason to believe that persistent labor market divides are more likely today because of secular trends such as deindustrialization, globalization, and the feminization of labor markets. Since the 1970s, we are witnessing steep decreases in the level of employment in manufacturing (Kollmeyer 2009), while new employment tends to be created in the service sector. However, as argued by Iversen and Wren (1998), based on Baumol's (1967) famous cost-disease problem, wage inequality is a necessary condition for the expansion of *private* service sector employment, as productivity increases are more difficult to achieve in the service sector compared to manufacturing. In parallel, the massive entry of women into the labor market has created a pool of workers who predominantly work in the service sector and whose working life suffers from more career interruptions (Estevez-Abe 2005). Thus we assume that the likelihood of labor market divides, especially gendered ones, is much higher in the twenty-first century than some thirty years ago.

Labor market economists further developed this approach, emphasizing the micro-level and highlighting the rationale of firms, employers, and unions. The work on *insider-outsider politics* and strategic bargaining emphasized differences between the employed and the unemployed (Blanchard and Summers 1986; Lindbeck and Snower 1988; Saint-Paul 1996, 2002). Most importantly, these authors stressed that labor market insiders face incentives to seek higher wages at the cost of jobs for outsiders. The notion of dualism has also gained prominence in the literature on industrial relations and the future of corporatism (Goldthorpe 1984). Most of this literature has been devoted to identifying insiders and outsiders and analyzing the logic of their behavior. One of the major conclusions of this literature is that insiders and outsiders have partly conflicting interests and that there is potential for cross-class coalitions between labor market insiders and employers.

Recent work by political economists and political scientists has once again focused on insider-outsider politics from a more macro-political perspective, in an attempt to understand the mechanisms and processes leading to the creation of outsiders, understood more broadly as both the unemployed and workers in non-standard employment relationships (cf. Rueda 2005; Seeleib-Kaiser et al. 2008; Emmenegger 2009). The focus of this research goes beyond the mere labor market to also include the analysis of party politics, elections, and various policies (including labor market and welfare state reforms). Rueda

(2005) highlights the electoral dilemmas faced by social democratic parties that simultaneously need to cater to the interests of insiders (maintaining the status quo) and reform labor markets in order to facilitate the integration of outsiders. Similarly, but for the realm of pension reform, Häusermann (2010a, 2010b) shows that social democratic parties in Continental Europe are torn between the interests of insiders and outsiders in terms of pension retrenchment and redistributive outsider protection. This line of research has also highlighted the role of labor market institutions—such as employment protection (Rueda 2005; Emmenegger 2009) and different labor market policies (Rueda 2006)—that have contributed to the *persistence* of labor market divides or to the creation of *new* divides. For instance, by deregulating non-standard contracts, governments have contributed to an increasing bifurcation between standard and non-standard employment.

Beyond the field of labor market theory, *critical welfare state analyses* have focused on the concept of a "dual welfare system" (Tussing 1975) in the United States for some time. According to this line of research, different social protection policies are geared to the poor and the non-poor (cf. Weir et al. 1988). Very much in line with this argument, Leibfried and Tennstedt (1985) have argued that historically, the German welfare state has systematically differentiated between *Armenpolitik* (policy for the poor) and *Arbeiterpolitik* (policy for workers). More recently, the work by Hacker (2002) has emphasized the divided nature of the American welfare state. In the meantime, analyses of the development of the welfare state in Europe (Flora and Heidenheimer 1981, Flora 1986–1993) have shown that during their golden age, welfare systems were aimed at harmonizing and unifying social protection, either through a unique encompassing model (Scandinavia cf. Korpi and Palme 1998), or through (the multiplication of similar) social insurance schemes (Bleses and Seeleib-Kaiser 2004; Palier 2010). Thus, what seems to be new is the return to and expansion of dual social policies that treat different groups of citizens in different and uneven ways.

Finally, we draw on the literature on *welfare regimes* (Esping-Andersen 1990) and *varieties of capitalism* (Hall and Soskice 2001). Earlier research has tended to focus on single dimensions of outsiderness only, thus not addressing the interconnectedness and interrelationships of labor market participation, social protection, and political participation. More recent research aims at analyzing the links between these different domains and at introducing a multidimensional approach. Rueda (2005) has shown the connections between divisive labor market policies and political representation. Palier and Thelen (2010) hypothesize that, based on the institutional complementarities argument of the varieties of capitalism literature, there is some connection between processes of dualization on the labor market and within social protection. But the precise links between lacking integration in the labor market, insufficient social rights, and the political articulation of the insider-outsider divide have yet to be explored. Since it is clear that the individual labor market situation matters for social rights (e.g., eligibility as a function of contribution periods), while social policies influence labor market interactions (e.g., the social wage), one should further analyze these interactions and their effect on labor market, social, and political divisions.

Moreover, we take from this literature its focus on how policies and institutions mediate the effect of structural drivers on national policies. Approaches by many sociologists or economists have often ignored the crucial role of institutions. As argued by Esping-Andersen (1993a: 8), these approaches are "nested in an institutionally 'naked' world, an Adam Smithian world of unfettered markets." Thus, rather than expecting convergence as a result of common challenges, institutions are likely to shape the direction of change. For instance, the high social wage in Continental and Northern Europe is said to price low-skill service sector jobs out of the market, if these jobs are not publicly subsidized. Similarly, welfare state institutions that help reconcile work and family life, such as free and encompassing child care, allow women to participate in the labor market on more equal terms with men.

With reference to such institutional effects, the existing literature in political economy has hypothesized the likelihood of diverse policy responses. Following Iversen and Wren (1998), three possible labor market and social policy strategies can be distinguished in the advent of deindustrialization and Baumol's (1967) cost disease problem. If market forces are left to their own, low-skill service employment are likely to expand, as well as inequalities, due to the fact that low wages correspond to the low levels of productivity of these jobs. Alternatively, a high and rigid social wage may price these jobs out of the market and lead to high levels of unemployment and low levels of employment, but avoids too much increase in inequalities. Finally, governments may step in and subsidize low-skill service sector jobs, primarily in the public sector, which leads to high levels of employment and a relatively high level of equality, but also high levels of taxation. The important point is that, rather than convergence as a function of common challenges, diverse reactions with unequal distributional consequences can be expected.

According to Esping-Andersen et al. (1993: 36), social divides are likely to be more prominent in Liberal and Continental welfare regimes than in the Nordic countries. In the former case, the residual nature of the welfare state and decentralized industrial relations should facilitate the development of a large low-wage service sector segment. In the absence of comprehensive employment and training systems, these workers are likely to remain in this labor market segment. In Continental European welfare regimes, the high social wage and centralized industrial relations will inhibit the development of a large low-wage service sector segment—however, at the price of creating a large "outsider surplus population" with no access to the labor market. In contrast, the Northern European welfare regimes are best suited to prevent the development of a secondary labor market, as they create employment through the welfare state and the public sector. Thus, although social divisions are likely to be found everywhere (King and Rueda 2008), existing labor market and social policy institutions make their development more probable in Liberal and in Continental European welfare states (Esping-Andersen et al. 1993; Blossfeld et al. 1993; Iversen and Wren 1998; Scharpf 2000; Bonoli and Emmenegger 2010).

We take Esping-Andersen's (1993a: 27) argument, whereby "the relative size of the outsider surplus population is a function of the combined effect of welfare state policy and the cost-disease problem" as a starting point for our analysis of insider-outsider divides during the last decades. We analyze whether his hypothesis still holds up in light of more recent labor market and welfare reforms. In many countries, new (active) labor market policies (Bonoli 2011) and structural welfare reforms have been implemented—even in Continental Europe (cf. Bleses and Seeleib-Kaiser 2004; Palier 2010; Häusermann 2010a; Vail 2010)—during this time period, which may have contributed to changed social outcomes, such as the increase in the number of working poor.

However, we contend that the literature has so far underestimated the variation *within* welfare state regimes that can be related to specific policy innovations (and not only to welfare regimes' persistent institutions). More concretely, we argue that there are not only inter-regime differences, but also important intra-regime differences. Not all countries within a regime are equally characterized by processes of dualization, and some countries have managed to avert or moderate social divides. The policies of these countries can contribute to policy learning of how to avoid, or at least minimize, insider-outsider divides. In order to learn from these countries, we need to broaden our perspective and turn our focus somewhat away from the core labor market and welfare state programs and also to center our attention on the margins as well as on the new public/private social protection mix. Moreover, we need to analyze which policies have contributed to the development of insider-outsider divides in the first place.

Putting these four literatures together leads us to the core thesis of this book. We argue that the translation of structural pressures into policies and outcomes must be understood as a political process, in which politically and economically stronger groups are using their power resources to insulate themselves from the negative effects of these structural pressures, and in which governments make deliberate choices in favor or against outsiders. Thereby, changes in the labor market are translated into the social policy realm, where new distinctions arise or old institutional distinctions are re-activated. Feedback effects and vicious circles are likely to strengthen this effect because weak labor attachment and social exclusion are associated with weaker political representation.

This book makes three major contributions to the literature. First, we stress the role of politics and political choice. Contrary to those who claim that inequalities are primarily the result of economic trends and necessities (Wright and Dwyer 2003; Goos and Manning 2007; Autor et al. 2008), we show that *policies matter*. Instead of mainly being the result of liberalization processes, achieved through a gradual retrenchment of labor market regulation and social protection across the board (see, for instance, Streeck 2009), we argue that current policies tend to differentiate between different social groups: some portions of the society are insulated from growing risk and inequality through various labor market and social policies, while others are exposed to new or greater risks through policy reforms. In a nutshell, we claim that the last two to three decades can be characterized in many countries as "the age of dualization," in which new and/or deepened divides have surfaced between various groups of insiders and outsiders. Our systematic comparative perspective underlines the varieties of dualization, both between and within welfare regimes.

Second, we emphasize the multidimensionality of dualization. There are at least three dimensions along which dualization processes can vary: (1) across time in their intensity, prevalence, and respective importance; (2) across policy fields (labor market regulation, social protection regulation, migration policies, etc.); and (3) across countries and regimes. Our book integrates all three dimensions of comparison. Based on our comparative perspective, we are able to grasp the varieties of dualization across rich OECD countries.

Finally, we stress the complementarities between the different dimensions of outsiderness and the interconnectedness of different political realms. Labor market policies and social policies can no longer be analyzed in isolation. The individual labor market situation matters for social rights (cf. eligibility as a function of contribution periods), while social policies influence labor market interactions (cf. social wage). Changes in one realm are likely to trigger reforms in the other realm (Palier and Thelen 2010). In a similar vein, labor market policy and social policy reforms are likely to be influenced by political representation (Rueda 2005).

STRUCTURE OF THE BOOK

The primary focus of this book is on Continental European countries, since dualization is a trend, as we will show empirically, that has developed particularly rapidly and strongly in this region over the last two decades, whereas in Liberal countries dualization has existed for a longer time period. However, we deliberately offer broad comparisons in a number of chapters to situate the Continental European countries within a larger context, and we narrow our focus to specific topics and specific countries in other chapters. Although most of the chapters include Continental European welfare states, five chapters include Liberal welfare states and two chapters focus on Asian and Scandinavia countries, clearly showing that dualization goes beyond Liberal and Continental European countries.

The book is structured in four parts. The first part of the book focuses on the conceptualization and measurement of dualization, while the second part decomposes dualization by looking at the private service sector, the public sector, and immigration. Part III of this book maps varieties of dualization by analyzing policy change in a diverse set of countries. Finally, the fourth part discusses the politics underlying processes of dualization.

In Part I of the book, of which this introduction is the first chapter, we develop a conceptual framework for the analysis of dualization, and we identify insiders and outsiders using various methods and angles. More specifically, we address the following questions: Who are the outsiders? What types of social divides and divisions do we find in different countries? Chapters in this section offer a systematic mapping of insider-outsider cleavages and conditions. Instead of providing a static snapshot they provide a dynamic analysis, based on new class analysis as well as original panel data.

In Chapter 2, Silja Häusermann and Hanna Schwander show that labor markets in Western democracies have changed profoundly. Across all countries, they observe a trend toward a segmentation of the workforce: ever fewer people's work biographies correspond to the industrial blueprint of protected, stable, full-time, and fully insured insider employment, while a growing proportion of the population are outsiders, whose employment status and employment biographies deviate from the insider model. For the outsiders, this deviation may potentially result in specific disadvantages, such as poor job perspectives, poverty, welfare losses, and a lack of social and political integration. The extent to which segmentation results in actual insider-outsider divides depends on the institutional context, that is, it varies across countries and across welfare regimes.

In Chapter 3, Mark Tomlinson and Robert Walker analyze labor market and poverty dynamics at the micro level. Analyzing longitudinal individual data from Great Britain (British Household Panel Survey) and Germany (Socio-Economic Panel) they explore the relationship between segmentation in the labor market and its longer term implications for recurrent poverty experience. According to their findings, there is a degree of correspondence between the two countries in both the proportions of insiders and outsiders and also the relative probability of transfer between insider and outsider status. In both countries, previous poverty experience remains the strongest determinant of future poverty experience. However, the analysis also shows that the German welfare state seems to be significantly more able than the British state to reduce the risks of recurrent poverty, all other things being equal.

Part II of the book decomposes dualization by analyzing three social areas that are said to be particularly prone to dualization processes. Chapters 4 and 5 focus on employment structures in private services and in public social services, respectively, in Continental Europe. Chapter 6 discusses the social and economic status of immigrants in the three biggest "reluctant countries of immigration" of Western Europe.

Werner Eichhorst and Paul Marx, in Chapter 4, compare employment structures in five Continental European welfare states, with a focus on private services. Despite a common trend to overcome institutional employment barriers by creating a more flexible labor market, a closer look reveals considerable differences between national patterns of standard and non-standard work. They identify five transformative pathways toward a more flexible and cheaper use of labor in Continental European welfare states and show that by relying on one or several of these options, each country developed a distinct solution for the labor cost problem in the service sector, which corresponds to a particular form of dualization.

In Chapter 5, Daniela Kroos and Karin Gottschall compare the situation of employment and job structures in the public social services in France and Germany. This chapter reveals varying degrees of labor market dualization in Germany and France. The different legacy of a "high road" of social service provision and employment allowing for labor market integration of mothers in France contrasts with a more semi-professional "low road" based on a strong male breadwinner model in Germany, generating less pronounced insider-outsider divides in France than in Germany. Nevertheless, precarious employment in expanding social services, such as elder care, is on the rise in both countries, challenging the role of the welfare state as a model employer.

In Chapter 6, Patrick Emmenegger and Romana Careja discuss the social and economic status of immigrants in France, Germany, and Great Britain. They show that immigrants continue to be worse off with respect to virtually all socioeconomic indicators, despite multiple attempts to integrate them into their host societies. They argue that these socioeconomic differences are the result of three processes, which contribute to the persistence of inequalities between the citizen population and immigrants. First, migration policies are changed to encourage the arrival of "desired" workers, while barriers to entry for "undesired" immigrants are erected. Paradoxically, these restrictions have contributed to the extension of the pool of immigrant cheap labor. Second, immigrant-specific social security schemes are reformed in order to reduce the incentive for immigrants to come in the first place. Finally, immigrants are disproportionately affected by the cutbacks in social security programs since the 1990s. Higher levels of conditionality, tighter eligibility criteria, and more demands on individual recipients are likely to increase the pressure on individuals with weak labor market attachments, many movements in and out of work, and few skills. As the authors show, these criteria apply to most immigrants in the "reluctant countries of immigration": France, Germany, and Great Britain.

Part III of the book focuses on the mechanisms and processes of dualization. More specifically, this part addresses the following question: To what extent do institutional reforms and policy change contribute to the deepening, widening, and creation of new social, economic, and political divides? The section encompasses comparative analyses of Liberal, Conservative, and Social-democratic welfare systems, small and large countries, and also East Asian countries. It thus provides a comprehensive mapping of the diverse processes of dualization.

In Chapter 7, Martin Seeleib-Kaiser, Adam Saunders, and Marek Naczyk concentrate their analysis on the development of the public-private mix in welfare systems in two Liberal countries (the UK and the U.S.) and two Conservative welfare systems (Germany and France), taking an explicitly temporal approach. They argue that institutional dualisms have always been a part of social protection arrangements in Liberal and Conservative welfare systems. Although institutional dualism was particularly evident in Liberal welfare systems, the proportion of social protection outsiders declined during the era of industrial welfare capitalism as more workers became entitled to occupational welfare. In Conservative welfare systems, social insurance became more encompassing, making these systems quasi-universal. With the onset of post-industrial welfare capitalism since the mid-1970s, however, the processes were reversed, leading to higher proportions of social protection outsiders within the workforce. This process becomes fully evident only if trends in both public and private social protection are analyzed.

Herbert Obinger, Peter Starke, and Alexandra Kaasch, in Chapter 8, analyze various *policy responses* to labor market divides in three small open economies (Austria, New Zealand, and Sweden). They argue that different welfare state regimes generate distinctive patterns of insider-outsider divides and that the three countries developed quite different, albeit mainly path-dependent coping strategies. In other words, none of the three countries significantly departed from previous labor market policies in response to growing labor market inequalities.

In Chapter 9, Bruno Palier and Kathleen Thelen demonstrate that the French and German political economies have been significantly reconfigured over the past two decades. Although the changes have often been incremental, their cumulative effects are profound. They argue that what gives contemporary developments a different character from the past is that they are now explicitly underwritten by state policy. Furthermore, they emphasize complementarities across institutional realms, and show how these linkages have facilitated the spread of dualization—beginning in the field of industrial relations, moving into labor market dynamics, and finally finding institutional expression in welfare state reforms. The result in France and Germany has led to an institutionalization of a stable but distinctly less egalitarian model.

Pursuing a similar approach in Chapter 10, Ito Peng analyzes the developments in the two East Asian political economies of Japan and Korea. She argues that both countries have been going through a re-articulation of their political economies since the 1990s. Similar to France and Germany, labor market dualization in Japan and Korea has been a continuous process since the 1990s, not a sudden shift in direction. However, unlike some Continental European countries, the changes of the labor market have spurred the respective governments to expand the welfare state, particularly in social care, to compensate for increased economic insecurity.

Part IV of the book deals with political processes (e.g., cross-class alliances) and governance structures, as well as with the political dilemmas and trade-offs imposed by insider-outsider cleavages. More specifically, this part addresses the following question: Which political actors are deepening and widening institutional dualisms, and which actors are trying to prevent dualization or to smooth its distributional consequences?

In Chapter 11, Daniel Clegg explores the political dynamics behind the contrasting institutional and distributive choices in the unemployment benefit reforms of Belgium and France, two otherwise similar countries, in the process shedding light on the politics of dualization more generally. In particular, he suggests that rather fine-grained differences in social governance have had a crucial impact on processes of unemployment policy preference formation in Belgian and French trade unions, whose influence has driven policy down distinctive paths. More generally, the impact of such proximate institutional environments on preference formation implies that common structural tendencies toward a post-industrial employment structure can be expected to elicit diverse social policy responses in different countries, even within the same welfare-production regime.

Johannes Lindvall and David Rueda, in Chapter 12, focus on the political implications of insider-outsider divides. They show that outsiders react to the policy agenda that political parties advocate in electoral campaigns. If political parties abandon their focus on employment-related issues, outsiders either support more radical parties or exit politics. They argue further that this electoral response creates a dilemma for social democratic parties: if they focus on outsider-interests, they risk losing support among insiders, and vice versa. They demonstrate their arguments through the analysis of novel data on voter attitudes and electoral campaigns from four national Swedish elections (1994–2006). Sweden is investigated as a least-likely case, given that labor market divides are less pronounced in Sweden than in most Continental or Anglo-Saxon countries. By showing that insider-outsider divides affect electoral dynamics even in Sweden, they make a strong point for similar trends in more divided societies.

Finally, the last chapter returns to the main findings of this book, by answering the following questions: Who are the outsiders? What divides do we observe cross-nationally, and to what extent are they new or different from the ones that have characterized our societies throughout the postwar era? What is driving dualization and insider-outsider divides? What are the mechanisms behind new and/or growing insider-outsider inequalities? What is specific to our approach and in our understanding of the "age of dualization"? Will dualization be a

lasting reality? Under which economic and political conditions could dualization processes be mitigated or even reverted? We argue that increasing
inequalities are not a straightforward consequence of globalization or deindustrialization. Rather, this volume demonstrates that increasing inequalities are
the result of policy and thus, at least to some extent, are avoidable.

NOTES

1 URL: http://www.oecd.org/document/4/0,3343,en_2649_33933_41460917_
   1_1_1_1,00.html (accessed September 5, 2011).
2 Leigh (2007) shows that top income shares are a good predictor of
   broader inequality measures.
3 URL: http://www.oecd.org/document/34/0,3343,en_2649_33927_40917154_
   1_1_1_1,00.html (accessed September 5, 2011).
4 This distinction is necessary for the sake of analytical clarity. The
   literature has so far tended to conflate these different dimensions. See
   Davidsson and Naczyk (2009) for a review of the literature.

REFERENCES

Autor, David H., Katz, Lawrence F., and Kearney, Melissa S. (2008). "Trends in
   U.S. Wage Inequality: Revising the Revisionists," *Review of Economics and
   Statistics*, 90(2): 300–323.
Baumol, William J. (1967). "The Macroeconomics of Unbalanced Growth: The
   Anatomy of Urban Crisis," *American Economic Review*, 57(3): 415–426.
Berger, Suzanne, and Piore, Michael J. (1980). *Dualism and Discontinuity in
   Industrial Societies*, Cambridge: Cambridge University Press.
Blanchard, Olivier, and Summers, Lawrence H. (1986). "Hysteresis and
   the European Unemployment Problem," in Fischer, Stanley (ed.), *NBER
   Macroeconomics Annual 1986*, Volume 1, Cambridge: MIT Press, pp. 15–90.
Bleses, Peter, and Seeleib-Kaiser, Martin (2004). *The Dual Transformation of the
   German Welfare State*, Basingstoke: Palgrave.
Blossfeld, Hans-Peter, Giannelli, Gianna, and Mayer, Karl Ulrich (1993). "Is
   There a New Service Proletariat? The Tertiary Sector and Social Inequality in
   Germany," in Esping-Andersen, Gøsta (ed.), *Changing Classes: Stratification
   and Mobility in Post-Industrial Societies*, London: Sage, pp. 109–135.
Bonoli, Giuliano (2011). "The Political Economy of Active Labor-Market Policy,"
   Politics and Society, 38(4): 435–457.
Bonoli, Giuliano, and Emmenegger, Patrick (2010). "State-Society Relationships,
   Social Trust and the Development of Labour Market Policies in Italy and
   Sweden," *West European Politics*, 33(4): 829–850.
Brady, David, Beckfield, Jason, and Seeleib-Kaiser, Martin (2005). "Economic
   Globalization and the Welfare State in Affluent Democracies, 1975–2001,"
   American Sociological Review, 70(6): 921–948.

Bridgen, Paul, and Meyer, Traute (2008). "Politically Dominant but Socially Flawed," in Seeleib-Kaiser, Martin (ed.), *Welfare State Transformations: Comparative Perspectives,* Basingstoke: Palgrave, pp. 111–131.

Davidsson, Johan B., and Naczyk, Marek (2009). "The Ins and Outs of Dualisation: A Literature Review," *RECWOWE Working Paper,* No. 02/2009.

Doeringer, Peter B., and Piore, Michael J. (1971). *Internal Labor Markets and Manpower Analysis,* Lexington MA: Heath Lexington Books.

Eardley, Tony, Bradshaw, Jonathan, Ditch, John, Gough, Ian, and Whiteford, Peter (1996). *Social Assistance in OECD Countries,* DSS Research Reports Nos. 46 and 47 (two volumes), *Country Reports* and *Synthesis Report,* HMSO, London.

Ebbinghaus, Bernhard (2006). *Reforming Early Retirement in Europe, Japan and the USA,* Oxford: Oxford University Press.

Emmenegger, Patrick (2009). "Barriers to Entry: Insider/Outsider Politics and the Political Determinants of Job Security Regulations," *Journal of European Social Policy,* 19(2): 131–146.

Esping-Andersen, Gøsta (1990). *The Three Worlds of Welfare Capitalism,* Cambridge: Polity.

Esping-Andersen, Gøsta (1993a). "Post-industrial Class Structures: An Analytical Framework," in Esping-Andersen, Gøsta (ed.), *Changing Classes: Stratification and Mobility in Post-Industrial Societies,* London: Sage, pp. 7–31.

Esping-Andersen, Gøsta (1993b). "Mobility Regimes and Class Formation," in Esping-Andersen, Gøsta (ed.), *Changing Classes: Stratification and Mobility in Post-Industrial Societies,* London: Sage, pp. 225–241.

Esping-Andersen, Gøsta (1996). "After the Golden Age," in Esping-Andersen, Gøsta (ed.), *Welfare States in Transition: National Adaptations in Global Economies,* London: Sage, pp. 1–31.

Esping-Andersen, Gøsta (1999). *Social Foundations of Postindustrial Economies,* Oxford: Oxford University Press.

Esping-Andersen, Gøsta, van Kersbergen, Kees, and Assimakopoulou, Zina (1993). "Trends in Contemporary Class Structuration: A Six-Nation Comparison," in Esping-Andersen, Gøsta (ed.), *Changing Classes: Stratification and Mobility in Post-Industrial Societies,* London: Sage, pp. 32–57.

Estevez-Abe, Margarita (2005). "Gender Bias in Skills and Social Policies: The Varieties of Capitalism Perspective on Sex Segregation," *Social Politics,* 12(2): 180–215.

Fleckenstein, Timo, Saunders, Adam M., and Seeleib-Kaiser, Martin (2011). "The Dual Transformation of Social Protection and Human Capital: Comparing Britain and Germany," *Comparative Political Studies,* 44(12).

Flora, Peter (ed.) (1986–1993). *Growth to Limits: The European Welfare States since World War II,* five volumes, Berlin: De Gruyter.

Flora, Peter, and Heidenheimer, Arnold J. (eds.) (1981). *The Development of Welfare States in Europe and in America,* London: Transaction Book.

Genschel, Phillip (2002). "Globalization, Tax Competition and the Welfare State," *Politics and Society,* 30(2): 245–275.

Gilbert, Neil (2002). *Transformation of the Welfare State,* Oxford: Oxford University Press.

Goldthorpe, John H. (1984). "The End of Convergence: Corporatist and Dualist Tendencies in Modern Western Societies," in Goldthorpe, John H. (ed.), *Order and Conflict in Contemporary Capitalism*, Oxford: Clarendon Press, pp. 315–343.

Goos, Maarten, and Manning, Alan (2007). "Lousy and Lovely Jobs: The Rising Polarization of Work in Britain," *Review of Economics and Statistics*, 89(1): 118–133.

Hacker, Jacob S. (2002). *The Divided Welfare State: The Battle over Public and Private Social Benefits in the United States*, Cambridge: Cambridge University Press.

Hall, Peter, and Soskice, David (2001). *Varieties of Capitalism: The Institutional Foundations of Comparative Advantage*, Oxford: Oxford University Press.

Häusermann, Silja (2010a). *The Politics of Welfare Reform in Continental Europe: Modernization in Hard Times*, New York: Cambridge University Press.

Häusermann, Silja (2010b). "Solidarity with Whom? Why Trade Unions Are Losing Ground in Continental Pension Politics," *European Journal of Political Research*, 49(2): 233–256.

Held, David, McGrew, Anthony, Goldblatt, David, and Perraton, Jonathan (1999). *Global Transformations: Politics, Economics and Culture*, Stanford: Stanford University Press.

Iversen, Torben, and Cusack, Thomas R. (2000). "The Causes of Welfare State Expansion: De-industrialization or Globalization?," *World Politics*, 52(3): 313–349.

Iversen, Torben, and Wren, Anne (1998). "Equality, Employment, and Budgetary Restraint: The Trilemma of the Service Economy," *World Politics*, 50(4): 507–546.

King, Desmond, and Rueda, David (2008). "Cheap Labor: The New Politics of 'Bread and Roses' in Industrial Democracies," *Perspectives on Politics*, 6(2): 279–297.

Kollmeyer, Christopher (2009). "Explaining Deindustrialization: How Affluence, Productivity Growth, and Globalization Diminish Manufacturing Employment," *American Journal of Sociology*, 114(6): 1644–1674.

Korpi, Walter, and Palme, Joakim (1998). "The Paradox of Redistribution and Strategies of Equality: Welfare State Institutions, Inequality, and Poverty in the Western Countries," *American Sociological Review*, 63(5): 661–687.

Leibfried, Stephan, and Tennstedt, Florian (1985). "Armenpolitik und Arbeiterpolitik. Zur Entwicklung und Krise der traditionellen Sozialpolitik der Verteilungsformen," in Leibfried, Stephan, and Tennstedt, Florian (eds.), *Politik der Armut und die Spaltung des Sozialstaats*, Frankfurt am Main: Suhrkamp, pp. 64–93.

Leigh, Andrew (2007). "How Closely Do Top Income Shares Track Other Measures of Inequality," *Economic Journal*, 117(524): F619–F633.

Lindbeck, Assar, and Snower, Dennis J. (1988). *The Insider-Outsider Theory of Employment and Unemployment*, Cambridge: MIT Press.

Martin, Cathie Jo, and Thelen, Kathleen (2007). "The State and Coordinated Capitalism: Contributions of the Public Sector to Social Solidarity in Postindustrial Societies," *World Politics*, 60(1): 1–36.

Mullaly, Bob (2006). *The New Structural Social Work: Ideology, Theory, Practice,* 3rd ed., New York: Oxford University Press.

OECD (2008). *Growing Unequal? Income Distribution and Poverty in OECD Countries,* Paris: OECD.

OECD (2010). *Employment Outlook 2010,* Paris: OECD.

Oesch, Daniel (2006). *Redrawing the Class Map: Stratification and Institutions in Germany, Britain, Sweden and Switzerland,* London: Palgrave Macmillan.

Palier, Bruno (ed.) (2010). *A Long Good Bye to Bismarck? The Politics of Welfare Reforms in Continental Europe,* Amsterdam: Amsterdam University Press.

Palier, Bruno, and Thelen, Kathleen (2010). "Institutionalizing Dualism: Complementarities and Change in France and Germany," *Politics and Society,* 38(1): 119–148.

Pierson, Paul (ed.) (2001). *The New Politics of the Welfare State,* Oxford: Oxford University Press.

Piore, Michael J. (1980). "An Economic Approach," in Berger, Suzanne, and Piore, Michael J. (eds.), *Dualism and Discontinuity in Industrial Societies,* Cambridge: Cambridge University Press, pp. 13–81.

Rueda, David (2005). "Insider-Outsider Politics in Industrialized Democracies: The Challenge to Social Democratic Parties," *American Political Science Review,* 99(1): 61–74.

Rueda, David (2006). "Social Democracy and Active Labour-Market Policies: Insiders, Outsiders and the Politics of Employment Promotion," *British Journal of Political Science,* 36(3): 385–406.

Saint-Paul, Gilles (1996). "Exploring the Political Economy of Labour Market Institutions," *Economic Policy,* 11(23): 265–315.

Saint-Paul, Gilles (2002). "The Political Economy of Employment Protection," *Journal of Political Economy,* 110(3): 672–704.

Saraceno, Chiara (2010). "'Concepts and Practices of Social Citizenship in Europe: The Case of Poverty and Income Support for the Poor," in Alber, Jens, and Gilbert, Neil (eds.), *United in Diversity? Comparing Social Models in Europe and America,* New York: Oxford University Press, 151–175.

Scharpf, Fritz W. (1991). *Crisis and Choice in European Social Democracy,* Ithaca, NY: Cornell University Press.

Scharpf, Fritz W. (2000). "The Viability of Advanced Welfare States in the International Economy: Vulnerabilities and Options," *Journal of European Public Policy,* 7(2): 190–228.

Scruggs, Lyle (2004). Comparative Welfare Entitlements Dataset, University of Connecticut. Online, available from http://sp.uconn.edu/~scruggs/ (Last accessed: October 13th 2011).

Seeleib-Kaiser, Martin (1995). "The Development and Structure of Social Assistance and Unemployment Insurance in the Federal Republic of Germany and Japan," *Social Policy and Administration,* 29(3): 269–293.

Seeleib-Kaiser, Martin, van Dyk, Silke, and Roggenkamp, Martin (2008). *Party Politics and Social Welfare,* Cheltenham: Edward Elgar.

Sengenberger, Werner (1981). "Labour Market Segmentation and the Business Cycle," in Wilkinson, Frank (ed.), *The Dynamics of Labour Market Segmentation,* London: Academic Press, pp. 243–259.

Standing, Guy (2009). *Work after Globalization*, Cheltenham: Edward Elgar.

Stinchcombe, Arthur L. (1979). "Social Mobility in Industrial Labor Markets," *Acta Sociologica*, 22(3): 217–245.

Streeck, Wolfgang (2009). *Re-Forming Capitalism: Institutional Change in the German Political Economy*, Oxford: Oxford University Press.

Swank, Duane (2010). "Globalization," in Castles, Francis G., Leibfried, Stephan, Lewis, Obinger, Jane, Herbert and Pierson, Christopher (eds.), *The Oxford Handbook of the Welfare State*, Oxford: Oxford University Press, pp. 318–330.

Tussing, A. Dale (1975). *Poverty in a Dual Economy*, New York: St. Martin's Press.

Vail, Mark (2010). *Recasting Welfare Capitalism: Economic Adjustment in Contemporary France and Germany*, Philadelphia: Temple University Press.

Weir, Margaret, Orloff, Ann Shola, and Skocpol, Theda (1988). *The Politics of Social Policy in the United States*, Princeton NJ: Princeton University Press.

Wood, Adrian (1994). *North-South Trade: Employment and Inequality*, Oxford: Clarendon Press.

Wright, Erik Olin, and Dwyer, Rachel E. (2003). "The Patterns of Job Expansion in the USA: A Comparison of the 1960s and 1990s," *Socio-Economic Review*, 1(3): 289–325.

2

VARIETIES OF DUALIZATION?

LABOR MARKET SEGMENTATION AND INSIDER-OUTSIDER DIVIDES ACROSS REGIMES

SILJA HÄUSERMANN AND HANNA SCHWANDER

INTRODUCTION

Over the past decades, labor markets in the Western democracies have changed profoundly. Across all countries, we observe a trend toward a segmentation of the workforce:[1] ever fewer people's work biographies correspond to the industrial blueprint of protected, stable, full-time, and fully insured insider employment, while a growing proportion of the population are outsiders, whose employment status and employment biographies deviate from the insider model. For the outsiders, this deviation may potentially result in specific disadvantages, such as poor job prospects, poverty, welfare losses, and a lack of social and political integration. As we argue and demonstrate in this chapter, the extent to which segmentation results in actual insider-outsider divides depends on the institutional context, that is, it varies across countries and across welfare regimes. Hence, while labor market segmentation is a fairly universal trend, the appearance of actual insider-outsider divides is not: it is contingent on policies.

We argue that it is crucial to study not only the segmentation of labor markets in insiders and outsiders, but also its translation in economic, social, and political outcomes for two reasons. First, it emphasizes the importance of *policies*. Welfare state research has shown that social policies do not always benefit the poorest, and that they may have stratifying, rather than redistributive, effects (Esping-Andersen 1990; Bradley et al. 2003). With regard to the insider-outsider divide, this insight is crucial: welfare states may compensate for labor market segmentation, but—conversely—they may also perpetuate labor market

27

inequalities or even reinforce occupational divides. While recent studies indeed show that welfare states become increasingly dualized, that is, they apply different policies to insiders and outsiders (e.g., Häusermann 2010; Palier 2010; Seeleib-Kaiser et al., Chapter 7 of this volume; Palier and Thelen, Chapter 9 of this volume; and Clegg, Chapter 11 of this volume), we analyze the effect of these policies in a cross-national and cross-regime perspective.

Second, it is crucial to look at outcomes in order to assess the *political relevance* of insider-outsider divides. If unemployment or atypical employment is not linked to concrete disadvantage in terms of labor market power, welfare rights, or political integration, the insider-outsider divide may well remain a purely sociological distinction without further political relevance. If, however, labor market segmentation correlates with job market closure, poverty, and poor welfare coverage, the insider-outsider divide might become the socio-structural basis of political mobilization. The chances of this divide being politicized depend, of course, on the presence of a political actor drawing on this potential, but the empirical analysis of actual economic, social, and political divides across regimes is a pre-condition for understanding the politics of dualization.

In this chapter, we proceed in three steps. In a first step, we develop our theoretical argument on the link between institutions, welfare regimes, and insider-outsider divides. In a second step, we identify insiders and outsiders empirically on the basis of their relative risk of being unemployed or atypically employed. In a third step, we compare earnings power, job prospects, social rights, and political integration of insiders and outsiders across countries and regimes.

POST-INDUSTRIALISM, LABOR MARKET SEGMENTATION, AND INSIDER-OUTSIDER DIVIDES

Over the past 30 years, the industrial economies of the developed world have transitioned to the era of post-industrialism, with ever growing shares of the workforce being employed in the third sector. Much of the literature characterizes the industrial era of Western societies as "the golden age," since it was characterized by relatively stable families and stable labor markets (Esping-Andersen 1999b). And even though the rhetoric of the golden age may paint a somewhat too rosy picture of the distribution of economic and social opportunities in Western societies, it is certainly true that the exceptional economic growth during the three postwar decades allowed for full male employment, the development of the Western welfare states, and a relatively high degree of status homogenization.

Three structural developments have, however, profoundly altered this "industrial equilibrium": the tertiarization of the employment structure, the educational revolution, and the feminization of the workforce (Oesch 2006). The rise of the service sector is a major trend in all OECD countries. While Continental Europe remained predominantly industrial until the 1990s, service sector employment was already more important than the industrial sector in the United Kingdom and Sweden in the 1970s. After 2000, service sector employment outdid industrial employment throughout the OECD by a factor of 2 to 3 (Oesch 2006: 31). Jobs in the service sector tend to differ from industrial employment because they are either very low-skilled or highly skilled, and because service sector employment has a lower potential for productivity gains (Iversen and Wren 1998; Kroos and Gottschall, Chapter 5 of this volume). The educational revolution—as the second structural change of the post-industrial era—denotes the massive expansion of tertiary education throughout the OECD countries, leading to a broader and more heterogeneous middle class. Finally, the increasing feminization of the workforce is both a consequence of and a driver for the educational revolution and tertiarization. The massive entry of women into paid labor is also related to the increasing instability of traditional family structures (Esping-Andersen 1999a).

This shift toward post-industrial employment has led to labor markets that are increasingly segmented, which means that they are increasingly divided in standard jobs on the one hand, and non-standard jobs on the other hand. Unemployment and formerly "atypical" employment relations have become more and more widespread. Unemployment increased in all OECD countries throughout the 1980s and 1990 and has remained on a higher level than in the late 1970s since. Especially in Continental Europe, unemployment rates have remained high, around 10 percent in some countries, such as France and Belgium. Atypical employment denotes all employment-relations that deviate from the Standard Employment Relation (i.e., full-time, stable, fully insured employment). Part-time and temporary employment contracts are among the most prominent types of atypical employment (see Eichhorst and Marx, Chapter 4 of this volume). According to Standing (1993: 433), the number of workers on temporary contracts across the entire European Union (EU), for instance, has been growing by 15–20 percent annually since the 1980s, which is about ten times the overall rate of employment growth (see also Esping-Andersen 1999a and OECD 2006). Similarly, part-time employment counted for close to 80 percent of the net job creation in the EU since the mid-1990s (Plougmann 2003). Atypical employment is also clearly gendered in many countries (Esping-Andersen 1999b). For women in Continental Europe, atypical employment is generally the norm rather than the exception. Similarly, atypical employment has become more and more widespread among labor market entrants in a range of Continental and Southern European countries (e.g., Chauvel 2009).

Hence, the segmentation of labor markets in "inside labor," that is, people in standard employment, and "outside labor," that is, people in atypical and precarious employment, is a structural trend that affects all advanced post-industrial economies. To what extent, however, can we expect these structural changes to result in actual social divides, that is, in specific disadvantages of outsiders in terms of outcomes? Indeed, if most people repeatedly move back and forth between standard and non-standard employment or between unemployment and employment, new employment patterns must not result in actual new divides. However, research shows that social mobility has *not* increased in post-industrial societies (Erikson and Goldthorpe 1993; Breen 2004) and that unemployment and atypical employment risks are concentrated in clearly identifiable social groups (Häusermann and Schwander 2009a). Therefore, the segmentation of labor markets may indeed result in structural disadvantages with regard to economic, social and political outcomes. This is what we explore in this chapter.

To analyze outcomes, we distinguish between three types of insider-outsider divides. *Labor market divides* refer to structural disadvantages of outsiders in terms of earnings possibilities and access to training. We will speak of *social protection divides* if outsiders are structurally disadvantaged with regard to welfare coverage and benefits. And we identify *political integration divides* if labor market outsiders are politically underrepresented and alienated from democratic decision making. None of these three divides are *necessary* consequences of labor market segmentation, since countries can counterbalance the increasing segmentation of labor markets.

In this chapter, we analyze empirically to what extent the translation of segmentation into outcomes varies across welfare regimes. As recent research has shown that welfare regimes increasingly become hybrids and more heterogeneous (e.g., Palier 2010), one might ask whether it still makes sense to focus on between-regime differences. We do so in this chapter, because regimes reflect long-standing institutions, policies, and underlying ideological foundations that shape political outcomes in the long run (Esping-Andersen 1990, 1999a). In addition, given the increasing within-regime heterogeneity of welfare states, any observed between-regime differences reflect a "hard test" of the impact of regimes. Nevertheless, we also show cross-country variation, thereby preparing the ground for further contributions in this book (e.g., see Chapter 4 by Eichhorst and Marx, Chapter 7 by Seeleib-Kaiser et al., Chapter 8 by Obinger et al., and Chapter 9 by Palier and Thelen), which will explore within-regime differences in detail.

How do we expect regimes to differ in the extent to which they translate labor market segmentation into economic, social, and political outcomes? The Liberal countries generally have flexible and Liberal labor markets and relatively high levels of income inequality. Their welfare states are means-tested and focused on poverty prevention (Esping-Andersen 1990). Hence, while we expect marked labor market divides, we also expect the welfare state to have a compensating effect on these inequalities. Further, as political participation depends inter alia on individual resources like time, money, and civic skills (Brady et al. 1995), a compensating welfare state may help in preventing strong political divides. Nordic welfare states are quite the opposite: they have generally low levels of income inequality despite strongly gendered labor markets, as well as encompassing trade unions and an egalitarian, universalistic profile of welfare state policies (Esping-Andersen 1990, 1999a). We thus expect weak insider-outsider divides on all three dimensions, since the institutions of the Nordic countries countervail segmentation. Finally, we expect pronounced divides in Continental and Southern European welfare regimes for two reasons. The first reason is that Continental labor market and social policy institutions were strongly marked by industrial trade unions, which tend to represent inside labor (Palier and Thelen 2010). The second reason relates to the social insurance welfare states typical of Continental Europe (Esping-Andersen 1990). Social insurance implies that welfare benefits are proportional to contributions. Therefore, unemployment and non-standard work tend to lead to incomplete and insufficient social rights (Esping-Andersen 1999b: 83). In that sense, Continental and Southern European welfare states reproduce market inequalities (Bradley et al. 2003). Consequently, we expect to observe comparatively strong insider-outsider divides in these regimes.

WHO ARE THE OUTSIDERS? IDENTIFYING INSIDERS AND OUTSIDERS ACROSS REGIMES

In order to analyze the consequences of labor market segmentation, we first need to define labor market insiders and outsiders. In line with our previous work (Häusermann and Schwander 2009a, 2009b; Häusermann and Walter 2010), we consider labor market outsiders those individuals who incur a particularly high risk of being in atypical employment or unemployment. People differ in their risk profile, that is, in the likelihood that they will be affected by unemployment or atypical employment. We share this idea of atypical employment and unemployment as determinants of outsiderness with the main contributions to this literature in political science (e.g., Rueda 2005, 2007; Emmenegger 2009). The question is, of course, how we can *measure* this risk. Most of the literature simply takes the current labor market status of an individual as the basis for measurement. This means that the existing literature (e.g., Lindbeck and Snower 2001; Saint-Paul 2002; Rueda 2005; Emmenegger 2009) uses a snapshot categorization of outsiders at a particular point in time. This measure implies various misclassification risks (see Häusermann and Schwander 2009a and Emmenegger 2009 for a discussion). Hence, in this chapter, we deviate from this measure by defining outsiders as belonging to occupational groups, which are "typically" affected by atypical work and unemployment. This implies that people are categorized based on the characteristics of their reference group. This approach relies on the idea that people form identities and preferences *not* on the basis of a momentary labor market status, but with regard to their occupational reference group, and this is what we need to capture if we want to talk about the social and political relevance of insider-outsider divides.[2]

How then can we measure the *risk* of unemployment or atypical employment? The probability of experiencing these forms of outsiderness obviously depends on their rate of occurrence within the relevant occupational category. Post-industrial societies are still structured in different, relatively stable occupational groups, which share similar employment and risk profiles. Classes are occupational groups characterized by a particular situation in the labor market, which shapes their resources and preferences. Class schemes are based on occupational profiles (Erikson and Goldthorpe 1993; Oesch 2006) because people in similar professions tend to have similar employment biographies. Class is therefore a meaningful starting point for the identification of group-specific risks of unemployment and atypical employment. We rely on the class schema by Oesch (2006), which is explicitly developed to reflect post-industrial societies, since it takes into account a heterogeneous middle class and it distinguishes between different types of low-skilled employees who can no longer be reasonably subsumed under a single category of workers (Oesch 2006). Individuals are categorized on the basis of their current or last occupation (by means of ISCO88 codes). Kitschelt and Rehm (2005) have regrouped Oesch's schema into five classes: Capital accumulators are high-skilled managers and self-employed. Sociocultural professionals are high-skilled professionals in interpersonal professions, most of them in the public and private service sector. Lower-skilled workers are differentiated in three groups: blue-collar workers are unskilled and skilled workers mostly in the industry. Low service functionaries are unskilled and skilled employees in interpersonal services, and mixed service functionaries denote a residual class of routine and skilled workers in jobs with mostly organizational work logic. Table 2-1 represents the location of these five classes in the class schema that is both vertically structured by skill levels, and horizontally by work logic.[3]

These five classes are a good starting point for the assessment of group-specific rates of unemployment and atypical employment. Capital accumulators are consistently the most privileged members of the workforce. For the other four classes, however, we need to go more into detail. In addition to class, employment trajectories are strongly structured by gender and age.[4] Post-industrial labor markets are strongly gendered (Esping-Andersen 1999a: 308; Emmenegger 2010). They also—at least in some regimes (Esping-Andersen 1999a)—tend to hold different occupational prospects for young and older workers.[5] Consequently, we further distinguish the socio-structural classes according to gender and age. We distinguish between two age groups, below

Table 2-1: The post-industrial class schema

Independent work logic	Technical work logic	Organizational work logic	Interpersonal work logic	
Large employers, liberal profes- sionals, and petty bourgeoisie with employees *(e.g., entrepreneurs, lawyers)* **Capital accumulators CA**	Technical experts *(e.g., executive engineers)* **Capital accumulators CA** Technicians *(e.g., engineers)* **Mixed service functionaries MSF**	Higher-grade and associate manag- ers *(e.g., financial and managing executives)* **Capital accumulators CA**	Socio-cultural (semi)-professionals *(e.g., teachers, health professionals)* **Sociocultural professionals SCP**	**Professional/ managerial** **Associate professional/ managerial**
Petty bourgeoisie without employ- ees *(e.g., small shopkeepers)* **Mixed service functionaries MSF**	Skilled crafts and routine opera- tives *(e.g., machine operators, laborers in construction)* **Blue-collar workers BC**	Skilled and routine office workers *(e.g., office clerks)* **Mixed service functionaries MSF**	Skilled and unskilled service *(e.g., sales- persons, waiters)* **Low service functionaries LSF**	**Generally/ vocationally skilled and unskilled**

Note: Based on Oesch (2006) and Kitschelt and Rehm (2005). For the classification of occupations (ISCO88-2d codes), see Häusermann (2010).

and above the age of 40. The combination of 4 classes, 2 sexes, and 2 age groups leaves us with 16 occupational groups. For each of them, we have computed the group-specific rate of unemployment and the rate of atypi- cal employment (including part-time employment—both voluntary and involuntary[6]—as well as temporary or fixed-term employment, depending on the data availability in the respective survey), compared it to the average in the country's workforce, and tested whether the difference is significant. Occupational groups that have a significantly higher rate of either unem- ployment or atypical employment (i.e., significant at a 0.01 percent level of error) are defined as outsider-groups. Consequently, all individuals in these groups are then treated as outsiders.

In order to make our measurement robust, we have computed these mean- comparisons throughout the range of those six surveys that are most widely used in this research area (ISSP Role of Government III and IV [1996, 2006], ISSP Work Orientations III 2005, European Social Survey 2002 and 2008, Eurobarometer 44.3 1996) as well as three household panel datasets (for the UK, Switzerland, and Sweden, 2007). Only those occupational groups that were sig- nificantly more strongly affected by unemployment or atypical employment in a *majority* of the surveys were eventually defined as outsider-groups. The temporal and geographical variation of these surveys increases robustness. Some groups (e.g., elderly female blue-collar workers) are very small, which obviously influences significance tests. However, since we define outsiders on the basis of significantly higher probabilities of unemployment and atypical employment, our operationalization produces conservative results for these small groups. Table 2-2 shows the resulting classification.

Comparing the distribution of insiders and outsiders across welfare regimes, we note two main points. First, women and young labor market participants are over-represented among outsiders in all regimes, which fits well with what we know from previous analyses (Esping-Andersen 1999a, 1999b; Emmenegger 2010; Kroos and Gottschall, Chapter 5 of this volume). Second, however, the composition of insiders and outsiders also differs across regimes: in the Nordic and Continental countries, gender is the most important criterion, while in the Southern European regime, outsiderness concerns mostly young labor market participants, and in the Liberal countries, outsiders are predominantly found among the low-skilled.

In the subsequent section of this chapter, we will analyze empirically to what extent insiders and outsiders—as identified in Table 2-2—differ in terms of their incomes, job prospects, social rights, and political integration. While doing so, we systematically conduct a series of robustness-tests: first, we recalculated the results including only part-timers who work less than 30 hours per week. Second, we controlled for the effect of retirement by re-running the analyses without pensioners; and finally, we controlled for household composition. Indeed, one might argue that many female outsiders may be married to male insiders, which is why insider-outsider gaps in income, welfare entitlements, or labor market chances may not reflect economic precariousness directly, and married outsiders might even partly adopt the preferences of the male breadwinner.[7] On the other hand, defining insiders and outsiders at the household level only entails a risk of masking inequalities and neglecting the implications of family instability. Also, we follow Iversen and Rosenbluth (2006) in arguing that divorce rates approaching 50 percent in most OECD countries create strong incentives to evaluate one's life chances as individuals. Therefore, we perform our main analyses at the individual level. However, we re-test all results with a focus on households. When doing so, we define as outsiders only those individuals living in single households or in "pure" outsider households (i.e., where both spouses are outsiders). Where detailed information on the spouse's occupation is lacking (mostly with regard to income data), we check for household effects by defining outsider-households on the basis of the occupational profile of the head of the household. None of these robustness tests alters our results markedly. Where we do find important differences, we discuss them in more details in the respective section.

Table 2-2: Insiders and outsiders in the four welfare regimes

	Liberal regimes	Nordic regimes	Continental regimes	Southern regimes
Outsiders	Young female LSF	Young female LSF	Young female LSF	Young female LSF
Insiders	Young male LSF	Young male LSF	Young male LSF	Young male LSF
	Older female LSF	Older female LSF	Older female LSF	Older female LSF
	Older male LSF	Older male LSF	Older male LSF	Older male LSF
	Young female SCP	Young female SCP	Young female SCP	Young female SCP
	Young male SCP	Young male SCP	Young male SCP	Young male SCP
	Older female SCP	Older female SCP	Older female SCP	Older female SCP
	Older male SCP	Older male SCP	Older male SCP	Older male SCP
	Young female BC	Young female BC	Young female BC	Young female BC
	Young male BC	Young male BC	Young male BC	Young male BC
	Older female BC	Older female BC	Older female BC	Older female BC
	Older male BC	Older male BC	Older male BC	Older male BC
	Young female MSF	Young female MSF	Young female MSF	Young female MSF
	Young male MSF	Young male MSF	Young male MSF	Young male MSF
	Older female MSF	Older female MSF	Older female MSF	Older female MSF
	Older male MSF	Older male MSF	Older male MSF	Older male MSF
	CA	CA	CA	CA
% outsiders	52.7%	40.2%	43.0%	40.1%
% female outsiders	69.7%	96.2%	100%	77.2%
% young outsiders	31.0%	21.8%	33.8%	59.7%
% low-skilled outsiders	65.7%	47.5%	46.6%	45.0%
% immigrant outsiders (1st and 2nd gen.)	14.0%	9.7%	18.4%	11.2%
N	7334	4491	5319	3522

Notes: Highlighted groups are significantly more strongly affected by unemployment and/or atypical employment than not highlighted groups; based on the following data sources: ISSP Role of Government III and IV, ISSP Work orientations III, European social survey 2002 and 2008, Eurobarometer 44.3 as well as three household panel datasets (for the UK, Switzerland and Sweden); descriptive statistics from ISSP RoG IV 2006 (for reasons of data availability, the numbers regarding immigrants stem from the ESS round 4 2008 survey).

EMPIRICAL ANALYSIS: FROM SEGMENTATION TO DIVIDES

In the following sections, we analyze the distribution of earnings power, job perspectives and social rights between insiders and outsiders as well as their respective political integration.

Labor Market Divides Between Insiders and Outsiders

Labor market divides, that is, the distribution of economic advantages and disadvantages between insiders and outsiders, has two sides: income and job prospects. If outsiders receive a similar income to insiders, and if they have the same access to training and professional development as do insiders, then labor market segmentation must not necessarily become an actual social divide. In other words, atypical jobs *can* be "good jobs." However, there is a considerable chance that in regimes that are characterized by generally high levels of inequality (the Liberal regimes) and selective insider corporatism (the Continental regimes), segmentation leads to specific inequalities between insiders and outsiders. We examine this question by looking at gross income gaps on the one hand, and by investigating access to training on the other hand.

Figure 2-1 shows the results in terms of gross income inequalities. For the countries available in the Luxemburg Income Study Dataset, we computed the average gross income of insiders and outsiders.[8] Thereby, we want to capture the earnings power of insiders and outsiders *before* taxes and transfers. We rely on the most recent comparative data available, which is from 2000. Figure 2-1 shows how much less outsiders earn in comparison with insiders. The higher the number, the bigger the gap between insiders and outsiders.

Income differentials are on average highest in Liberal and Continental countries, where outsiders earn gross salaries that lie between 25 and 45 percent below those of insiders. The result is particularly consistent across the three Continental countries in our sample—France, the Netherlands, and Germany— where the market income of outsiders is on average more than a third below that of insiders. In the Nordic countries, in contrast, income differentials are somewhat lower—even though they approach Continental levels in Sweden. Finally, the low gross income gap between insiders and outsiders in Spain may come as a surprise at first glance. Rather than indicating "good incomes" for outsiders, however, the result merely evidences relatively poor incomes for insiders, too. This results in a rather narrow gap between insiders and outsiders.[9]

Income is just one side of labor market divides. Access to vocational training is an equally important indicator of labor market (dis)advantage. Indeed, if outsiders have opportunities similar to those of insiders to improve their job situation, income differentials may be transitory only. The results, however, just add evidence to the pattern detected in Figure 2-1. Figure 2-2 shows the percentage of respondents who say that they had some form of job training over the last 12 months.

Figure 2-1: Gross income gap (before taxes and transfers)

Average gross income
difference between
insiders and outsiders
in %

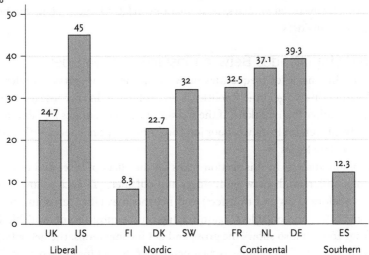

Note: Reading example: in the UK, outsiders have an average market income that is 24.7% lower than the average market income of insiders

Source: Luxemburg Income Study Data, own calculations. Data refers to 2000 with the exceptions of the Netherlands and the UK, where data refer to 1999.

Figure 2-2: Gap in access to vocational training for insiders and outsiders

Share of respondents who
had job training over the last
12 months

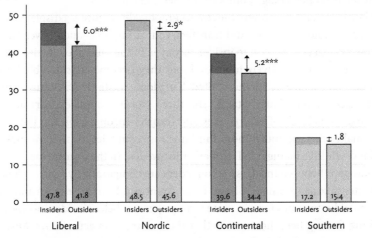

Note: Liberal N=6616 (AUS, UK, US, IRE, NZ, CA); Nordic N=4539 (NO, SW, DK, FI); Continental N=3319 (GER, F, SWI); Southern N=2433 (SP, PO)

Source: ISSP Work orientations III 2005 (see appendix for question wording).

In all countries, outsiders fare worse on this indicator than insiders. In the Liberal and Continental countries, this difference is significant at the 0.01 level. Another striking result is the poor level of training for all respondents in the Southern regimes (Spain and Portugal). As with gross income differentials, Southern European labor markets seem to be relatively precarious for both insiders and outsiders.[10]

Welfare State Divides Between Insiders and Outsiders

A second dimension of inequalities between insiders and outsiders refers to social rights. This is a genuinely political source of inequality because it depends on policies rather than markets. If the welfare state compensates for labor market disadvantages, for instance, poor job conditions must not necessarily translate into welfare losses.

Our main analysis in this section relies on the effect of taxes and transfers on income differentials between insiders and outsiders. Table 2-3 shows gross incomes (before taxes and transfers) and net incomes (after taxes and transfers) for insiders and outsiders, again relying on the most recent available LIS data from 2000. It also shows the gross and net income ratios: the net outsider income in the UK, for example, is 84.6 percent of the net insiders income. The higher the ratio, the more equal insider and outsider incomes. A welfare state that compensates labor market divides between insiders and outsiders should raise this ratio, thereby attenuating societal divides. The effect of taxes and transfers in the highlighted row in Table 2-3 corresponds to the *reduction in the insider-outsider divide due to taxes and transfers* in percentage points. In the United Kingdom, for example, the income gap between insiders and outsiders narrows by 9.3 percentage points after taxes and transfers.

Figures 2-3 and 2-4 present the results graphically. Figure 2-3 displays income gaps before and after taxes and transfers, indicating how much lower outsider incomes are in comparison to insider incomes. In the Liberal countries, income gaps start from a relatively high level, but they become considerably lowered by taxes and transfers in the United Kingdom, while they remain virtually unchanged in the United States. The three Nordic countries start at rather heterogeneous levels of before taxes and transfer-income gaps, but the welfare state makes this gap much more similar across countries, raising inequality in Finland, while reducing it in Denmark and Sweden. In the Continental regimes, income gaps between insiders and outsiders are comparatively high both before *and* after taxes and transfers in all three countries. Even after taxes and transfers, outsider incomes remain more than 30 percent below insider incomes. The striking finding here, however, is that the welfare state actually *reinforces* the insider-outsider divide in France and Germany (while slightly reducing it in the Netherlands). Finally, the Spanish welfare state massively increases inequality between insider and outsider incomes through taxes and transfers.

Table 2-3: Effect of taxes and transfers on income ratios between insiders and outsiders

	UK	US	DK	FI	SW	FR	DE	NL	ES
Gross income insider	17,179	41,875	131,200	97,022	118,074	69,880	50,014	52,995	1,738,164
Gross income outsider	12,931	23,354	101,378	88,990	80,242	47,143	30,346	33,329	1,523,881
Ratio gross income	75.3	55.8	77.3	91.7	68.0	67.5	60.7	62.9	87.7
Net income insider	16,039	35,334	110,613	99,906	108,293	113,742	59,731	39,670	2,684,702
Net income outsider	13,563	19,660	93,779	82,760	81,377	67,786	33,418	27,074	1,577,510
Ratio net income	84.6	55.6	84.8	82.8	75.1	59.6	55.9	68.2	58.8
Effect of T&T (gross-net)	-9.3	0.1	-7.5	8.9	-7.2	7.9	4.7	-5.4	28.9

Note: Incomes are in units of national currency, data refer to 2000 with the exception of the Netherlands and Britain where data refer to 1999.
Data source: Luxembourg Income Study, 2000; own calculations.

Figure 2-3: Income gaps between insiders and outsiders before and after taxes and transfers

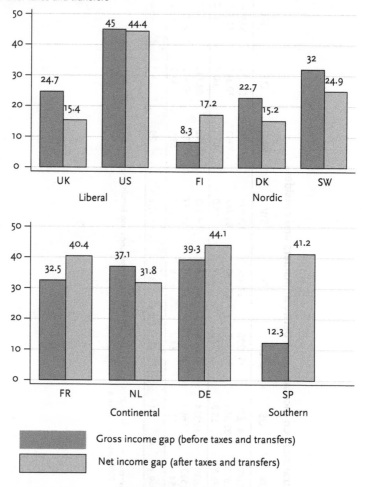

Average income difference
between insiders and outsiders
before and after taxes and transfers

Reading example: in the UK, before taxes and transfers, outsiders have an average gross income that is 24.7% lower than the average gross income of insiders; after taxes and transfers, outsiders have an average net income that is 15.4% lower than the average net income of insiders.
Source: Luxemburg Income Study Data, 2000, own calculations.

To emphasize the differential distributive effects of social and tax policy, we display the effect of welfare states again in Figure 2-4. In the Liberal and Nordic countries (except for Finland, which has strong gross income equality from the outset), the welfare state *reduces* the insider-outsider income divide.[11] In some countries of the Continental and Southern European regimes, in contrast—and this is the striking result of this analysis—the

Figure 2-4: The effect of welfare states (taxes and transfers) on income differences between insiders and outsiders

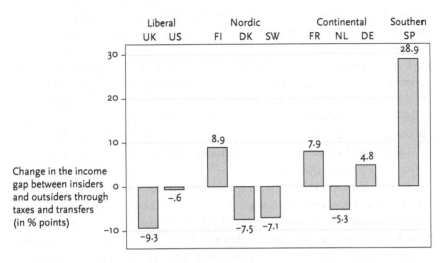

Reading example: in the UK, taxes and transfers reduce the income gap between insiders and outsiders by 9.3 percentage points, while taxes and transfers increase the income gap by 7.9 percentage points in France.
Source: Luxemburg Income Study Data, 2000, own calculations.

welfare state tends to *reinforce* inequalities between insiders and outsiders. The exception of the Netherlands seems plausible with regard to the literature (see, e.g., Hemerijck et al. 2000 on the increasing outsider-reorientation of the Dutch welfare state), and it points to an interesting variance within Continental Europe.

We again performed robustness tests for these results by defining outsiders and insiders at the household, rather than the individual level.[12] The effect of the welfare state remains largely the same: in Spain, Germany, and to a smaller extent also in Finland, the welfare state increases inequalities also at the household level. The Liberal welfare states, as well as the Swedish, Danish, and Dutch welfare states, reduce inequalities at both levels. We also control for the effect of old age pensions. When we exclude old age pensions from the income data, the effect of the welfare states indeed changes in Finland, Germany, and Spain. The Finnish welfare state now reduces inequality, while the German and Spanish welfare states are neutral. This shows that it is mainly the pension systems that are responsible for the dualizing effect of taxes and transfers. People who worked in outsider-jobs during their active life are considerably worse off than people who worked in insider occupations.

The fact that Continental and Southern European welfare regimes do not compensate insider-outsider divides comes, of course, not as an utter surprise. Christian Democratic welfare regimes are based on the insurance principle, which distributes benefits proportional to contributions (Esping-Andersen

1990). Social insurance—especially in the field of pensions—is thus an inadequate instrument to cover outsiders because outsiders have incomplete contribution records. Consequently, outsiders oftentimes have to rely on the general minimum security (or on derived benefits if they are—and stay—married). If this minimum is very low as compared to the average insurance benefits, the welfare state indeed reinforces insider-outsider divides. We explore this institutional effect of dualization further by comparing the pension replacement rates of a worker earning the average income over his entire (full) employment biography and the replacement rate of a worker earning a low income, that is, half of the average income, expressed as percentage of average earnings. The higher this difference between the replacement rates, the more dualized is the pension system of a particular country.

Table 2-4 clearly shows that institutional dualization through the pension regime is and will remain strongest in Continental Europe and lowest in the Liberal countries. Differences exceed the overall mean in the Finland, Norway, and Sweden, as well as in all Northern and Southern Continental countries, except France.[13] Despite its social insurance logic, the French pension system does not lead to a strong divide between average and low-income earners, because of a comparatively high minimum pension. This finding adds evidence to the hypothesis that the regressive effect of Continental welfare regimes is a result of social insurance policies. The French case shows, however, that high social minima may be a way to counter-balance the inequality effect of social insurance systems (on this, see Chapter 4 by Eichhorst and Marx, as well as Chapter 9 by Palier and Thelen, in this volume).

Political Integration Divides Between Insiders and Outsiders

A third dimension of insider-outsider divides in terms of outcomes refers to political integration, that is, democratic representation. We start with an analysis of trade union membership.

In some initial conceptualizations of the insider-outsider divide, weak trade union organization was almost a part of the definition of outsiders (Lindbeck and Snower 2001). Here, however, we want to see whether and to what extent outsiders are actually underrepresented. Figure 2-5 demonstrates that there is no direct link between labor market segmentation and trade union representation. In Liberal countries—where the insider-outsider divide is most clearly skill related (see Table 2-2)—outsiders are even significantly more likely to be union members. In the Nordic states, there is no significant difference between insider and outsider representation, since trade union density is nearly universal. Again, the Continental and Southern European regimes provide a different picture: here, outsiders are clearly, strongly, and significantly less represented in organized labor. The labor market segmentation thus translates into clear differences in terms of power resources.[14]

Table 2-4: Projected gross replacement rates as proportion of average earnings, difference between average and low-income earners

Liberal regimes	Ave-rage earner	Low-income earner	Diff. in % points
Australia	43.1	35.4	7.7
Canada	43.9	37.7	6.2
Ireland	32.5	32.5	0
UK	30.8	21.7	9.1
USA	41.2	27.6	13.6
New Zealand	39.7	39.7	0
Mean			6.10
Standard dev.			5.33

Nordic regimes	Ave-rage earner	Low-income earner	Diff. in % points
Denmark	75.8	59.8	16
Finland	63.4	35.6	27.8
Norway	59.3	33.2	26.1
Sweden	78.9	41.5	37.4
Mean			26.83
Standard dev.			8.77

Continen-tal regimes	Ave-rage earner	Low-income earner	Diff. in % points
Austria	80.1	40	40.1
Belgium	57.1	28.6	28.5
France	51.2	31.9	19.3
Germany	56	20	36
Netherlands	81.9	40.3	41.6
Switzerland	58.4	31.2	27.2
Italy	67.9	34	33.9
Spain	81.2	40.6	40.6
Mean			32.12
Standard dev.			8.61

Note: Numbers reflect *projected* gross replacement rates as proportion of average earnings. The projection includes the full effects of all reforms adopted until 2007. Highlighted are differences over 22.8 percentage points (the overall mean across all countries). It is assumed that average-earning workers in Germany and Belgium contribute fully to the voluntary second pillar pension schemes, while low-income earners do not. If we exclude voluntary second pillar pensions, the differences for these countries are lowered to 11.8 % points (Belgium) and 19.9 % points (Germany).
Source: OECD (2007).

Figure 2-5: Gap in union membership of insiders and outsiders

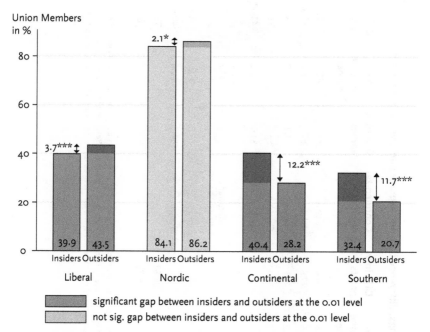

Note: Liberal N=7134 (AUS, UK, US, IRE, NZ, CA); Nordic N=4438 (NO, SW, DK, FI); Continental N=4430 (GER, NL, F, SWI); Southern N=3486 (SP, PO).
Source: ISSP Role of Government IV 2006 (see appendix for question wording).

Finally, we look at abstention from elections as an indicator of political alien-ation. Figure 2-6 shows that abstention is indeed stronger among outsiders in all regimes but the Nordic one.

Abstention is generally low in the Nordic countries for both insiders and out-siders. Participation is unequal, however, in Liberal, Continental, and Southern regimes. The difference is about 5 percentage points in Liberal and Continental countries, but it is nearly 13 percentage points in Southern Europe.[15] The gap in political participation raises doubts on whether politics in these countries will steer policies toward narrowing the existing labor market or social protection divides.

CONCLUSION

In this chapter, we analyzed the extent to which the segmentation of the post-in-dustrial labor markets in insiders and outsiders translates into actual economic, social, and political divides. While the trend toward a structural segmentation of employment relationships into inside and outside labor is almost universal across the advanced post-industrial economies, its distributive implications

Figure 2-6: Gap in voting abstention between insiders and outsiders

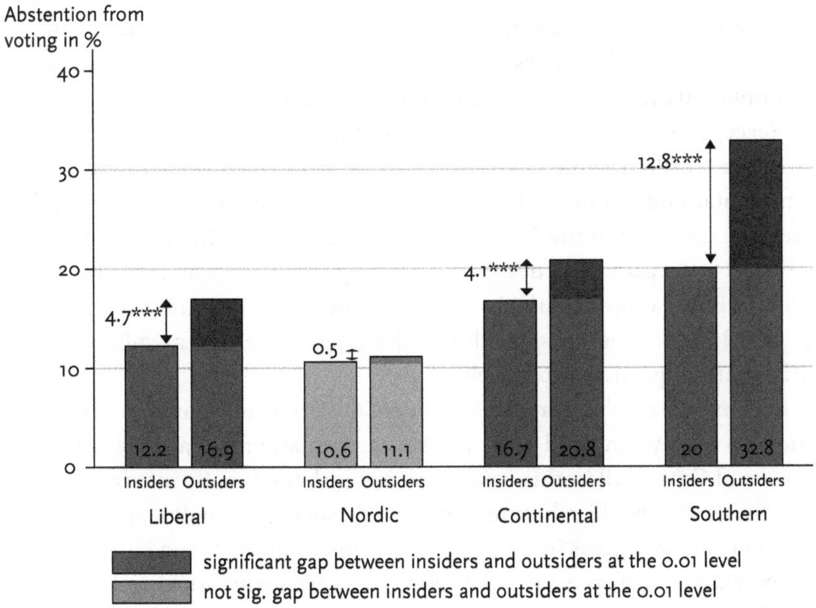

Note: Liberal N=6225 (AUS, UK, US, IRE, NZ, CA); Nordic N=4361 (NO, SW, DK, FI); Continental N=5035 (GER, NL, F, SWI); Southern N=3198 (SP, PO).
Source: ISSP Role of Government IV 2006 (see appendix for question wording).

are neither universal nor obvious. Segmentation must not necessarily lead to inequality and social divides. If atypical work is well paid and fully integrated into the welfare state, segmentation may have only limited social and political implications. Whether segmentation leads to inequality is therefore an empirical question, the answer to which depends on the existing policies and the reforms that different countries have adopted. Empirically, we found both considerable differences between regimes, as well as within them. In the following, we summarize the main findings.

For the countries belonging to the Liberal regime type, we showed that outsiderness is more clearly biased toward the low-skilled. This results generally in strong gross income gaps and poorer access to training for outsiders. Public transfers in the Liberal welfare state either reduce these labor market inequalities (in the UK) or are neutral in their effect (in the U.S.),[16] reflecting different political choices (see, e.g., Seeleib-Kaiser et al., Chapter 7 of this volume). In the political realm, outsiders abstain from voting more often than insiders, but at the same time, they are more likely to be organized in trade unions.

The picture looks very different in the Nordic countries, where labor market segmentation is less widespread and more strongly biased toward women. Even though we also observe a considerable gross income gap between insiders and outsiders in countries such as Denmark and Sweden, the gaps in access to training and promotion prospects are far narrower than in the other regimes, which means that atypical employment is less strongly penalized in the labor market. In addition, the Nordic welfare state tends to counterbalance gross income inequalities by means of taxes and transfers (except for Finland). The net income gap between insiders and outsiders in the Nordic regime is around 15–25 percent, against 30–40 percent in Continental and Southern European countries. The redistributive effect of taxes and transfers in the Nordic countries seems to be the result of a more universal and egalitarian design of welfare policies, as well as of the strong political integration of outsiders: indeed, there is no significant difference between insiders and outsiders both with regard to union membership and with regard to participation in elections.

The reverse is true for the Continental European countries. Here, we observe a highly gendered labor market segmentation (see also Chapter 5 by Kroos and Gottschall in this volume) that translates directly into insider-outsider divides in the distribution of economic, social, and political opportunities and resources: gross income gaps reach 30–40 percent, and outsiders have far lower chances of access to training. What is even more striking, however, is that the Continental welfare regimes—notably through pensions—in France and Germany seem to *reinforce* labor market inequalities by means of taxes and transfers: net income gaps lie between 5 and 8 percentage points *above* gross income gaps. This means that the welfare state "actively" contributes to social protection inequalities (see also Palier and Thelen, Chapter 9 of this volume). The Dutch welfare state may be singled out as an exception: here, welfare reforms aimed at integrating outsiders have been adopted (Hemerijck 2003), and taxes and transfers indeed reduce labor market inequalities. Intra-regime variation is generally large in the Continental regimes. It seems that governments in these countries are choosing different "routes" in dealing with labor market transformation. Several chapters in this book (e.g., Chapter 7 by Seeleib-Kaiser et al., Chapter 8 by Obinger et al., Chapter 9 by Palier and Thelen, and Chapter 10 by Clegg) shed light on precisely these different political choices in a dynamic perspective.

Finally, Southern European countries provide a somewhat more complex picture. Labor markets are less dualized than in Continental Europe, both with regard to gross income gaps and training prospects. However, the lower levels of inequality simply reflect the poor job conditions *even* for insiders. The welfare state, however, considerably worsens the situation for outsiders, because it strongly widens the net income gap. After taxes and transfers, we observe a strong social protection divide. The insiders-bias in the institutional policy design fits with the poor political integration of outsiders, who are less organized and abstain from elections much more frequently.

APPENDIX

Variables	Operationalization
Insiders/outsiders	Outsiders are all individuals who belong to occupational groups (defined by class, gender, and age) that are significantly more strongly affected by unemployment or atypical employment.
Gross income of insiders and outsiders	Luxembourg Income Study, 2000 PGWAGE: gross income and salaries
Net income insiders and outsiders	Luxembourg Income Study, 2000 Net income = PGWAGE + PSELF + PCHBEN + PSTSICK + PFAMLV + PPENSTL + PUNEMPTL − PYTAX − PMEEC
Training over the last 12 months	ISSP Work Orientations III 2005; Dummy variable measuring whether the respondent had any training to improve job skills ("Over the past 12 months, have you had any training to improve your job skills, either at the workplace or somewhere else?"); V48 and V76
Union membership	ISSP RoGIV 2006; Dummy variable measuring current or past trade union membership; UNION 1,2=1; UNION 3=0;
Abstention	ISSP RoGIV 2006; Dummy variable measuring whether the respondent abstained from the last national elections; VOTE_LE 2=1; VOTE_LE 1=0;

NOTES

1 In the early literature in labor market economics, the term "segmentation" denoted structural disadvantage for outsiders as compared to insiders (Berger and Piore 1980). In this chapter, we use the term "segmentation" in a more neutral way, i.e., as merely a trend toward more unstable and atypical work relations.

2 See Häusermann and Schwander (2009a, 2009b) for a detailed discussion of different measures of outsiderness and the comparison of their empirical leverage in explaining individual social policy preferences.

3 We do not differentiate between employment sectors, because it is not the sector that matters but the daily work experience. Oesch cites the example of a cleaning lady in a large industrial company who—despite being employed by a manufacturing firm—is clearly a member of the routine service class (Oesch 2006: 69).

4 Skill levels are already integrated in the class schema.

5 As Emmenegger and Careja (Chapter 6 of this volume) and Table 2-1 in this chapter show, the migration background is also an important determinant of outsiderness. Immigrants incur a high risk of being labor market outsiders. However, we do not include immigration background

in the operationalization of outsiderness because most surveys contain very low numbers of immigrants.

6   The question of whether or not to include voluntary part-time work in the category of atypical work is answered differently by different authors. Rueda (2005) includes involuntary part-time work only, while Emmenegger (2009) uses all part-time work. We decide deliberately not to distinguish between the two categories because we investigate to what extent disadvantage is correlated with atypical work, irrespective of the motivations of atypical work. In addition, part-time work is particularly widespread among women in Continental Europe, for cultural and institutional reasons, which makes the distinction between voluntary and involuntary somewhat meaningless.

7   Emmenegger (2010) has analyzed household effects on individual preferences for job security. He finds that living in a couple household does indeed increase outsider preferences for job security as compared to outsiders living alone. However, married outsiders do not simply adhere to their main earners' insider preferences, since the latter remain significantly more favorable to job security than the former. These results provide evidence that defining insiders at the individual level does make sense.

8   We did not pool the individual countries in regimes here, because of the small number of countries for which data is available. For example, no data was available for Portugal or Italy.

9   Defining insiders and outsiders at the household level somewhat increases gross income gaps in some countries—Great Britain, Finland, Sweden, the Netherlands, and Spain—because of narrower definition of outsiders (only households with an outsider as the household head).

10 Robustness tests for the effect of retirement and different part-time definitions on job training do not change the results. When we look at the household level (pure insider- and mixed households vs. pure outsider households), differences increase considerably in the Nordic and Continental countries (from 2.9 to 6.7 percentage points in the Nordic countries, resp. from 5.2 to 10.6 percentage points in the Continental countries), while they remain more or less unchanged in the liberal and Southern regimes. This implies that outsiders who are married to insiders tend to have "better" jobs than outsiders who are single or married to outsiders. This may be due to the high share of middle-class women working part-time in relatively good jobs (they are outsiders only at the individual, but not at the household level), and the higher share of low-skilled workers in the more narrow outsider category. Furthermore, low-skilled workers are more often in unemployment, which reduces the possibility for job training.

11 Figures 2-3 and 2-4 do not—and cannot—take into account the effects of private social benefits, which may be important especially in liberal regimes (see Seeleib-Kaiser et al., Chapter 7 of this volume).

12   Robustness tests were not possible for France because of a lack of the gross income data at the household level.

13   The low values for Switzerland and Denmark might be partly misleading, because they are based only on the universal first pillar public pension.

14   Robustness tests for household level, pensioners, and work-hours do not change the results. The only notable change is a lower insider-outsider gap in unionization in Continental Europe when controlling for households. This implies that outsiders married to insiders are particularly weakly organized.

15   Robustness tests (household level, pensioners, and work-hours) yield consistent results. When we focus on households only (pure insider- and mixed households vs. pure outsider households), the gaps become slightly larger in all regimes, which means that single outsiders or outsiders living in pure outsider households are particularly likely to abstain.

16   Private insurances, which are a typical characteristic of the liberal regime, are, however, likely to reinforce insider-outsider divides.

REFERENCES

Berger, Suzanne, and Piore, Michael J. (1980). *Dualism and Discontinuity in Industrial Societies*, Cambridge: Cambridge University Press.

Breen, Richard (ed.) (2004) *Social Mobility in Europe*, Oxford: Oxford University Press.

Bradley, David, Huber, Evelyne, Moller, Stephanie, Nielsen, François, and Stephens, John D. (2003). "Distribution and Redistribution in Postindustrial Democracies," *World Politics,* 55(2): 193–228.

Brady, Henry E., Verba, Sidney, and Schlozman, Kay Lehman (1995). "Beyond SES: A Resource Model of Political Participation," *American Political Science Review,* 89(2): 271–294.

British Household Panel Survey (2007).

Chauvel, Louis (2009). "Comparing Welfare Regime Changes: Living Standards and the Unequal Life Chances of Different Birth Cohorts," in Jones, Ian Rees, Higgs, Paul, and Ekerdt, David J. (eds.), *Consumption and Generational Change: The Rise of Consumer Lifestyles*, New Brunswick. NJ: Transaction Publishers.

Emmenegger, Patrick (2009). "Barriers to Entry: Insider/Outsider Politics and the Political Determinants of Job Security Regulations," *Journal of European Social Policy,* 19(2): 131–146.

Emmenegger, Patrick (2010). "Gendering Insiders and Outsiders: Labor Market Status and Preferences For Job Security," *RECWOWE working paper* 2/2010.

Erikson, Robert, and Goldthorpe, John H. (1993). *The Constant Flux*, Oxford: Oxford University Press.

Esping-Andersen, Gosta (1990). *The Three Worlds of Welfare Capitalism*, Princeton: Princeton University Press.

Esping-Andersen, Gosta (1993). *Changing Classes: Stratification and Mobility in Post-Industrial Societies*, London: Sage.

Esping-Andersen, Gosta (1999a). "Politics Without Class? Post-industrial Cleavages in Europe and America," in Kitschelt, Herbert, Lange, Peter, Marks, Gary, and Stephens, John D. (eds.), *Continuity and Change in Contemporary Capitalism*, Cambridge: Cambridge University Press, pp. 293–316.

Esping-Andersen, Gosta (1999b). *Social Foundations of Postindustrial Economies*, Oxford: Oxford University Press.

Eurobarometer Data, Survey 44.3, 1996.

European Social Survey, waves 2002 and 2008.

Häusermann, Silja (2010). *The Politics of Welfare State Reform in Continental Europe: Modernization in Hard Times*, Cambridge: Cambridge University Press.

Häusermann, Silja, and Walter, Stefanie (2010). "Restructuring Swiss Welfare Politics: Post-Industrial Labor Markets, Globalization and Attitudes Towards Social Policies," in Hug, Simon, and Kriesi, Hanspeter (eds.), *Value Change in Switzerland*, Lexington: Lexington Press, pp. 143–168.

Häusermann, Silja, and Schwander, Hanna (2009a). "Identifying Outsiders Across Countries: Similarities and Differences in the Patterns of Dualization," *RECWOWE Working Paper* 09/2009.

Häusermann, Silja, and Schwander, Hanna (2009b). "Who Are the Outsiders and What Do They Want? Welfare State Preferences in Dualized Societies," paper presented at the American Political Science Association, annual conference, September 3–6, 2009, Toronto, Canada.

Hemerijck, Anton (2003). "A Paradoxical Miracle: The Politics of Coalition Government and Social Concertation in Dutch Welfare Reform," in Jochem, Swen, and Siegel, Nico A. (eds.), *Konzertierung, Verhandlungsdemokratie und Reformpolitik im Wohlfahrtstaat—Das Modell Deutschland im Vergleich*, Opladen: Leske und Budrich, pp. 95–113.

Hemerijck, Anton, Unger, Brigitte, and Visser, Jelle (2000). "How Small Countries Negotiate Change: Twenty-Five Years of Policy Adjustment in Austria, the Netherlands and Belgium," in Scharpf, Fritz W., and Schmidt, Viven A. (eds.), *Welfare and Work in the Open Economy*. Volume II. *Diverse Responses to Common Challenges*, Oxford: Oxford University Press, pp. 175–263.

International Social Survey Programme, Role of Government III (1996).

International Social Survey Programme, Role of Government IV (2006).

International Social Survey Programme, Work Orientation III (2005).

Iversen, Torben, and Wren, Anne (1998). "Equality, Employment and Budgetary Restraint: The Trilemma of the Service Economy," *World Politics*, 50(4): 507–546.

Iversen, Torben, and Rosenbluth, Frances (2006). "The Political Economy of Gender: Explaining Cross-National Variation in the Gender Division of Labor and the Gender Voting Gap," *American Journal of Political Science*, 50(1): 1–19.

Kitschelt, Herbert, and Rehm, Philip (2005). "Work, Family and Politics. Foundations of Electoral Partisan Alignments in Postindustrial Democracies," paper prepared for delivery at the Annual Meeting of the American Political Science Association, Washington, DC, September 1–4, 2005.

Lindbeck, Assar, and Snower, Dennis J. (2001). "Insiders versus Outsiders," *Journal of Economic Perspectives*, 15(1): 165–188.

Luxembourg Income Study Data, wave V (2000).

OECD (2006). *OECD Employment Outlook*, Paris: OECD.

OECD (2007). *Pensions at a Glance*, Paris: OECD.

OECD (2008). *Growing Unequal? Income Distribution and Poverty in OECD Countries*, Paris: OECD.

Oesch, Daniel (2006). *Redrawing the Class Map: Stratification and Institutions in Germany, Britain, Sweden and Switzerland*, London: Palgrave Macmillan.

Palier, Bruno (ed.), (2010). *A Long Goodbye to Bismarck? The Politics of Welfare Reforms in Continental Europe*, Amsterdam: Amsterdam University Press.

Palier, Bruno, and Thelen, Kathleen (2010). "Institutionalizing Dualism: Complementarities and Change in France and Germany," *Politics & Society*, 38(1): 119–148.

Plougmann, Peter (2003). "Internationalisation and the Labour Market in the European Union," in Goul Andersen, Jorgen, and Jensen, Per H. (eds.), *Changing Labour Markets, Welfare Policies and Citizenship*, Bristol: The Policy Press, pp. 15–38.

Rueda, David (2005). "Insider-Outsider Politics in Industrialized Democracies: The Challenge to Social Democratic Parties," *American Political Science Review*, 99(1): 61–74.

Rueda, David (2007). *Social Democracy Inside Out*, Oxford: Oxford University Press.

Saint-Paul, Gilles (2002). "The Political Economy of Employment Protection," *Journal of Political Economy*, 110(3): 672–704.

Scruggs, Lyle (2004). *Summary Dataset Welfares Entitlements: A Comparative Institutional Analysis of Eighteen Welfare State*, Version 1.2.

Standing, Guy (1993). "Labor Regulation in an Era of Fragmented Flexibility," in Buechtemann, Christoph F. (ed.), *Employment Security and Labor Market Behaviour*, Ithaca, NY: ILR Press, pp. 425–441.

Swedish Level-of-Living Survey (2007).

Swiss Household Panel (2007).

3

LABOR MARKET DISADVANTAGE AND THE EXPERIENCE OF RECURRENT POVERTY

MARK TOMLINSON AND ROBERT WALKER

INTRODUCTION

This chapter analyzes longitudinal panel data from Great Britain and Germany to identify outsiders in the labor market and explores ways in which this status affects their future well-being in terms of poverty experience. The panels are largely comparable with each other, enabling a direct comparison of two welfare regimes: one Liberal and one Conservative. In addition to investigating the influence of being an insider or outsider in the labor market, other factors are also taken into account, such as household circumstances, age, gender, and educational endowments. Previous poverty is also included to account for the well-established finding that poverty is somewhat "sticky"—that is, poverty, once experienced, is a strong predictor of future poverty occurrence.

It is postulated that labor market divides (by which we refer to the existence of upper and lower strata in employment conditions and opportunities) have an impact on social divides: that is, those in unstable labor market positions may have an increased tendency to experience recurrent poverty episodes. Social divides, defined as the coexistence of poor versus non-poor individuals, are essentially determined by recourse to standard poverty measures. The existence of these dualist structures within different policy regimes can then be explored by comparing equivalent longitudinal panel data from different countries (in this case, Great Britain and Germany). One regime may perpetuate a dualist structure while another type of welfare regime may not (see Häusermann and Schwander, Chapter 2 of this volume). The risks associated with being an outsider on the periphery of the labor market are assessed, as well as the likelihood of an outsider being able to move to insider status.

SEGMENTED LABOR MARKET THEORIES
AND DUALIZATION

Standard economic theory generally postulates that there is one labor market and all buyers and sellers compete on the basis of perfect information in this market, while another set of institutional theories argues that there is not a single labor market at all, but generally two. This set of theories in economics has also been very influential in the sociology of labor markets, but as far as social policy is concerned, there has been relatively little exploration of how this type of phenomenon is relevant to discussions of poverty experience or marginalization in more general areas of life. The initial growth of this type of theory was in part a response to the failings of neoclassical theory (although it was usurped back into the neoclassical fold later; see Fine 1998). According to Rosenberg (1989: 363):

> Neoclassical economists have been unable to explain satisfactorily the structure and functioning of labor markets in North America and Europe. A rich non-neoclassical labor market analysis has evolved to fill this void. It goes under the rubric of "labor market segmentation." Segmented labor market theories argue that distinct labor market segments characterise the advanced industrial economies. This is in contrast with traditional competitive labor market analysis which pictures the labor market as relatively unified.

Rosenberg shows how segmentation theory developed out of the initial American dual labor market (DLM) theory. DLM theory was initially concerned to address the problem of ethnic minority underemployment in the United States. The basic position was that the labor market consisted of primary and secondary sectors. The primary sector was characterized by good working conditions, high wages, job security, and promotion prospects, while the secondary sector consisted of poorly paid, unstable work with generally poor working conditions. This was the view put forward by Piore (1970) and Edwards (1975), among others.

Workers were to some extent said to be caught in a trap if they fell into the secondary sector. Contrary to human capital theories, even if they had skills and ability, they would still find it difficult to escape into the primary sector due to the intermittent nature of their current employment. This leads in turn to increasing poverty and deprivation among this group, which finally results in these workers falling behind their primary counterparts in terms of labor discipline and skills, leading to a higher incidence of unemployment.

We can think of the two main developments of this early theory of DLM, leading to two different and more sophisticated though obviously related strands. Piore, with Doeringer, developed a more advanced segmentation theory (see Doeringer and Piore 1971; Piore 1975, referred to below as SLM, or segmented labor market theory) and another theory of a "core" and "peripheral" economy was also developed (see Bluestone 1970; Harrison 1972). In SLM theory there are essentially two labor markets: internal and external. Internal labor markets can exist within firms or occupations and are characterized by stable, quality employment with recognized career ladders and high stability. Those labor markets outside this labor market (external or secondary labor markets) are the ones in which the prospects for advancement are low or nonexistent. Employment here is casual or temporary, low paid, and unstructured. The major distinction that SLM makes over DLM theories is the notion that the segmentation can occur anywhere: within firms, within industries, within certain types of job, or a combination (e.g., a particular firm may have a dualist structure, even though labor market divides are not prevalent in that firm's particular industry).

Building on this early literature, later commentators have noted that, in the era of post-industrialization, labor markets have become even more segmented. Unemployment has become much more prevalent in post-industrial societies, and the rise of the temporary contract has become a central feature of many European countries (Standing 1993). Part-time employment is also a more prominent feature of European labor markets than before, especially for women (Esping-Andersen 1999a). Thus segmentation is now a more entrenched feature of modern economic structures than was previously the case.

In terms of labor market insiders and outsiders, segmentation theory can assist in the development of typologies for inclusion in statistical models. We can identify employees who have deleterious working conditions and unstable or temporary contracts, as well as those who are unemployed or completely excluded from the labor market altogether. Atypical employment and unemployment are often used to determine outsiderness in the contemporary literature (Rueda 2005, 2006; Emmenegger 2009). Thus the contemporary literature is to some extent building on the tradition established by earlier scholars in segmentation theory.

The analysis that follows attempts to show whether there is any relationship in a statistical sense between a person's labor market segment and his or her future income poverty experience. Thus we are testing the strength of the relationship between being a labor market insider or outsider with being prone to economic hardship in the future, as measured by experiencing spells of poverty (or economic outsiderness). The impact of different regimes can be tested, as we have comparable data for Great Britain and Germany.

DUALIZATION AND RECURRENT POVERTY

While research has drawn attention to the importance of recurrent poverty, there is as yet insufficient understanding of the mechanisms involved in perpetuating poverty in order to develop an effective policy response. However, there is evidence that recurrent poverty is often linked to the so-called "low-pay-no-pay cycle," to labor market conditions, and to specific household level changes (Smith and Middleton 2007). In other words, occupying the lower strata of the labor market or being excluded altogether from labor market activity has a tendency to exacerbate the occurrence of poverty in the following years. This can be compounded by family structure. For instance, being part of a single parent household or having a family with large numbers of dependents may combine to make matters worse.

Smith and Middleton also have drawn attention to the comparative neglect of the "low-pay-no-pay cycle" in the United Kingdom and the associated prevalence of "recurrent poverty." The policy emphasis has been more on job entries than the quality of the jobs themselves—although one of the guiding principles underpinning the previous Government's welfare reform proposals was "retention and progression, not just job entry" (DWP 2007)—but the policy manifestation of this principle remains poorly articulated. This lack of focus may partly be due to a limited understanding of the causes of recurrent poverty and, indeed, to the difficulty of adequately defining it. Smith and Middleton also stress the strong links between recurrent poverty and labor market factors—a distinguishing characteristic of the United States (Walker and Collins 2003), but also the role of household circumstances as demonstrated by Jenkins's (2000) analysis of the impact of additional children. Moreover, it is clear that the triggers associated with changing income trajectories differ in kind and effect between different individuals and families in varying circumstances, probably due partly to individual resilience and agency (Rigg and Sefton 2006; Kemp et al. 2004; Furlong and Cartmel 2004). Research to date has generally not sought to explore this multiple causality or therefore to assess the relative importance of these different determinants and protecting factors. Therefore variables related to household circumstances are also included in the models presented.

If the existence and identification of different segments within the labor market can be operationalized using panel data, then the relationships between these labor market strata and the repeated occurrence of poverty are then open to detailed statistical analysis (thus labor market outsiderness can be analyzed in relation to a dimension of economic outsiderness). The comparative dimension that an investigation of analogous panel data between countries can bring will allow us to ascertain the impact of different policy regimes on poverty alleviation after other factors have been taken into consideration. Here we will be comparing a Liberal regime (Great Britain) with the corporatist regime of Germany (Esping-Andersen 1990, 1999a). In the Liberal regime, where benefits are thought to be means-tested and focused on poverty alleviation, we might expect that people trapped in peripheral employment or unemployment eventually move out of poverty as they change jobs or move back into better labor market positions over time. In the German regime, we might expect to see more segmentation due to the corporatist nature of business, where trade unions assist in perpetuating and protecting insiders (see Palier and Thelen, Chapter 9 of this volume), and we may also perceive the greater impact of that segmentation on poverty outcomes due to the fact that the welfare regime's generosity is based on social insurance rather than being means-tested. The restrictions in social rights generated by this type of system might perpetuate inequalities rather than diminish them. Thus the impact of segmentation should be greater in Germany than in Great Britain.

On the other hand, Fleckenstein et al. (2011) argue that several changes in the German system have allowed a degree of convergence with the British system from the 1990s onward. Although the German system is still different, there are several changes taking place in both the composition of the labor force and the welfare system. Deindustrialization has potentially altered the assumptions implicit in the derivation of traditional typologies of welfare states (Estevez-Abe et al. 2001; Iversen and Stephens 2008). There has been a polarization of skills in the service sector, which has generated a group of highly skilled professionals along with an army of lower skilled white-collar workers (predominantly women and often part-time rather than full-time). This, coupled with the trend toward increased means-testing and the institutionalization of an employment-oriented family policy in Germany, for example, has had the potential to alter the assumptions underlying the Conservative welfare regime (cf. Fleckenstein et al. 2011; Bleses and Seeleib-Kaiser 2004). If there has been a degree of convergence between the British and German systems then we might not expect to see very significant differences in the impact of labor market divides on economic hardship between the two countries, and levels of segmentation might in fact be similar in the two regimes. Unfortunately the fact that data employed here only begin in the late 1990s does not allow us to test a convergence hypothesis, but it does allow us to explore the genuine similarities and differences between the regimes in more recent times.

This chapter then seeks to develop a taxonomy of labor market strata based on labor market segmentation theory and shows that there are relationships between these different strata and recurrent poverty experience. It is indeed the case that there is a large proportion of the UK and German working population in what could be defined as peripheral or unstable labor markets (or "outsiders") often characterized as having low pay, few benefits and short term contractual arrangements.

DATA, VARIABLE CONSTRUCTION, AND METHODS

The analysis utilizes data from the British Household Panel Study (BHPS) and the German Socio-Economic Panel (SOEP). The BHPS commenced in 1991 with an initial sample of around 10,000 individuals resident in some 5,000 house-holds. These individuals have subsequently been re-interviewed each year, and the sample has also been extended to include more households from Scotland and Wales and to embrace Northern Ireland. While the data can be weighted to provide an accurate picture of life in Great Britain or the United Kingdom at different points in time, this analysis is restricted to Great Britain. The analysis covers the period 1999 to 2005 where it is comparable to the German data. Individuals under 18 years of age are excluded from the sample analyzed and also those over 60 at any point during their participation in the panel.

The German SOEP data commenced in 1984 and comprised around 4,500 households in West Germany. Over time, eight additional panels have been merged with the original (including an East German panel and a panel of high earners). The panel currently has over 20,000 individuals included for analysis. Several of the questions in the SOEP are identical or very similar to those in the BHPS, thus allowing a modicum of comparative panel data analysis to be undertaken.

Defining Poverty

The main analysis uses panel regression techniques to examine the factors that determine the experience of poverty (or economic outsiderness), with a partic-ular focus on labor market and family experiences. The basic analytic approach is to use a person's situation at one point in time to predict their poverty status. Previous poverty experience is also included in the models. Thus the impact of being poor and remaining poor over time (a measure of a structural trend in poverty persistence) is explored after controlling for several other variables. If previous poverty is significant, it implies that there are perpetuating divides in society and confirms the existence of a poverty trap that binds people into a life of hardship. Poverty is defined as falling into the bottom quartile of the dis-tribution of equivalized household income. Equivalization was undertaken by dividing total household income by the square root of the number of household members. This gives us a relative and comparable poverty measure between the two regimes although it must be borne in mind that the United Kingdom had higher rates of both overall poverty and in-work poverty in the early 2000s (the period we are analyzing here). For example, in 2001, Germany had a pov-erty rate of 11 percent compared to the UK's 15 percent, and in-work poverty rates were 4 percent and 6 percent, respectively (Eurostat 2005).[1] The United Kingdom was in fact very close to the EU-15 average at this time.

Defining Labor Market Segmentation and Dualization

As discussed above, we are exploring the impact of labor market segmenta-tion on poverty recurrence. By segmentation we are referring essentially to the quality of employment. A method is therefore required that distinguishes the segment to which a person belongs by recourse to the nature of his or her employment terms and conditions. The employed respondents in the BHPS and

SOEP are categorized into various labor market strata based on their current job or the lack of one. An insider in the BHPS is defined as having a permanent job and either or both of the following job characteristics:

- A pay structure that includes an annual incremental pay increase;
- Self-reported real prospects for promotion.

In the BHPS these questions are asked every year. In the SOEP the questions on contractual status are collected annually, but the other two questions are asked in broadly alternate years and differ slightly in wording. The question on pay asks for the likelihood of a pay raise in the next two years (as a percentage from 10 percent, 20 percent, 30 percent, and so on), and the question on promotion also asks for percentage likelihood rather than a yes/no answer. We have treated these questions as equivalent to the British data if the respondent stated a percentage greater than zero. As the data are not collected annually in Germany, we are therefore restricted in our analysis to alternate years (1999, 2001, 2003, and 2005).

The insider status defined here therefore represents the better strata of the labor market in terms of prospects for advancement and job stability. An outsider, on the other hand, is defined as someone who has either:

- No permanent employment contract;
- A permanent job, but with none of the benefits mentioned above (what might be termed a "dead-end job");
- Someone who is unemployed (and looking for work);
- Someone who is out of work and not looking for work (referred to hereafter as non-employed).[2]

Thus we have an indication of the labor market segment that the employed respondents in the survey occupy. The self-employed are included in the insider category, as they are not asked the questions that the employees are asked, and career and pay questions cannot be easily applied to this group. The impact of these dualization variables on poverty experience will reveal the extent to which social divides are perpetuated by and reinforced by labor market divides. We also at certain points attempt to disaggregate the outsiders into those with and without jobs to show that the risks associated with these categories are not invariable between groups within the outsider stratum.

THE EXTENT OF LABOR MARKET SEGMENTATION

The extent of labor market segmentation in the two countries and the degree to which it is perpetuated can be seen in Table 3-1, which shows the numbers of respondents in 2003 broken down into segments cross-tabulated with the numbers remaining in the panels in 2005 (with the outsiders being disaggregated

Table 3-1: Transitions between different strata, 2003–2005

2003	Insider	Outsider employed	Unemployed	Non-employed	Total
a) Great Britain					
Insider	3141	900	78	192	4311
	73%	21%	2%	4%	100%
Outsider employed	850	2318	88	208	3464
	25%	67%	3%	6%	100%
Unemployed	77	91	99	113	380
	21%	24%	26%	30%	100%
Non-employed	165	227	80	1500	1972
	8%	12%	4%	76%	100%
Total	4233	3536	345	2013	10,127
	42%	35%	3%	20%	100%
b) Germany					
Insider	3664	1471	164	218	5520
	67%	27%	3%	4%	100%
Outsider employed	1293	3015	302	422	5032
	25%	60%	6%	8%	100%
Unemployed	145	207	418	224	994
	14%	21%	42%	23%	100%
Non-employed	268	466	152	1742	2628
	11%	18%	6%	66%	100%
Total	5373	5159	1036	2606	14,174
	38%	36%	7%	18%	100%

(The column header "2005" spans Insider, Outsider employed, Unemployed, Non-employed, Total.)

into employed, unemployed, and non-employed respondents). In other words, we can observe the transitional probabilities of moving between segments in the two countries in a two-year period of observation.

In terms of the numbers of people occupying the segments, there is a remarkable degree of similarity between the two countries. In the region of 40 percent of respondents are insiders in both regimes. The outsiders in employment are also at similar levels in both countries, at around a third of the total in 2005. The German data appear to include more respondents in the unemployed category (7 percent versus 3 percent in Great Britain). Thus the actual levels of insider/outsider divides appear similar within the different regimes. This appears to contradict the notion that Germany has more entrenched labor market divides than Great Britain.

Moreover, of those people in work in 2003 there is a certain degree of similarity in the transition probabilities. Taking the insiders, for example, in Great Britain, 73 percent of respondents in this segment in 2003 remained so in 2005, 21 percent became employed outsiders, and just 6 percent lost their jobs altogether. In Germany the figures are 67 percent, 27 percent and 14 percent, respectively. Again, this reinforces the perception that there are not major differences between German employees and British employees in terms of life chances, although the German system actually seems more fluid than the British, which does not fit the stereotypical picture of a rigid German labor force with little mobility out of the core sectors.

The table also tells us that labor market divides are persistent in both countries. The diagonal percentages for the different employed segments are all higher than 50 percent, implying that it is relatively difficult to leave the outsider categories and relatively stable for the insiders of both countries. The other conspicuous findings are the transition probabilities of the unemployed and non-employed in 2003. In Great Britain a quarter of unemployed respondents moved into the outsider employed group, while even more moved into economically inactive positions (30 percent). A quarter remained unemployed after two years. Only 21 percent had acquired an insider job in 2005. In Germany the situation with respect to the unemployed was similar, although a much greater proportion remain in unemployment (42 percent), but again only 14 percent make it into the insider group and 23 percent drop into non-employment. The fact that the Germans can remain unemployed for longer (rather than ceasing to search for work and becoming non-employed) suggests that there is more leeway in the German system for an unemployed person to wait until a suitable job can be found. In the British system, many respondents stop looking for work. However, in both countries it is very difficult to move out of non-employment in general. The higher percentage remaining in unemployment in Germany does reinforce the idea that the benefit system still protects and allows a degree of flexibility in job choice, whereas in Britain, people are more likely to stop looking for work and to become economically inactive.

These figures, however, do not take into account the level of occupation. In order to do this, we enhance the segmentation data by combining it with occupational status. Occupations are separated into three levels based on the ISCO classification. Level 1 refers to unskilled and semi-skilled labor (ISCO group 9), while level 3 refers to associate professionals, professionals, and managerial occupations (ISCO groups 1, 2, and 3). All other occupations are referred to as level 2 (intermediate ISCO groups 4, 5, 6, 7, and 8). The breakdown is shown in Table 3-2.

Table 3-2 reveals once more that the levels of segmentation appear to be very similar between the two countries, even when taking occupation into consideration. Furthermore, the relationship between occupational level and segmentation is not straightforward. There is a significant number of employees in high-level occupations in the outsider segment of the labor market (18 percent of British and 21 percent of German workers). So there is a high degree of uncertainty and risk involved in the labor markets of both regimes, even among many professionals and associated technical and managerial occupations. Thus

Table 3-2: Dualization and occupational categories, 2005, employed (%)

	Great Britain	Germany
Insider level 3	25.8	26.7
Insider level 2	27.2	22.1
Insider level 1	2.4	2.4
Outsider level 3	18.3	21.0
Outsider level 2	23.3	23.1
Outsider level 1	3.1	4.1

having elevated skills and relatively prestigious jobs does not necessarily guarantee stable and favorable working conditions and benefits.

Thus the initial observations are that people are somewhat trapped in terms of labor segmentation in both countries, and the extent of segmentation is very similar and not generally occupationally specific. People on the outside are also much more likely to remain outsiders than to become insiders within a two-year window of opportunity. Thus there appears on the surface to be little difference between the two regimes in terms of this labor market categorization, and there is ample evidence for a structural trend occurring that will perpetuate divides and perhaps provide a material and social basis for political mobilization in the future (as suggested by Häusermann and Schwander, Chapter 2 of this volume). However, a more sophisticated analysis is undertaken below, which takes supplementary factors into consideration and relates the labor market divides identified above with social divides in the form of poverty experience.

PROBIT ANALYSIS

As we stated above, we are interested in predicting poverty as a function of labor market divides, human endowments, and family circumstances. We essentially take the poverty position of someone in a given year and use this position to predict his or her poverty experience during the next period of observation (which in this case is every two years), in addition to other circumstances. These additional factors are labor market divides, human capital, gender, household characteristics and age. Table 3-3 lists the variables that will be included in the models.

We include labor market divides in two ways: first, as a simple insider/outsider dichotomy; and second, by disaggregating the outsiders into employed, unemployed, and non-employed to ascertain whether there are differences between these outsider sub-groups. It might be the case that even being an outsider with employment is somewhat less risky than being out of work altogether. This is tested in the models that follow.

As we demonstrated above, there was only a tenuous relationship between occupational level and insider/outsider status, using our definition. Therefore,

Table 3-3: List of independent variables in the models

Independent variables

Previously poor (lagged dependent variable)
Female
Germany (country dummy in pooled models)
Age 18–24
Age 25–34
Age 35–44
   Reference: Age 45+
Higher level education (ISCED 5)
College level (ISCED 4)
Ordinary level (ISCED 3)
Elementary or no education (less than ISCED 3)
   Reference: Postgraduate (ISCED 6)
Couple no children
Couple with dependent children
Mixed adult households
Single parent
   Reference: Single adult
Insider versus outsider
Labor market status:
Outsider employed
Unemployed
Non-employed
   Reference: Insider

it might be the case that human capital does not have an independent effect on labor market status and therefore on poverty experience. Human capital theory would predict that those with better endowments in terms of education would be more resilient and therefore more likely to escape the effects of poverty in future years than those without such endowments, all else being equal. Thus we include a measure of educational attainment as a proxy for a person's human capital in the models.

Other variables included represent various socio-demographic influences that are known to have an impact on poverty in other literatures. A female dummy variable will reveal whether women are more likely than men to experience poverty. Women are more likely to be poor than men on aggregate, but whether they are after taking the other factors into consideration here remains to be seen. Age is also known to affect poverty (younger people in general whose earnings are generally lower are more likely to be poor, as are the elderly who have retired). There are also other life cycle issues to be considered. This is covered in the models by using family structure variables. For example, we can test whether having children increases the likelihood of poverty, as there are more mouths to feed, or is this only the case within struggling single-parent households where it is difficult for the parent to work full-time and look after children simultaneously? As we stated in the introduction, the impact of various family structure variables has not been explored in great detail in the context of recurrent poverty (although research does show that large families and single-parent households are more likely to be poor at any given time in the UK).

The most traditional way of analyzing recurrent events in the economic literature is the type of panel regression model that includes dynamic probit models. The probit model takes a state at time t (such as poverty status) and predicts the state based on characteristics of the individual at time t and often also at time t-1 (lagged variables that can include a previous poverty state—this is referred to as a lagged dependent variable). There are numerous variations of this model to deal with the fact that the individuals are repeatedly observed in a panel, as is the case in our analysis.

The main statistical problem that must be taken into account in this type of investigation is that there are repeated observations of the same people in the data over time and thus observations within the data are not independent (many statistical models assume that cases are in fact independent). However, the fact that we have these repeated observations allows us to use more advanced methods that can take account of unobserved characteristics of the respondents in the panel survey (known as unobserved heterogeneity). Thus we employ random effects probit modeling in the analysis. This adds an extra person-specific random term in the model to deal with the repeated observations over time. In models where we have combined the two countries together, we employ a dummy variable to measure the difference between regimes.

RESULTS

The models estimated combine the data within each country from four waves (1999, 2001, 2003 and 2005). As already noted, this is because the labor market variables are not asked in every wave in the SOEP from 1999. The dependent variable is poverty experience. Further models pool the country data together and include a country level dummy variable. Results are shown in Tables 3-4 and 3-5. Table 3-4 includes all the respondents aged 18–60 to restrict the analysis to working age individuals, while Table 3-5 uses various subsamples: first, a sample of employed respondents; and second, of economically active respondents (defined as employed or unemployed and looking for work rather than non-employed).

In all cases there is a strong effect from previous poverty experience. Previous poverty experience is an extremely strong predictor of future poverty experience in both countries, and the size of the impact is broadly the same in both regimes, but higher in Germany in every case. Thus those prone to poverty in the present will be much more likely to experience or remain in poverty in future periods, all other things being equal.

Gender is not significant in any of the models, although it is marginally significant in the economically active models in Germany and the pooled

Table 3-4: Models predicting poverty, 1999–2005 (all adults aged 18–60)

Independent variable	Great Britain	Germany	Pooled	Great Britain	Germany	Pooled
Previously poor	1.65***	1.92***	1.86***	1.63***	1.87***	1.82***
Female	0.05 ns	0.00 ns	0.02 ns	−0.00 ns	−0.02 ns	−0.01 ns
Germany	–	–	−0.06**	–	–	−0.10***
Age 18–24	0.38***	0.18***	0.21***	0.33***	0.19***	0.20***
Age 25–34	0.16***	0.37***	0.32***	0.16***	0.36***	0.32***
Age 35–44	−0.07 ns	0.20 ***	0.13***	−0.05 ns	0.23 ***	0.16***
Reference: Age 45+						
Higher level education	0.23 ns	0.28***	0.19***	0.22 ns	0.26***	0.16***
College level	0.52***	0.36***	0.40***	0.52***	0.30***	0.36***
Ordinary level	0.58***	0.51***	0.50***	0.58***	0.45***	0.45***
Low or no education	0.88***	0.68***	0.69***	0.85***	0.63***	0.64***
Reference: Postgraduate						
Couple no children	−0.78***	−0.76***	−0.77***	−0.77***	−0.77***	−0.77***
Couple with dependent children	−0.42***	−0.79***	−0.71***	−0.40***	−0.81***	−0.72***
Single parent	0.29***	0.02 ns	0.07 ns	0.28***	0.00 ns	0.06 ns
Mixed adult households	−1.08***	−0.79***	−1.00***	−1.08***	−0.83***	−1.03***
Reference: Single adult						
Outsider vs. insider	0.60***	0.50***	0.52***	–	–	–
Peripheral				0.30***	0.17***	0.20***
Unemployed				0.98***	0.96***	0.98***
Non-employed				0.77 ***	0.64***	0.67***
Reference: Insider						
N	19,489	45,919	65,408	19,489	45,919	65,408

Note: *** p-value < 0.001, ** p-value < 0.01, * p-value < 0.05, n.s. = not significant.

economically active models. Age in general, across the two countries, shows that the young are more at risk of poverty than those over 45 years of age. Educational level greatly reduces the likelihood of experiencing income poverty, thus reinforcing the role of human capital in determining the life-chances of individuals. The higher the education, the lower the chances of experiencing repeated spells of income poverty. Even relatively modest qualifications provide some protection. However, the impact of human capital as measured by educational qualifications appears generally stronger in Great Britain than in Germany. The gradient is also much steeper: that is, in the United Kingdom the lower the qualification, the much greater the impact; whereas in Germany the

Table 3-5: Models predicting poverty, 1999–2005 (employed and economically active, aged 18–60)

Independent variable	Great Britain employed	Germany employed	Pooled employed	Great Britain economically active	Germany economically active	Pooled economically active
Previously poor	1.70***	1.92***	1.87***	1.70***	1.96***	1.89***
Female	−0.00 ns	−0.04 ns	−0.03 ns	−0.03 ns	−0.07**	−0.06**
Germany	–	–	−0.07**	–	–	−0.01 ns
Age 18–24	0.23***	0.45***	0.36***	0.28***	0.25***	0.24***
Age 25–34	0.13*	0.49***	0.39***	0.15**	0.35***	0.31***
Age 35–44	−0.06 ns	0.31***	0.21***	−0.07 ns	0.22***	0.15***
Reference: Age 45+						
Higher level education	0.24 ns	0.26***	0.18***	0.27 ns	0.26***	0.19***
College level	0.41**	0.28***	0.32***	0.46***	0.33***	0.35***
Ordinary level	0.55***	0.49***	0.48***	0.60***	0.51***	0.51***
Low or no education	0.80***	0.64***	0.67***	0.88***	0.70***	0.71***
Reference: Postgraduate						
Couple no children	−0.73***	−0.80***	−0.79***	−0.72***	−0.79***	−0.77***
Couple with dependent children	−0.28***	−0.69***	−0.59***	−0.32***	−0.74***	−0.64***
Single parent	0.46***	0.15**	0.21***	0.41***	0.09 ns	0.16***
Mixed adult households	−0.95***	−0.69***	−0.94***	−0.99***	−0.72***	−0.96***
Reference: Single adult						
Outsider vs insider	0.41***	0.23***	0.29***	0.48***	0.40***	0.42***
N	15,607	32,390	47,997	16,171	35,738	51,909

Note: *** p-value < 0.001, ** p-value < 0.01, * p-value < 0.05, n.s. = not significant.

increased impact of higher qualifications is less discernible as the educational level decreases.

Being an outsider increases the risks of poverty in all the models and to a high degree. However, the impact appears to be substantially more pronounced among the British employed than the German employed (Table 3-5). Disaggregation of the outsider category in Table 3-4 also reveals that being in employment is somewhat better in terms of outcomes than being an unemployed or non-employed outsider. Nevertheless, being an outsider—even in work—significantly reduces an employee's future chances.

The impact of labor market divides then is crucial in determining a person's chances in terms of income poverty outcomes, even when human capital and other factors are accounted for. However, being out of work or economically inactive is generally worse reinforcing the findings of the transition matrices (Table 3-1). There is then a significant labor market divide effect at work within the German and British systems that also reinforces the perpetuation of social divides. Once someone is an outsider, the odds are against a future transition to insider status.

Furthermore, the effect of household composition is also significant in both countries. In general, most household types are significantly less likely to experience poverty than single adults. The exception to this is single parents with dependents. In the British data overall (Table 3-4), single parents are much more likely to experience poverty, whereas in the German case this is not significant, implying more social protection for single adult families in the Conservative regime. But even in Germany, when we only look at employees, there is also an effect here (Table 3-5). This implies that the German welfare system is much better equipped to help single parents escape the ravages of poverty commonly associated with single parents in Britain, especially if the parent is not in employment. One explanation for these findings might be the German Parental Leave Benefit, which can be accumulated with other social assistance benefits during the leave period, providing relatively high wage replacement rates for low-income earners (cf. Bleses and Seeleib-Kaiser 2004: 88). Parents who return to work full-time lose these benefits.

Finally, perhaps the most interesting finding is that in almost every single model where the data from the two countries were merged together, there is a reduced likelihood of experiencing poverty in Germany rather than Britain. In other words, *ceteris paribus*, the German welfare system prevents the onset of poverty experience slightly more effectively than the British system does. The effect is relatively small, but statistically significant.

DISCUSSION AND CONCLUSIONS

We have shown that it is possible to partition employment into strata along the lines of labor market segmentation theory using data from the BHPS and

SOEP. This reveals a reasonable degree of similarity between the two countries. Unlike what might be expected from a standard typology along the lines of Esping-Andersen (1990, 1999a), there is a degree of correspondence between the two regimes in both the proportions of insiders and outsiders and also the relative probability of transfer between insider and outsider status within the two regimes. This may be because the time period available for analysis is post-1999, when many of the policies adopted by Germany could have converged to a greater degree with a Liberal economy like Britain. Unfortunately, we cannot assess the pre-1999 state of affairs, so this hypothesis remains unexplored.

However, it still remains the case that there is a small but significant difference between German and British systems in terms of the likelihood of experiencing poverty. As might be expected, the pooled statistical models show that the German welfare system is statistically superior with respect to the prevention of poverty spells (as it is more generous) after controlling for the other factors we have considered. Thus, despite any convergence that may have taken place, the German welfare structure is still more effective. In both nations, previous poverty experience remains the strongest determinant of future poverty experience. However, the analysis also shows quite clearly that the German welfare state seems to be significantly more able than the British state to reduce the risks of recurrent poverty, all other things being equal. The impact of previous poverty in Britain is marginally weaker than in Germany, implying that any stigmatizing effects of poverty are not so prevalent in the former.

We have demonstrated that when labor market divides are used to predict poverty experience, there are significant effects that imply that superior labor market conditions such as those characterized by being an insider rather than an outsider decrease the likelihood of becoming poor, even after accounting for a person's human capital and family situation, along with other factors. However, those who are employed, even in outsider labor market positions, generally do better on average than those who are not working at all at any point in time. In both countries, the transition matrices reveal that there appears to be a reinforcing and entrenchment of outsiderness.

What this analysis confirms is that structural factors, opportunities presented by the labor market, are as important, and often more important, than personal attributes and circumstances in determining the risk of poverty. Policies that simply encourage people to find work, without paying attention to the kind of jobs that are available, cannot secure a marked reduction in recurrent poverty or a sustained decline in the poverty rate. The analysis underlines the importance of seeking to ensure the availability of high-quality core jobs offering security and prospects, as well as policies that foster job search and improved skills, whether in a Liberal or Conservative regime.

Education and human capital also undoubtedly play a role, as predicted by human capital theory. But the educational effect appears to be stronger in the British context. This is perhaps because the return on investment in a Liberal market economy would be higher than in a Conservative one, where skills are more attached to a corporation and labor mobility is supposedly lower (see Estevez-Abe et al. 2001, for example). But the transition matrices discussed above also call into question the notion that Germany has a more rigid labor market than Britain. There was actually slightly more fluidity in the German matrix than the British one. Nevertheless, education is a significant off setting component of poverty alleviation in both regimes.

The structural reinforcement of dualization seen in the two countries, be it founded on an economic or a labor market basis, provides evidence for the possibility of a shared political or social identity that cuts across traditional class lines and is founded on poor labor conditions (insecurity) and low income (relative poverty) rather than occupation. There is little evidence for the notion postulated in the introduction that the different welfare regimes would result in quite different segmentation impacts in the two countries. There are many more similarities than differences. There is some diversity, but it is not as extensive as might be expected. Therefore, the ideas proposed by Fleckenstein et al. (2011) that there has been a degree of convergence between the welfare systems and employment structures of the two countries and that the impact of deindustrialization in the 1990s and 2000s has had profound effects on the assumptions implicit in traditional typologies of welfare regimes seem to be highly plausible. A longer time frame for analysis would have to be employed to verify these issues.

NOTES

1 Poverty was measured by Eurostat as being below 60 percent of equivalized median income.
2 Part-time is not included as a separate category, as it does not *per se* provide any information about the quality of the employment relationship. Nevertheless, those employed part-time are included in the category of outsiders, if they have no prospects of promotion or pay increase.

REFERENCES

Bleses, Peter, and Seeleib-Kaiser, Martin (2004). *The Dual Transformation of the German Welfare State*, Basingstoke: Palgrave.

Bluestone, Barry (1970). "The Tripartite Economy: Labor Markets and the Working Poor," *Poverty and Human Resources*, 5(4): 15–35.

Doeringer, Peter, and Piore, Michael (1971). *Internal Labor Markets and Manpower Analysis*, Lexington: D.C. Heath and Co.

DWP (2007). *Opportunity, Employment and Progression: Making Skills Work*, Department of Work and Pensions, Norwich: HMSO.

Edwards, Richard (1975). "The Social Relations of Production in the Firm and Labor Market Structure," in Edwards, Richard, Reich, Michael, and Gordon, David (eds.), *Labor Market Segmentation*, Lexington: D.C. Heath and Co., pp. 3–26.

Emmenegger, Patrick (2009). "Barriers to Entry: Insider/Outsider Politics and the Political Determinants of Job Security Regulations," *Journal of European Social Policy*, 19(2): 131–146.

Esping-Anderson, Gosta (1990). *The Three Worlds of Welfare Capitalism*, Princeton, NJ: Princeton University Press.

Esping-Anderson, Gosta (1999a). *Social Foundations of Post-industrial Economies*, Oxford: Oxford University Press.

Esping-Anderson, Gosta (1999b). "Politics Without Class? Post-Industrial Cleavages in Europe and America," in Kitschelt, Herbert, Lange, Peter, Marks, Gary, and Stephens, John (eds.), *Continuity and Change in Contemporary Capitalism*, Cambridge: Cambridge University Press, pp. 293–316.

Estevez-Abe, Margarita, Iversen, Torben, and Soskice, David (2001). "Social Protection and the Formation of Skills," in Hall, Peter, and Soskice, David (eds.), *Varieties of Capitalism*, Oxford: Oxford University Press, pp. 145–163.

Eurostat (2005). "In-Work Poverty," *Statistics in Focus*, 5/2005, Eurostat: Luxembourg.

Fine, Ben (1998). *Labour Market Theory*, London: Routledge.

Fleckenstein, Timo, Saunders, Adam and Seeleib-Kaiser, Martin (2011). "The Dual Transformation of Social Protection and Human Capital: Comparing Britain and Germany," *Comparative Political Studies*, 44(12).

Furlong, Andy, and Cartmel, Fred (2004). *Vulnerable Young Men in Fragile Labour Markets: Employment, Unemployment and the Search for Long-Term Security*, York: Joseph Rowntree Foundation.

Harrison, Bennett (1972). *Education, Training and the Urban Ghetto*, Baltimore, MD: John Hopkins University Press.

Iversen, Torben, and Stephens, John (2008). "Partisan Politics, the Welfare State and Three Worlds of Human Capital Formation," *Comparative Political Studies*, 41(4/5): 600–637.

Jenkins, Stephen (2000). "Modelling household income dynamics," *Journal of Population Economics*, 13(4): 529–567.

Kemp, Peter, Bradshaw, Jonathan, Dornan, Paul, Finch, Naomi, and Mayhew, Emese, (2004). *Routes Out of Poverty: A Research Review*, York: Joseph Rowntree Foundation.

Piore, Michael (1970). "Jobs and Training," in Beer, Samuel, and Barringer, Richard (eds.), *The State and the Poor*, Cambridge: Winthrop, pp. 53–83.

Piore, Michael. (1975). "Notes for a Theory of Labor Market Segmentation," in Edwards, Richard, Reich, Michael, and Gordon, David (eds.), *Labor Market Segmentation*, Lexington: D.C. Heath and Co, pp. 125–150.

Rigg, John, and Sefton, Tom (2006). "Income Dynamics and the Life Cycle," *Journal of Social Policy*, 35(3): 411–435.

Rosenberg, Samuel (1989). "From Segmentation to Flexibility," *Labor and Society*, 14(4): 363–407.

Rueda, David (2005). "Insider-Outsider Politics in Industrialized Democracies: The Challenge to Social Democratic Parties," *American Political Science Review*, 99(1): 61–74.

Rueda, David (2006). *Social Democracy Inside Out*, Oxford: Oxford University Press.

Smith, Noel, and Middleton, Sue (2007). *A Review of Poverty Dynamics Research in the UK*, York: Joseph Rowntree Foundation.

Standing, Guy (1993). "Labor Regulation in an Era of Fragmented Flexibility," in Buechtemann, Christoph (ed.), *Employment Security and Labor Market Behaviour*, New York: ILR Press, pp. 425–441.

Walker, Robert, and Collins, Claire (2003). "Families of the Poor," in Scott, Jaqueline, Treas, Judith, and Richards, Martin (eds.), *Blackwell Companion on the Sociology of the Family*, Malden: Blackwell Publishers, pp. 192–217.

PART II

DECOMPOSING DUALIZATION

4

WHATEVER WORKS

DUALIZATION AND THE SERVICE ECONOMY IN BISMARCKIAN WELFARE STATES

WERNER EICHHORST AND PAUL MARX

INTRODUCTION

This chapter deals with a group of countries that are, in a comparative perspective, generally seen as prime examples of dualized welfare states and labor markets. What makes Continental European or Bismarckian welfare states such as Austria, Belgium, France, Germany, and the Netherlands particularly interesting for the analysis of labor market change and dualization is that in the 1990s they were still regarded as major cases of institutional inertia and resilience despite structural problems (Esping-Andersen 1996; Pierson 1996). A major structural problem identified by the literature was the alleged incapacity of Bismarckian systems to create low-skilled service jobs because of the inherent cost of labor associated with the Continental European welfare regime, due in particular to the mode of financing social expenditure via social contribution (Scharpf 1997; Iversen and Wren 1998).

More recent contributions, however, have identified remarkable transformations of Bismarckian welfare states and labor markets. It is usually argued that overcoming the Continental European service sector job deficit has come at the cost of new inequalities at the margin of the labor market in terms of a significant growth of so-called atypical jobs and low-pay work (Boeri and Garibaldi 2007; Clegg 2007; Eichhorst and Marx 2011; Eichhorst and Hemerijck 2010; Palier and Thelen, Chapter 9 of this volume; Davidsson and Naczyk 2009).

We refer directly to this strand of research by analyzing how selected Continental European countries moved beyond "welfare states without work" and to what extent this was accompanied by a process of dualization. We furthermore identify and explain intra-regime variation with respect to labor market divides in the private service sector. Despite broad similarities, recent developments in particular revealed major differences across Continental European countries in terms of labor market change and employment patterns. We argue that this variation can partly be explained by institutional legacies: labor market institutions create different constraints and opportunities for employment relationships in our cases. What we try to understand is how economic actors—employers, workers, and job seekers—overcome country-specific obstacles to job creation and how this contributes to the process of dualization. Therefore, we extend the scope of our analysis beyond politically controlled forms of change to creative strategies at the micro-level, for example, exploiting legal loopholes or converting regulations to conform to new strategies.

We focus our analysis on the development in low-skilled work, especially on low-productivity services in the private sector.[1] This area of economic activity is particularly exposed to pressures for cheaper labor, which makes it an interesting object for studies in dualization. Furthermore, we understand our contribution as being complementary to Chapter 5 by Kroos and Gottschall in this volume, which deals with developments in the public sector.

The chapter is organized as follows: after presenting the argument, the comparative section provides empirical data on labor market divides in our five Continental European cases (Austria, Belgium, France, Germany, and the Netherlands) along a typology of cheap labor options. The idea is to identify and assess the prevailing labor market divides in each country setting as well as to explain diverging patterns by including the general institutional framework.

DIFFERENT RESPONSES TO A COMMON PROBLEM

With a considerable degree of simplification, it can be said that over the recent decades all developed economies have been exposed to a common trend: the growing pressure in favor of differentiation and employment flexibility, particularly at the lower end of labor markets. In the course of globalization and skill-biased technological change, low-productivity jobs in manufacturing industries have increasingly been put under pressure. At the same time, structural change affects working conditions. To exploit employment potentials in the service economy, labor market institutions have to allow for remuneration corresponding to relatively low productivity levels.

Continental European welfare states were for a long time seen as plagued by a persistent jobs deficit, which mainly emerged from a severe inability to create employment in the service sector. Researchers saw high non-wage labor costs, demanding minimum wages, generous social benefits, and strict employment protection as major institutional obstacles to job creation (Hemerijck 2002; Samek Lodovici 2000). They were perceived as particularly problematic for private sector employment characterized by levels of productivity lower than in the core manufacturing sector. All countries in the sample have insurance-based social security systems, which are financed by employer and employee contributions. The problem for low-productivity occupations with remuneration levels close to the minimum wage (as defined by law, collective agreement, or implicitly by the benefit system) is that these costs cannot be transferred to the employee. Hence, social contributions can impede job creation in low-skilled services (Scharpf 1997). Esping-Andersen basically argued in the same direction by stating that:

> [the] upshot is prohibitively heavy fixed labour costs which, in turn, discourage employment growth or, alternatively, spur the growth of informal sector jobs or self-employment. In brief, these systems find themselves locked into a self-reinforcing negative spiral, and are today particularly ill-suited to address pressures for greater labour market flexibility and women's demand for economic independence. In brief, the continental Western European welfare states are coming into conflict with the emerging needs of a postindustrial economy. (Esping-Andersen 1996: 68)

How did Continental European welfare states react to this challenge over the past decade? It may be illustrative to recall Iversen and Wren's (1998) famous "trilemma of the service economy" in order to understand the implications for the integration of low-skilled workers into the labor market. Since productivity of many workers cannot be improved easily and since neither low employment levels nor increased public spending are sustainable solutions, the pressure to allow for more inequality also increased in traditionally egalitarian societies. Against this background, the process of welfare state or labor market recalibration should be primarily interpreted from a labor cost perspective, which is closely related to the discussion about labor market flexibility (see, e.g., OECD 1994). The creation of more "flexible" or "cheaper" labor can take many forms, all of which deviate from the institutional provisions regulating the standard employment relationship.

The question of why different patterns prevail in different countries is at the core of the cross-country variation in the degree of dualization. In a stylized fashion, one can argue that Liberal market economies typically ensure labor market inclusiveness by allowing wage levels to correspond to productivity, so that inequality is reflected in a dispersed wage scale. In Continental European economies, this is impeded by institutionalized downward "rigidities," such as minimum wages and collective bargaining, as well as non-wage labor costs and higher reservation wages due to more generous systems of unemployment protection. Together with turnover costs created by employment protection, these institutions render standard employment too expensive for low-skilled work. At the same time, however, already high levels of labor taxation and social insurance contributions make an expansion of public employment following the Scandinavian trajectory virtually a non-issue. Moreover, core labor market institutions are not only detrimental to employment creation in the service sector, but, as we know from the "new politics" literature, they also create strong path dependencies, as those covered form a constituency against liberalization (Palier and Martin 2007; Pierson 2001; Saint-Paul 1996).

In this highly constraining and path-dependent context, we expect, first, that policy makers prefer to design solutions that do not directly challenge the institutional core but which create employment options circumventing it. This implies a process of partial deregulation, as we observe in many European countries in the field of employment protection. Second, we expect that the actual behavior of economic actors is an important source of institutional change. Employers and job seekers have various options to circumvent standard labor market regulation, too, because there is some inevitable institutional leeway to create flexible and cheap jobs, even within the institutional arrangements in place. By definition, such indirect solutions to the labor cost problem lead to the creation of labor market segments with inferior job quality (in terms of wages, employment stability, or social security coverage). Continental European welfare states, with their strict dismissal regulations and contributory unemployment benefit systems, are "usual suspects" for this two-tier pattern of employment.

Hence, we argue that neither the Scandinavian nor the Anglo-Saxon path was pursued in Continental Europe, but rather policy makers and—even more importantly—economic actors created different types of non-standard employment, thereby effectively circumventing or converting existing regulations, without dismantling the institutional core. These new divides between different types of jobs and workers also produced new inequalities in terms of remuneration, job stability, and social security coverage.

In order to account for variation within the group of Continental European welfare states, it is important to acknowledge that different types of "cheap labor" can serve as functional equivalents (King and Rueda 2008; Maurin and Postel-Vinay 2005). For example, the most straightforward way to create cheaper jobs—via an increase in low-pay employment—is not an option if a statutory minimum wage imposes a downward limitation. Yet alternative types of contracts that are not covered, say freelance, may compensate for this; or temporary contracts—which usually involve a wage penalty as well—help to at least save costs associated with dismissal. This means that Continental European welfare states, even if starting from a similar problem, have various options to boost demand for low-skilled and cheap labor. In this sense, all strategies that (explicitly or implicitly) address wage rigidities, non-wage labor costs, or turnover costs can be considered functionally equivalent solutions to a common problem. It goes without saying that in real-world labor markets, combinations of different flexibility types exist. Our analysis focuses on five types of deviation from standard employment relationships, which can be seen as such strategies. In our understanding, standard employment relationships are characterized by (1) open-ended (2) full-time (3) dependent employment with (4) substantial earnings and therefore (5) are not subsidized by government. Correspondingly, the five options are:

1. *Defection from open-ended contracts* by way of fixed-term contracts and agency work. This can be seen as a second-best solution to the problem of high turnover cost in regimes with strict dismissal protection: temporary work only becomes necessary on a large scale because of the typical difficulties associated with a more general liberalization of dismissal law in highly regulated labor markets. In principle, fixed-term contracts and agency work only affect turnover costs and therefore cannot compensate for rigid wages and non-wage labor costs. In practice, however, they typically come with a wage penalty because of a lack of effective equal pay principles and lower tenure.

2. *Defection from full-time jobs.* This path implies the relative growth of part-time work, which is often characterized by lower hourly wages and a more informal reliance on (frequently unpaid) overtime. Furthermore, some countries have established distinct part-time segments with only few weekly working hours, usually called "marginal part-time work." This type of employment features major advantages in terms of taxation and non-wage labor costs, so that employers acquire access to an additional type of cheap and flexible labor.

3. *Defection from dependent employment.* Hiring freelancers for tasks that could have been performed by dependent workers is an effective way to reduce labor costs, as in Bismarckian systems the self-employed are not, or only partially, integrated into social insurance. Hence, non-wage labor costs tend to be significantly lower. At the same time, wage rigidities usually do not apply and there are no dismissal costs. There are obvious limitations to this approach: often it is simply not feasible because of the nature of work, and furthermore, it is located in a legal grey area ("bogus" self-employment, i.e., quasi-dependent freelance jobs for one client only). Yet, in many occupations in the service sector, it is a viable option if firms reorganize work accordingly.

4. *Wage dispersion.* The most straightforward way to decrease employment barriers is stronger wage dispersion at the lower end of the earnings distribution. Of course, this approach is contingent on institutional prerequisites, in particular on the existence and actual character of statutory or collectively agreed wage scales. Low-pay jobs can only be expanded if there are no statutory minimum wages or, if they exist, are not adjusted to the general wage development or lowered by explicit political intervention. Furthermore, in many countries the private service sector is characterized by lower collective bargaining coverage and only limited

bargaining power of trade unions, so that in some service sub-sectors low pay can occur both within and outside collective agreements.

5. *Government-sponsored labor cheapening.* A significant contribution to the reduction of labor costs in the low-skill segments can stem from subsidization, that is, in-work benefits topping up earnings, tax breaks, or exemptions from social insurance contributions, so that part of the labor cost otherwise borne by employers is transferred to the public budget. As this can help create low-pay jobs without necessarily having to lower workers' earnings, governments can buy themselves out of the trade-off between labor market efficiency and equality but have to accept higher budget deficits or taxes.

The five options for the reduction or avoidance of labor costs are summarized in Table 4-1. As becomes clear from the stylized presentation, the advantages of each option in terms of labor cost are mirrored in one or several labor market divides. For instance, temporary work reduces turnover costs but, in turn, makes employment inherently unstable for a segment of workers. Part-time does not reduce labor costs per se, but if marginal jobs are exempt from social insurance, affected workers do not enjoy social protection. Wage dispersion increases the chances of some workers to persistently end up in a low-wage segment, and the self-employed may be simultaneously affected by all dimensions. The subsidization option does not necessarily produce labor market divides, but in practice, limited upward mobility and in-work poverty often remain problems. In any case, the costs of such schemes to the society are an additional issue.

The bottom line is that we can observe a general pressure for lower labor costs and more flexibility at the margin of the labor market, but that different trajectories exist as functionally equivalent solutions to this common problem. In combination, these solutions can lead to different national or sectoral

Table 4-1: Paths toward labor cost reduction

Paths toward labor cost reduction	Type of labor costs affected	Types of employment	Dimension of labor market divide
Defection from open-ended contracts	Turnover costs	Fixed-term contracts, agency work	Employment stability
Defection from full-time jobs	Non-wage labor costs in some countries	Part-time, particularly marginal	Social security coverage
Defection from dependent employment	Wage, non-wage and turnover costs	Self-employed without employees	Emp. stability, wages, and social security
Wage dispersion	Wage costs	All	Wages
Government-sponsored labor cheapening	Wage costs	All, special contracts/programs	Limited mobility to unsubsidized jobs

patterns, but to a greater or lesser degree they all reflect the creative strategies of economic actors and policy makers to flexibilize the labor market.

MAPPING PATHWAYS OF LABOR MARKET CHANGE IN CONTINENTAL EUROPE

In the following section we provide a cross-sectional overview on labor market divides in the five countries covered by this chapter. The intention is to show empirically that each case developed a distinct solution for the labor cost problem in the service sector, with each solution corresponding to a particular form of dualization.

A significant part of the jobs in private services are non-standard forms of employment. This includes (marginal) part-time, fixed-term contracts, agency work, freelance, and low-wage jobs. To understand why countries predominantly rely on one form of non-standard work or another, we have to consider the level of regulation, remuneration, and social protection of these segments in comparison to standard contracts. The qualifications and productivity matter, the more we expect employers to exploit the "cheapest" available option in terms of labor cost (including turnover cost such as severance pay and non-wage labor costs). Hence, the relative cost attractiveness of non-standard work will be determined by the configuration of three elements:

- regulation of temporary work vis-à-vis permanent contracts;
- wage setting (i.e., coverage by collective agreements or minimum wages) and the resulting actual pay distribution;
- coverage of atypical jobs by the social security system and related non-wage labor costs (particularly marginal part-time and freelance).

To explain the various patterns of labor market divides in Continental European welfare states, indicators for each of the three domains are presented below. Unfortunately, limitations of the EU Labor Force Survey (EU-LFS) and the Survey on Income and Living Conditions (EU-SILC) hamper the analysis of complex dynamics and multiple characteristics, such as type of job and low-pay incidence at the sectoral level. Hence, we supplemented our analysis with national studies and more qualitative work.

Without exaggerating the homogeneity of the group, it should be made clear that it makes sense to talk of a Continental European cluster when we analyze the conditions for cheap and flexible work—at least for our starting point in the 1990s. At that time, the Continental countries featured broad similarities in terms of labor market regulation and welfare financing. They all had rather strict job security regulations (Venn 2009; Emmenegger 2011), predominantly relied on social insurance contributions to finance welfare (Manow 2010), and had a rather compressed wage structure as a consequence of collective bargaining institutions (OECD 2004). As mentioned above, it has been argued in the literature that these institutional conditions amounted to an adversarial context for employment growth, particularly in the service sector (Esping-Andersen 1996; Iversen and Wren 1998; Scharpf 1997). Indeed, labor market performance was sluggish in most Continental countries throughout the 1990s. As a consequence of declining industrial employment, extensive early-retirement programs, and low service sector growth, employment rates lagged behind Scandinavian or Liberal welfare states (Eichhorst and Hemerijck 2010). However, Figure 4-1 shows that the picture changed over the last 15 years, and that labor markets became more inclusive throughout Continental Europe. In each of the countries, employment rates grew significantly stronger than the OECD average. In the aftermath of the 2008–2009 economic crisis, the Netherlands, Austria, and Germany even performed better than the United States, which had long served as a benchmark. Belgium and France started from a lower level, but growth has been equally strong.

Even more surprising than this unexpected catch-up is the fact that employment was created in those sectors considered the weak spot of Continental countries. Table 4-2 shows that, in contrast to the gloomy perception of the 1990s, private services were not only able to compensate for the decline

Figure 4-1: Employment rates in selected OECD countries (15–64 years), 2009, and change since 1994

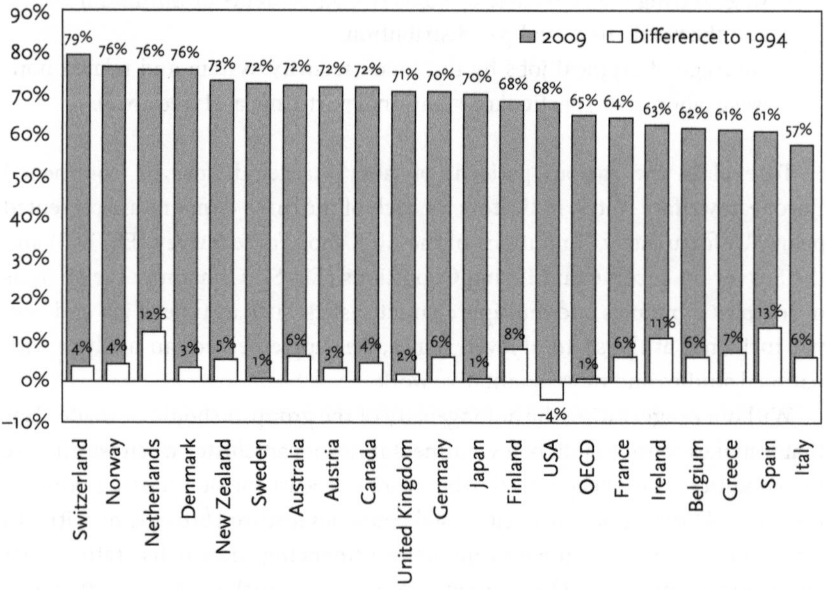

Source: OECD.

Table 4-2: Employment by sector, 2008 (1995=100)

	BE	DE	FR	NL	AT
Total	117	108	118	126	111
Manufacturing (D)	95	95	94	91	86
Services (excluding public administration) (G-K)	120	122	125	130	127
Trade and repair (G)	99	102	116	106	116
Hotels and restaurants (H)	114	139	120	142	135
Transport, storage and communication (I)	117	104	118	128	101
Other community, social, personal service activities (O)	128	119	129	146	136

Notes: Letters in parentheses refer to NACE (Nomenclature statistique des activités économiques dans la Communauté européenne) categories.
Source: Eurostat.

of manufacturing but even spurred overall growth. Moreover, low-wage/low-productivity branches, such as hotels and restaurants or personal services, contributed to this development with a quite dynamic expansion. Thus, Continental welfare states were able to overcome the "welfare without work" problem of the 1990s.

It is usually argued that this employment growth was at the expense of the traditional egalitarian model (based on the standard employment relationship), as non-standard contracts account for a large share of the newly created jobs (e.g., Clegg 2007; Eichhorst and Marx 2011; Palier and Thelen, Chapter 9 of this volume). For instance, the use of temporary work more or less increased over the last 20 years in all of the countries observed (see Figure 4-2). Accordingly, on a rather abstract level we can speak of a common trend in Continental Europe to redefine labor market outsiders: while they were typically kept outside the labor market in the 1990s (as expressed in high shares of long-term unemployment and inactivity), they now increasingly participate in the labor market, but in inferior jobs that deviate from the rule of the standard employment relationship. However, as we argue in this contribution, there are important differences in the trajectories of change, which lead to a variety of divides in Continental European labor markets.

A more detailed examination of the employment structures in our cases reveals such differences. Data on the distribution of types of jobs across selected occupational groups is shown in Figure 4-3. The classification is based on Häusermann and Schwander (Chapter 2 of this volume). The figure compares lower service functionaries (LSF), that is, service occupations with a rather low-skill requirement, such as personal and protective ones, with mixed service functionaries (MSF), for example, office clerks, and with blue collar jobs (BC). The comparison reveals obvious sectoral cleavages. Low-skilled service jobs (LSF) are characterized by the largest variation of employment contracts in all countries, especially in Germany, where almost 20 percent work in a marginal part-time job, and the Netherlands. Here, marginal part-time as well as

Figure 4-2: Share of temporary contracts in total dependent employment, 1985–2008

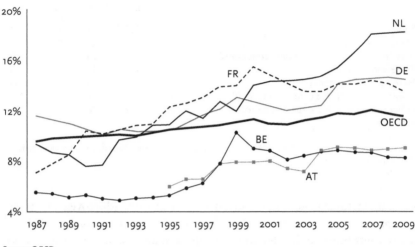

Source: OECD.

fixed-term contracts are important forms of flexible work (both 15 percent). The latter are also quite common in France (16 percent). The least divided structure is found in the Austrian LSF category: while a non-negligible share of 8 percent work in marginal part-time positions, 83 percent are on a permanent contract (full or part-time). One should note, however, that apprentices, who typically hold fixed-term contracts, are excluded from the sample in order to remove the bias of the dual training system in Austria and Germany.

In all countries the self-employed play a smaller role in services compared to the rest of the economy. However, the EU Labor Force Survey data neither provide information on the number of employees nor on income, which would be necessary in order to assess the contribution of self-employment to reducing labor costs (see section Defection from Dependent Employment).

Notwithstanding similar institutional backgrounds and common overarching trends in terms of employment growth and dualization, a closer look at our cases reveals considerable cross-country variations. The differences are most pronounced in the segment of low-skilled private services, the main subject of our study. Thus, it appears that the countries followed different pathways in coping with the common labor cost problem. In order to analyze these trajectories, the remainder of the chapter deals with the various "paths" outlined in the previous section in more detail: defection from open-ended, full-time employment, and dependent employment, as well as wage dispersion and government subsidies. The idea is to assess the relative importance of the different paths for each country and, as a result, to provide a detailed picture of the various ways to tackle the Continental European labor cost problem.

Figure 4-3: Types of contract (%) by sector, 2007

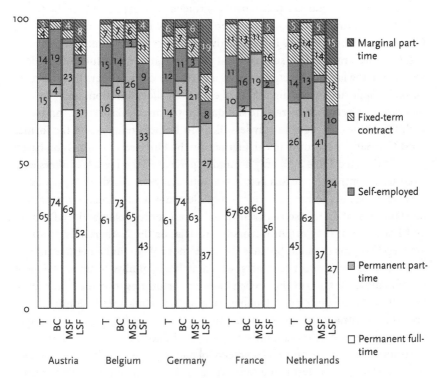

Note: Only values from 5 percent upward are displayed. The classification is based on ISCO-88 (two digits) and the concept of Häusermann and Schwander (Chapter 2 of this volume). Legend: BC = blue collar (ISCO 61, 71–83, 92, 93), MSF = mixed service functionaries (ISCO 41, 42), LSF = low service functionaries (ISCO 51, 52, 91). Apprentices are excluded.
Source: EU-LFS.

Defection from Open-Ended Contracts

As argued by King and Rueda (2008), as well as by Maurin and Postel-Vinay (2005), temporary employment can be seen as a second-best solution for high labor costs. Fixed-term contracts and agency work reduce turnover costs and usually feature a wage gap to permanent employment, even if individual characteristics are controlled for (Brown and Sessions 2005; evidence for Germany is provided by Giesecke 2009; for France by Blanchard and Landier 2002; and for the Netherlands by Zijl 2006). One reason for this could be that equal pay regulation is absent or ineffectively enforced. According to this, temporary contracts should not only be attractive in countries with very strict dismissal protection (in our sample France, Germany, and the Netherlands) but in all cases with a labor cost problem.

However, fixed-term contracts can fulfill quite different functions. Besides being a source of external flexibility or cheap labor, they can also serve as a means of personnel policy to screen workers over an extended period of time. In the latter case, the quality of the job and—most importantly—the perspectives of making a transition to a permanent contract can be expected to be best.

Table 4-3 provides indicators for the use of fixed-term contracts, referring to the entire labor market. Involuntarily temporary jobs are most frequent in Belgium and France. This suggests that they primarily constitute a secondary segment in the labor market, serving as a flexible or cheap buffer. This interpretation is supported by the high share of extremely short durations and—at least for France—low transition rates to standard employment. Gash (2008) finds that such transitions are significantly less likely in France compared to the former West Germany. According to calculations by the European Commission based on EU-SILC (see Table 4-3), only around 15 percent of the French workers on a fixed-term contract move to a permanent job each year. The share is greatest in Austria, at almost 50 percent. Here, as in Germany, educational purposes are most prominent. In that sense, fixed-term jobs are more problematic in Belgium and France than they are in Germany, Austria, or the Netherlands. Workers are largely in this segment because they were not able to find a permanent job; they have relatively short contracts, which makes eligibility to unemployment benefits difficult; and (in the French case) opportunities to make a transition to a better job are quite poor. Further striking indicators are the dominance of very short contracts (less than six months) as well as the high share of younger workers in France. Although only 20 percent of fixed-term contracts are used for training in France, around 50 percent of all temporary workers are younger than 25. Hence, fixed-term contracts are extensively used for younger workers, without involving any educational purpose.

Table 4-3: Selected indicators on fixed-term contracts, 2008

	BE	DE	FR	NL	AT
OECD Index strictness of regulation	1.5	0.75	4	0.75	1.75
change since 1990	(−3.75)	(−2.75)	(0)	(−0.75)	(0)
Share of involuntary contracts*	78.5%	24.1%	54.8%	35.2%	12.5%
change since 1990, % points	(+22.4)	(+8.4)	(−)	(−17.9)	(−3)
Share of education or training*	9.9%	57.0%	20.5%	3.3%	49.3%
Duration less than 6 months*	49.1%	18.4%	49.6%	N.A.	23.5%
Duration 7–18 months*	30.9%	28.7%	24.2%	N.A.	22.6%
Duration 19–36 months*	8.0%	39.5%	16.9%	N.A.	34.8%
Duration more than 36 months*	11.8%	11.3%	2.8%	N.A.	18.7%
Annual transition rate to permanent job (average 2004–2007)	38.7%	28.5%	14.7%	22.0%	48.7%
Share of fixed-term contracts among					
Young workers (15–24)	29.5%	56.6%	51.5%	45.2%	34.9%
Prime-age workers (25–49)	7.0%	10.2%	11.2%	14.2%	4.8%
Older workers (50–64)	3.6%	4.7%	6.3%	6.9%	2.7%

Notes: According to Eurostat, some data are to be interpreted with caution. * In total fixed-term employment.
Source: Eurostat and European Commission (2009) except for EPL (OECD, Venn 2009).

It is interesting to note that France, in contrast to most other neighbors, did not significantly deregulate fixed-term contracts. The French reform process as such was rather inconsistent and, as far as labor law is concerned, not clearly directed toward dualization (see Palier and Thelen, Chapter 9 of this volume). The OECD indicator for the strictness of employment protection legislation even shows a small tightening of regulations for fixed-term contracts between 1985 and 2008, which is against the trend in most OECD countries. Armour et al. (2009), who provide an alternative measure, come to a similar result: after a steep increase of regulation in the 1982 "lois Auroux," fixed-term contracts were slightly de- and re-regulated in various steps. They remained, however, at the very high level of the early 1980s. Yet, according to Eurostat, the share of fixed-term contracts in total employment had increased in France from 3 to 14 percent between 1983 and 2008. The fact that fixed-term employment developed into a secondary segment in the labor market, despite relatively strong restrictions, points to the importance of non-political dynamics. Clearly, the development was affected by regulatory changes, but it also originates in the way in which these contracts are actually used (and how the use changes over time). The increase of temporary work has to be interpreted against the background of the overall institutional framework. The French procedure for individual dismissals is even stricter than in Germany, making alternative contracts particularly attractive. Hence, compared within the national institutional setting, fixed-term contracts, even if heavily regulated, are an important source of external flexibility. This particularly concerns young labor market entrants and the formerly unemployed who have had difficulties in qualifying for a permanent job. There are now a set of temporary and subsidized forms of employment in France to "insert" unemployed into the labor market (Barbier and Kaufmann 2008).

A similar situation can be observed in the Netherlands. Although the country has been praised for its "flexicurity" approach (Wilthagen and Tros 2004), in terms of labor law the country features the typical Continental dual structure. The system of dismissal protection, which either demands ex-ante permissions by an official body or rather high severance pay, is among the strictest in the OECD. Although this legislation has been strongly criticized and although there have been several attempts to change it, liberalizing reforms have so far been very modest. The consequence has been a reform process mainly targeted at atypical workers. Evaluations have shown that this led to a deterioration in conditions for workers with fixed-term contracts, especially in terms of transition rates.

Although the expansion of fixed-term contracts in the Netherlands has clearly been politically facilitated, initially it also goes back to an uncontrolled dynamic on the micro-level. In the 1990s strict employment protection gave rise to peculiar practices to circumvent restrictions on fixed-term contracts. At the time, it became common to rely on what was called "revolving door

construction": since consecutive fixed-term contracts were automatically transformed into permanent ones, employers hired workers with an expired contract
via temporary work agencies for a short time, just to rehire them on another
fixed-term contract. This allowed for an extensive use of temporary workers.
The "flexicurity" legislation can be partly seen as reaction to this trend. Thus,
it was not only designed to liberalize temporary work but also to counter its
uncontrolled use by creative employers (Houwing 2010). Accordingly, the share
of involuntary fixed-term contracts has clearly declined since 1990.

In the Belgian low-skill service sector, fixed-term contracts are less widespread than in the French or Dutch one (see Figure 4-3). One obvious explanation is the more flexible labor law, which does not create to the same degree
incentives for employment outside statutory dismissal protection. However,
one should note that in Belgium collective agreements create significant additional barriers for dismissals. Nevertheless, fixed-term contracts are attractive
to Belgian employers. As a consequence, they make up more than two-thirds
of all involuntary separations (Cockx and van der Linden 2009). And in fact,
deregulation has been considerable over the last 20 years. Also, in a qualitative
sense, one can observe an exacerbated divide between permanent and fixed-
term employment: involuntary fixed-term contracts increased dramatically
and now approach 80 percent, while educational purposes hardly play a role.
As in France, contracts typically are relatively short, which demands even more
flexibility from workers; and hence, fixed-term contracts are less common in
Belgium but clearly constitute a secondary segment.

It is different in Germany, where fixed-term employment is less problematic
from a qualitative perspective. About half of all temporary contracts are dual
apprenticeships, and a major part of the remaining ones are used as extended
probationary periods, mostly for high-skilled labor market entrants. It is fair
to say that fixed-term jobs do not produce a major labor market divide in the
German private sector (Boockmann and Hagen 2006; Hohendanner 2010). This
also applies to Austria, where the share of involuntary contracts is the lowest,
while transition to permanent contracts is relatively likely.

A second prominent form of temporary employment is agency work. It now
plays a small but crucial role in all of the five countries. While some countries
use it merely as a source of numerical flexibility, but effectively enforce equal pay,
others use it in addition as a segment of cheap labor. Therefore, it is important
to note that deviations from the equal pay principle are possible in Germany
and the Netherlands via collective agreements. It is interesting to see that the
growth of agency work in both countries has been particularly dynamic and
deregulation most intense (see Table 4-4). In the Netherlands collective agreements allow a deviation from agreed wages in the first 26 weeks of an assign-
ment, which leads to a wage gap for this group of workers (Houwing 2010).
A similar—but probably even more pronounced—tendency can be observed in
Germany, where a legal loophole led to collective agreements for agency workers,

Table 4-4: Selected indicators on agency work

	BE	DE	FR	NL	AT
Share in total employment (2007)	2.2%	1.6%	2.5%	2.8%	1.5%
Growth number of workers (2004–07)	27.1%	53.6%	11.9%	48.4%	34.3%
OECD Index strictness of regulation (2008)	3.75	1.75	3.25	1.63	1.25
change since 1990	(−0.25)	(−2.25)	(+0.62)	(−1.62)	(0)
Maximum duration in months	3–18	No	6–24	38	No
Deviation from equal pay possible	No	Yes	No	Yes	No

Source: Eurofound (2009); CIETT; EPL: OECD, Venn (2009).

with wages significantly below the standard rates in major manufacturing sectors. The German development serves as an example for dualization caused by the unintended consequences of political reform. Because there has been some unexpected competition between different trade unions in the agency work sector, employers could implement an enormous wage gap to their core workforce. However, this mainly affects manufacturing (Kvasnicka 2008) and therefore is of limited interest for the present study. In the other countries, and particularly in the Netherlands, agency work is strongly focused on services.

Defection from Full-Time Jobs

In all countries (but least so in France) the stock of part-time workers is considerable in low-skilled private services. Yet it is debatable whether regular part-time employment provides much cost-saving potential for employers. Regulations such as minimum wages, dismissal protection, or social insurance apply to this kind of work as well. Very often it is not clear whether low working hours serve the interests of the worker, those of the employer, or both. In the Netherlands involuntary part-time work is virtually nonexistent, and it also is very limited in Austria and Belgium. This optimism could be related to a rather beneficial treatment by the welfare state: generosity of unemployment insurance for low incomes (67 percent of the average wage) is highest in Belgium (for singles) and the Netherlands (for families). In addition, the Belgian and Dutch systems have a strong redistributive component, resulting in higher replacement rates for low-wage earners (which is also true to lesser degree for Austria).

In France the share of involuntary part-time employment is around one-third. This comparatively high value reflects the fact that part-time is much less popular among French women than in countries with a more "conservative" legacy of female labor market participation and family policies. The provision of child care in France is more developed than in the other Bismarckian welfare states, and the general orientation of women is more in favor of full-time employment. Accordingly, the low-skill service sector is much less dominated by part-time work than in each of the four other countries (see also Figure 4-3).

In fact, we find more regular full-time employment at the minimum wage or slightly above that level in France.

Because of the regulatory situation in some of the countries, it is necessary to differentiate between regular and marginal part-time employment. The distinction is, however, not made explicitly in all countries, so there is no general definition of the two forms of part-time work. While for comparative purposes, marginal part-time can be defined as part-time with low weekly working hours (usually less than 15), national regulation may also establish wage thresholds. This is the case in Austria and Germany. It is important to note that the tax and benefit treatment of marginal part-time work crucially increases options for low-wage work in both countries. In Austria and Germany, employers are largely exempted from social insurance contributions up to a wage threshold of €366 and €400, respectively. Particularly in Germany, marginal part-time work (*geringfügige Beschäftigung*, also called "mini-jobs") has become a typical employment pattern in private services. This development is another example of labor market change that is rather driven by economic actors than by policy makers.

In Germany, the exemption of part-time work with few weekly hours from social insurance was designed in the nineteenth century to reduce the administrative burden of workers with only a marginal or irregular attachment to the labor market. This employment opportunity was of minor importance for a long time, and it was only in the 1990s that it was used extensively. Firms started to exploit the gap in social insurance coverage and taxation as a possibility to reduce labor costs in low productivity jobs, for example by dividing regular jobs into several marginal ones. One should note that the reinterpretation of marginal part-time employment as a source of cheap labor was only possible because Germany lacks an institutional constraint found in many other countries. Private service-sector firms typically operate outside collective bargaining and in the absence of binding minimum wages. Only recently, attempts to introduce statutory minimum wages into service sectors have become stronger. This effort has so far had a limited impact. Such attempts have been more successful in Austria, partly because strongly institutionalized social partnership has allowed for a negotiated solution. Similar to Germany, the exemption of marginal part-time workers from social insurance facilitated the growth of a flexible (female) labor force segment. However, the incidence of low pay in this group is lower than in Germany (see Table 4-5), and in 2009 a general monthly gross minimum wage of €1,000 was introduced. Based upon a general political agreement of the Grand Coalition with the social partners in 2006, this is being implemented via sectoral collective agreements.

In addition, marginal part-timers benefit from an indirect subsidy in Germany via social insurance (see section Government-Sponsored Labor Cheapening). This type of work is particularly attractive for married women because in the German social security system, insurance is provided by the insider status of their spouses.

Table 4-5: Selected indicators on part-time work, 2008

	BE	DE	FR	NL	AT
Share of involuntary part-time*	14.4%	22.8%	33.6%	4.5%	11.2%
Share of part-timers working 1h-19h*	43.5%	56.9%	39.3%	57.7%	41.3%
Share of low-pay jobs* (2001)	16%	38%	20%	34%	16%
UI coverage (earnings threshold)	Yes	€400	Yes	Yes	€366
Net replacement rates relative to national average wage					
67%: one-earner, two kids	69%	81%	82%	85%	73%
67%: single, no kids	77%	61%	74%	71%	55%
67–150%: one-earner, two kids	27%	11%	13%	27%	19%
67–150%: single, no kids	35%	0%	5%	16%	10%

Notes: According to Eurostat, some data are to be interpreted with caution. * In total part-time employment.
Source: Eurostat; OECD; low-pay: Salverda/Mayhew (2009); UI coverage: MISSOC.

Table 4-6: Selected indicators on self-employment, 2007

	BE	DE	FR	NL	AT
Own-account SE (% of total employment)	9%	6.1%	5.8%	8.7%	6.8%
Share of low-skilled (LSF only)	42%	12%	18%	36%	17%
UI coverage	No	Mostly no	No	No	Yes

Source: EU-SILC; UI coverage: MISSOC.

Defection from Dependent Employment

The problem in interpreting data on self-employment is that this form of employment is obviously not per se precarious: it includes, for example, cab drivers as well as factory owners. Comparable data on income are difficult to obtain or to interpret because many respondents in surveys are reluctant to declare it. To approximate the extent to which self-employment serves a source of cheap labor, we therefore include two further variables. The first one is the number of employees. Own-account self-employed often do not have a strong position in the market. In many cases they fulfill tasks that could be performed by dependent employees as well. However, as they operate outside wage-setting institutions, they potentially have to accept lower income than that which a wage would provide. They also have to bear the immediate entrepreneurial risk of their economic activity, including fluctuations of income. Thus, not having further employees indicates that self-employment is used as a flexible and cheap type of work. At 9 percent, the share of own-account self-employment in total employment is highest in Belgium and only slightly lower in the Netherlands. Self-employment in low-skilled services (the LSF sector, see Figure 4-3) is particularly high in the Netherlands, Belgium, and Germany, while it is smaller in Austria and negligible in France.

Within the group of own-account self-employed there still is considerable variation, and we have to differentiate between "necessity start-ups" (of workers who lack alternatives) and "opportunity start-ups" (which are pre-ferred options over dependent employment) (Schulze Buschoff and Schmidt 2009). As the latter is more plausible for academics, a second interesting variable is the skill composition of the self-employed in the LSF. At 42 percent, the share of low-skilled (ISCED 0–2) is extremely high in Belgium as well as in the Netherlands (36 percent). An interpretation could be that necessity start-ups are more strongly pronounced in these countries, since self-employment is taken up by many workers with low productivity as an opportunity to enter the labor market.

The only country that tries to balance the high-risk profile of self-employment is Austria, since freelancers are included in unemployment insurance (in Germany, in some cases voluntary insurance is possible). However, in recent years there has been a growing awareness of this problem. In Belgium several reforms aimed at reducing the disadvantaged status of self-employed workers. This was done by improving access to health insurance, increasing minimum pensions, and introducing maternity leave, as well as measures to tackle "bogus" self-employment. However, as social security harmonization mainly relies on tax funding, incorporation into the unemployment system does not seem to be on the agenda (Van Gyes and Vaes 2009).

As opposed to attempts at limiting precarious self-employment, France has recently implemented policies fostering the growth of this segment. The "auto-entrepreneur" scheme created in 2008 encourages start-ups by simpli-fied administrative procedures as well as beneficial tax and social contribution treatment (up to a variable turnover threshold amounting to €32,000 per year for service jobs). There has been an immediate response to these incentives with approximately 320,000 new "auto-entrepreneurs" in 2009. However, so far most jobs in the scheme seem to be of rather low quality as the average earnings of auto-entrepreneurs lies even below the French poverty threshold (although this could be biased by some workers using the scheme for a secondary activity only). Moreover, there have been concerns that dependent jobs are transformed into more flexible "bogus" self-employment (Jeanneau 2010).

Wage Dispersion

Wage flexibility has a pivotal role in our argument, since the straightforward way to facilitate job creation in low-skilled services is to allow for sufficient wage dispersion. On the one hand, restrictions for wages to respond to productivity differentials create incentives to use (cheaper) non-standard work in the first place; on the other hand, wage dispersion can also be an effect of dualization if labor market segments are created that are outside the traditional wage-setting regime. What complicates matters in the empirical analysis is that aggregate data disguise the difference between general wage dispersion and wage inequal-ity that stems from divided labor markets, that is, from wage penalties for non-standard workers. Although disentangling the effects of the two is not always possible due to data limitations, we discuss both aspects separately in this chapter. Having touched on the issue of remuneration of flexible jobs in the preceding subsections, we now compare general wage dispersion as it is defined by institutions like minimum wages and collective bargaining.

Although the results must be treated with caution,[2] OECD data on wage dispersion reveal significant differences across our cases. We include information on the ratio of the median and the first wage decile, since we are interested in how low-skilled workers perform compared to the standard. In this respect, Germany clearly exceeds the levels of the other cases. Moreover, growth of wage inequality since the early 1990s has been particular strong. Table 4-7 also provides information on the institutional background, which helps to explain why Germany stands out. The data on wage dispersion reflects two crucial institutional differences between the countries. First, collective bargaining is rather weakly developed in market-related services. Coverage (across the economy as well as in commercial services) is much higher in Belgium and Austria, as well as in France, where bargaining results are regularly extended to all firms in a sector. Second, cases with general and high minimum wages tend to have narrower wage dispersion. In 2008 the French statutory minimum wage (SMIC) amounted to 63 percent of the median wage, which is by far the most generous level in the OECD and certainly helps to limit wage dispersion. A statutory minimum wage also applies for the Netherlands, however, at a much lower rate. Belgium and—more recently—Austria have generally binding, collectively agreed minimum wages covering the whole economy. Given a large number of companies outside collective bargaining and the absence of a binding wage floor, it is fair

Table 4-7: Selected indicators on wage flexibility

	BE	DE	FR	NL	AT
Minimum wage as % of median (2008)	50.6%	–	62.7%	42.8%	–
change since 1990, % points	(−4.9)		(+6.9)	(−9.4)	
Employer social insurance contributions (2008)	23.4%	16.2%	29.7%	13.8%	22.5%
Collective bargaining coverage (2006)					
Overall coverage	96%	61%	90%	84%	98%
Industry	H	M	H	–	H
Service I	H	L	H	–	H
Service II	H	H	H	–	H
Wage dispersion (decile ratio) 2005					
Decile 5/1	1.4	1.89	1.47	1.65	1.7
change since 1990	(–)	(+0.28)	(−0.17)	(+0.08)	(–)

Notes: Service I = Trade, repair, hotels, restaurants, logistics and telecoms, financial and business services. Service II= Public, social and other non-commercial services. VL=very low (0–25%), L=low (26–50%), M=medium (51–75%), H=high (76–100%).
Source: OECD; collective bargaining: Eurofound, EIRO: Industrial Relations Country Profile.

to say that the German institutional setting is the least prepared to contain pressure for wage inequality.

A further important aspect of wage flexibility—particularly in Bismarckian welfare states—is the level of non-wage labor costs, as payroll taxes can impede job creation in low-skilled services (Scharpf 1997). Data from the OECD show that all countries have considerable contribution levels (Table 4-7). As we argued in section Defection from Full-Time Jobs, the burden of non-wage labor costs directly explains a severe labor market divide in Austria and Germany, where it creates strong incentives to rely on exempted marginal part-time jobs.

Government-Sponsored Labor Cheapening

The strategy of employment subsidization is closely related to the issue of wage dispersion. It offers a possibility to overcome the various labor market entry barriers for low-skilled individuals while avoiding the problem of in-work poverty.

France is a case in point. As shown earlier, it illustrates the effects of a generous minimum wage. Because of the existence and the regular increases of the SMIC, France is an exception to the general trend of increasing wage dispersion observed in many European countries. In addition, the widespread extension of collective agreements imposes binding wage rates above the SMIC, also in private services. This contributes to the containment of low-pay work in services. Nevertheless, there is now a relatively high level of employment of low-skilled people in France. This can be explained by massive wage subsidies in the form of reduced social insurance contributions for employment at (or close to) the SMIC rate. This policy was launched in the early 1990s by the Balladur government to offset the labor cost problems generated from minimum wage increases based on political grounds (Jamet 2006). Subsequent governments incrementally expanded the measure, with the effect of a growing gap between the relatively generous take-home pay for low-skilled workers and the actual labor costs for the employer (Pisani-Ferry 2003). Hence, to limit wage dispersion and to counter an erosion of collective bargaining, minimum wages are increased regularly—but part of the cost for creating or maintaining jobs in the low-wage segment is shifted to the public budget. Albeit implying considerable costs, this policy brings about obvious advantages in terms of employment policy and social equity. In particular, subsidization reduces the employers' need to search for alternative sources of cheap labor and therefore limits wage dispersion. However, besides costliness, subsidized jobs create further problems: while they are rather stable and most often full-time, the subsidy scheme hampers upward mobility. As higher hourly wages imply a disproportionate increase in employers' labor costs, barriers to higher remuneration levels are quite high. This persistence can be seen as one major labor market divide in France. A similar policy exists in Belgium, where wage dispersion is also very limited. Here, the *plan d'embauche* subsidizes low-skilled employment by providing reductions in social insurance contributions for different target groups. Furthermore, in both countries, services delivered to private households, that is, in a field where labor cost is a particular concern, publicly subsidized service vouchers have been introduced and gradually expanded. Low-wage work is subsidized more implicitly in Germany. Since marginal part-time workers who have an employed spouse are insured via their partner (which is rather common), the exemption of marginal part-time employment from contributions is cross-subsidized within the social insurance system.

In-work benefits, that is, employment-conditional transfers paid to the worker, are a further possibility to subsidize employment. In 2001 the French government introduced the *prime pour l'emploi*, which currently provides up to €960 per year for workers with a wage below two-thirds of the average (Immervoll and Pearson 2009). Since 2009, unemployed who take up low-pay work remain eligible for the minimum income scheme *revenu de solidarité active*, which now provides an additional in-work benefit. A similar mechanism (Arbeitslosengeld II) exists in Germany, whereby workers with low earnings can top up their income with cash transfers. In the Netherlands there are in-work benefits, but they are less generous and more limited, as they are targeted at low-wage earners with young children (Immervoll and Pearson 2009).

Finally, Germany has implemented a more implicit yet widely used in-work benefit in the course of the "Hartz reforms." Accordingly, unemployed persons receiving transfers from the minimum income scheme can top up their benefits with additional earnings. Up to a threshold of €1,200 per month (€1,500 for recipients with children), they can keep between 10 and 20 percent of the additional wage. In 2009, approximately 1.3 million persons used this subsidization of low-paid work. In the majority of cases, unemployment benefits are combined with a marginal part-time job. Moreover, marginal part-timers with a working spouse benefit from free inclusion into health insurance.

FIVE PATHS TOWARD LABOR COST REDUCTION

From the empirical material gathered in this study, we can now try to place our cases within the different transformative pathways outlined at the beginning. This exercise cannot lead to a clear-cut attribution of the cases to one specific path but to a rather complex picture. As the country evidence shows, the alternative routes toward cheapening labor are not mutually exclusive, and national cases exhibit eclectic combinations of several options. We place the countries as follows:

1. *Defection from permanent contracts* by way of fixed-term employment or temporary agency work can be observed in all of the countries in our

analysis. These types of contracts have been substantially deregulated in most cases over recent decades and now provide employment alternatives with lower turnover costs. Fixed-term contracts, however, play a particular role in labor market dualization in France and the Netherlands. In both cases, not only political actions contributed to the development but also the changing behavior of employers and job seekers. Agency work is still a relatively small segment in Continental European labor markets. It has grown most dynamically in the Netherlands and Germany; although in Germany this type of employment is mainly concentrated in manufacturing.

2. *Defection from full-time jobs* is particularly pronounced in the Netherlands, where part-time employment is most prominent. However, this does not necessarily mean a deep labor market divide. Rather, this is the case in Germany and Austria, which have established distinct part-time segments with only few weekly working hours (marginal part-time work).

3. While the divide between *self-employed* and dependent employment in European labor markets deserves more empirical research, particularly in terms of income stability, we have presented preliminary evidence that the self-employed serve as a highly flexible but also insecure segment. In the low-skill service sector this problem seems to be most pronounced in Belgium. More recently, France has shown some signs of increasingly precarious self-employment as well.

4. With respect to *wage dispersion,* our study finds that in particular Germany and Austria rely on a relatively high dispersion of wages to integrate low-skilled workers into the labor market. This approach is contingent on institutional prerequisites. In Germany the flexible wage-setting regime and low bargaining coverage in critical sectors is crucial in understanding growing wage inequality. In Austria even private services are fully incorporated into the collective bargaining process, but a tradition of competitiveness-oriented social partnership and the various institutionalized negotiations have rendered wage rigidity less problematic. Both countries, however, are currently reinforcing binding minimum wage provisions. Given the institutional context of the other countries, in particular the existence of statutory or generally binding minimum wages at a substantial level, it is rather unlikely that they will follow the path of growing wage dispersion.

5. *Government-sponsored labor cheapening* can be observed in most countries of our study to a certain extent. Belgium and France have developed the largest schemes of this subsidization approach, in which the government takes over part of the non-wage labor cost of low-pay work. France is also a major Continental European example of in-work

benefits. This is also true for Germany, where the possibility to combine minimum income support and part-time work is equivalent to an in-work benefit.

On the basis of the labor market indicators we have presented in this chapter, it is difficult to provide a normative assessment of labor market divides in the five countries. To evaluate which labor market is "most divided" would require more detailed micro-level evidence, in particular on variables such as income, job satisfaction, and mobility (as it is partly provided by Häusermann and Schwander in Chapter 2 of this volume). This being said, our results suggest that Austria stands out from the rest of the sample, with relatively moderate labor market divides. This concerns the size of the secondary segment as well as the quality of the divides. Against the background of its sound labor market performance and political attempts to limit dualization (see Obinger et al., Chapter 8 of this volume), Austria can be considered a good-practice example in the Continental European group. On the other hand, one could argue that Germany is the case with the most severe departure from an egalitarian employment model because the fragmentation of its labor market is accompanied by an enormous growth of wage inequality.

CONCLUSIONS

The chapter has compared employment structures in five Continental welfare states. It showed that these countries feature broad similarities in their reliance on a more divided employment model. Particularly in service occupations with low skill requirements, economic actors are constrained by institutional barriers to work or hire at low wage levels. In all of our cases, more or less efficient strategies emerged to bypass these barriers. As we have shown, the consequence of this development is a trend toward a more divided labor market. In this sense, each case has its "skeleton in the closet." If one looks closer, there are considerable differences between the national patterns of standard and non-standard work. We have identified five transformative pathways toward more flexible and cheaper labor market segments: growing wage dispersion, defection from permanent contracts and from full-time employment, as well as from dependent employment and government-sponsored labor cost reductions.

As we have argued, intra-regime variation can be best understood if country-specific institutional constraints are included in the analysis as well as the creative (and destructive) behavior of economic actors to overcome such constraints. We have presented some preliminary evidence pointing to the importance of micro-level dynamics for the process of dualization. Investigating how patterns of institutional defection and compliance affect labor market change will be a useful task for future research.

NOTES

1 Please note that, due to data limitations in many cases, we are not able to break down our empirical results by sector. Thus, although the argument focuses on private services, our data often refer to the entire economy, assuming that results are at least partly driven by developments in the service sector. To avoid confusion, all results refer to the entire labor market unless indicated otherwise.

2 Unfortunately, the applied micro data sets do not provide information on wages. Therefore, we cannot break down results for wage dispersion by sector. For further information on the limitations of international wage data and of the OECD approach in particular, see Lucifora et al. (2005).

REFERENCES

Armour, John, Deakin, Simon, Lele, Priya, and Siems, Mathias M. (2009). "How Do Legal Rules Evolve? Evidence from a Cross-Country Comparison of Shareholder, Creditor and Worker Protection," *American Journal of Comparative Law*, 57(3): 579–629.

Barbier, Jean-Claude, and Kaufmann, Otto (2008). "The French Strategy Against Unemployment: Innovative but Inconsistent," in Eichhorst, Werner, Kaufmann, Otto, and Konle-Seidl, Regina (eds.), *Bringing the Jobless into Work? Experiences with Activation Schemes in Europe and the US*, Berlin: Springer, pp. 69–120.

Blanchard, Olivier, and Landier, Augustin (2002). "The Perverse Effects of Partial Labour Market Reform: Fixed—Term Contracts in France," *Economic Journal*, 112(480): 214–244.

Boeri, Tito, and Garibaldi, Pietro (2007). "Two Tier Reforms of Employment Protection: A Honeymoon Effect?," *Economic Journal*, 117(521): 357–385.

Boockmann, Bernhard, and Hagen, Tobias (2006). "Befristete Beschäftigungsverhältnisse? Brücken in den Arbeitsmarkt oder Instrumente der Segmentierung," *ZEW-Wirtschaftsanalysen*, Band 80, Baden-Baden.

Brown, Sarah, and Sessions, John G. (2005). "Employee Attitudes, Earnings and Fixed-Term Contracts: International Evidence," *Review of World Economics*, 141(2): 296–317.

Clegg, Daniel (2007). "Continental Drift: On Unemployment Policy Change in Bismarckian Welfare States," *Social Policy and Administration*, 41(6): 597–617.

Cockx, Bart, and Van der Linden, Bruno (2009.) "Flexicurity in Belgium: A Proposal Based on Economic Principles," *IZA Policy Paper* No. 9, Bonn.

Davidsson, Johan, and Naczyk, Marek (2009). "The Ins and Outs of Dualisation: A Literature Review," *RECWOWE Working Paper* No. 2, Edinburgh.

Eichhorst, Werner, and Marx, Paul (2011). "Reforming German Labor Market Institutions: A Dual Path to Flexibility," *Journal of European Social Policy*, 21(1): 73–87.

Eichhorst, Werner, and Hemerijck, Anton (2010). "Welfare and Employment: A European Dilemma?," in Alber, Jens, and Gilbert, Neil (eds.), *United in Diversity? Comparing Social Models in Europe and America*, New York: Oxford University Press, pp. 201–236.

Emmenegger, Patrick (2011). "Job Security Regulations in Western Democracies: A Fuzzy-Set Analysis," *European Journal of Political Research*, 50(3): 336–364.

Esping-Andersen, Gøsta (1996). "Welfare States Without Work: The Impasse of Labour Shedding and Familialism in Continental European Social Policy," in Esping-Andersen, Gøsta (ed.), *Welfare States in Transition: Social Security in the New Global Economies*, London: Sage, pp. 66–87.

European Commission (2009). "Indicators for monitoring the Employment Guidelines including indicators for additional employment analysis. 2009 compendium." Retrieved on 25/06/2009 from http://ec.europa.eu/social/main.jsp?catId=477&langId=en.

Gash, Vanessa (2008). "Bridge or Trap? Temporary Workers' Transitions to Unemployment and to the Standard Employment Contract," *European Sociological Review*, 24(5): 651–668.

Giesecke, Johannes (2009). "Socio-Economic Risks of Atypical Employment Relationships: Evidence from the German Labour Market," *European Sociological Review*, 25(6): 629–646.

Hemerijck, Anton, and Marx, Ive (2010). "Continental Welfare at a Crossroads. The Choice Between Activation and Minimum Income Protection in Belgium and the Netherlands," in Palier, Bruno (ed.), *A Long Goodbye to Bismarck? The Politics of Welfare Reform in Continental Europe*, Amsterdam: Amsterdam University Press, pp. 129–155.

Hemerijck, Anton (2002). "The Self-Transformation of the European Social Model(s)," in Esping-Andersen, Gøsta (ed.), *Why We Need a New Welfare State*, Oxford: Oxford University Press, pp. 173–214.

Hohendanner, Christian (2010). "Befristete Arbeitsverträge zwischen Auf- und Abschwung: Unsichere Zeiten, unsichere Verträge?," *IAB Kurzbericht* 14/2010, Nürnberg.

Houwing, Hester (2010). "A Dutch Approach to Flexicurity? Negotiated Change in the Organization of Temporary Work," Doctoral thesis, University of Amsterdam: Amsterdam.

Immervoll, Herwig, and Pearson, Mark (2009). "A Good Time for Making Work Pay? Taking Stock of In-Work Benefits and Related Measures Across the OECD," *IZA Policy Paper*, No. 3, Bonn.

Iversen, Torben, and Wren, Anne (1998). "Equality, Employment, and Budgetary Restraint: The Trilemma of the Service Economy," *World Politics*, 50(4): 507–546.

Jamet, Stéphanie (2006). "Improving Labour Market Performance in France," *OECD Economics Department Working Papers*, No. 504, Paris.

Jeanneau, Laurent (2010). "Auto-entrepreneurs: Arnaque ou miracle?," *Alternatives économiques*, 5/2010: 16.

King, Desmond, and Rueda, David (2008). "Cheap Labor: The New Politics of 'Bread and Roses'," in Industrial Democracies, *Perspectives on Politics*, 6(2): 279–297.

Kvasnicka, Michael (2008). "Does Temporary Help Work Provide a Stepping Stone to Regular Employment?," *NBER Working Paper* 13843, Cambridge.

Lucifora, Claudio, McKnight, Abigail, and Salverda, Wiemer (2005). "Low-wage Employment in Europe: A Review of the Evidence," *Socio-Economic Review*, 3(2): 259–292.

Manow, Philip (2010). "Trajectories of Fiscal Adjustment in Bismarckian Welfare Systems," in Palier, Bruno (ed.), *A Long Goodbye to Bismarck? The Politics of Welfare Reform in Continental Europe*, Amsterdam: Amsterdam University Press, pp. 279–299.

Maurin, Eric, and Postel-Vinay, Fabien (2005). "The European Job Security Gap," *Work and Occupations*, 32(2): 229–252.

OECD (1994). *The OECD Jobs Study*, Paris: OECD.

OECD (2004). *OECD Employment Outlook*, Paris: OECD.

Palier, Bruno, and Martin, Claude (2007). "Editorial Introduction From 'a Frozen Landscape' to Structural Reforms: The Sequential Transformation of Bismarckian Welfare Systems," *Social Policy and Administration*, 41(6): 535–554.

Pierson, Paul (1996). "The New Politics of the Welfare State," *World Politics*, 48(2): 143–179.

Pierson, Paul (2001). "Coping with Permanent Austerity: Welfare State Restructuring in Affluent Democracies," in Pierson, Paul (ed.), *The New Politics of the Welfare State in Continental Europe*, Oxford: Oxford University Press, pp. 410–456.

Pisani-Ferry, Jean (2003). "The Surprising French Employment Performance: What Lessons?," *CESifo Working Paper*, No. 1078, Munich.

Saint-Paul, Gilles (1996). "Exploring the Political Economy of Labour Market Institutions," *Economic Policy*, 11(23): 265–300.

Samek Lodovici, Manuela (2000). "The Dynamics of Labour Market Reform in European Countries," in Esping-Andersen, Gøsta, and Regini, Marino (eds.), *Why Deregulate Labour Markets?*, Oxford, Oxford University Press, pp. 30–65.

Salverda, Wiemer, and Mayhew, Ken (2009). "Capitalist Economies and Wage Inequality," *Oxford Review of Economic Policy*, 25(1): 126–154.

Schank, Thorsten, Schnabel, Claus, and Stephani, Jens (2009). "Geringverdiener: Wem und wie gelingt der Aufstieg?," *Jahrbücher für Nationalökonomie und Statistik*, 229(5): 584–614.

Scharpf, Fritz W. (1997). "Employment and the Welfare State: A Continental Dilemma," *MPIfG Working Paper* 97/7, Cologne.

Schulze Buschoff, Karin, and Schmidt, Claudia (2009). "Adapting Labour Law and Social Security to the Needs of the 'New Self-Employed': Comparing the UK, Germany and the Netherlands," *Journal of European Social Policy*, 19(2): 147–159.

Van Gyes, Guy, and Vaes, Tine (2009). "Belgium: Self-Employed Workers," http://www.eurofound.europa.eu/comparative/tno801018s/be0801019q.htm.

Venn, Danielle (2009). "Legislation, Collective Bargaining and Enforcement: Updating the OECD Employment Protection Indicators," *OECD Social, Employment and Migration Working Papers* 89, Paris.

Wilthagen, Ton, and Tros, Frank (2004). "The Concept of 'Flexicurity': A New Approach to Regulating Employment and Labour Markets," *Transfer*, 10(2):166–186.

Zijl, Marloes (2006). "Economic and Social Consequences of Temporary Employment," Doctoral thesis, University of Amsterdam, Amsterdam.

5

DUALIZATION AND GENDER IN SOCIAL SERVICES

THE ROLE OF THE STATE IN GERMANY AND FRANCE

DANIELA KROOS AND **KARIN GOTTSCHALL**

INTRODUCTION

Against the background of a shrinking manufacturing sector, erosion of standard family formation, and demographic change, the burgeoning social service sector evokes high expectations for job growth and the settlement of pressing societal needs such as elderly care and education. Moreover, the sector is expected to promote women's integration into the labor market, not least due to the welfare state's role both as a provider of services and as a model employer (Esping-Andersen et al. 2002).

At the same time, the social service sector always has been characterized by a variety of employment structures. Typically, these range from informal to formal work, including low-skilled, low-wage jobs on the one hand and professional jobs on the other. In the current era of deregulating labor markets, the growth of social services reinforces labor market divides, weakening the standard of full-time, lifelong employment of a male breadwinner prominent in the golden age of the welfare state (Deakin 2002). This holds true especially for Bismarckian welfare systems such as Germany and France, as both tend to promote dual labor market structures in order to gain pockets of flexibility in an otherwise highly regulated labor market (Palier and Thelen 2010 and Chapter 9 of this volume; Eichhorst and Marx, this volume). Indeed, recently these countries have seen an increase of non-standard employment in social services, albeit from different starting points. In France, where social service provision for a long time has been characterized by high professional standards, already since the mid-1990s reforms aimed at flexibility in elder home care and child care labor markets contributed to an increase of mostly marginal non-standard employment (Morel 2007; Méhaut 2007; Hamandia 2007). Germany, too, exhibits an increase of part-time and low-wage work, but the tradition of semi-professional occupations in social services loses ground as early child care and health care call for higher levels of professionalization (Bahle 2007; Gottschall 2008). Not least against the background of a different tradition of state intervention in social services and a different earner model in both countries, the question arises whether the changes mentioned above really indicate a common trend toward precarious employment patterns in social services, reinforcing or establishing divided structures detrimental to the dominant female workforce and women's career perspectives.

This chapter examines employment dynamics in social services during the last two decades and investigates how to account for commonalities and differences in the dualization of this sector and their gender consequences in Germany and France. By addressing social services and the role of the state as employer, our chapter complements the study by Eichhorst and Marx (Chapter 4 of this volume), which analyzes the private service sector and the role of the state as regulator of employment. Moreover, our analysis emphasizes the potential occupational bias of dualization, reflecting that the occupational status is likely to impact employment careers over the life course and that social services host occupational classes (groups of so-called "sociocultural semi-professionals" as well as "routine service workers") that are regarded as particularly prone to an outsider status (see Häusermann and Schwander, Chapter 2 of this volume).

The chapter unfolds in four main sections. The first section discusses the role of the state as employer in the Bismarckian welfare systems of Germany and France. Here we argue that they represent different cases with respect to the organization of social services. We then map the field of social services in both countries, using a cross-sectional analysis of employment growth and employment structures, with special emphasis on the emergence of non-standard employment. In order to assess potential long term-effects of precarious employment on individual career trajectories, the third section addresses how changes in established training and career patterns might contribute to dualization in the sector. Concluding remarks evaluate the observed changes, reflecting the role of state as either promoting or constraining dual employment structures.

THE STATE AS EMPLOYER AND GENDER RELATIONS IN BISMARCKIAN WELFARE SYSTEMS

Comparative welfare state research mainly has addressed the role of the state as service provider. Yet the state as an employer shapes the structure of labor markets and the social position of men and women. With respect to social services, two insights are of relevance here: first, that different ways of social service provision (public, private, or by households) influence female labor market integration; and second, that (varying) quality of service provision and employment structure are interrelated.

Following the notion of the "three worlds of welfare capitalism," Social-democratic and Liberal welfare regimes host a more post-industrial economy with a large state-run social service sector in Social-democratic regimes and a more market-driven service sector in Liberal regimes, both easing women's integration into the labor market. Conservative regimes, however, are more likely to be rooted in (Fordist) industrial capitalism and therefore are less service intensive. Favoring financial transfers to families, they exhibit low female labor market integration and tend to put women at risk of becoming part of a "large outsider surplus population" (Esping-Andersen 1999; Davidsson and Naczyk 2009: 11). Feminists argue that welfare capitalism has supported a gendered division of labor, discharging men from household and care work, which negatively affects women's social status in two ways. First, the "standard worker" norm, entailing a living (family) wage, requires full-time and lifelong market availability in accordance with a male standard life course. Second, household and care work and the related skills informally performed by women tend to be devalued, which has hampered their transfer to the market sphere as a "professional project" (Ostner and Lewis 1995). Also relevant is the insight from comparative labor market research identifying a "high road" and "low road" of service provision. In this case, we argue that the state plays a crucial role in defining the social standards and professional level of employment in social services. Welfare regimes characterized by a large public social service sector providing high-quality services as an entitlement to all citizens call for standard employment and a skilled workforce. Regimes with a more pronounced commercial provision of social services tailored to the different demands and purchasing power of customers, in contrast, tend to generate a more polarized wage and skill structure (Schmid and Ziegler 1993; Fligstein 2001; Shire and Gottschall 2007).

In this framework, Germany and France figure as "conservative corporatist" or, more specifically, Bismarckian welfare systems emphasizing job and income security for male workers, based on standard employment and high labor market regulation. Access to benefits is linked to work position, and most benefits are in cash instead of flat-rate benefits or social services in kind, restricting both public and private service sector expansion (Palier and Martin 2007). Complementary to the male breadwinner standard of full-time, lifelong employment, women are seen primarily as mothers and wives, rather than as workers. In turn, maternal employment rates are low and women's labor market position is tenuous (Ostner and Lewis 1995; Offe and Hinrichs 1984).

This ideal type assessment captures basic institutional similarities of both countries, including a well-established bureaucracy sustained by civil servants whose privileged status served as a model for standardizing employment in the private economy (Kroos 2010; Tepe et al. 2010). However, in the field of social services, the Conservative welfare regime classification fits Germany more than France. In Germany the subsidiarity principle, in combination with a strong male breadwinner model, has favored the provision of social services by family or third-sector organizations, allowing for deviations from standard employment with respect to wages and interest representation, especially in the dominant church-run social service organizations where informal work has been prevalent for a long time (Gottschall 2008). In contrast to this "low road" of service provision, the French model of service provision resembles the Social democratic welfare regime, fostering a dual earner rather than a male breadwinner model. Not only is the laic state a strong social service provider of child care and education, with comprehensive elementary education and all-day schooling that allows for professional careers in the field, but also mothers' high labor market participation is based on the norm of full-time employment (Morgan 2005; Bahle 2007).

Obviously, the role of the state as employer makes a difference for both the structure of social services and female employment patterns in this sector. We assume that different legacies affect changes in the social service sector and therefore have to be taken into account when investigating the emergence of non-standard employment in both countries.

If we consider the change capacity of welfare states, that is, their potential to induce employment growth and safeguard standard employment, Bismarckian welfare states are expected to have a lower capacity to promote service employment than Social-democratic welfare states that have been boosting public service provision or Liberal welfare states fostering the expansion of private service provision (Scharpf 1997; Esping-Andersen 1991). In light of current economic challenges, it is argued that Bismarckian welfare states attempt to gain flexibility in their currently highly regulated labor markets by allowing the emergence of a secondary labor market segment. The secondary market contrasts with the primary labor market segment; the former exhibits less employment protection and higher flexibility in wages and working time, and it mainly applies to expanding service employment and new entrants into the labor market (Eichhorst and Marx 2009 and Chapter 4 of this volume; Davidsson and Naczyk 2009). This trend seems especially pronounced in Germany and France: in both countries labor market divides have been triggered by the erosion of traditional industrial relations, as well as labor market and social policy reforms (Palier and Thelen 2010). Recent developments in social service labor markets in both countries seem to support the dualization argument: growing services and services undergoing organizational transformation such as elder care and child care indeed are characterized by an increase of non-standard work, that is, fix-term, low-wage, and part-time work. This trend seems to align with the increasing private service provision and the dwindling power of unions even in the public sector.

However, again the picture is less uniform than the expansion of non-standard work might suggest. State employment expanded over the last two decades in France, while the state retreated from its role as employer in Germany. And although an increase of precarious work might indicate a "low quality" trend of service provision, at least in Germany some occupational upgrading in social services such as nursing and child care can be observed. In addition, job expansion in the service sector has been accompanied by rising female labor market participation. This indicates that employment flexibility might take on different forms between and within countries and calls for a more in-depth analysis of the growth and structural dynamics of employment in this field, which we present in the next section.

MAPPING THE SECTOR: EMPLOYMENT DIVIDES IN SOCIAL SERVICES

Social services are an economically dynamic sector. While the whole service sector expanded in both Germany and France, this was especially true for social services. Between 1992 and 2007, the share of jobs in social services increased from 13.3 percent to 19.1 percent in France and increased from 10.8 percent to 17.3 percent in Germany, mainly based on job growth in health and social work occupations.[1] This job expansion is of special interest because the state as dominant employer in the sector set an example both for the provision of secure employment relationships and for the integration of women into the labor market. Moreover, public employers set the standard for employment in the private sector with respect to working conditions, wage structures, and social security on the one hand and securing career tracks on the other. The status and regulatory frameworks of civil servants in Germany (*Beamte*) and France (*fonctionnaires*) established in the nineteenth century served as a blueprint for designing the standard employment relationship in each country. This was successfully implemented in general only after World War II during the "golden age of the welfare state" (Gottschall 2009). Subsequently, the significance of the state as a model employer has been challenged in social services in particular, both in terms of the ascendance of private employers delivering social services and with regard to the characteristics of public jobs. The impact of these changes in public employment on female employment patterns and gender equity in the labor market cannot be underestimated, given that social services account for a large share of women's overall employment (15.9 percent in Germany and 14.9 percent in France, compared to slightly more than 2 percent of men) in 2007.[2]

Although the relative dominance of public employment in the sector had guaranteed stable jobs and sufficient hourly wages, this positive impact of the state on social services employment seems to have weakened. Non-public social services grew with a corresponding decline of public jobs in the sector. At the same time, financial constraints induced local and state-level authorities to introduce greater flexibility of the remaining workforce, translating into a significant rise of non-standard work in child care, health, and social care services. This section argues that both public and private social services exhibit dualization of employment structures. However, as we will see, public employment still mitigates this development with employment relationships that are less often part-time, non-permanent, or badly paid than in private social services. Therefore, the existence of non-standard employment relationships along with the public-private mix of social services can be considered as indicating tendencies toward dualization of social services.

In the following section, we highlight the divided employer structure of social services and analyze its significance for the affected workforce. The remainder of this section presents an analysis of non-standard employment in social services. Data on employment structures in the sector are derived from the German *Mikrozensus* and the French *Enquête Emploi*. Data analysis covers the time span from 1990–1991 to 2007, in order to fully acknowledge the development of German social services after reunification. We differentiate between health services, social care services, and child care services.[3]

Employer and Workforce Divides in Social Services

Social services feature divided labor market structures. Not only are social services characterized by a juxtaposition of public and private employers, but even within public employment different employment models exist. In both Germany and France, three forms of standard employment can be distinguished that are of different significance on the labor market. They differ with respect to their legal foundation as well as job security, social security, and pay systems (see Table 5-1). German *civil servants* enjoy lifelong employment and generous social security provisions, and mainly execute public core tasks in administration, public security, or education. Social services are delivered by *public employees*, whose employment conditions are not as beneficial as those of civil servants. Nonetheless, employment security is usually higher than in the *standard employment relationship of the private economy*, which applies to employment in social services provided by nonprofit or private organizations. The differentiation between employment forms is basically similar in France. However, French social services are to a larger degree integrated into the civil service employment model.

Due to these different employment models inherent to social services, the public-private mix of service provision and its dynamics strongly impact the dualization of the sector. While new data show that many OECD countries so far have been subject to moderate public sector downsizing only (Tepe 2009), social services are particularly prone to public personnel cuts. The share of public social services jobs is shrinking in both Germany and France since 1990, after dominating the sector for a long time. Germany sustained a substantial

Table 5-1: Main employment characteristics of civil service, other public employment, and the standard employment relationship (SER) of the private economy in Germany and France

	Civil service		Other public employment		SER of the private economy	
	Beamte in Germany	Fonctionnaires in France	Germany	France	Germany	France
Legal basis of employment relationships	Statutory regulation that creates a life-long employment relationship with the state	Statutory regulation that creates a life-long employment relationship with the state	General labor law	Statutory regulation (special section of civil service law)	General labor law	General labor law
Job security	Lifelong employment and seniority-based career development	Lifelong employment and seniority-based career development	Dismissals possible, based on general labor law; after 15 years of service dismissal is no longer possible	Dismissals possible, based on statutory regulation (special section of civil service law)	Dismissals possible, based on general labor law	Dismissals possible, based on general labor law
Social security	Tax-based exclusive social security schemes	Exclusive social security schemes	General social security schemes based on social insurance	General social security schemes based on social insurance	General social security schemes based on social insurance	General social security schemes based on social insurance
Pay systems	Seniority-based pay system and incremental pay increases	Seniority-based pay system and incremental pay increases	Seniority-based pay system and incremental pay increases, based on collective bargaining	Different ways of pay-setting are possible	Based on collective bargaining or individual negotiation or legal minimum wages in a small number of occupations (including out-patient care services)	Based on collective bargaining, individual negotiation or the national minimum wage

Table 5-2: Share of public jobs in health services, social care services, and child care services (excluding teachers), %

	Health services		Social care services		Child care services	
	France	Germany	France	Germany	France	Germany
1990/91*	54.1	54.1	62.5	58.0	#	78.3
2000	51.5	41.5	63.0	43.2	#	64.6
2007	48.5	31.4	58.0	36.0	#	56.7

* France 1990, Germany 1991.
# Data underestimate the share of public jobs and are thus not reported here, compare comment on child care data in footnote 3.
Sources: *Enquête Emploi* and *Mikrozensus*, own calculations.

decrease in public jobs, while the loss of public social services jobs in France was less dramatic (see Table 5-2). The above-mentioned job growth in social services thus can be attributed to job creation in the private social services.

In Germany, nonprofit associations carry out a large share of social tasks and act as an intermediary between citizens and the state in line with the subsidiarity principle inherent to the German welfare state, whereas the French state is more directly accountable for the needs of its citizens (Kroos 2010). These different ideologies informing the provision of social services imply divides both within public social services employment and across the whole sector. Within public social services, the differentiation between civil servants and other public employees creates distinct workforces in both countries, but the different state commitment to social services also is visible in the higher significance of the civil servant status in French social services (see Table 5-3). Though the share of civil servants has been decreasing in French health services and social care services between 1990 and 2007, civil servants still made up almost half of all workers in these two subsectors of social services in 2007. In Germany, however, the share of civil servants is negligible in health services, social care services, and child care services alike, indicating that social tasks are considered as inferior to tasks such as the ensuring of public safety. In contrast, in France large numbers of former employees have become civil servants with the incorporation of municipal services—providing many services in the realm of social care—into the public service in 1984, as well as with the incorporation of the health sector into the public service in 1986 (Kroos 2010). For social services workers, these status distinctions imply crucial differences with regard to job security, social security, and pay levels, as civil service positions are associated with employment security and higher income than public employee positions or private jobs in both countries.

However, not only is the state a more significant employer in French social services quantitatively, it also exerts more influence on the *third sector*, that is, on that part of the welfare economy that can be considered as neither public nor

Table 5-3: Share of civil servants in health services, social care services, and child care services (excluding teachers), %

	Health services		Social care service		Child care services	
	France	Germany	France	Germany	France	Germany
1990/91*	46.5	0.5	51.5	2.9	#	0.3
2000	44.1	0.1	53.5	1.8	#	0.2
2007	46.0	0.1	49.4	1.3	#	0.2

* France 1990, Germany 1991.
# Data underestimate the share of civil servants and are thus not reported here, compare comment on child care data in footnote 3.
Sources: Enquête Emploi and Mikrozensus, own calculations.

as part of the private for-profit economy.[4] Whereas the egalitarian orientation of French social policies (Laville 2000) places direct responsibility for social services on the state and involves a close regulation of other welfare providers, in Germany the subsidiarity principle turns welfare institutions into more autonomous actors despite their dependency on the state for funding. Welfare associations dominating non-public social services in Germany account for almost three-quarters of employment in this segment of the sector (Kühnlein and Wohlfahrt 2006), and experienced a tremendous employment growth between 1990 and 2008 (Bundesarbeitsgemeinschaft der Freien Wohlfahrtspflege 2009: 18).[5] Employer structures in French social services are more homogenous, with the state clearly in the lead. However, as in Germany, there is evidence that social services have seen an increase in non-public employment, especially in social care services outsourced by the municipalities to the third sector (Archambault 2001; Conseil National des Chambres Régionales de l'Economie Sociale 2009: 10). But whereas in France the state as employer and the civil service as employment model still dominate social services, in Germany third-sector organizations responsible for less favorable employment conditions are more significant.

The partial withdrawal of the German state out of social services implies a stronger dualization of the social services labor market than in France. This has implications not only for the integration of women into the labor market, but also for the design of typically female jobs. The sector is characterized by a highly feminized workforce, with women making up more than three-quarters of the workforce in both Germany and France in 2007 (86.3 percent in France, 85.5 percent in Germany; Enquête Emploi and Mikrozensus, own calculations). Therefore, the diminishing role of the state in the provision of social services and of employment opportunities in the sector affects women to a larger extent than men. Indeed, of all women working in French social services in 1990, 64.6 percent were employed in the public sector, as compared to only 52.9 percent in 2007. In Germany, the decrease of public employment relationships among female social service workers was even more substantial, as their share has fallen from 59.6 percent to 36.7 percent between 1991 and 2007, respectively (*Enquête Emploi* and *Mikrozensus*, own calculations).

The dominance of women in social services is linked to a degradation of the sector and low professional profiles in Germany; in France professional profiles of social services workers are more diverse (see Figure 5-1). A vast majority of social service workers in Germany hold a degree obtained through vocational training or schooling, while higher qualifications are more prominent in France.

All in all, French and German social services feature the coexistence of private for-profit, private nonprofit, and public employers, which to a lesser degree applies in other segments of the service sector. As to cross-country variation, the German and French states are not only unevenly involved in the provision of social services, but also differ concerning the employment status they link to social services. It is the distinction between the civil servant status, other public employment, and private employment relationships, in combination with the dynamic development of the sector, that makes it particularly prone to dualization. However, rather than deduce the emergence of divided structures

Figure 5-1: Distribution of educational degrees within social services

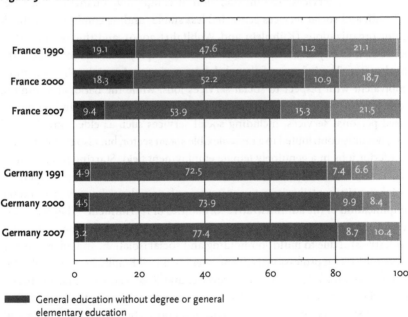

General education without degree or general
elementary education

Basic to full secondary vocational training or
schooling

Intermediate to full secondary general training
without vocational training or schooling

Lower or higher tertiary education

No answer

Sources: Enquête Emploi and Mikrozensus,own calculations.

solely from privatization in social services, it is necessary to examine the actual quality of employment relationships in both public and private social services.

Non-standard Employment in Public and Private Social Services

For a long time, public sector employment in both countries was a synonym for stable employment relationships offering sufficient income and reliable prospects for career development in social services as well as in other parts of the public sector (Gottschall 2009; Rouban 2008). Yet this role is threatened not only by privatization of public tasks, but also by labor market and welfare state policies that contribute to the dualization of the sector in an indirect way. In Germany, the deregulation of the labor market (see Eichhorst and Marx, Chapter 4 of this volume) through the gradual facilitation of fixed-term employment, the extension of marginal employment, and the introduction of means-tested unemployment benefits in 2003 set the course for general labor market dualization. Social services were hit by this process more thoroughly than other parts of the economy due to union weakness in the sector (see Dølvik and Waddington 2005) and the decreasing financial commitment of the state to social services. The introduction of competitive financing structures in health and social services generated less stable funding conditions of third-sector organizations (Kühnlein and Wohlfahrt 2006), and thus welfare state policies indirectly fostered the deterioration of employment relationships in the third sector. The balance of French labor market and social policies is more ambivalent with respect to social services jobs: while the national minimum wage protects income standards, policies fostering job creation in household-based personal services, including social services such as elder care or child care, not only contributed to a more flexible social sector, but also to the creation of inferior jobs in a genuinely female employment field. Starting in 1993, these policies included reductions of value added tax, exemptions from employers' social security contributions, tax exemptions for employer-households, and the simplification of the administrative formalities of recruitment.[6] They were successful in terms of job creation, but jobs in this field are mostly part-time, low paid, stressful due to multi-job-holding and social isolation, and offer minimal opportunities for professional advancement (Conseil Emploi Revenus Cohésion sociale 2008; Devetter et al. 2009; Devetter and Rousseau 2009). Labor market and social policies thus contributed to the emergence of non-standard employment in social services in both Germany and France, but with a focus on private employment relationships.

Increasing shares of *low-wage jobs* are one indicator of divided service sector labor markets (standard vs. non-standard employment) in Germany and France. France provides one of the highest national minimum wages in Europe (as January 1, 2011, it was fixed at €9.00 per hour gross). Whereas 10.6 percent of the private sector workforce earned the national minimum wage in 2009, low-wage work at the national minimum wage was below average in the field of education (5.0 percent) and slightly above average in "health and social work" (12.2 percent).[7]. Similarly, in 2007, 9.4 percent of workers received the national minimum wage in the *Fonction publique*, that is, in central government, public hospitals, and local collectivities, which was below the private sector average of that year (12.9 percent), but still surprisingly high given that the state is understood as a model employer (Berry and Variot 2008). Nonetheless, despite the application of the national minimum wage, social service workers suffer from a wage penalty when compared to other sectors. For example, day nannies (*assistantes maternelles*) can earn far less than the legal minimum wage, depending on the number of children under their care (Blanpain and Momic 2007). Additionally, low-wage work is quite common in household-based services where legal stipulations are more difficult to enforce (Caroli et al. 2008).

In Germany, where a national minimum wage does not exist, the share of low-wage recipients is notably higher and growing. In 1995, about 15 percent of all German employees worked for low wages, compared to 20.7 percent in 2008, according to data of the German Socio-Economic Panel Study (Kalina and Weinkopf 2008, 2010).[8] This development also applies to social services and in particular to social services occupations that require low qualifications (Rhein and Stamm 2006). However, as a result of the political debate over the introduction of a (national) minimum wage, workers in the fields of elderly care and out-patient nursing services are covered by a sectoral gross minimum wage of €8.50 (West) or €7.50 (East) since mid-2010. These hourly wages are only slightly above the statistical low-wage threshold for the year 2008 in Eastern Germany and even below the 2008 low-wage threshold in Western Germany (see footnote 8). The implementation of this minimum wage thus can only be considered a partial success in the fight against a divided social sector.[9] Nonetheless, it might signal the end of a downward spiral of low-wage developments in private and public social services that had started with nonprofit welfare organizations cutting wages and outsourcing jobs from the mid-1990s onward. Subsequently, public employers followed suit by outsourcing jobs, for instance in hospitals (Jaehrling 2007).

When assessing the role of *part-time employment* in social services, the historical development of this employment form in Germany and France has to be considered. Indeed, part-time employment was poorly developed in France until the 1980s due to the fostering of female full-time employment by both labor market and family policies. Part-time employment in Germany builds upon a different tradition of female employment. While female full-time employment became the official norm in the former German Democratic Republic, a traditional male breadwinner model, fostered by political regulation, prevailed in the Federal Republic of Germany. In the latter case, women worked only if it was necessary for economic reasons (Oertzen and Rietzschel 1997).

Accordingly, health services and social services exhibit lower degrees of part-time employment in France than in Germany. Nonetheless, with 23.8 percent in the public sector and 22.5 percent in the private sector (see Figure 5-2), the share of part-time employment in French health services was much higher than in other sectors in 2007 (*Enquête Emploi*). The same is true for French social care services. Early child care services (excluding preschool teachers), however, show much higher shares of part-time employment, especially in the private sector. This is probably due to the increase of home-based child care (Blanpain and Momic 2007). For Germany, however, part-time shares were much higher in health services as well as in social care services and child care services in 2007. These figures single out social services as a sector with an immense significance of part-time work.

Figure 5-2: Shares of part-time jobs in health services, social care services, and child care services in public sector and private economy, 2007 (and 1990/1991), %

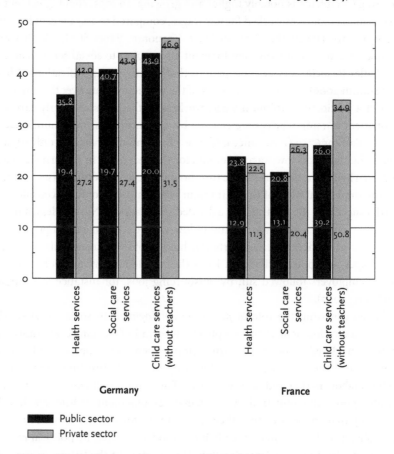

Notes: Underlined figures refer to 2007, figures not underlined refer to 1990 (France) or 1991 (Germany).
Sources: Enquête Emploi and Mikrozensus, own calculations.

The shares of part-time jobs in German public social services, lower than in private social services but still reaching 36 percent to 44 percent, underscore the ambivalence of this employment form in the German public sector. On the one hand, the majority of child care facilities (*Kindergarten*) hardly offers full-time positions due to the German half-day model of public child care (Hagemann 2006) and therefore tend to produce involuntary part-time work. On the other hand, in other parts of the public sector, the granting of opportunities for part-time work is considered an employee-friendly policy, especially in public administration. The role of the state as a "good employer" also is evident in the hesitant use of marginal part-time employment in public social services. Marginal part-time employment, that is, short part-time employment relationships without full social insurance coverage (for details see Eichhorst and Marx, Chapter 4 of this volume), made up smaller shares of employment in public than in private services in 2007 (*Mikrozensus*, own calculations). Although social services are one of the economic sectors in which increasing numbers of marginally employed workers can be found (Minijob-Zentrale 2009: 10), the public sector attenuates this development.

With respect to *non-permanent employment*, the German public sector hosts a more strongly divided workforce than its French counterpart, too (see Figure 5-3). Although shares of non-permanent employment in German public social services were either similar to or considerably lower than in private social services, ranging from 14.4 percent (health services) to 18.1 percent (child care services), they are still much higher than in other sectors. This reflects the poor financial situation of many German municipalities responsible for the provision of social care services. In private social care or child care services, though, even more than one-fifth of workers had a non-permanent job in 2007. Similarly, French public early child care services and social care services are the responsibility of the municipalities. They showed higher degrees of non-permanent employment than the respective sectors of the private economy and of central-state provided public services like health services. Overall, the preponderance of non-permanent employment relationships in both German and French public social services contributes to segmentation of the sector into high-quality and low-quality jobs.

In summary, the cross-sectional analysis has shown that social services in Germany and France do indeed exhibit a divide between workforces with permanent or non-permanent, full-time or part-time, and well-paid or badly paid jobs. Non-standard employment relationships have become a regular part of public employment in most German cities as well as in French municipalities (Kroos 2010; Czerwick 2007). Nonetheless, this employment flexibilization appears more prominent in the German than in the French public sector. Moreover, flexibility extends out to the large, mainly religious nonprofit organizations providing social services in Germany, whereas the

Figure 5-3: Shares of non-permanent jobs in health services, social care services, and child care services in public sector and private economy, 2007 (and 1990/1991), %

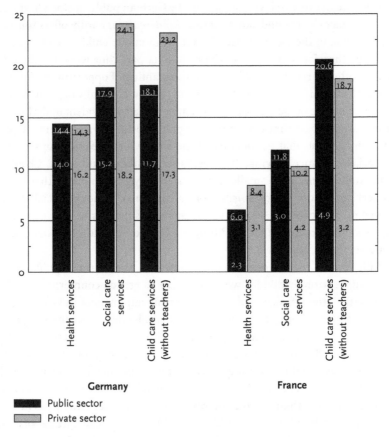

French state, as the major and model employer especially in health services and education, still exerts a safeguarding influence on employment in the sector. Finally, the larger share of public jobs and civil servants in France and the existence of the national minimum wage diminish the number of non-standard workers in France as compared to Germany. These developments leave open the question of whether or not the divided structure of social services is a (new) permanent feature of the sector or if the dualization trend can be reversed. This question is closely linked to education and training and professional dynamics within the sector, which will be addressed in the next section.

PROFESSIONAL PROFILES AND THE STATE
IN SOCIAL SERVICES

From an institutional (meso) perspective, a stable career path despite phases of non-standard employment is more likely when social services are linked to clear professional profiles and to a conception of social services as high-quality. Here again, the state plays a crucial role, not only as provider of services, but also as a regulator of training and provider of training opportunities. Training structures for social service occupations and their impact on career patterns had differed substantially between Germany and France, while recent changes seem to indicate some convergence.

In general, the French system of vocational training can be characterized as a general skill system, as compared to a specific skill system prevalent in Germany. The main features of the French general skill system also apply to social services occupations with a school-based vocational training for social workers, nurses, and physiotherapists and a (tertiary) university-based education for teachers in elementary schools (écoles maternelles). In contrast, the training regime for social service occupations deviates from the highly praised firm- and school-based apprenticeship system, covering manufacturing and administrative and commercial services in Germany. It is mainly school-based and so far has lacked a higher tertiary education track. These differences in skill structure and coherence of training systems account for a far more professional character of social service occupations in France than in Germany.

In France many of the training institutions are state-run, and access relies on competitive entry exams. In some health occupations such as nursing, state regulation even stipulates annual nation-wide quotas that define the number of available training positions for the entire county. The large extent of state regulation has pushed a high degree of standardization of training in social services—extending to the private sector—and has enhanced professional development of particular social services, both in health care and child care. Thus, nursing occupations, preschool education, and child care are based on well-defined sets of job and task hierarchies (Méhaut et al. 2008). Career prospects are well-defined, and are fostered not only by the dominance of civil servant status and full-time employment, but also by the integrated educational system. For example, the high level of training in the field of education involves university education for teachers in écoles maternelles and primary schools.

The German system of training and career patterns in social services represents a semi-professional rather than a professional path. Partly, this can be attributed to the fact that training for social services deviates from the three-year firm-based apprenticeship-type of vocational training, secured by law since 1969, allowing for smooth transitions from training to employment and providing well-defined career ladders both within and across firms and industries. In contrast, training for social services operates within a vocational school system oriented toward health occupations, child care, and household services. This second vocational tier historically served to prepare women for a housewife and mother role and voluntary work in the respective fields. It has been backed up by the subsidiarity principle in the German social security system and the mixed provision of social services, prioritizing nonprofit rather than state-run organizations (Krüger 1995). This type of school-based vocational training sets off a very different career path, with its governance subject to the regional (the German *Länder*) and not national bodies, resulting in a lack of or belated (in the case of nurses) standardization in training and certification as well as a privatization of training costs. Moreover, health care, child care, and social work occupations are shaped as semi-professions, with relatively low wages (corresponding to a three- to five-year training period) and part-time work patterns, attuned to the half-day culture, especially in public education (Hagemann 2006; Gottschall 2008). Additionally, this type of training and framing of the respective occupations until recently did not allow for advancement to management positions or entering university education. Due to the weaker standardization of certifications and qualifications, the respective sectors also are more open to low-skilled and low-wage work characterized by so-called assistant positions such as child minders or care helpers. Thus, the segmentation of training in Germany, affecting mainly the social service sector, might account for important differences highlighted earlier: namely, a higher share of part-time work on average and a higher level of low-wage work in social services in Germany than in France.

While the regimes of training for social services have differed, recent changes indicate some convergence. In Germany, an ambivalent mixture of upgrading and reinforcement of semi-professionalism can be observed. Against the background of expanding societal demands for high-quality care, new tracks of tertiary education (in public health and more recently in elementary education) have been established. Though the rising number of graduates of these programs will not replace the still dominant vocational training, they might provide an academically trained workforce for training and leading positions in care services and enhance the insertion of elementary education in child care services. At the same time, however, short-term (one- and two-year) training tracks in the expanding fields of elder care and child care are gaining importance (see Gottschall 2008). Both trends have been backed by family, education, and health care policies over the last decade. On the one hand, Germany's poor performance in the PISA study as well as the interest of mothers and parents for combining work and family favored upgrading policies for elementary education (alongside an expansion of child care and after-school care facilities). On the other hand, the budget problems on the local level as well as strong forces upholding the subsidiarity principle lead to a preference for a mixed road of service provision including informalized work. For example, the 2008 reform for the expansion of nursery care designates 30 percent of the places as family care (*Tagesmütter*) with very low and not yet legally established training requirements for the mostly female workforce (Gottschall 2008; Bahle 2007).

The German academic upgrading in training for health care and preschool education occupations indicates a belated professionalization already well established in France. However, the high and rising general skill levels in social services in France (Beynier and Tudoux 2005) do not give the whole picture, as short, low-level training programs also are on the rise in French social services. This applies in particular to elder care services, which are characterized by a lack of institutional structures for out-patient care and a mixed structure of public and private providers (Leitner 2009; Ledoux 2011). Controversial debates on the need for professionalization of the expanding elder care services (Bressé 2003) so far only have been met by the introduction of low-level training programs and the issuing of state diplomas that are to a large extent based on' practical experience in the field (Grenat 2006; Pinaud 2004). In this respect, German elder care and ambulant care services provide better training and more distinct occupational profiles, not least stimulated by the integration of elder care in the social insurance system already in 1994, thus providing funding for standardized ambulant care (and home care) services (Ledoux 2011).

In summary, whereas German social services have to handle a difficult legacy of semi-professionalism that is partly due to the comparatively low commitment of the state in the sector, French social services are more strongly characterized by a tradition of state-based professionalization and serve better to integrate women into the labor market. However, occupational dualization is on the rise in both countries. In Germany, the parallel trends of academic upgrading and downgrading of training requirements are resulting in a more polarized training structure in care services. In France, we can observe the failure to fully incorporate new training programs in the field of elder care in the otherwise successful training system for social services, which is also true for home-based early child care. Thus, in both countries, expanding social services provide the terrain for dualization, lowering but not offsetting path dependency in training.

CONCLUSION

The state no longer guarantees homogeneous and exemplary employment, a conclusion that can be drawn from three trends in social services: the shrinking role of the state as an employer and provider of services; the increased recourse to non-standard employment relationships also in the public sector; and the erosion of the state's model role due to social polices increasingly based on competitive financing structures in Germany and the promotion of home-based child and elder care in France. However, the German state, less devoted to the provision of social services in the first place, has retreated from the role as a model employer more thoroughly, evident not least in more pronounced divided structures in employment and training.

The different commitment of the state as an employer in social services also affects its capacity to integrate women into the labor market. In restraining from investments in public service provision and the promotion of non-public employers in expanding fields of the social sector, both Germany and France diminish the potential of the public sector to facilitate female employment. Nevertheless, the French public sector offers more high-quality employment to women due to stratified and profession-based career patterns. In Germany, cleavages between occupational classes continue to be more strongly pronounced, and the observed polarization in training and employment in the sector probably will generate more occupational inequality among women.

Irrespective of the observed convergence toward lower state commitment in the social services, the comparison of France and Germany shows that the state as employer can either promote or hinder high-quality provision of services and employment in the sector. Since demand for social services in areas such as home-based elder care, which so far represent an under-regulated field enhancing illicit and low-wage work, is rising, the provision and regulation of social services will continue to stay on the public agenda.

NOTES

1 Source: Eurostat 2010, Labour Market, downloaded August 24, 2010, from http://epp.eurostat.ec.europa.eu/portal/page/portal/employment_ unemployment_lfs/data/database. The category "health and social work" refers to health services, social care services, and child care services. In France, only child care services that are not part of the national educational system are included.

2 *Mikrozensus* and *Enquête Emploi*, own calculations.

3 Whereas health services exclude medical doctors and include nursing occupations and other health services, social care services refer to a heterogeneous field comprising social work, assistance provided to families and youth, and care provided to the elderly and to the physically impaired. Data on child care services in France comprise *early* child care only, due to structural reasons as well as data restrictions: in France, preschool child care largely is provided by teachers in so-called *écoles maternelles*, while it is provided by child minders with a lower level of qualification in Germany. Additionally, teachers had to be excluded from the category of child care services due to data restrictions.

4 Unfortunately, comparative data on the size and structure of the third sector are not readily available due to different definitions and data shortages on the national level; see Zimmer/Priller 2007.

5 However, there is no systematic data on the relative weight of the state, nonprofit welfare associations and private for-profit providers in German social services.

6 The main instruments have been the creation of service checks issued by the employer or public authorities, namely *Chèque Emploi Service* in 1993 and *Chèque Emploi Service Universel* in 2005.

7 Source: INSEE 2009, downloaded 4 March 2010 from http://www.insee. fr/fr/themes/tableau.asp?ref_id=NATTEF04112&reg_id=0 .

8 Low wages are defined as less than two-thirds of the median hourly wage, which is differentiated between Eastern and Western Germany. The low-wage threshold of the year 2008 was fixed at 9.50 € for Western Germany and 6.87 € for Eastern Germany (Kalina and Weinkopf 2010).

9 The German service sector trade union Ver.di for a long time rather neglected the negative wage development in social services and only recently started to campaign for better pay in the sector. In France this issue has been of lower importance due to the national minimum wage.

REFERENCES

Archambault, Edith (2001). "Frankreichs Dritter Sektor: Stellung im Wohlfahrtsmix und Rolle in der Arbeitsmarktpolitik," in Priller, Eckhard, and Zimmer, Annette (eds.), *Der Dritte Sektor international. Mehr Markt - weniger Staat?*, Berlin: Edition sigma, pp. 179–195.

Bahle, Thomas (2007). *Wege zum Dienstleistungsstaat. Deutschland, Frankreich und Großbritannien im Vergleich*, Wiesbaden: VS Verlag für Sozialwissenschaften.

Berry, Jean-Baptiste, and Variot, Nathalie (2008). "Les bénéficiaires de la revalorisation du SMIC au 1er juillet 2007," Premières Synthèses Premières Informations 10.3, Paris: Direction de l'Animation de la Recherche, des Etudes et des Statistiques.

Beynier, Dominique, and Tudoux, Benoît (2005). "Les métiers du travail social hors aide à domicile," Etudes et Résultats 441/Novembre 2005, Paris: Direction de la Recherche, des Etudes, de l'Evaluation et des Statistiques.

Blanpain, Nathalie, and Momic, Milan (2007). "Les assistantes maternelles en 2005," *Etudes et Résultats* 581/Juin 2007, Paris: Direction de la Recherche, des Etudes, de l'Evaluation et des Statistiques.

Bressé, Sophie (2003). "L'enjeu de la professionnalisation du secteur de l'aide à domicile en faveur des personnes âgées," *Retraite et société*, 39(2): 119–143.

Bundesarbeitsgemeinschaft der Freien Wohlfahrtspflege (2009). *Gesamtstatistik 2008. Einrichtungen und Dienste der Freien Wohlfahrtspflege*, Berlin: Bundesarbeitsgemeinschaft der Freien Wohlfahrtspflege.

Caroli, Ève, Gautié, Jérôme, and Askenazy, Philippe (2008). "Low-Wage Work and Labour Market Institutions in France," in Caroli, Ève and Gautié, Jean (eds) *Low-Wage Work in France*, New York: Sage, pp. 28–87.

Conseil Emploi Revenus Cohésion sociale (2008). *Les Services à la Personne,* Paris: Conseil Emploi Revenus Cohésion sociale.

Conseil National des Chambres Régionales de l'Economie Sociale (2009). *Atlas de l'économie sociale et solidaire en France et dans les régions,* Paris: Conseil National des Chambres Régionales de l'Economie Sociale.

Czerwick, Edwin (2007). *Die Ökonomisierung des öffentlichen Dienstes: Dienstrechtsreformen und Beschäftigungsstrukturen seit 1991,* Wiesbaden: VS Verlag für Sozialwissenschaften.

Davidsson, Johan, and Naczyk, Marek (2009). "The Ins and Outs of Dualisation: A Literature Review," Working Papers on the Reconciliation of Work and Welfare in Europe REC-WP 02/2009, Edinburgh: RECWOWE Publication.

Deakin, Simon (2002). "The Evolution of the Employment Relationship," in Auer, Peter, and Gazier, Bernard (eds.), *The Future of Work, Employment and Social Protection: The Dynamics of Change and the Protection of Workers,* Geneva: International Labour Organization, pp. 191–205.

Devetter, François-Xavier, Jany-Catrice, Florence, and Ribault, Thierry (2009). *Les services à la personne,* Paris: La Découverte.

Devetter, François-Xavier, and Rousseau, Sandrine (2009). "The Impact of Industrialization on Paid Domestic Work: The Case of France," *European Journal of Industrial Relations,* 15(3): 297–316.

Dølvik, Jon Erik, and Waddington, Jeremy (2005). "Can Trade Unions Meet the Challenge? Unionisation in the Marketised Services," in Bosch, Gerhard, and Lehndorff, Steffen (eds.), *Working in the Service Sector: A Tale from Different Worlds,* London: Routledge, pp. 316–341.

Eichhorst, Werner, and Marx, Paul (2009). "Reforming German Labor Market Institutions: A Dual Path to Flexibility," IZA Discussion Paper 4100, Bonn: Forschungsinstitut zur Zukunft der Arbeit.

Esping-Andersen, Gøsta (1999). *Social Foundations of Postindustrial Economies,* Oxford: Oxford University Press.

Esping-Andersen, Gøsta (1991). "Three Postindustrial Employment Regimes,'" in Kolberg, Jon Eivind (ed.), *The Welfare State as Employer,* New York: M.E. Sharpe, pp. 149–188.

Esping-Andersen, Gøsta, Gallie, Duncan, Hemerijck, Anton, and Myles, John (2002). *Why We Need a New Welfare State,* Oxford: Oxford University Press.

Fligstein, Neil (2001). *The Architecture of Markets: An Economic Sociology of Twenty-First Century Capitalist Societies,* Princeton: Princeton University Press.

Gottschall, Karin (2008). "Soziale Dienstleistungen zwischen Informalisierung und Professionalisierung," *ARBEIT - Zeitschrift für Arbeitsforschung, Arbeitsgestaltung und Arbeitspolitik,* 17(4): 254–267.

Gottschall, Karin (2009). "Der Staat und seine Diener: Metamorphosen eines wohlfahrtsstaatlichen Beschäftigungsmodells," in Obinger, Herbert, and Rieger, Elmar (eds.), *Wohlfahrtsstaatlichkeit in entwickelten Demokratien: Herausforderungen, Reformen und Perspektiven,* Frankfurt: Campus, pp. 462–491.

Grenat, Pascale (2006). "Les étudiants et les diplômés des formations aux professions sociales de 1985 à 2004," *Etudes et Résultats* 513/Août 2006, Paris: Direction de la Recherche, des Etudes, de l'Evaluation et des Statistiques.

Hagemann, Karen (2006). "Between Ideology and Economy: The 'Time Politics' of Child Care and Public Education in the Two Germanys," *Social Politics*, 13(2): 217–260.

Hamandia, Akima (2007). "Germany: Towards a Dual Labour Market?," in Eyraud, Francois, and Vaughan-Whitehead, Daniel (eds.), *The Evolving World of Work in the Enlarged EU. Progress and Vulnerability*, Geneva: International Labour Office, pp. 269–318.

Jaehrling, Karen (2007). "The Polarization of Working Conditions: Cleaners and Nursing Assistants in Hospitals," in Bosch, Gerhard, and Weinkopf, Claudia (eds.), *Low-Wage Work in Germany*, New York: Sage, pp. 177–213.

Kalina, Thorsten, and Weinkopf, Claudia (2008). "Weitere Zunahme der Niedriglohnbeschäftigung: 2006 bereits rund 6,5 Millionen Beschäftigte betroffen," IAQ-Report 2008-01, Duisburg: Institut Arbeit und Qualifikation.

Kalina, Thorsten, and Weinkopf, Claudia (2010). "Niedriglohnbeschäftigung 2008: Stagnation auf hohem Niveau—Lohnspektrum franst nach unten aus," IAQ-Report 2010-06, Duisburg: Institut Arbeit und Qualifikation.

Kroos, Daniela (2010). "Warum hat 'Marianne' so viele Diener? Zum Wachstum des französischen öffentlichen Dienstes entgegen internationalen Trends," Transtate Working Paper 115, Bremen: Universität Bremen, Sonderforschungsbereich 597.

Krüger, Helga (1995). "Prozessuale Ungleichheit. Geschlecht und Institutionenverknüpfungen im Lebenslauf," in Berger, Peter A., and Sopp, Peter (eds.), *Sozialstruktur und Lebenslauf*, Opladen: Leske + Budrich, pp. 133–153.

Kühnlein, Gertrud, and Wohlfahrt, Norbert (2006). "Soziale Träger auf Niedriglohnkurs?—Zur aktuellen Entwicklung der Arbeits- und Beschäftigungsbedingungen im Sozialsektor," *WSI-Mitteilungen*, 59(7): 389–395.

Laville, Jean-Louis (2000). "Le tiers secteur. Un objet d'étude pour la sociologie économique," *Sociologie Du Travail*, 42(4): 531–550.

Ledoux, Clémence (2011). "La construction des métiers féminisés d'intervention dans la sphère privée, une comparaison France—République Fédérale d'Allemagne," in Jacquot, Lionel (ed.), *Formes et structures du salariat: crise, mutation, devenir*, Tome 1: De la construction sociale du rapport salarial, Nancy: Presses universitaires de Nancy, pp. 243–258.

Leitner, Sigrid (2009). "Von den Nachbarn lernen? Care-Regime in Deutschland, Österreich und Frankreich," *WSI-Mitteilungen*, 62(7): 376–382.

Méhaut, Philippe (2007). "France: Patchwork - Tensions between Old and New Patterns," in Eyraud, Francois, and Vaughan-Whitehead, Daniel (eds.), *The Evolving world of Work in the Enlarged EU: Progress and Vulnerability*, Geneva: International Labour Office, pp. 231–267.

Méhaut, Philippe, Arborio, Anne Marie, Bouteiller, Jacques, Mossé, Philippe, and Causse, Lise (2008). "Good Jobs, Hard Work? Employment Models for

Nurse's Aides and Hospital Housekeepers," in Gautié, Jerome and Caroli, Ève (eds.), *Low-Wage Work in France*, New York: Sage, pp. 127–167.

Minijob-Zentrale (2009). *Aktuelle Entwicklungen im Bereich der geringfügigen Beschäftigung. IV. Quartal 2009*, Essen: Deutsche Rentenversicherung Knappschaft-Bahn-See.

Morel, Nathalie (2007). "From Subsidiarity to 'Free Choice': Child- and Elderly-Care Policy Reforms in France, Belgium, Germany and the Netherlands," *Social Policy & Administration*, 41(6): 618–637.

Morgan, Kimberly J. (2005). "The Production of Child Care: How Labor Markets Shape Social Policy and Vice Versa," *Social Politics*, 12(2): 243–263.

Oertzen, Christine von, and Rietzschel, Almut (1997). "Comparing the Post-War Germanies: Breadwinner Ideology and Women's Employment in the Divided Nation," *International Review of Social History*, 42(Supplement 5): 175–196.

Offe, Claus, and Hinrichs, Karl (1984). "Sozialökonomie des Arbeitsmarktes: primäres und sekundäres Machtgefälle," in Offe, Claus (ed.), *Arbeitsgesellschaft. Strukturprobleme und Zukunftsperspektiven*, Frankfurt a.M./New York: Campus, pp. 44–86.

Ostner, Ilona, and Lewis, Jane (1995). "Gender and the Evolution of European Social Policy," in Pierson, Paul, and Leibfried, Stephan (eds.), *European Social Policy. Between Fragmentation and Integration*, Washington, DC: Brookings, pp. 159–193.

Palier, Bruno, and Martin, Claude (2007). "Editorial Introduction. From 'a Frozen Landscape' to Structural Reforms: The Sequential Transformation of Bismarckian Welfare Systems," *Social Policy & Administration*, 41(6): 535–554.

Palier, Bruno, and Thelen, Kathleen (2010). "Institutionalizing Dualism: Complementarities and Change in France and Germany," *Politics & Society*, 38(1): 119–148.

Pinaud, Michel (2004). *Le Recrutement, la Formation et la Professionalisation des Salariés du Secteur Sanitaire et Social*, Paris: Rapport du Conseil Economique et Social.

Rhein, Thomas, and Stamm, Melanie (2006). "Niedriglohnbeschäftigung in Deutschland. Deskriptive Befunde zur Entwicklung seit 1980 und Verteilung auf Berufe und Wirtschaftszweige," IAB-Forschungsbericht 12/2006, Nürnberg: Institut für Arbeitsmarkt- und Berufsforschung.

Rouban, Luc (2008). "Reform without Doctrine: Public Management in France," *International Journal of Public Sector Management*, 21(2): 133–149.

Scharpf, Fritz W. (1997). "Employment and the Welfare State: A Continental Dilemma," MPIfG Working Paper 07/97, Cologne: Max-Planck-Institut für Gesellschaftsforschung.

Schmid, Günther, and Ziegler, Christine (1993). "Die Frauen und der Staat— Beschäftigungspolitische Gleichstellung im internationalen Vergleich," *Zeitschrift für Sozialhilfe und Sozialgesetzgebung*, 32(3/4): 126–139, 69–85.

Shire, Karen, and Gottschall, Karin (2007). "Understanding Employment Systems from a Gender Perspective: Pitfalls and Potentials of New Comparative Analytical Frameworks," ZeS-Arbeitspapier 6/2007, Bremen: Universität Bremen, Zentrum für Sozialpolitik.

Tepe, Markus (2009). "Public administration employment in 17 OECD nations from 1995 to 2005," RECWOWE Working Paper 12/2009, Edinburgh: Working Papers on the Reconciliation of Work and Welfare in Europe.

Tepe, Markus, Gottschall, Karin, and Kittel, Bernhard (2010). "A Structural Fit between States and Markets? Public Administration Regulation and Market Economy Models in the OECD," *Socio-Economic Review*, 8(4): 685–707.

Zimmer, Annette, and Priller, Eckhard (2007). *Gemeinnützige Organisationen im gesellschaftlichen Wandel*, Wiesbaden: VS Verlag für Sozialwissenschaften.

6

FROM DILEMMA TO DUALIZATION

SOCIAL AND MIGRATION POLICIES IN THE "RELUCTANT COUNTRIES OF IMMIGRATION"

PATRICK EMMENEGGER AND **ROMANA CAREJA**

INTRODUCTION

Industrialized democracies rely on "cheap labor," here defined as jobs with low levels of pay, benefits, and employment protection, for a variety of economic activities. Immigrant workers are an important source of cheap labor (King and Rueda 2008). However, due to their limited political and, especially in case of illegal immigration, civil rights as well as language problems and widespread discrimination, immigrants form a qualitatively different segment within the group of cheap labor. Consequently, immigrants cannot be simply lumped together with non-immigrant cheap labor. Put bluntly, if non-immigrant cheap labor risks precariousness, much immigrant cheap labor risks precariousness and expulsion.

Immigration poses a dilemma for Western European governments. On the one hand, the immigrant population in their countries is growing because of the economy's need for labor market flexibility and skills, demographic aging, and illegal immigration, as well as the constitutional rights to family and to political asylum. On the other hand, the public opposes large-scale immigration and wants to restrict immigrants' access to social benefits. In the decades after World War II, this tension was solved by guest worker programs, which brought in immigrant workers willing to accept jobs associated with low social status, poor salaries, and without chances of advancement (Piore 1979). As the term "guest" implies, these programs did not envision that immigrant workers would remain in the country, and severely restricted their social rights (Soysal 1994).

However, the extension of immigrants' rights has rendered the classical guest worker programs impossible. In recent decades, the status of migrants has become a legitimate concern for domestic and international actors, who have argued that migrants have rights independent of their citizenship status (Joppke 2001). For economic migrants, this meant that host states were no longer allowed to treat them as mere instruments for economic production. Most importantly, this new attitude toward immigrants undermined the basic criteria of eligibility for community support (citizenship and work) and thereby opened immigrants' access to welfare benefits (Emmenegger and Careja 2011). As a result, Western European governments once again face the dilemma between immigration realities and population preferences.

Although France, Germany, and the United Kingdom (UK) have been recipients of large-scale immigration for many decades, they have never endorsed this fact—hence their label "reluctant countries of immigration" (Cornelius et al. 2004). Faced with noticeable immigrant populations, all three countries have created programs to integrate them (Hollifield 2000). Nevertheless, immigrants continue to be, on average, worse off with respect to virtually all socioeconomic indicators. In this chapter, we document the particularly precarious labor market status of immigrants, and we argue that these socioeconomic differences are the result of three processes, which contribute to the persistence of inequalities between the native population and immigrants in these societies.

First, France, Germany, and the UK actively encourage the immigration of "desired" workers to satisfy business needs (Caviedes 2010), while erecting barriers to entry for "undesired" immigrants. Paradoxically, these restrictions have contributed to the *extension* of the pool of immigrant cheap labor as they have led to an increase in illegal immigration and have forced many economic migrants into clandestine employment (King and Rueda 2008). Thus, rather than being stopped, net immigration has remained positive and the pool of available low-skilled, irregular immigrant labor has considerably increased (Favell and Hansen 2002).

Second, all three countries have reformed their social security systems in order to reduce the incentive to immigrate, for instance by temporarily restricting the newly arrived immigrants' access to social security programs. These reforms are inspired by the widespread fear that immigration from poorer countries is a function of available benefits in receiving countries (Kvist 2004). Consequently, governments attempt to regulate migration flows by reducing Western Europe's image as welfare heaven.

Finally, immigrants have disproportionately suffered from welfare retrenchment since the 1990s. Higher levels of conditionality, tighter eligibility criteria, and more demands on individual recipients are likely to increase the pressure on individuals with weak labor market attachments, many movements in and out of work, and few skills. As we show in the next section, these criteria apply to most immigrants in the "reluctant countries of immigration." Thus, although these reforms retrench social rights for both citizens and immigrants, they hit immigrants harder.

Due to these three processes, most immigrants continue to be considerably worse off compared with citizens in terms of labor market integration and social protection *despite* considerable improvements with regard to legal immigrants' rights and public programs aimed at their integration into the host societies. Thus, these dualizing policy reforms have contributed to the persistence of insider-outsider divides in Western European societies, in which many citizens and some high-skilled immigrants reap the benefits of the European social model, while some citizens and many immigrants carry the burden of economic adjustment.

We acknowledge that immigrants are not the only source of cheap labor and that there are also other processes that contribute to new social inequalities. However, we argue that several significant attributes distinguish immigrant cheap labor from non-immigrant cheap labor. By bringing to the fore this specific issue, our chapter is complementary to the other chapters of this volume, which stress the age, class, and gender (see Häusermann and Schwander, Chapter 2, and Kroos and Gottschall, Chapter 5, in this volume).

In the next section, we present evidence on the overrepresentation of immigrants among cheap labor in Western Europe. We then discuss the three processes that contribute to this outcome. Our analysis focuses on France, Germany, and the UK, the three biggest receivers of immigrants among the "reluctant countries of immigration." Our goal is to demonstrate that despite completely different points of departure in terms of immigration regimes (jus sanguinis vs. jus soli), welfare state regimes (Liberal vs. Conservative), and varieties of capitalism (liberal vs. coordinated), these three countries have reformed their social and migration policies in broadly similar ways. In a final section, we address the issue of intentionality: Do governments deliberately target immigrants, or is the persistence of the divide between the citizens and immigrant population an unintended consequence of recent reform activities?

THE ROLE OF IMMIGRANTS IN THE LABOR MARKET

Immigrants, here understood as both foreigners (residents without citizenship) and foreign-born residents (persons born outside the country of residence), constitute a considerable share of the labor force in all European countries. In France, Germany, and the UK, 5 to 10 percent of the legal labor force are not citizens of the respective country (SOPEMI 2008: 378). The share of workers not born in the country where they work is, in function of naturalization rates, considerably higher. Thus, immigrant workers are an important source of labor supply. Figure 6-1 displays the net legal immigration rate per 1,000 inhabitants. It shows that net legal immigration turned negative immediately after France and Germany suspended labor migration at the beginning of the 1973 oil price crisis. In the UK, net legal immigration turned negative after the passage of the 1962 Commonwealth Immigrants Act. Figure 6-1 also shows that net *legal* immigration has been positive since 1985 in all three countries. In addition, *illegal* immigration into the European Union (EU) has been estimated to be around 500,000 individuals per year (King and Rueda 2008: 285). Thus, despite the professed restrictive policies, considerable annual intakes can be observed.

The first decades following World War II were characterized by a strong interest in foreign manpower and the creation of guest worker programs. The term "guest" implied that workers were not to stay, but were supposed to leave after a designated period of time. Guest workers were mostly used as cheap labor. Native workers were reluctant to accept jobs in the so-called secondary labor market, characterized by low pay, low status, and few chances of advancement toward the primary labor market (Piore 1979: 17). However, these jobs needed to be done. According to Piore, immigrants brought in by guest worker programs were the most likely candidates to take these jobs.

Although flux and uncertainty are inherent to economic activity, they are at odds with labor's desire for security. According to Piore (1980: 24), "dualism within the labor market arises when portions of the labor force begin to be insulated from uncertainty and variability in demand." These workers—insiders—belong to the primary labor market and enjoy the benefits of stable

Figure 6-1: Net legal immigration rate per 1,000 inhabitants (1955–2007)

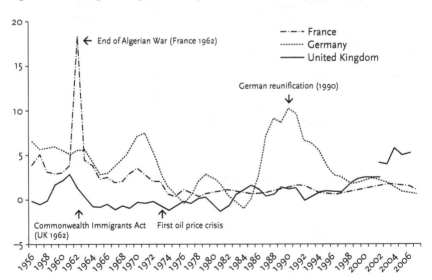

Sources: OECD (2009) and SOPEMI (2008: 295–296). 5-year moving averages have been used for the German data in order to increase readability. Break in series: UK in 2002.

employment relationships and high wages, while those in the secondary labor market—outsiders—bear the brunt of economic adjustment. The allocation of workers in the primary and secondary labor market is not random, but is a function of their economic, political, and social resources. Groups that lack representation in the political arena or possess fewer civil and political rights, such as immigrants, are more likely to find themselves in the secondary labor market (see Häusermann and Schwander, Chapter 2 of this volume).

Piore conducted most of his research on immigration and secondary labor markets in the 1970s. Nevertheless, major differences between citizens and immigrants are still observable today (see Table 6-1). In 2006, the ratio of the unemployment rates of foreign-born to native-born residents was 1.8 in France, 1.7 in Germany, and 1.5 in the UK. In France, 35 percent of all foreign-born aged 15 to 24 are unemployed. With regard to labor market participation rates,

Table 6-1: Labor market participation of immigrants

	France	Germany	UK
Unemployment rate (2006):			
a) Native-born (men and women)	9.0%	9.4%	5.1%
b) Foreign-born (men and women)	16.1%	16.2%	7.6%
c) Foreigners (men and women)	18.7%	18.3%	8.4%
d) Foreigners (women)	20.6%	17.6%	8.9%
e) Foreign-born (15 to 24 years old, data from 2003–2004)	34.9%	16.4%	15.3%
Labor market participation rate (2006):			
a) Native-born (men and women)	69.9%	76.5%	75.9%
b) Foreign-born (men and women)	66.5%	70.4%	71.6%
c) Foreigners (men and women)	62.1%	65.6%	72.6%
d) Foreigners (women)	50.1%	53.6%	63.7%
Immigrant share of low-skilled occupations in 2007 (ISCO level 9):			
a) Among all immigrants	21.2%	27.5%	14.4%
b) Among recent immigrants (arrived during the previous ten years)	25.9%	45.4%	38.1%
Share of temporary employment in total employment in 2005:			
a) Native-born	12.1%	13.8%	4.9%
b) Foreign-born	15.0%	14.8%	9.7%
Predicted percent differences in earnings of immigrants at arrival and natives with the same characteristics (1994–2000):			
a) Men (all foreigners)	−41.8%	−15.3%	−16.5%
b) Men (non-EU foreigners)	−50.6%	−18.1%	−53.9%
c) Women (all foreigners)	−33.7%	−1.7%	−22.1%
d) Women (non-EU foreigners)	−34.6%	−11.2%	−38.3%

Sources: Unemployment rates and labor market participation rates: SOPEMI (2008: 89–92) except unemployment rate of young workers (SOPEMI 2006: 55); low-skilled occupations: SOPEMI (2009: 88); temporary employment: SOPEMI (2007: 76); earning differences: Adserà and Chiswick (2006: 97).

immigrant women fare particularly poorly, with participation rates 20 percentage points below the rates of native-born men and women in France and Germany.

Likewise, immigrant workers earn significantly less than native-born, even when educational attainment is taken into account (SOPEMI 2008: 78–86). Adserà and Chiswick (2006) estimate the percent differences in earnings of immigrants at arrival and natives with the same characteristics to be up to 50 percent. Non-EU foreigners, in particular, earn significantly less than one might expect given their educational attainments. The earnings differences are particularly pronounced in France. Moreover, immigrants work in less favorable conditions (SOPEMI 2007: 75), are more often overqualified (SOPEMI 2006: 54), and are more often employed on a temporary contract (see Table 6-1). It should be emphasized that these numbers are likely to underestimate the true difference between immigrant and native-born workers, as illegal immigrants are underrepresented in the data on which these numbers are based. Thus, although significant within-group differences can be observed, migrant status continues to be one of the major determinants of poverty and social exclusion even after controlling for other socioeconomic variables (Schierup et al. 2006).[1]

Similarly, research has shown that immigrant employment is more volatile than average employment (SOPEMI 2008: 68, 2009: 19). While immigrant employment increases steeply in times of economic growth, immigrants are more quickly fired in economic crises. As shown by Kogan (2004), immigrant status is a significant determinant of the likelihood to be fired during economic downturn, even if other sociodemographic characteristics are kept constant. Thus, immigrant cheap labor is an important source of labor market flexibility and therefore highly desired by employers (Caviedes 2010).

Finally, the sectoral distribution of foreign-born employment shows that immigrants are disproportionately employed in sectors affected by outsourcing of services to the secondary labor market. A comparison of data provided by the Organisation for Economic Co-operation and Development (OECD) on the sectoral distribution of foreign-born workers (SOPEMI 2009: 73, 120) with the sectors most affected by dualization processes (Palier and Thelen 2010: 127) shows an almost perfect match (construction, restaurants, goods delivery, household work, cleaning, personal care). Similarly, immigrants are more often employed in low-skilled occupations (see Table 6-1). In Germany, 45.4 percent of immigrants who arrived after 1997 worked in low-skilled occupations in 2007. We thus conclude that with regard to both individual and sectoral characteristics, immigrants face a disproportionate employment risk.

These differences in labor market participation are reflected in standards of living (see Table 6-2). In France, immigrant households are 3.57 times more likely to have a household income below the poverty line than citizen households. In case of immigrant households from an ethnic minority group,[2] the

Table 6-2: Social rights of immigrants (mid-1990s)

	France	Germany	UK
Share of households below the poverty line:			
a) Citizen households	6.7%	6.3%	9.1%
b) Migrant households	23.9%	23.6%	–
c) Ethnic minority households	36.2%	–	24.4%
Social assistance as a share of households			
a) Citizen households	23.7%	14.0%	30.7%
b) Migrant households	45.4%	34.7%	49.3%
c) Ethnic minority households	62.8%	–	–
Unemployment benefits as a share of unemployed households			
a) Citizen households	73.0%	30.5%	46.9%
b) Migrant households	70.3%	27.3%	21.2%
Pensions as a share of elderly households			
a) Citizen households	97.9%	90.2%	88.2%
b) Migrant households	92.1%	83.3%	62.6%
c) Ethnic minority households	75.0%	–	–

Source: Morissens and Sainsbury (2005).

likelihood increases to 5.40. Similar patterns can be observed in Germany and the UK. Table 6-2 further shows that immigrants are more often dependent on social assistance. The participation rate is 1.61 times higher in the UK, 1.92 times higher in France, and 2.48 times higher in Germany among immigrant households than among citizen households.

In contrast, despite higher unemployment rates, immigrant households receive less often unemployment benefits than citizen households, especially in the UK. Similarly, fewer elderly immigrant households receive old-age pensions. As the data on France show, ethnic minority households are particularly often poor and are not eligible for social insurance.

Immigrant workers are largely seen as a source of cheap labor. However, this view hides considerable variations. Most importantly, Western European countries no longer confine themselves to low-skill immigrants (Caviedes 2010). Due to skill-biased technological change, demand for high-skilled workers has increased in recent years. According to Autor et al. (2003), skill-biased technological change has led to a polarized pattern of job expansion. While many jobs in the middle of the wage distribution have disappeared, high-skill jobs and low-skill jobs depending on physical proximity have continued to soar. These developments are also reflected in immigration policies. Western European countries have started to actively compete for high-skilled immigrants, who are often able to directly access the primary labor market.

In parallel, numerous low-skilled immigrants are trying to enter Western Europe on their own, many of them attracted by the opportunity to work

(Favell and Hansen 2002: 589; Thielemann 2006). There are plenty of work opportunities for low-skilled immigrants in Western Europe. Schneider (2005: 611) estimates the size of the shadow economy as a percentage of GDP in 2002–2003 to be between 12.3 percent (UK) and 16.8 percent (Germany), which suggests that there is a significant illegal space, which is likely to employ immigrants. Governmental estimations of the extent of illegal immigration for France, Germany, and the UK range between 100,000 and one million individuals per country (SOPEMI 2009: 121–122). The UK government estimates that more than 20 percent of all immigrant residents do not have the right to stay in the UK. The European Commission (2008: 89) estimates the number of illegal immigrants in Germany to be almost 2 percent of the total population. Finally, all three countries allow asylum seekers to work after a designated period of time (UK) or after receiving a temporary residence permit (CESifo 2009; Gower 2010).

In sum, Western European economies continue to rely on immigrant cheap labor. However, as we show below, the big guest worker programs have been replaced by smaller programs seeking to attract high-skilled and some clearly delimited categories of low-skilled immigrants, and by policies aimed at restricting the inflow of undesired immigrants. These policies, however, have failed to suppress the inflow of low-skilled immigrants. Rather, low-skilled immigrants have entered through other, often illegal, channels. As a result, we continue to observe a divide between immigrants and native-born citizens with regard to living and working conditions, even though some (high-skilled) immigrants are able to enter the primary labor market right away.

SOCIAL AND MIGRATION POLICY REFORMS IN THE "RELUCTANT COUNTRIES OF IMMIGRATION"

The postwar labor shortages confronted Western European governments with the tension between the economy's need for workers and the public's opposition to large-scale immigration. Governments solved this dilemma by developing guest worker programs (Piore 1979; Soysal 1994). It was assumed that guest workers would come only to work and would leave when work would no longer be available. It was argued that they would not be a burden for social security systems because they were expected to be young and healthy, to have no families to support, and to be enrolled in paid jobs. Moreover, in order to preserve social benefits for the national community, the guest worker programs entitled the participants only to a limited range of benefits.

If the Western governments were the initiators of the guest workers programs and had the upper hand in deciding the conditions attached to these programs, the same cannot be said about the subsequent developments, in particular family reunification, asylum seeking, and European integration, which forced the hand of European governments in unexpected directions. The right of migrants who entered either through family reunification provisions or as recognized asylum seekers to access social benefits has been developed and enforced through court decisions and under the pressure of international and national organizations concerned with individual rights. The interaction of these institutions with national ones and the development of far-reaching anti-discrimination policies (Soysal 1994; Joppke 2001) has led to an incremental extension of immigrants' social rights, a process that has taken place outside public scrutiny. EU integration and the eastward enlargement follow a similar pattern in that they are driven by forces outside the control of national governments (Scharpf 2010). These are top-down processes, which force the European countries to open their labor markets and national welfare systems to citizens of other EU member states. In both situations, EU member states counteracted these liberalizing pressures through national re-regulation (Menz 2002).

The demand for migrant workers, court decisions, post-nationalism, and EU integration and enlargement can been visualized as a network of contracts that limit the room of maneuver of European governments, pushing them to open their labor markets and granting immigrants access to social benefits. In face of these pressures, the Western European governments have adapted their strategy. In order to regain control and satisfy a public opposed to large-scale immigration, they are relying on two main approaches to control immigration. First, Western European governments differentiate between groups of migrants with unequal rights. Second, they reform social security programs in order to decrease the incentive to immigrate.[3]

Migration Policy: Making a Difference and Unintended Consequences

In the decades following World War II, France, Germany, and the UK had a strong interest in recruiting immigrant guest workers. As the first oil price crisis struck, numerous immigrant workers became unemployed, but did not leave the country. Although unanticipated by policy makers, guest workers had acquired the right to stay. Governments reacted to this new situation by suspending economic immigration. In the aftermath of the first oil price crisis, immigration was to be limited to political asylum and family reunification, both of which were numerically not as important as they are today (Geddes 2003).[4]

Despite the end of the guest worker programs, immigration for work reasons continued, through derogations or on the basis of work permit systems, which allowed companies to recruit migrant workers under certain conditions (Geddes 2003). The major administrative hurdle was the need to justify to the immigration offices that nationals could not be found for the respective jobs. Although the work permit system allowed companies to fill their immediate needs, it was not flexible enough, as it impeded firms to plan in advance their personnel needs and did not allow the recruitment of third-country nationals graduating from Western universities (Rollason 2001: 329). In general, low-skilled workers could not be recruited through work permit schemes (SOPEMI 2006: 182; Rollason 2001: 329). The obvious inadequacy of these schemes to tend to the needs of the economy forced the governments to adopt more flexible and targeted programs.

For bringing in low-skilled workers, governments created seasonal or temporary work permits based on bilateral contracts for labor in agriculture, construction, or hospitality (SOPEMI 2006). These schemes set country quotas and employment conditions in terms of duration, salary, and work conditions. Since under this type of contract workers can be employed up to a certain limit per calendar year and since most social benefits are related to longer employment contracts and permanent residence permits, the holders of seasonal worker contracts cannot access welfare benefits other than those related to the work conditions as prescribed by law. However, it must be mentioned that part of these low-skill jobs are occupied by asylum seekers who are granted refugee status or temporary residence permits associated with the right to work.

For attracting high-skilled workers, governments developed a wider array of instruments, from administrative measures to more targeted programs (SOPEMI 2001, 2003, 2006; Hamilton et al. 2004; OECD 2004: 61–62; Rollason 2001: 335; Caviedes 2010). To the first category belong measures that enable the authorities to process employment requests faster, to gradually reduce the barriers faced by potential employers of high-skilled migrants, or to liberalize the rules allowing foreign graduates to apply for jobs in their host countries. To the second category belong the point-based systems, which assess the qualifications of potential immigrants and which can be oriented toward filling specific needs of the economy. The UK has enacted such a program in 2002, and Germany tried (unsuccessfully) to implement a similar one in 2003 (Caviedes 2010). Other programs in this category define the type of skills sought for, such as the IT Green Card program deployed in Germany (SOPEMI 2001). It should be noted that the high-skilled employed under these programs are treated differently from country to country: while in the UK and Germany (since 2005) they are given permanent residence permits after a certain period, their stay is limited in France (EMN 2007: 5; SOPEMI 2007: 246).

In addition to these "desired" immigrants, Western European countries are confronted with continuous waves of asylum seekers and illegal immigrants. These immigrants form a very heterogeneous group. However, Western governments act mainly under the assumption that they come for work and welfare benefits (Thielemann 2006). Therefore, the policies focus on reducing the attractiveness of Western countries through measures targeting the right to work, the residence permits, and the access to welfare. First, residence permits are rendered difficult to obtain without legal documents and proofs of serious reasons for asylum request. Second, permission to work is not given automatically, but is attached to certain types of residence permits. Third, the waiting period for the clarification of the situation is made difficult: the asylum seekers have no right to work, receive only minimal social support, and in some countries restrictions to move are imposed. The UK is an exception, as it allows the asylum seekers to apply for work permits if their situation is not clarified within one year (Thorp 2009).

The application of the concept of "safe country of origin" is another means to prevent the inflow of asylum seekers. As of 2005, France, the UK, and Germany used this concept or its equivalents to distinguish "real" from "bogus" asylum seekers (ECRE 2005). Similarly, the "safe third country" concept has been used to sort asylum requests (Liedtke 2002). The application of these concepts leads to the situation that, although the right to asylum is formally recognized and upheld, the de facto possibility to apply for it is severely limited (Geddes 2003).

Finally, Western European countries increasingly restrict family migration despite the constitutional right to family. In her discussion of recent policy changes in EU member states, Block (2009) identifies three strategies used to restrict family migration. First, governments reduce the categories of eligible family members by using a narrow definition of family. Second, governments tie various conditions to both the sponsor (e.g., independence from the welfare state) and the incoming family (e.g., acquisition of language skills prior to arrival). Third, governments question the familial relationship as such, by demanding DNA tests or qualifying some marriages as improper.

The strategies for recruiting low-skilled workers and for dissuading asylum seekers and family migration reveal a common concern for maintaining a tight control over the inflow, while the more diversified strategies for recruiting high-skilled workers are the response to competitive pressures in the economy. Menz (2002) argues that these programs reflect a reinvention of the guest worker concept. The difference is that they are much more targeted and careful at specifying the conditions in which work permits are given.

Despite the focus of these policies on regulating and restricting the inflow of "undesired" immigrants, they have largely failed to achieve their goal for mainly two reasons. First, the constitutional rights to family and political asylum—upheld by national courts—and intra-EU migration have undercut most attempts to restrict inflows. Moreover, despite increasingly restrictive regulations, ever more people attempt to reach Western Europe (Favell and Hansen 2002). Governments' capabilities are reaching their limits, especially in the area of political asylum. For instance, Schuster (2003: 219) reports that in 1999, Germany accepted only 3 percent out of about 100,000 requests for political asylum. At the same time, only about 40,000 could be sent back. This leaves 57,000 immigrants who received temporary residence permits (and therewith the right to work) or who disappeared before expulsion.

Second, increasing levels of illegal immigration have accompanied the process of restricting the inflow of legal immigrants. As King and Rueda (2008:

285) report, there is a strong positive correlation between the tightening of legal immigration and the amount of illegal immigration, a pattern visible also in the countries analyzed here. Brücker et al. (2002: 19) report that illegal immigration to Germany has increased by 150 to 300 percent in the 1990s. Similarly, the number of *detected* illegal entrants in the UK doubled from 7,500 in 1994 to 14,300 in 1997. As regards the situation in France, Brücker et al. (2002: 21) note that in the late 1990s, 143,000 illegal immigrants have applied for a legal status during a regularization campaign,[5] while every year since 2008, the French government has announced the expulsion of about 25,000 illegal immigrants per year (*Le Monde*, November 5, 2010).

These migration policy reforms have contributed in two ways to the persistence of inequalities between citizens and immigrants in Western European societies. First, by attempting to restrict immigration to mostly skilled foreigners, these reforms have created a distinction between "desired" and "undesired" immigrants. Second, by failing to effectively curb the overall inflow of "undesired" immigrants, they have failed to improve the living conditions of these "undesired" immigrants. They have increased the vulnerability of many immigrant workers by forcing them into illegality or awarding them only temporary residence permits. As a result, these reforms have inadvertently contributed to the extension of the pool of cheap immigrant labor.

Social Policy: Retrenchment of Immigrant-Specific Social Security Programs

Western governments and public alike share the fear that social benefits and services encourage people from other countries to come and live in Western Europe (Kvist 2004; Thielemann 2006). Consequently, governments have attempted to decrease the incentive to immigrate in the first place. For instance, governments have retrenched social benefits for asylum seekers. As argued by Schuster (2000: 125):

> The response [to the] question "How low can the lowest denominator go?" would seem to be very low. The governments of the European Union are opting for offering the barest minimum possible to asylum seekers—the acceptance of a few token, carefully chosen refugees who will be entitled to minimal support from host governments.

Similarly, Liedtke (2002: 493) concludes that in Germany, "welfare state instruments are used rather to minimize or limit than to maximize asylum seekers' well-being." As documented in Emmenegger and Careja (2011), in all three countries social benefits for asylum seekers have been gradually retrenched over the last 20 years. The results of these reforms are low recognition rates, the increased usage of vouchers instead of cash benefits (if any benefits at all), and extensive restrictions of the freedom of movement.

Less often, reforms have targeted the whole group of immigrants. Among the three countries covered by this study, the UK has been most active in restricting the access to certain social security schemes, for example through five-year bars for newly arrived immigrants. The list of social benefits, from which immigrants, in some cases even EU citizens (Kvist 2004), are barred includes income support, housing support, and council tax benefit. In 1996, the list has been extended to include attendance allowance, disability living allowance, disability working allowance, family credit, invalid care allowance, and severe disablement allowance (Banting 2000: 24; Fix and Lagragaron 2002: A16). Policy makers have justified these restrictions by portraying immigrants as abusers of the British social security system. As MP Edward Garnier (Conservatives) noted (cited in Schuster and Solomos 1999: 65): "Our duties to our citizens include the duty to protect our welfare and benefit budgets and our housing system at a time of economic stringency. [...] Those who should not be here but who have got round the system by false applications are of no benefit to our own people."

That France and Germany did not enact such restrictions is the result of the existence of general eligibility criteria, which presuppose active labor market participation for a certain time before an individual becomes eligible for social support (Banting 2000: 23). Nonetheless, in France, Minister of Interior Charles Pasqua tried in 1993 to restrict foreigners' social rights by denying access to health care. However, after intense debates, Pasqua had to soften his plans and introduced only legal residence as a prerequisite for access to health care (Guiraudon 2000: 78; Hollifield 2000: 124).

The anti-discrimination laws, which prohibit discrimination on the basis of ethnicity or nationality, generally impede reforms restricting the social rights of *all* immigrants. Social rights can only be restricted for certain designated categories of immigrants, such as asylum seekers, or certain time periods, such as the first years after immigration. If governments want to limit the redistribution of resources from native citizens to immigrants, they would have to reform those social security programs that provide benefits to both immigrants and the native population. The next section thus addresses the distributional consequences of recent reforms of social security programs that are not immigrant-specific.

Social Policy: Activation and Tighter Eligibility Conditions

There is considerable evidence that immigrants are disproportionately affected by the cutbacks in social security programs since the 1990s (Handler 2004; Sainsbury 2006; Schierup et al. 2006). As argued by Menz (2006: 400): "Migrants are much more likely to be on the receiving end of the 'sticks' implied by the logic of the second wave of welfare retrenchment of the 1990s: tighter eligibility, lower absolute levels of transfer payments, more pressure and demands on the individual recipients." One example is the introduction of higher levels of conditionality of social benefits (Clasen and Clegg 2007). Conditionality implies that recipients need to fulfill certain conditions and to respect behavioral requirements in order to be entitled to benefits. Since immigrants are more often unemployed and more likely to work in the secondary labor market than citizens, it can be expected that reforms which increase the level of conditionality of social protection systems disproportionately negatively affect the welfare of immigrants (Schierup et al. 2006; King and Rueda 2008). Moreover, conditionality and activation policies are increasingly used to "test" the willingness to work rather than to promote reintegration into standard employment (see Seeleib-Kaiser et al., Chapter 7 of this volume).

Another example is social spending on particular programs. As shown in Table 6-2, migrant households are particularly dependent on social assistance. However, as Nelson (2007) shows, means-tested benefits such as social assistance have been retrenched to a larger extent than social insurances. For instance, the yearly social assistance standard rates standardized for the development of wages (average for a single adult below retirement age without children, for a single parent with two children, and a two-parent family with two children) have decreased by 8 percent (Germany), 13 percent (UK) and 17 percent (France) in the period 1990 to 2005 (Nelson 2009). Thus, benefit generosity has decreased in programs that disproportionately provide benefits to migrants, such as social assistance.

Research on the distributional effects of recent social policy reforms is scarce, but the available evidence shows that immigrants have been among the main losers of these reforms. For instance, Butterwegge and Reißlandt (2005) argue that immigrants were disproportionately hit by the Hartz reforms in Germany. In particular, the reduction of benefit duration complicates family reunification and the prolongation of residence permits. Although the Hartz reforms have increased the income of some social assistance recipients,[6] it generally reduced the level of social protection of cheap labor and liberalized labor market regulation at the margins of the labor market (Palier and Thelen, Chapter 9 of this volume; Vail 2010). Since immigrants are twice as likely to be in need of financial support—in some German cities, more than 50 percent of all needy persons have an immigration background—these reforms strongly affect the welfare of immigrants in Germany (Knuth et al. 2009: 14). Most importantly, the Hartz reforms have reinforced the institutionalization of the divide between unemployment benefit and social assistance recipients (Palier and Thelen, Chapter 9 of this volume).

Although the Hartz reforms had also a negative effect on the level of social protection of workers in the primary labor market, they are less likely to suffer from these changes (Palier and Thelen 2010: 136–137; Seeleib-Kaiser et al., Chapter 7 of this volume). First, high levels of employment protection and the massive usage of short-time work during economic recessions mean that workers in the primary labor market are unlikely to become unemployed. Second, the insurance coverage for long-time contributing, and therefore deserving, "standard" workers was (re-)extended in 2007 after heavy criticism of the reforms.

In the UK, social policy reforms inspired by the idea of contractual workfare have also worsened the situation of the poor. According to Jones and Novak (1999: 71), the poor have been "squeezed by unemployment, low pay and casualisation on the one hand, and an increasingly parsimonious and brutalising social-security system on the other." In the words of King (1999: 257), recent social policy reforms have relegated "unemployed persons, and some other recipients of assistance, to second-class status in the polity." Since migrant households are much more likely to be poor than native citizen households and since migrants are more often unemployed than natives, these welfare-to-work programs have a disproportionately negative effect on immigrants.

Seeleib-Kaiser et al. (in Chapter 7 of this volume) document several reforms of the British unemployment insurance, which decreased overall generosity and led to a significant decline in the percentage of the unemployed receiving benefits. Again, the difference between citizen and migrant households is striking. According to Morissens and Sainsbury (2005: 650), 46.9 percent of all unemployed citizen households receive unemployment benefits, while only 21.2 percent of all unemployed migrant households receive unemployment benefits. With regard to old-age pensions, the difference is somewhat smaller, with 88.2 percent of the elderly citizen households and 62.6 percent of the elderly migrant households receiving a pension (see Table 6-2).

It should also be noted that non-EU immigrants are subject to an additional "Habitual Residence Test" for benefit entitlement, which aims to stop "benefit tourism" (Patterson 2002: 168). If subject to the test, applicants have to *prove* that they are voluntarily in the UK, have their place of residence in the UK, intend to remain in the UK, and have already resided in the UK for a considerable period.

In France, immigration is most clearly linked to the problem of youth unemployment. Unemployment is particularly high among young immigrants and children of immigrants (see Table 6-1) and is often considered an important source of social problems (Fougère et al. 2009). Successive French governments have attempted to tackle this problem by liberalizing labor market regulation and reducing the social protection of young people. In some cases, these reforms have clearly targeted the main "problem group," namely the young unemployed from the immigrant-heavy *banlieues*. For instance, a new employment contract for young people, which loosened restrictions on firing workers under the age of 26, was introduced by the de Villepin government just a few months after the *banlieues* had erupted in violent riots, for which immigrants had been blamed by many (Snow et al. 2007). Ultimately, the government had to withdraw the measure after violent protests (Vail 2010: 28).

The effects of the main French social assistance scheme (RMI before being transformed into RSA in 2010) on cheap labor were mixed. While the scheme was likely to avoid poverty, it fails to insert the socially excluded into the labor market (Handler 2004: 186). Likewise, recent pension reforms in France have extended the contributory period needed for a full pension (see Seeleib-Kaiser et al., Chapter 7 of this volume). Already before these reforms, the share of elderly households from ethnic minority groups receiving an old-age pension was 29.9 percentage points lower than the share of elderly citizens households (see Table 6-2). These recent reforms are likely to have accentuated that difference.

In sum, immigrants have been disproportionately affected by the cutbacks in social security programs since the 1990s. The next section discusses the question of whether this outcome was the deliberate choice of reforming governments or whether it was an unintended consequence caused by immigrants' generally inferior socio-economic status.

Do Governments Deliberately Target Immigrants?

Research on welfare state reforms has highlighted the role of the public perception of target groups (Schmidt 2002). A central argument is that reforming governments can rely on existing popular images or can alter the public's perception of different groups' worthiness in order to create public support for welfare state reforms. Thus, by portraying a group of recipients as lazy or indocile, popular resistance to welfare state reforms can be decreased. For instance, using an experimental setting, Slothuus (2007) shows that the framing of recipients' deservingness in news stories has a strong effect on popular support for welfare state reforms. Similarly, Larsen (2008) demonstrates that social assistance recipients are considered less deserving than unemployed people in general and elderly unemployed in particular, and that these deservingness frames are also used in political justifications of social assistance reforms.

These studies point to a possible relationship between public attitudes and public policy. Even though these studies do not suggest a one-to-one relationship between public attitudes and public policy, they assert that it is very likely that there is at least a positive correlation between public preferences on the one hand and migration and social policies on the other. Moreover, research on agenda setting has shown that a correspondence between public preferences and public policy is more likely, the higher these issues are on the political agenda and the more prominent they are in the popular debate (Mortensen 2010).

Both migration and social policies have been high salience issues in recent decades (Emmenegger and Careja 2011). In addition, survey research has shown that being part of the national community continues to be perceived as a major criterion for deserving community-funded social support in times of need. As van Oorschot (2006) shows, migrants are consistently reported as the least deserving group, which indicates that respondents, although approving the principle of redistribution, invariably judge that groups associated to their national community are more deserving than groups explicitly not associated with their community.

Interestingly, this remains true even when the neediness of immigrants is acknowledged. Appelbaum (2002) shows in her analysis of 2000 German students that, although refugees from Kosovo and asylum seekers from Bosnia were identified as the least responsible for their need of aid, they were nonetheless thought to be the least deserving of receiving aid. In contrast, Germans were considered most deserving of receiving aid, although Germans were considered to be the most responsible for their need. Thus, there can be no doubt that many Western Europeans draw a clear line between citizens and immigrants.

Although immigrants constitute a very heterogeneous group, public opinion does not take these diverse backgrounds into account. Table 6-3 shows that in France, Germany, and the UK, a majority of citizens thinks that immigrants take out more than they put in and are attracted by available social benefits, that immigrants should work and pay taxes for at least a year before becoming eligible for social benefits, and that minority groups abuse the system of social benefits. Thus, the stereotypical perception of immigrants is one of individuals who abuse the welfare state, cost extra tax money, and take away jobs from natives. Moreover, this stereotypical perception seems to be applied indiscriminately to the entire group of immigrants. Furthermore, as Boeri (2009) shows, the number of people with critical opinions about immigrants is steadily increasing.

Consequently, we can observe a strong correspondence between public policy and public opinion. As shown earlier, recent welfare state retrenchment disproportionately disadvantages immigrants, an outcome that the majority of the population is likely to support. Moreover, there is a striking parallel to the retrenchment of immigrant-specific social policy programs and migration policy reforms that have complicated legal immigration. But do Western European governments really target resident immigrants?

The timing of these reforms, the salience of social and migration policy reforms in public debates, and the long history of welfare chauvinism in Western Europe (Emmenegger and Careja 2011) suggest a causal relationship. However,

Table 6-3: Welfare chauvinism (percentage of respondents agreeing or tending to agree with statement)

	France	Germany	UK
Taxes and services: Immigrants take out more than they put in.	67.3%	80.8%	74.6%
Social benefits and services encourage people from other countries to come and live here.	71.6%	81.5%	76.0%
Immigrants should only obtain the same rights to social benefits and services as citizens already living here after working and paying taxes for at least a year.	77.3%	79.4%	88.8%
People from these minority groups abuse the system of social benefits.	65.3%	56.9%	57.8%

Sources: Rows 1 and 4: Crepaz and Damron (2009: 448); rows 2 and 3: European Social Survey wave 4 (2009).

there are also other motivations for welfare state reforms. For instance, govern-ments might simply reform in order to save money. In this case, immigrants might suffer disproportionately because of their generally low socioeconomic status. Similarly, there is no need to resort to arguments based on welfare chau-vinism in order to explain why recent reforms have increased the contributory period needed for a full pension or retrenched social assistance benefits rather than lowered the benefit levels of full pensions (see, for example, Nelson 2007; Larsen 2008).

In general, recent welfare state reforms have not been accompanied by xeno-phobic or racist tones on the part of mainstream parties, although far-right par-ties have used xenophobic and racist rhetoric in their demands for such reforms (Bale 2003). This leads Menz (2006: 396) to reject a causal link between immi-gration and welfare state reforms. We believe that such a rejection is premature. In postwar Europe, the lighthearted usage of xenophobic and racist rhetoric in the justification of policy reforms cannot be expected from mainstream par-ties. Rather, mainstream parties resort to politically correct "code language" in order to justify certain measures (Marthaler 2008). Thus, we cannot expect to observe a "smoking gun."

Recent developments, however, show that mainstream parties are more and more willing to break the postwar consensus on the usage of xenophobic rheto-ric (Bale 2003). The current president of France is a particularly telling example. In his 2007 presidential campaign, Nicolas Sarkozy ran on a platform high-lighting both the need for tougher immigration laws and social policy reforms. On several occasions, he linked the need for social policy reforms to questions of immigration (Marthaler 2008). In doing so, he copied the rhetoric of the far-right *Front National* in order to win back voters lost in the early 2000s. While Sarkozy never justified social policy reforms using xenophobic rhetoric, the simultaneous highlighting of the need for migration and social policy reforms and the proclaimed causal link between immigration and social problems leave little room for interpretation. Similar developments can be observed in Germany and the UK (Schuster 2003; Craig 2007), as well as in countries with strong far-right parties in general (Bale 2003).

Thus, have recent welfare state reforms deliberately targeted immigrants? We find it hard to believe that governments attempt to deliberately hurt immi-grants (for the sake of being immigrants), a few exceptions notwithstanding. Such an interpretation could not explain why they simultaneously invest in the integration of immigrants. However, governments clearly care about the incen-tives for prospective immigrants to come to Western Europe in the first place. That said, we consider it equally unlikely that governments are not aware of the distributional consequences of their reforms. Rather, on the empirical grounds discussed above, we believe that they tacitly accept that their reforms contrib-ute to the persistence of a divide between immigrants and the native popula-tion. Moreover, we believe that welfare chauvinism plays an important *indirect* role in the politics of welfare state reform. The bad public image of immigrants contributes to the persistence of some bad target group images (e.g., social assistance recipients), which make certain reforms possible in the first place (Schmidt 2002; Larsen 2008). Thus, while it is not clear whether welfare chauvinism has a direct effect on welfare state reform, it is very likely to have at least an indirect effect.

CONCLUSIONS

Western Europe's "reluctant countries of immigration" are confronted with two contradictory demands. On the one hand, the economy pushes for more immigration because many industries rely on cheap labor and immigrant workers are one—if not the most important—source of it (King and Rueda 2008). On the other hand, the public opposes large-scale immigration and wants to restrict immigrants' access to social benefits. In the decades following World War II, this dilemma could be solved through the establishment of guest worker programs, which created a divide between immigrants and the native population by circumscribing immigrants' right to residence and access to social benefits. However, although guest worker programs have been largely abandoned and despite programs that aim at the better integration of immigrants, we continue to observe this divide.

We have shown that three dualization processes contribute to the persistence of this divide within the societies of France, Germany, and the UK. First, these countries have created a distinction between "desired," mostly high-skilled, immigrants and less desired, but more numerous low-skilled immigrants, some of which have been forced into clandestine employment. Second, these countries have engaged in the reform of social security programs that exclusively provide benefits to immigrants in general and asylum seekers in particular. Finally, immigrants have been disproportionately negatively affected by recent welfare state reforms.

How deliberately did these governments dualize their societies? It is clear that the creation of a divide between "desired" and "undesired" immigrants and the retrenchment of immigrant-specific social security schemes were both attempts to manage immigration. In contrast, it is unlikely that these governments intended to extend the pool of immigrant cheap labor. Rather, this is the unintended consequence of failing to effectively manage immigration. Finally, it is not clear whether the distributional consequences of recent social policy reforms were rather the result of the deliberate attempt to weaken the socio-economic position of immigrants or the unintended distributional consequence of reforms that put more pressure on some of the weakest members of society. That said, considering the recommendations made by economists (e.g.,

Sinn 2002) and the preferences of the public, it is unlikely that governments are unaware of the distributional consequences of their reforms. As a consequence, they at least tacitly accept that their reforms contribute to the persistence of a divide between immigrants and the native population.

In this chapter, we have shown that, despite numerous institutional differences, France, Germany, and the UK have moved in the same direction. However, it is important to note that significant cross-country differences can be observed. Most notably, it looks as if the UK sets the pace with regard to the development of programs for high-skilled migrants and the reform of its social security programs. The UK has gone furthest in adapting its immigration policy to labor market needs and in restricting access to social security programs. In contrast, France and Germany seem more hesitant. Even though they have been similarly active in restricting low-skilled immigration, they have not to the same extent developed programs to attract high-skilled immigrants. Similarly, France and Germany have been less pressed to introduce tougher eligibility criteria, not least because in Continental European welfare regimes general eligibility criteria already exist. Consequently, Continental European welfare regimes have a general tendency to reinforce insider-outsider divides (Häusermann and Schwander, Chapter 2 of this volume). However, these cross-national differences should not belie the fact that all three countries have introduced significant measures and are heading in a similar direction.

NOTES

1 Significant differences can also be observed for children of immigrants (SOPEMI 2007: 81–85).
2 For reasons of data availability, ethnic minority migrants are defined as those who are not from EU member countries (prior to the 2004 enlargement) or North America and Australasia (Morissens and Sainsbury 2005: 642).
3 Interestingly, these two approaches closely mirror recommendations made in the political economy literature (e.g., Sinn 2002).
4 This development started earlier in the UK. The three legislative acts adopted between 1962 and 1971 were justified by the need to protect the British island from overcrowding (Geddes 2003: 33).
5 The number of illegal immigrants who do not participate in legalization is likely to be much higher than the number of illegal immigrants who apply for legal status (Brücker et al. 2002: 21).
6 In fact, the average monthly income of long-term recipients of social assistance with migration background and the right of unlimited residence increased by €50 (Knuth et al. 2009: 18).

REFERENCES

Adserà, Alicia, and Chiswick, Barry R. (2006). "Divergent Patterns in Immigrant Earnings across European Destinations," in Parsons, Craig A., and Smeeding, Timothy M. (eds.), *Immigration and the Transformation of Europe*, Cambridge: Cambridge University Press, pp. 85–110.

Appelbaum, Lauren D. (2002). "Who Deserves Help? Students' Opinions About the Deservingness of Different Groups Living in Germany to Receive Aid," *Social Justice Research*, 15(3): 201–225.

Autor, David H., Levy, Frank, and Murnance, Richard J. (2003). "The Skill Content of Recent Technological Change: An Empirical Exploration," *Quarterly Journal of Economics*, 118(4): 1279–1333.

Bale, Tim (2003). "Cinderella and her Ugly Sisters: The Mainstream and Extreme Right in Europe's Bipolarising Party Systems," *West European Politics*, 26(3): 67–90.

Banting, Keith G. (2000). "Looking in Three Directions: Migration and the European Welfare State in Comparative Perspective," in Bommes, Michael, and Geddes, Andrew (eds.), *Immigration and Welfare: Challenging the Borders of the Welfare State*, London: Routledge, pp. 13–33.

Block, Laura (2009). "Controlling Marriage to Control Migration? Revisiting the Notions of Marriages of Convenience and Forced Marriages," paper read at the 5th General Conference of the European Consortium of Political Research, September 10–12, Potsdam.

Boeri, Tito (2009). "Immigration to the Land of Redistribution," IZA Discussion Paper No. 4273.

Brücker, Herbert, Epstein, Gil S., McCormick, Barry, Saint-Paul, Gilles, Venturini, Alessandra, and Zimmermann, Klaus (2002). "Managing Migration in the European Welfare State," in Boeri, Tito, Hanson, Gordon, and McCormick, Barry (eds.), *Immigration Policy and the Welfare System*, New York: Oxford University Press, pp. 1–167.

Butterwegge, Christoph, and Reißlandt, Carolin (2005). "Folgen der Hartz-Gesetze für Migrant(inn)en," *Gesundheits- und Sozialpolitik*, 59(1): 20–24.

Caviedes, Alexander A. (2010). *Prying Open Fortress Europe: The Turn to Sectoral Labor Migration*, Lanham, MD: Lexington.

CESifo (2009). "Migration Policies Concerning Refugees and Asylum Seekers, 2003/2004." Online, available from http://www.cesifo-group.de/portal/page/portal/DICE_Content/LABOUR_MARKET_AND_MIGRATION/MIGRATION/Non-labour%20Migration/migrat-pol-refug-asyl.pdf (accessed June 15, 2009).

Clasen, Jochen, and Clegg, Daniel (2007). "Levels and Levers of Conditionality: Measuring Change Within Welfare States," in Clasen, Jochen, and Siegel, Nico A. (eds.), *Investigating Welfare State Change: The 'Dependent Variable Problem' in Comparative Analysis*, Cheltenham: Edward Elgar, pp. 166–197.

Cornelius, Wayne A., Tsuda, Takeyuki, Martin, Philip L., and Hollifield, James F. (2004). *Controlling Immigration: A Global Perspective*, 2nd ed., Stanford, CA: Stanford University Press.

Craig, Gary (2007). "'Cunning, Unprincipled, Loathsome': The Racist Tail Wags the Welfare Dog," *Journal of Social Policy*, 36(4): 605–623.

Crepaz, Markus M. L., and Damron, Regan (2009). "Constructing Tolerance: How the Welfare State Shapes Attitudes about Immigrants," *Comparative Political Studies*, 42(3): 437–463.

ECRE (2005). *The Application of the Safe Country of Origin Concept in Europe*, Brussels: European Council on Refugees and Exiles.

Emmenegger, Patrick, and Careja, Romana (2011). "The Politics of Inclusion and Exclusion: Social Policy, Migration Politics and Welfare State Nationalism," in Suszycki, Andrzej Marcin (ed.), *Welfare Citizenship and Welfare Nationalism*, Helsinki: NordWel, pp. 151–186.

EMN (2007). *Conditions of Entry and Residence of Third Country Highly-Skilled Workers in the EU*, Brussels: European Migration Network.

European Commission (2008). *Quality in and Equality of Access to Healthcare Services*, Brussels: European Commission.

Favell, Adrian, and Hansen, Randall (2002). "Markets Against Politics: Migration, EU Enlargement and the Idea of Europe," *Journal of Ethnic and Migration Studies*, 28(4): 581–601.

Fix, Michael, and Laglagaron, Laureen (2002). *Social Rights and Citizenship: An International Comparison*, Washington, DC: Urban Institute.

Fougère, Denis, Kramarz, Francis, and Pouget, Julien (2009). "Youth Unemployment and Crime in France," *Journal of the European Economic Association*, 7(5): 909–938.

Geddes, Andrew (2003). *The Politics of Migration and Immigration in Europe*, Los Angeles: Sage.

Gower, Melanie (2010). "Asylum Seekers and the Right to Work." Online, available from http://www.parliament.uk/briefingpapers/commons/lib/research/briefings/snha-01908.pdf (accessed November 29, 2010).

Guiraudon, Virginie (2000). "The Marshallian Triptych Reordered: The Role of Courts and Bureaucracies in Furthering Migrants' Social Rights," in Bommes, Michael, and Geddes, Andrew (eds.), *Immigration and Welfare: Challenging the Borders of the Welfare State*, London: Routledge, pp. 72–89.

Hamilton, Kimberly, Simon, Patrick, and Veniard, Clara (2004). "The Challenge of French Diversity." Online, available from http://www.migrationinformation.org/Profiles/display.cfm?ID=266 (accessed March 4, 2009).

Handler, Joel F. (2004). *Social Citizenship and Workfare in the United States and Western Europe: The Paradox of Inclusion*, Cambridge: Cambridge University Press.

Hollifield, James F. (2000). "Immigration and the Politics of Rights: The French Case in Comparative Perspective," in Bommes, Michael, and Geddes, Andrew (eds.), *Immigration and Welfare: Challenging the Borders of the Welfare State*, London: Routledge, pp. 109–133.

Jones, Chris, and Novak, Tony (1999). *Poverty, Welfare and the Disciplinary State*, London: Routledge.

Joppke, Christian (2001). "The Legal-Domestic Sources of Human Rights: The United States, Germany, and the European Union," *Comparative Political Studies*, 34(4): 339–366.

King, Desmond (1999). *In the Name of Liberalism: Illiberal Social Policy in the USA and Britain*, New York: Oxford University Press.

King, Desmond, and Rueda, David (2008). "Cheap Labor: The New Politics of 'Bread and Roses' in Industrial Democracies," *Perspectives on Politics,* 6(2): 279–297.

Knuth, Matthias, Brussig, Martin, Neuffer, Stefanie, Dittmar, Vera, and Mosler, Bettina (2009). *Wirkungen des SGB II auf Personen mit Migrationshintergrund*, Duisburg: Universität Duisburg-Essen.

Kogan, Irene (2004). "Last Hired, First Fired? The Unemployment Dynamics of Male Immigrants in Germany," *European Sociological Review*, 20(5): 445–461.

Kvist, Jon (2004). "Does EU Enlargement Start a Race to the Bottom? Strategic Interaction among EU Member States in Social Policy," *Journal of European Social Policy*, 14(3): 301–318.

Larsen, Christian Albrekt (2008). "The Political Logic of Labour Market Reforms and Popular Images of Target Groups," *Journal of European Social Policy*, 18(1): 50–63.

Liedtke, Matthias (2002). "National Welfare and Asylum in Germany," *Critical Social Policy*, 22(3): 479–497.

Marthaler, Sally (2008). "Nicolas Sarkozy and the Politics of French Immigration Policy," *Journal of European Public Policy*, 15(3): 382–397.

Menz, Georg (2002). "Patterns of EU Labour Immigration Policy: National Initiatives and European Responses," *Journal of Ethnic and Migration Studies*, 28(4): 723–742.

Menz, Georg (2006). "'Useful' Gastarbeiter, Burdensome Asylum Seekers, and the Second Wave of Welfare Retrenchment: Exploring the Nexus between Migration and the Welfare State," in Parsons, Craig A., and Smeeding, Timothy M. (eds.), *Immigration and the Transformation of Europe*, Cambridge: Cambridge University Press, pp. 393–418.

Morissens, Ann, and Sainsbury, Diane (2005). "Migrants' Social Rights, Ethnicity and Welfare Regimes," *Journal of Social Policy*, 34(4): 637–660.

Mortensen, Peter B. (2010). "Political Attention and Public Policy: A Study of How Agenda Setting Matters," *Scandinavian Political Studies*, 33(4): 356–380.

Nelson, Kenneth (2007). "Universalism versus Targeting: The Vulnerability of Social Insurance and Means-tested Minimum Income Protection in 18 Countries, 1990–2002," *International Social Security Review*, 60(1): 33–58.

Nelson, Kenneth (2009). *Social Assistance and Minimum Income Protection Interim Data-Set, version 2.0 Beta*, Stockholm: University of Stockholm.

OECD (2004). *Global Knowledge Flows and Economic Development*, Paris: OECD.

OECD (2009). OECD Factbook 2009, Paris: OECD.

Palier, Bruno, and Thelen, Kathleen (2010). "Institutionalizing Dualism: Complementarities and Change in France and Germany," *Politics and Society*, 38(1): 119–148.

Patterson, Terry (2002). "From Safety Net to Exclusion: Ending Social Security in the UK for 'Persons from Abroad,'" in Cohen, Steve, Humphries, Beth, and

Mynott, Ed (eds.), *From Immigration Controls to Welfare Controls*, London: Routledge, pp. 157–184.

Piore, Michael J. (1979). *Birds of Passage: Migrant Labor and Industrial Societies*, Cambridge: Cambridge University Press.

Piore, Michael J. (1980). "An Economic Approach," in Berger, Suzanne, and Piore, Michael J. (eds.), *Dualism and Discontinuity in Industrial Societies*, Cambridge: Cambridge University Press, pp. 15–81.

Rollason, Nicolas (2001). "International Mobility of Highly Skilled Workers: The UK Perspective," in OECD (ed.), *International Mobility of the Highly Skilled*, Paris: OECD, pp. 327–342.

Sainsbury, Diane (2006). "Immigrants' Social Rights in Comparative Perspective: Welfare Regimes, Forms in Immigration and Immigration Policy Regimes," *Journal of European Social Policy*, 16(3): 229–244.

Scharpf, Fritz W. (2010). "The Asymmetry of European Integration, or Why the EU Cannot Be a 'Social Market Economy,'" *Socio-Economic Review*, 8(2): 211–250.

Schierup, Carl-Ulrik, Hansen, Peo, and Castles, Stephen (2006). *Migration, Citizenship, and the European Welfare State*, New York: Oxford University Press.

Schmidt, Vivien A. (2002). "Does Discourse Matter in the Politics of Welfare State Adjustment?" *Comparative Political Studies*, 35(2): 168–193.

Schneider, Friedrich (2005). "Shadow Economies Around the World: What Do We Really Know?" *European Journal of Political Economy*, 21(3): 598–642.

Schuster, Liza, and Solomos, John (1999). "The Politics of Refugee and Asylum Policies in Britain: Historical Patterns and Contemporary Realities," in Bloch, Alice, and Levy, Carl (eds.), *Refugees, Citizenship and Social Policy*, Houndmills: Palgrave Macmillan, pp. 51–75.

Schuster, Liza (2000). "A Comparative Analysis of the Asylum Policy of Seven European Governments," *Journal of Refugee Studies*, 13(1): 118–132.

Schuster, Liza (2003). *The Use and Abuse of Political Asylum in Britain and Germany*, London: Frank Cass.

Sinn, Hans-Werner (2002). "EU Enlargement and the Future of the Welfare," *Scottish Journal of Political Economy*, 49(1): 104–115.

Slothuus, Rune (2007). "Framing Deservingness to Win Support for Welfare State Retrenchment," *Scandinavian Political Studies*, 30(3): 323–344.

Snow, David A., Vliegenthart, Rens, and Corrigall-Brown, Catherine (2007). "Framing the French Riots: A Comparative Study of Frame Variation," *Social Forces*, 86(2): 385–415.

SOPEMI (several years). *Trends in International Migration/International Migration Outlook*, Paris: OECD.

Soysal, Yasemin Nuhoglu (1994). *Limits of Citizenship: Migrants and Postnational Membership in Europe*, Chicago, IL: University of Chicago Press.

Thielemann, Eiko R. (2006). "The Effectiveness of Governments' Attempts to Control Unwanted Migration," in Parsons, Craig A., and Smeeding, Timothy M. (eds.), *Immigration and the Transformation of Europe*, Cambridge: Cambridge University Press, pp. 442–472.

Thorp, Arabella (2009). "Asylum Seekers and the Right to Work," Information to the Members of Parliament, Library of House of Commons. Online, available from http://www.parliament.uk/commons/lib/research/briefing/snha-01908.pdf (accessed May 4, 2009).

Vail, Mark I. (2010). "Bending the Rules: Institutional Analysis, Political Change, and Labor Market Reform in Advanced Industrial Societies," *Comparative Political Studies*, 42(2): 21–39.

van Oorschot, Wim (2006). "Making the Difference in Social Europe: Deservingness Perceptions among Citizens of European Welfare States," *Journal of European Social Policy*, 16(1): 23–42.

PART III

VARIETIES OF DUALIZATION

7

SHIFTING THE PUBLIC-PRIVATE MIX
A NEW DUALIZATION OF WELFARE?¹

MARTIN SEELEIB-KAISER, ADAM SAUNDERS, AND MAREK NACZYK

INTRODUCTION

The concept of dualization poses a significant challenge to established approaches of social policy analysis, as much of the *comparative* political economy literature has focused its attention on differences in state welfare between countries (see, e.g., Esping-Andersen 1990; Estévez-Abe 2001; Iversen 2005; Pontusson 2005). In place of the one-dimensional notion of *welfare states*, we introduce the concept of *welfare systems* (cf. Seeleib-Kaiser 2001; 2008), which incorporates both public *and* private social protection, thereby giving a clearer picture of the extent of dualism within countries and a potential dualization of social protection over time. Critical welfare state analyses, focusing on single nation-states, have highlighted the concept of "dual welfare systems" whereby policies for the poor were historically differentiated from policies for workers (Tussing 1975; Liebfried and Tennstedt 1985; Weir et al. 1988). Yet, this literature largely neglected social policy provision through the market, that is, mainly employer-provided, occupational social policies, which could result in an even more profound bifurcation or division of welfare, as already noted by Titmuss (1958; cf. Hacker 2002). To some extent, our definition of institutional welfare dualism relates to the concept of dual welfare systems that differentiates between insiders (workers) and outsiders (the poor). Social protection insiders are defined as individuals covered either through comprehensive public/statutory social protection *or* those whose public/statutory entitlements are complemented or supplemented by private/occupational social protection to a level that maintains living standards. In contrast, outsiders are defined as those who would have to rely on modest (largely means-tested) public provision, primarily intended to ameliorate poverty. The concept of dualization refers to processes of deepening, widening, or the establishment of new welfare dualisms.

To investigate processes of dualization over the past three decades, a clear reference point is needed. Thus, in the first section of this chapter we present a stylized history of social protection in the era of industrial welfare capitalism, before analyzing welfare during post-industrial capitalism. Industrial welfare capitalism, which prevailed in affluent democracies in the first three decades of the postwar period, was underpinned by mass employment in the manufacturing sector (cf. Wilensky 1975). During the era of industrial welfare capitalism, direct *public* provision of social policy was perceived as the core element for the realization of "social citizenship" (Marshall 1950), social integration, or the reduction of poverty by a majority of political actors and social scientists in Western Europe. Nevertheless, labor market participation was essential for access to comprehensive social protection in both Conservative and Liberal welfare systems. Our analysis focuses on the development in two Conservative welfare systems, France and Germany, and two Liberal welfare systems, the United Kingdom and the United States. Despite full employment in France and Germany, dualism was *institutionally* embedded in the differentiation between earnings-related and means-tested social policy programs (Leibfried and Tennstedt 1985). In the United Kingdom and the United States, the limited availability of occupational benefits for core workers in certain industrial sectors resulted in significant welfare divisions (Hacker 2002). Nevertheless, in both Conservative and Liberal welfare systems, the social protection outsiderness declined during the era of industrial capitalism. Since the mid-1970s, deindustrialization has accelerated and has led to the development of post-industrial welfare capitalism (cf. Esping-Andersen 1999) and a reversal of the trend.

Our analysis focuses on *institutional* arrangements in relation to pensions, unemployment compensation, and health care. Across all four countries, a shift in the balance between public and private social protection arrangements has been unfolding to different degrees, which has resulted in varieties of welfare dualism. In the United Kingdom and the United States, overall coverage of occupational social protection has been declining as deindustrialization has progressed, leading to a greater reliance for many individuals on government programs. In France and Germany, the coverage of social insurance has been eroding over time for the same reason, and an increasing proportion of the population has become dependent upon means-tested welfare benefits. Furthermore, in certain sectors, occupational welfare has either proliferated or would seem poised to expand in the future.

DUALISM IN THE AGE OF INDUSTRIAL WELFARE CAPITALISM

Social Integration Through Social Insurance in Germany and France

In the age of industrial welfare capitalism, Continental welfare systems such as Germany and France relied on a wage-earner–centered approach to social policy to achieve social inclusion. Wage-earner–centered social policy was rooted in the belief that only the *standard* social risks of wage earners could be effectively insured. The definition of these standard risks was based on assumptions of what constitutes a "*standard* employment relationship" (Mückenberger 1985): (1) paid work is carried out as dependent work with a single employer, mainly by men; (2) paid work is full-time; (3) remuneration is higher than the subsistence level; (4) employment history is continuous as well as sufficiently long, at most interrupted by only short spells of unemployment; (5) the life course follows the education-work-retirement track. The standard employment relationship was not only perceived to be a normative goal, but it was also considered to be the foundation of the social insurance system. Only people unable to meet these criteria—generally through no fault of their own—would, in times of need, have to rely on tax-financed social assistance benefits.

Theoretically, such a social policy design could only function as a means of social integration as long as the overwhelming majority of (male) workers were in standard employment relationships, the family model was stable, and the economy generated full employment (cf. Standing 2009). The foremost aims of German and French social insurance schemes were inter-temporal redistribution within the life course (not interpersonal redistribution), and the entitlement of derived benefits to family members. The *leitmotiv* of postwar social policy expansion was to secure the "achieved living standard" of the male breadwinner and his family during old age, disability, sickness, and unemployment.

Germany: Quasi-Universalism Through Social Insurance

Historically, the German welfare state was based on a two-tiered system, differentiating between workers and the poor (Leibfried and Tennstedt 1985). While the main aim of postwar social policy expansions was to maintain the "achieved living standard" through more encompassing social insurance schemes, a very small minority of the population would continue to be dependent on social assistance. Hence, although the impact of the dual structure of social protection was minimized during this period, institutionally it was never abolished.

The pension reform of 1957 is the prime example of how the social insurance system aimed to guarantee that a worker would be able to maintain the achieved standard of living during retirement. The pension reform raised the old-age benefits on average by about 65 percent and indexed them to future increases in gross wages (cf. Schmähl 1999). Subsequently, pension benefits for male workers rose sharply as a result of the generally healthy performance of the economy and negotiated wage increases in the 1960s and early 1970s. By the mid-1970s, the net-income replacement ratio reached 70 percent for a standard pensioner (*Eckrentner*), a person with a prior average income and a work history of 45 years (Schmähl 1999: 405). This level of wage replacement symbolizes the core aim of the public old-age insurance scheme, namely to guarantee that the insured person maintains the same standard of living during retirement as enjoyed during employment. The overall success of the reformed pension insurance system was highlighted by the decreasing proportion of senior citizens dependent on social assistance (Leisering and Leibfried 1999).

Despite a long tradition, fringe or occupational benefits provided by employers played only a marginal role in insuring workers against social risks. Although a relatively high proportion of employees had some form of occupational old-age benefit coverage, the benefit amounts were rather small; the average replacement rate of occupational pension programs in the manufacturing sector was approximately 15 percent during the 1980s (Mitchell and Rojot 1992: 140).

The unemployment insurance (UI) system was normatively bound to insure the worker's standard of living against job loss. The UI benefit was intended to replace wage income and was supposed to be clearly separate from social assistance benefits. In 1969 crucial elements of active labor market policy (ALMP) were introduced with the aim to abolish "substandard" employment. By the mid-1970s, almost 70 percent of all unemployed workers received UI benefits that were set at 68 percent of prior net earnings. This level was to ensure a relatively stable income for workers during spells of unemployment. "Suitable work" was defined in such a way that an unemployed worker practically did not have to accept a job that either paid less or was in a different occupational field from his previous job. It must be emphasized that unemployment up to the 1970s was largely frictional and cyclical; the average unemployment rate for the period from 1964–1973 was 0.7 percent. Nevertheless, the long-term unemployed and those unemployed not qualified for UI benefits continued to depend on means-tested unemployment assistance or social assistance (Bleses and Seeleib-Kaiser 2004).

The predominance of standard employment relationships and the broad social insurance coverage of workers with benefits considerably higher than the level of subsistence significantly reduced the reliance on social assistance and thereby the effects of the institutionalized dual structure of the German welfare system. Thus, social protection outsiderness de facto became more or less residual. Statutory health insurance funds provided equitable access to health benefits and the state guaranteed access to those not insured. Leisering (2009:158) has coined this process as "the road to quasi-universalism."

France: The True Bismarckian Welfare System

As in Germany, the postwar French welfare system has overwhelmingly relied on social insurance to achieve generous income maintenance for standard workers in case of unemployment, old age, or sickness. However, it has been uniquely Bismarckian, since several social insurance schemes have been self-regulated by the social partners and have been often organized on an occupational basis, thereby complementing basic *statutory* provision. This has been a feature absent from other Bismarckian systems, even that of Germany.

This characteristic is best exemplified by the development of the pension system. When it was established in 1945, the statutory scheme covering all private-sector employees (called *régime général*) offered defined benefit (DB) pensions, but with limited replacement rates. Therefore, this first compulsory tier was complemented with occupational schemes set up through collective agreements. In 1947, representatives of management and technical staff in the private sector (*cadres*) negotiated the establishment of a national-level supplementary earnings-related scheme AGIRC (*Association Générale d'Institutions de Retraites des Cadres*) to top up their statutory benefits (Reynaud 1997; Friot 1998). From 1956, pay-as-you-go supplementary pension schemes were gradually extended to other categories of workers, first at the company and industry level and later at the national level, with the creation of ARRCO (*Association des Régimes de Retraite Complémentaire*) in 1961 and the extension of supplementary schemes to all private-sector companies in 1972. Once it reached maturity, the French mix of statutory and supplementary pay-as-you-go pensions was able to offer very high net replacement rates and contributed to decreasing the number of recipients of the *minimum vieillesse*, a special social assistance scheme for the elderly created in 1956. Thus, in 2001, private-sector workers born in 1934 and who had a full contributory record at retirement received on average 83 percent of their previous earnings, when combining benefits from *régime général* and ARRCO/AGIRC (DREES 2004).

The development of unemployment compensation also illustrates the reliance on statutory and non-statutory social protection in the post-war French welfare system. In 1958 the social partners negotiated a national-level collective agreement establishing a non-statutory unemployment insurance (UNEDIC) covering all firms belonging to the main employers' association, the CNPF (*Conseil National du Patronat Français*). Similarly to AGIRC, UNEDIC was managed by the social partners, who had decision-making power over adjustments to benefits and contributions, but the state contributed to extend coverage by UNEDIC to all private-sector workers in 1967. UNEDIC benefits served to supplement unemployment assistance, which provided flat-rate benefits with unlimited duration after a means test and, since 1967, a three-month basic income to all unemployed workers. UI benefits have traditionally been earnings-related, and until the end of the 1970s the duration of benefits depended on workers' age rather than on their contributory record (Daniel and Tuchszirer 1999). In 1976, when combined with unemployment assistance benefits, unemployment compensation could offer a 72.4 percent replacement rate for minimum wage workers and a 90 percent replacement rate for workers laid off for economic reasons (Daniel and Tuchszirer 1999: 251).

A majority of private-sector workers and their dependents were insured against health-related risks by the *régime général* since its inception in 1945. Those individuals who were not covered by the *régime général* or other statutory health insurance funds could join "voluntary" insurance schemes. Because the majority of such individuals were poor and were out of work, the state decided to partly subsidize their contributions beginning in 1967. However, even if coverage was large, benefit levels offered by statutory health insurance were limited, since co-payments of 20 percent were introduced as early as 1945 and were subsequently further increased, thereby opening up a market for supplementary private health insurance.

During the age of industrial welfare capitalism, the large majority of French standard workers could benefit from generous social protection, due to basic statutory benefits topped up by social insurance benefits introduced via the industrial relations system. Thus, despite the existence of various social assistance schemes, the degree of social protection outsiderness was rather small.

The Dual Structure of Liberal Welfare Systems

Welfare dualism has been most prevalent in the United Kingdom and in the United States, where employer-provided benefits have been used to supplement and complement public social policies. Private welfare provision sits awkwardly with the comparative literature's relatively narrow characterization of social protection in the United Kingdom and the United States as minimalist with a heavy reliance on means-testing (Esping-Andersen 1990; Estévez-Abe et al. 2001). The inclusion of occupational benefits provides a far more holistic picture of the kind of welfare dualism that has prevailed in Liberal welfare systems. In particular, it helps to reveal the extent to which American and UK insiders have been protected against social risks at a level similar to their counterparts in Bismarckian welfare systems (Brown 1999: 166). Due to long periods of job tenure, occupational social protection can be considered as a functional equivalent to social insurance guaranteeing the achieved standard of living. Job tenure was particularly high in many production industries and high value-added service industries. For instance, in 1968 average job tenure in the United Kingdom was 28 years in the insurance, banking, and finance industries, 26 years in the mining and quarrying industries, and 23 years in the automotive industry (Main 1982: 329).

America's Three Pillars of Welfare: Social Assistance, Social Insurance, and Occupational Welfare

The United States is usually considered a welfare state laggard, with a heavy reliance on means-tested programs. Nevertheless, it must be stressed that public social insurance programs have witnessed significant expansions in the era of industrial welfare capitalism. Although Social Security and UI initially were quite limited in coverage, they increasingly insured an ever larger proportion of workers. In the mid-1970s, about 90 percent of all full-time workers were covered (Seeleib-Kaiser 2001: 272). Nevertheless, compared to the replacement rates achieved in France and Germany, the wage replacement rate was rather modest at approximately 50 percent for the average worker in both programs (Hacker 2002: 143; Vroman 1990: 20). Furthermore, the poor had to rely on means-tested welfare programs, such as Aid to Families with Dependent Children (AFDC) or state-run general assistance.

Although the extent of welfare dualism declined through the parallel expansion of occupational welfare during the age of industrial welfare capitalism, it continued to be a major feature of the U.S. welfare system. At its peak, only about 70 percent of the workforce had occupational health care coverage, and occupational pension coverage barely surpassed 50 percent in the late 1970s (see Figure 7-1). The overwhelming majority of occupational pensions were DB plans, and the average replacement rate for workers formerly employed in the manufacturing sector was 42 percent during the 1980s (Mitchell and Rojot 1992: 140). Despite these achievements, coverage differed significantly by industry. In 1979, 79 percent of the workers in the automobile industry and 9 percent of workers in the hospitality sector were covered by occupational pensions (Kotlikoff and Smith 1983: Tables 3.2.9, 3.2.10).

Figure 7-1: Occupational social protection coverage in the U.S.: 1950–1974

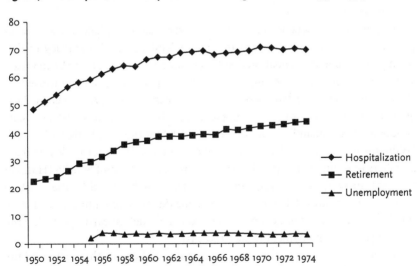

Note: Hospitalization: Percent of all wage and salary workers; Retirement and Unemployment: Percent of wage and salary workers in private industry.
Source: Skolnik 1976: 7.

Supplemental Unemployment Benefit (SUB) plans, occupational programs that provided workers with payments in addition to UI, were largely limited to the automobile, rubber, and steel industries. By the late 1960s, the automobile industry had the most generous SUB payments which, in conjunction with UI, replaced a worker's previous weekly earnings as much as 95 percent for 52 weeks (Skolnik 1976: 20).

Although occupational welfare provision became a "social obligation" for many employers during the era of industrial welfare capitalism (Allen 1969), a declining but significant proportion of the American workforce continued to lack social protection at a level providing the achieved living standard. Only America's core labor market insiders had access to social protection at comparable levels to their counterparts in Continental European countries.

Between Universalism and Dualism: The UK Case

The UK welfare system has been composed by an amalgamation of universal, social insurance, means-tested, and occupational social policies. Since the National Health Service (NHS) has provided universal access to health care, the two main pillars of the postwar social insurance system have been pensions and unemployment compensation. While a distinction was made between contributory-based social insurance and means-tested social assistance, pension and unemployment benefits were provided on a flat-rate basis for a significant proportion of the postwar period. The absence of an earnings-related link meant that the United Kingdom differed considerably from France, Germany, and the United States. During the postwar period, this void was increasingly supplemented by occupational schemes (Cutler et al. 1986: 44; Russell 1991: 128).

As growing numbers of contributory-based pension recipients without occupational benefits required means-tested supplements, the inadequacy of flat-rated provision and occupational voluntarism became apparent (Williamson and Pampel 1993: 52). The impoverishment of pensioners was addressed by the establishment of a two-tiered pension system in 1959. A universal Basic State Pension (BSP) was now supplemented by the earnings-related State Graduated Retirement Pension Scheme (SGRPS) for those with higher incomes (Williamson and Pampel 1993: 54; Blake 2003: 13). The reform also enabled members of occupational pension schemes to contract out of SGRPS (Hannah 1986: 57). In 1975, the earnings-related element was bolstered by the creation of the State Earnings-Related Pension Scheme (SERPS), providing a maximum supplementary benefit of 25 percent based on one's highest earnings during the final 20 years of employment (Blake 2003: 15).

Nevertheless, it was the receipt of occupational benefits that increased the probability of income protection at a level that maintained the achieved living standard. By 1967, 53 percent of the national workforce was entitled to occupational pension benefits, which were typically final salary schemes (GAD

1994: Table 2.1) and provided a gross replacement rate of 70 percent for the standard wage earner with 40 years of employment (Blake 2003: 170). Notable differences existed by gender and industry. While 93 percent of men employed in the mining industry were enrolled in occupational pension plans, only 13 percent of women employed in the wholesale and retail sector were covered in 1970 (Russell 1991: 211).

Like state pensions, postwar Unemployment Benefit (UB) was underpinned by a similar tension between being a contributory social insurance program yet one that provided flat-rate benefits. In 1965, the government introduced statutory redundancy payments that provided the involuntarily unemployed with additional compensation beyond their National Insurance entitlement. This was followed in 1966 by the creation of an Earnings-Related Supplement (ERS) to contributory-based UB, designed to support the incomes of higher earners (Clasen 1994; Saunders 2009). This legislation also prompted an expansion of extra-statutory redundancy pay schemes in private sector firms during the 1960s and 1970s (Root 1987). The most generous of such provisions predominated in the steel and coal mining industries (Fevre 1987: 66–69; Root 1987: 21). Redundancy pay became a key factor of institutional welfare dualism for the unemployed.

Britons employed in production industries and high value-added services notably had access to *both* earnings-related social insurance and occupational benefits. Consequently, many UK insiders had access to a comprehensive set of welfare entitlements during this period. Due to the significant expansion of both public and private social protection measures, the degree of social protection outsiderness declined significantly during the era of industrial welfare capitalism.

DUALIZATION IN AN AGE OF POST-INDUSTRIAL WELFARE CAPITALISM

Since the mid-1970s, all four welfare systems have undergone significant transformations. Institutional welfare dualism has widened and deepened in Germany, especially in relation to France, where social protection has remained *comparatively* less bifurcated. In the United Kingdom and the United States, we witness once again an increase of social protection outsiders in pensions largely as a result of declining occupational coverage. In the realm of unemployment protection dualism has widened and deepened in the United Kingdom, France, and Germany, whereas in the United States the extent and depth of dualism has remained relatively constant. With regard to health care, the large role played by private insurance in the United States and France has continued to entrench welfare dualism in these countries, although some efforts have been made to reduce it.

The Shifting Public-Private Balance in Pensions

Germany

Future pension entitlements in Germany will increasingly resemble those in the United Kingdom and the United States, especially due to the Pension Reform of 2001, which introduced a partial privatization of the statutory earnings-related pension system. Important elements of this reform were a significant reduction in future replacement rates and the introduction of public subsidies for certified private and occupational pension schemes. The net replacement ratio for a standard pensioner will decline from about 70 percent to 52 percent by 2030, forcing once again an increasing reliance on means-tested old-age benefits for those with insufficient occupational or individual private coverage. Workers contributing the maximum amount for which they can receive tax relief to private individual or occupational plans are "promised" a retirement income of 70 percent of their previous wage (Schmähl 2007). This change in policy has triggered an increase in occupational pension coverage, predominantly based on the principle of defined contributions (DC). As shown in Table 7-1, the coverage of occupational pensions in the private sector has risen from 38 percent (2001) to 52 percent (2007). However, stark differences in coverage rates can be seen, for instance, between individuals employed in financial intermediation with especially high levels of participation, manufacturing with medium to high levels, and hospitality and food services with relatively low levels of coverage.

Table 7-1: Percentage of employees in the German private sector covered by occupational pension plans by industry (2001–2007)

Industry	2001	2003	2005	2007
Manufacturing				
Production/Intermediate goods	43%	55%	73%	74%
Consumer durables	58%	59%	62%	62%
Food, alcohol & tobacco goods	30%	57%	62%	61%
Consumer goods	24%	39%	53%	53%
Mining, quarrying & energy	63%	72%	71%	73%
Construction	22%	30%	37%	42%
Services				
Financial intermediation	76%	83%	89%	90%
Wholesale/Retail & repair	27%	39%	47%	46%
Real estate & business services	16%	25%	28%	29%
Hospitality and food services	10%	25%	26%	28%
Total private sector coverage	38%	45%	52%	52%

Source: TNS Infratest Sozialforschung, *Situation und Entwicklung der betrieblichen Altersversorgung in Privatwirtschaft und öffentlichem Dienst 2001–2007.* [The Situation and Development of Occupational Pensions in the Private Sector and Public Service, 2001–2007], Untersuchung im Auftrag des Bundesministeriums für Arbeit und Soziales, Endbericht, München: 30. Oktober 2008: 42.

France

Although the French public pension system was retrenched, it has remained relatively more resilient to private encroachment. In the private-sector employees' statutory pension scheme (*régime général*), reforms legislated in 1993, in 2003, and in 2010 have shifted the indexation of benefits from wage inflation to price inflation, and have also extended the reference wage used to calculate benefits and the contributory period needed for a full pension from 37.5 years in 1993 to 41.5 years by 2020 (Mandin and Palier 2005; Bonoli and Palier 2007). Since the mid-1990s, current and future pensioners have also been affected by changes in the indexation of the AGIRC/ARRCO schemes, which have led to reductions in the purchasing power of benefits (Naczyk and Palier 2010). According to projections (COR 2007: 64) and depending on indexation assumptions in AGIRC and ARRCO, the net replacement ratio will decline from about 83.6 percent for a standard worker retiring in 2003 to about 76.8 percent in 2020 and 73.5 percent (based on optimistic assumptions) or 64.4 percent (based on pessimistic assumptions) in 2050.

To date, funded occupational pensions have played a minor role in France. Only a limited number of funded pension schemes exist at the firm level. Their distribution is very unequal and mostly advantages high-earners. Funded DB plans have been offered mainly to top executives in large companies, while DC plans, which are more encompassing in terms of coverage, have been mainly limited to large companies (Naczyk and Palier 2010). Firm-level DC schemes (called Art. 83) have been expanding in recent years. Approximately 12.3 percent of workers were covered by such plans in 2006 (DREES 2010), compared to 8 percent in 2004 (DREES 2006).

The United States

In parallel to the reduction of benefit generosity under the Social Security Act of 1983 (Munnell 2009: 18), occupational pension plans came under growing strain. Overall coverage declined significantly, especially for workers employed in low value-added industries. While in 1979, 50.6 percent of workers[2] were covered, the coverage rate declined to 43.7 percent in 1989. In 2006, only 42 percent of workers were enrolled in occupational pension plans (Mishel et al. 2009). Coverage differs significantly by sector. Workers employed in manufacturing and financial services are much more likely to be covered, compared to workers in low value-added sectors, such as hospitality and food services (Bureau of Labor Statistics 2008: Table 2.5). Second, the majority of employer-provided pensions have shifted from DB to DC plans (Mishel et al. 2009).

However, reductions in generosity were countered, if only temporarily, by rising pension fund assets during the stock market booms of the 1990s and the 2000s. Congress committed itself to supporting the public pension system during the credit crisis and recession of 2008–2009 as losses in pension savings mounted. In February 2009, the American Recovery and Reinvestment Act introduced a supplement to Social Security recipients to partially compensate for shortfalls in personal retirement income (CongressNow 2009). To some extent, the recent policy changes demonstrate the limits of a liberalization strategy and emphasize that the state has the ultimate responsibility for pensions.

The United Kingdom

Since the 1980s, reform of the UK public pension system has led to a significant decline in state benefits. The 1986 Social Security Act reduced the real value of SERPS to 20 percent of "pensionable earnings" and created incentives for individuals to opt out of the state scheme in order to enroll in personal or occupational alternatives (Creedy and Disney 1988: 61). By 2002, SERPS were replaced by the State Second Pension and became a fully flat-rate benefit by 2007. However, more importantly, overall occupational pension coverage has significantly declined over the past decade, with only 37 percent of the workforce in the private sector covered in 2008. As in Germany and the United States, coverage differs widely by industrial sector, with rates of high coverage in financial intermediation, medium coverage in manufacturing, and a low level of coverage in the hospitality sector (see Table 7-2). As in the United States, the United Kingdom has witnessed a shift from DB to DC plans.

As the percentage of insiders with occupational scheme coverage has declined, the United Kingdom has embarked on significant pension reform. In general, these changes will improve the access to and benefit levels of the private as well as public schemes and thereby will contribute to an increased overall adequacy of replacement rates. Based on the Pensions Act of 2007, the necessary contributory periods for a full Basic State Pension will be reduced from 44 years for men and 39 years for women to 30 years for everyone retiring on or after April 2010. In the medium term, the government will reintroduce earnings up-rating. A second

Table 7-2: **Percentage of employees in the UK private sector covered by occupational pension plans by major industry group: 1998–2008**

Industry	1998	2000	2002	2004	2006	2008
Manufacturing	57%	57%	61%	58%	57%	53%
Mining, quarrying & energy	85%	83%	82%	78%	83%	79%
Construction	37%	31%	42%	39%	36%	34%
Services						
Financial intermediation	77%	82%	80%	80%	81%	77%
Wholesale/Retail trade & repair	40%	42%	41%	34%	32%	29%
Real estate, renting & business services	39%	38%	45%	40%	38%	36%
Hospitality & food services	16%	13%	12%	13%	9%	8%
Total private sector coverage	45%	45%	47%	43%	41%	37%

Source: Authors' calculations derived from the Annual Survey of Hours and Earnings (ASHE) Pensions Analysis Tables (1997–2008), Office for National Statistics.

reform, to be implemented from 2012, is aimed at reversing the process of dualization in occupational pension coverage, as all workers with an income above a minimum threshold will be automatically enrolled into a qualifying workplace pension with an option to opt out. These two pension reforms to some extent reverse the previous strategy based on liberalization and voluntarism.

Comparing Pension Dualism

In Germany, the United Kingdom, and the United States, pension dualism has significantly widened over the last decades, whereas in France the process has been so far more limited. It is very likely that the proportion of poor pensioners (social protection outsiders) in Germany will increase significantly as the result of the significant reductions in the replacement rate and the low occupational coverage of workers employed in low value-added sectors. Both in the United Kingdom and the United States, the percentage of old-age social protection outsiders will increase, due to the significant decline in occupational coverage. The depth of welfare dualism becomes apparent when prospective replacement rates derived from public and occupational pension systems are examined for current workers. Based on OECD simulations, the average American worker enrolled in an occupational pension plan will have the highest replacement rate among the four countries. The average worker reliant solely on the public pension system will have the lowest replacement rate in the United Kingdom and the highest in France, while a pensioner dependent upon a means-tested minimum income will be the worst off in Germany. Comparing the gross replacement rate of the public systems with the combined gross replacement rate of public and voluntary occupational pensions, the depth of welfare dualism is highest in the United States (see Table 7-3).

Table 7-3: Prospective pension minima and replacement rates for current workers (2004 baseline)

Country	Minimum Income for Pensioners as % of Average Earnings	Gross Replacement Rate of Public System (AW)	Net Replacement Rate of Public System (AW)	Gross Replacement Rate of Public and Voluntary Occupational Pensions (AW)
France	24.0	64.7	78.1	N/A
Germany	19.3	39.9	58.0	56.0
United Kingdom	20.0	30.8	41.1	67.0
United States	22.0	41.2	52.4	81.2

Note: Minimum income provisions are based on means-tested programs available to pensioners. All replacement rates are based on the assumption of a full career. Gross replacement rates of public and voluntary occupational/private pensions are based on assumed contribution rates of 9 percent (currently the mean) in the United Kingdom and the United States. For Germany the assumed contribution rate is 4 percent, currently the maximum contribution to receive the full tax incentive.
Source: OECD (2007) *Pensions at a Glance*. Paris: OECD.

Dualizing the Unemployed

Germany

Since the late 1970s, the German UI system has seen incremental changes that have limited the access to unemployment insurance benefits for prime-aged workers. However, the de-commodification of older workers was significantly increased through the extension of benefit duration for older workers from 12 to 32 months in the mid-1980s. Among prime-age workers, the objective of status preservation was in effect increasingly restricted to the short-term unemployed, while a process of recommodification and workfare came to dominate the unemployment and social assistance schemes (Neyer and Seeleib-Kaiser 1995). For these social protection outsiders, ALMP was increasingly used to test the willingness to work and to provide temporary and "substandard" work instead of promoting reintegration into standard employment relationships. The Labor Promotion Reform Law of 1997–1998 vastly curtailed the ability of those receiving UI benefits to be selective in their choice of prospective employment opportunities, as the duration of unemployment progresses (Bieback 1997).

In late 2003, the federal government enacted a comprehensive reform of unemployment compensation payments. According to the new rules, the regular "Unemployment Compensation Payment I," that is, the earnings-related UI benefit, was limited to a maximum of 12 months.[3] Individuals who have either exhausted their UI benefit and are needy or are needy unemployed workers who do not qualify for the Unemployment Compensation Payment I are entitled to the "Unemployment Compensation Payment II." Unlike the "old" unemployment assistance benefit, this new payment constitutes a flat means-tested benefit. Consequently, this reform resulted in substantial benefit reductions for those long-term unemployed workers who had previously commanded a comparatively "high" income. Furthermore, the suitability requirements have been considerably tightened for those receiving the Unemployment Compensation II benefit, in effect defining any legal job offer as suitable (cf. Seeleib-Kaiser and Fleckenstein 2007). While the changes for the majority of short-term unemployed were rather minimal, the significant cutbacks for the long-term unemployed have deepened institutional welfare dualism. As the percentage of the long-term unemployed and those with insufficient contributory periods due to atypical employment have increased over time, we also witness a stark widening of institutional welfare dualism among the unemployed.

France

Since the 1980s, reforms in unemployment compensation have resulted in an increasingly dualized pattern of social protection (Daniel and Tuchszirer 1999; Clegg 2007; Palier 2010). While core workers with longer contribution records have continued to be relatively well protected, workers with shorter contribution records have been forced to rely on social assistance. They have also been most targeted by activation measures that, like those in Germany, have mostly provided temporary and "substandard" work (Clegg 2007). From 1979, the level of an individual's UI benefits was gradually decreased with time spent in unemployment. In 1982, benefit levels were tied to the duration of prior contributions, while in the past they had depended mainly on age. Dualism was institutionalized when, in 1984, unemployment insurance and unemployment assistance were separated, and the possibility to accumulate both was eliminated. Retrenchment has also occurred in unemployment assistance, since young workers and single mothers were no longer eligible for the *allocation d'insertion* from 1992. Indexation in the main unemployment assistance benefit—ASS (*allocation de solidarité spécifique*)—was suppressed beginning in 1994, but was later partially compensated. These developments and mass unemployment led to a heavy reliance of the unemployed on the national social assistance scheme (RMI) created in 1988 and replaced in 2009 by the *revenu de solidarité active* (RSA), which introduced a negative income tax for newly employed recipients of social assistance. However, reforms agreed to by the social partners between 1996 and 2002 led to small improvements in access to UI benefits. In particular, the link between prior contributions and the generosity of benefits was loosened, and the eligibility criteria for workers with incomplete contributory records were made more inclusive. A reform negotiated in 2009 led to an extension of benefit duration.

The United States

Historically, the American UI system has made a fundamental distinction between those unemployed individuals whose labor market participation has entitled them to benefits and those whose lack of it has made them altogether "undeserving," which is reflected in the continuously low UI beneficiary rate among the unemployed. Compared to the UK, France, and Germany, the U.S. UI system has experienced comparatively fewer changes since the demise of industrial welfare capitalism during the 1970s and 1980s. The most notable feature of the American system has been extensions to benefit duration during periods of high unemployment, providing extended and supplemental benefits for up to 65 weeks during the mid-1970s and 99 weeks during the 2008–2010 recession (Vroman 1990: 19; Luo 2010; cf. Figure 7-2). Although such provisions declined during the 1980s, Extended Benefits have continued to play an important role for insiders who have exhausted their regular benefit entitlements during economic downturns. The government's role in providing extended insurance to the unemployed has become more important as occupational provisions such as supplemental unemployment compensation plans have become even more peripheral.

The United Kingdom

One of the first successful retrenchment policies of the Thatcher government was the discontinuation of the Earnings-Related Supplement (ERS) to unemployment insurance. Restrictions over benefit receipt tightened during the 1980s and 1990s as successive Conservative governments made a concerted effort to link benefit payments to retraining and the active search for work for all claimants (King 1995: 170). In 1996, UB was transformed into a Job Seeker's Allowance (JSA). JSA created a flat-rate contribution-based benefit and a means-tested benefit. Whereas the benefit duration of the contributory benefit was reduced from 52 weeks to 26 weeks, the duration of the means-tested benefit continues to be in principle indefinite (Clasen 2010). Since the mid-1990s, a significant decline in the percentage of the unemployed receiving contributory benefits can be observed (Figure 7-2). Despite these liberalizing policies, which ended the previous duality in benefit provision generated by graduated and earnings-related schemes, welfare dualism for the unemployed has persisted, as many insiders have been able to supplement paltry JSA benefits with both public and private redundancy pay provisions.

Although statutory redundancy pay had been aimed at lower earners when it was originally introduced in 1965 (Clasen 1994: 76), eligibility criteria based on job tenure have prevented many unemployed from benefit entitlements. While a mere 24 percent of the UK's unemployed received redundancy pay in 1973, this figure would rise only to 36 percent in 1981, a year with exceptionally high unemployment.[4] Since the mid-1990s, the rate has fluctuated between 23 and 35 percent.[5] Core labor market insiders continue to be entitled to extra-statutory redundancy payments based on collective bargaining agreements or unilaterally determined by management, as the overwhelming majority of large employers continue to offer these benefits (Booth 1987; Clasen 2010). However, sectors that traditionally offered very generous extra-statutory redundancy payments, such as mining and quarrying, have seen a significant decline of employment over the past three decades, which suggests that the overall coverage of unemployed workers receiving this benefit has also declined.

Comparing Social Protection Dualization for the Unemployed

The dualization of unemployment protection has taken different paths in each country. Although the percentage of contributory benefit claimants as a percentage of total unemployed in the United Kingdom has historically been similar to the low levels in the United States, we have witnessed a significant decline since the 1980s. However, unemployment protection dualism in the United Kingdom since the mid-1990s is largely a function of those receiving statutory or extra-statutory redundancy benefits and those that have to rely on low flat-rate state benefits, as the ERS was abolished. In the United States, policies have historically differentiated between those short-term unemployed entitled to earnings-related benefits and the long-term unemployed with very

Figure 7-2: Unemployment insurance claimants as a percentage of total unemployed, 1971–2009

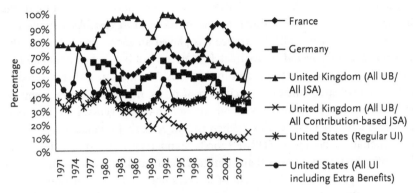

Note: The average annual number of unemployed is based on comparable labor force surveys as reported by the OECD and hence might differ from national definitions of unemployment; the average annual number of claimants is derived from national administrative statistics. There is a break in the German data because of unification.

Sources: Authors' calculations of OECD Labour Force Statistics for "Harmonized Total Unemployment"; BMAS (2010) Statistisches Taschenbuch 2010, Arbeits-und Sozialstatistik, Berlin: BMAS; Assedic "Bénéficiaires en fin de mois"; "Claimant Count—Seasonally Adjusted," Nomis, UK Office for National Statistics; Archived data, Department for Work and Pensions (DWP); Work and Pensions Longitudinal Study, DWP; UI Weekly Claims Reports, U.S. Department of Labor (DOL), Current Population Survey, U.S. Bureau of Labor Statistics, DOL.

residual or no support, demonstrating a clear institutional welfare dualism (see Figure 7-2).

Germany has witnessed a widening of dualism, as the percentage of UI claimants among the unemployed has been in steep decline since unification, dropping below U.S. levels since 2006. Furthermore, as benefit levels for the long-term unemployed have been significantly reduced, we have witnessed a deepening of dualism. Dualization in Germany is especially striking when compared to developments in France where, following a process of dualization during the mid-1980s and the early 1990s, the percentage of UI recipients has once again increased markedly in the late 1990s and early 2000s, before once again declining.

Inequalities in Health Care

Germany and the United Kingdom

In both Germany and the United Kingdom, health care coverage has continued to be universal. As a consequence, the role of private health insurance has remained relatively negligible. According to the OECD (2004: 50, 52), in 2000 only 9 percent of the German population and 10 percent of the UK population were covered by private health insurance schemes. Such arrangements are typically preferred by high-income individuals and not by a majority of insiders in the two countries.

France

Since the end of the 1970s, co-payments have been gradually increased, reaching 30 percent for medical consultations and 35 percent or 65 percent for drugs in 1993, while a flat-rate hospital fee was introduced in 1982. As a result, private supplementary health insurance has played an increasing role in health expenditure and covered approximately 85 percent of the French population in the 2000s, compared to 50 percent in the 1970s. Workers are either covered by individual private plans or by occupational plans, negotiated at the company level, which can be mandatory or remain voluntary. In general, occupational plans, which pool risk, are more generous, particularly for dental care and eye care, than individual plans (DREES 2008). Mandatory occupational plans similarly offer better guarantees than voluntary occupational plans (IRDES 2006). In 2006, approximately 61 percent of workers obtained supplementary health insurance through a firm-level plan. Coverage varies with skills and industry; while 77 percent of management and technical staff (*cadres*) were covered by compulsory occupational plans, this was the case for only 44 percent of employees in the retail industry (IRDES 2008).

The introduction of a specific health insurance scheme for the poor aimed at universalizing health care coverage in France (*CMU*, see Palier 2005a; 2005b), which offers free statutory health insurance for recipients of social assistance and free supplementary health insurance for individuals falling below a certain income threshold (634 Euros in 2010), has not solved inequalities in access. This free supplementary health insurance does not cover all fees, and individuals who are not claimants of social assistance benefits and whose income is higher than the CMU threshold continue to be excluded from such schemes (IRDES 2008). Moreover, beneficiaries of the CMU are significantly more likely to be refused treatment when they present themselves as CMU recipients, thereby potentially deepening social divides (Chadelat 2006; IRDES 2009).

The United States

One of the major developments in U.S. health care coverage has been the decline in employer-provided plans. While 69 percent of all workers were enrolled in employer-provided health care plans in 1979, the percentage declined to 55 percent in 2006 (Mishel et al. 2009). As might be expected, coverage among the various sectors of the economy is very unequal, with high coverage in the utilities, manufacturing, and finance, and low coverage in retail and the hospitality sectors (see Table 7-4). The percentage of those not covered has subsequently risen to almost 16 percent of the population in 2006 (DeNavas-Walt et al. 2007: 58).

As occupational health care coverage has declined over the past three decades, the government has expanded *public* health care coverage, especially through the expansion of Medicaid and the introduction of the State Children's Health Insurance Program (S-CHIP). The federal government has also strengthened

Table 7-4: Percentage of U.S. employees in the private sector covered by health insurance by industry group, 2008

	Health Insurance Coverage
Industry	
Manufacturing	75%
Utilities	84%
Construction	56%
Services	
Finance & insurance	70%
Wholesale trade	71%
Retail trade	41%
Real estate & rental & leasing	52%
Hospitality & food services	24%

Source: "National Compensation Survey," Bureau of Labor Statistics, Department of Labor, March 2008: Tables 2, 5.

the regulatory framework for unemployed workers previously covered by occupational health care plans. In 1985, Congress introduced legislation, known as COBRA, which continued occupational health insurance for unemployed workers followed by an additional provision in 1996 that enabled workers to maintain their health care coverage when changing employers (Seeleib-Kaiser 2001: 329; Hacker 2002: 258). The 2009 Recovery Act provided further COBRA funding, subsidizing nine months of health insurance to UI recipients (Solis 2009). Health care reform became a focus of the Obama administration and resulted in the 2010 health care act (the Healthcare and Education Reconciliation Act of 2010), which should eventually extend health care coverage to some 30 million uninsured Americans. In doing so, it will cover an additional 16 million individuals through the nation's means-tested Medicaid program and financially support the participation of millions of low and middle earners in private health insurance plans (Stolberg and Pear 2010).

It is important to highlight the limitations of the U.S. liberal approach to health care, which has eventually triggered greater government intervention, providing better access to health care for the previously uninsured. In France, government intervention has been limited to protect the poor and working poor, thus not making access to health care fully equitable. Whether the 2010 health care reform in the United States will *fully* eliminate the dualism in access to health care can only be assessed in the future.

CONCLUSION

Analyzing institutional welfare dualism in all four countries during the periods of industrial and post-industrial welfare capitalism has highlighted the importance of taking into account *private* and *public* social policy. Private social protection can under specific conditions constitute a functional equivalent of public social protection for certain workers and can result in a profound bifurcation of welfare. It should be emphasized that institutional welfare dualism is not new and has been a constituent part of Liberal *and* Conservative welfare systems. All four countries have witnessed processes of dualization, although different in their breadth and depth in the various social protection domains, during the era of post-industrial welfare capitalism.

In both Liberal countries occupational pension coverage (and in the United States healthcare coverage) increased during the era of industrial welfare capitalism. At the height of this period, private social protection in the United Kingdom and the United States significantly supplemented minimal to moderate public social protection during old age, covering more than 50 percent of the workforce. Occupational health care coverage reached almost 70 percent of the American workforce during the late 1970s. Although supplemental occupational unemployment protection was also available for workers in core manufacturing industries, the overall coverage of the workforce was rather minimal. For those covered, however, the provision was roughly similar to public provision in France and Germany, especially for those U.S. and UK workers employed in standard employment relationships, which applied to most of the industrial workforce. The key difference between the two Liberal and two Conservative welfare systems was that a substantial percentage of the workforce in the Liberal economies did not have sufficient coverage for certain social risks, even at the height of industrial welfare capitalism, and institutional welfare dualism was quite deep. In contrast, in France and Germany, the percentage of those excluded from social insurance protection was rather small, and public policy was geared toward including all employees into the social insurance systems, thereby reducing institutional welfare dualism.

Since the mid-1970s and with accelerating speed since the mid-1990s, the inclusionary process in France and Germany was reversed and subsequently has led to a widening and deepening of institutional welfare dualism, especially in Germany. For significant proportions of workers in financial and manufacturing industries, the reduction in public old-age social protection coverage has been mitigated by an expansion of occupational coverage in Germany. Conversely, a very large proportion of workers employed in the hospitality sector will have to rely solely on the public system, which for many future retirees will no longer provide a pension sufficient to secure the achieved standard of living. In the United Kingdom and the United States, the most important changes have occurred in the coverage of occupational pension programs. This has led to a widening of dualism and an increase of outsiders, as fewer pensioners will be able to rely on employer-provided benefits to maintain the achieved living standard. Although affecting most workers, the decline in coverage has been most dramatic for workers employed in low-value added sectors. Recent legislation in both countries was designed to counteract the declining occupational coverage, demonstrating the limits of Liberal approaches to welfare based on voluntarism.

With regard to the risk of unemployment, processes of dualization have been most pronounced in the United Kingdom and Germany. Whereas in the United Kingdom unemployed workers in high-value added sectors can rely on extra-statutory redundancy payments sufficient to maintain their standard of living during short spells of unemployment, most workers can no longer rely on earnings-related benefits, but have to cope with benefits at the social assistance level. In Germany unemployment insurance benefits for the short-term unemployed still secure the achieved standard of living; however, the majority of the unemployed, that is, those with insufficient work histories to qualify and the long-term unemployed, have become reliant on benefits at the social assistance level. In the United States, welfare dualism in the domain of unemployment has historically been very prevalent and has not substantially changed over time, as even during industrial welfare capitalism, only a very limited number of workers were entitled to SUB provided by employers.

Within the domain of health care coverage, institutional welfare dualism has been limited largely to the United States, although there has been some prevalence of welfare dualism in France, with relatively high co-payments for those workers not covered by supplementary plans. The United States has witnessed a significant decline in occupational health care coverage. Again welfare dualism primarily seems to occur along sectoral lines, with workers in the retail sector having the lowest level of coverage. In the United States, the Obama administration has introduced policies to limit institutional dualism. In France, the introduction of a universal health insurance for the poor entrenches dualism. In the United Kingdom and Germany, access to health care coverage has continued to be more or less universal.

To conclude, welfare dualism is not new and has been especially prevalent in Liberal welfare systems, primarily due to the importance of supplemental and complementary occupational social protection. Although social protection outsiderness has increased in all four countries during the era of post-industrial welfare capitalism, the breadth and depth of the dualization processes differ between countries and along social policy domains within countries.

NOTES

1 The authors gratefully acknowledge the generous support provided by the John Fell OUP Research Fund.
2 Private sector, wage and salary workers aged 18–64, who worked at least 20 hours per week and 26 weeks per year.
3 Workers above the age of 58 are currently entitled to a maximum benefit duration of 24 months instead of the previous 32 months.

4 Authors' calculations of figures provided by Booth (1987: 403) and OECD Stat harmonized unemployment data.
5 Authors' calculations of UK Labour Force Survey data.

REFERENCES

Allen, Donna (1969). *Fringe Benefits: Wages or Social Obligation?* Ithaca, NY: Cornell University Press.

Bieback, Karl-Jürgen (1997). "Der Umbau der Arbeitsförderung," *Kritische Justiz*, 30(1): 15–29.

Blake, David (2003). *Pension Schemes and Pension Funds in the United Kingdom*, Oxford: Oxford University Press.

Bleses, Peter and Seeleib-Kaiser, Martin (2004). *The Dual Transformation of the German Welfare State*, Basingstoke, UK: Palgrave.

Bonoli, Giuliano, and Palier, Bruno (2007). "When Past Reforms Open New Opportunities," *Social Policy and Administration*, 41(6): 555–573.

Booth, Alison L. (1987). "Extra-statutory Redundancy Payments in Britain," *British Journal of Industrial Relations*, 25(3): 401–418.

Brown, Michael K. (1999). *Race, Money, and the American Welfare State*, Ithaca, NY: Cornell University Press.

Bureau of Labor Statistics (2008). "National Compensation Survey," March 2008, Washington, DC: Bureau of Labor Statistics, Department of Labor.

Chadelat, Jean-François (2006). *Les Refus de soins aux bénéficiaires de la CMU. Rapport pour le Ministre de la Santé et des Solidarités*, Paris: Ministère de la Santé et des Solidarités.

Clasen, Jochen (1994). *Paying the Jobless*, Aldershot, UK: Avebury.

Clasen, Jochen (2010). "The United Kingdom," in de Beer, Paul, and Schils, Trudie (eds.), *The Labour Market Triangle*, Cheltenham, UK: Edward Elgar, pp. 70–95.

Clegg, Daniel (2007). "Continental Drift," *Social Policy and Administration*, 41(6): 597–617.

COR—Conseil d'Orientation des Retraites (2007). *Retraites: Vingt Fiches d'Actualisation pour le rendez-vous de 2008. Cinquième Rapport.* November 2007.

CongressNow (2009). "Preliminary Overview of Stimulus Conference Report," *CongressNow*, February 12, 2009.

Creedy, John, and Disney, Richard (1988). "The New Pension Scheme in Britain," *Fiscal Studies*, 9(2): 57–71.

Cutler, Tony, Williams, Karel, and Williams, John (1986). *Keynes, Beveridge and Beyond*, London, UK: Routledge & Kegan Paul.

Daniel, Christine, and Tuchszirer, Carole (1999). *L'Etat face aux chômeurs*, Paris: Flammarion.

DeNavas-Walt, Carmen, Proctor, Bernadette D., and Smith, Jessica C. (2007). *Income, Poverty, and Health Insurance Coverage in the United States: 2006*, US Census Bureau, Current Population Reports, P60–233, Washington, DC: GPO.

DREES (2004). "Le taux de remplacement du salaire par la retraite pour les salariés de la génération 1934 ayant effectué une carrière complète," *Etudes et résultats*, 312, June 2004.

DREES (2006). "L'épargne retraite en 2004," *Etudes et résultats*, 518, September 2006.

DREES (2008). "Typologie des contrats les plus souscrits auprès des complémentaires santé en 2006," *Etudes et résultats*, 663, October 2008.

DREES (2010). "Les retraités et les retraites en 2008," *Etudes et Résultats*, 722, April 2010.

EBRI—Employee Benefit Research Institute (2010). *EBRI Notes*. 31(1), January 2010, Washington, DC: EBRI.

Esping-Andersen, Gøsta (1990). *The Three Worlds of Welfare Capitalism*, Princeton, NJ: Princeton University Press.

Esping-Andersen, Gøsta (1999). *Social Foundations of Postindustrial Economies*, Oxford: Oxford University Press.

Estévez-Abe, Margarita, Iversen, Torben, and Soskice, David (2001). "Social Protection and the Formation of Skills," in Hall, Peter A., and Soskice, David (eds.), *Varieties of Capitalism*, Oxford: Oxford University Press, pp. 145–183.

Fevre, Ralph (1987). "Redundancy and the Labour Market," in Lee, Raymond M. (ed.), *Redundancy, Layoffs and Plant Closures*, Beckenham, UK: Croom Helm, pp. 62–83.

Friot, Bernard (1998). *Puissances du salariat*, Paris: La Dispute.

GAD (1994). *Occupational Pension Schemes 1991: Ninth Survey by the Government Actuary*, London, UK: GAD.

Hacker, Jacob S. (2002). *The Divided Welfare State*, Cambridge, UK: Cambridge University Press.

Hannah, Leslie (1986). *Inventing Retirement*, Cambridge, UK: Cambridge University Press.

IRDES (2006). "Complémentaire maladie d'entreprise," *Questions d'économie de la santé*, 115, November 2006.

IRDES (2008). "La complémentaire santé en France en 2006," *Questions d'économie de la santé*, 132, May 2008.

IRDES (2009). "Le refus de soins à l'égard des bénéficiaires de la Couverture maladie universelle complémentaire à Paris," *Etude commandée et financée par le Fonds CMU*, 2009/07.

Iversen, Torben (2005). *Capitalism, Democracy, and Welfare*, Cambridge, UK: Cambridge University Press.

King, Desmond (1995). *Actively Seeking Work?* Chicago: University of Chicago Press.

Kotlikoff, Laurence J., and Smith, Daniel E. (1983). *Pensions in the American Economy*, Chicago: University of Chicago Press.

Leibfried, Stephan, and Tennstedt, Florian (1985). "Armenpolitik und Arbeiterpolitik," in Leibfried, Stephan, and Tennstedt, Florian (eds.), *Politik der Armut und die Spaltung des Sozialstaats*, Frankfurt/M.: Suhrkamp, pp. 64–93.

Leisering, Lutz (2009). "Germany: A Centrist Welfare State at the Crossroads," in Alcock, Peter, and Craig, Gary (eds.), *International Social Policy*, 2nd ed., Basingstoke, UK: Palgrave, pp. 148–170.

Leisering, Lutz, and Leibfried, Stephan (1999). *Time and Poverty in Western Welfare States*, Cambridge, UK: Cambridge University Press, 1999.

Luo, Michael (2010). "99 Weeks Later, Jobless Have Only Desperation," *New York Times*, August 2, 2010.

Main, Brian G. M. (1982). "The Length of a Job in Great Britain," *Economica*, 49, 195: 325–333.

Mandin, Christine, and Palier, Bruno (2005). "The Politics of Pension Reform in France," in Bonoli, Giuliano, and Shinkawa, Toshimitsu (eds.), *Ageing and Pension Reform Around the World*, Cheltenham, UK: Edward Elgar, pp. 74–93.

Marshall, T. H. (1950). *Citizenship and Social Class and Other Essays*, Cambridge, UK: Cambridge University Press.

Mishel, Lawrence, Bernstein, Jared, and Shierholz, Heidi (2009). *The State of Working America 2008/2009*, Ithaca, NY: ILR Press.

Mitchell, Daniel J. B., and Rojot, Jacques (1992). "Employee Benefits in the Single Market," in Ulman, Lloyd, Eichengreen, Barry, and Dickens, William T. (eds.), *Labor and an Integrated Europe*, Washington, DC: Brookings, pp. 128–166.

Mückenberger, Ulrich (1985). "Die Krise des Normalarbeitsverhältnisses," *Zeitschrift für Sozialreform*, 31: 415 ff. and 457 ff.

Munnell, Alicia H. (2009). "Retirements at Risk." in Orenstein, Mitchell (ed.), *Pensions, Social Security, and the Privatization of Risk*, New York: Columbia University Press, pp. 10–39.

Naczyk, Marek, and Palier, Bruno (2010). "Complementing or Replacing Old Age Insurance?," *RECWOWE Working Paper*, 08/2010.

Neyer, Jürgen, and Seeleib-Kaiser, Martin (1995). "Bringing the Economy Back In," *ZeS-Arbeitspapier*, No. 16/95, Bremen: Zentrum fuer Sozialpolitik.

OECD (2004). *Private Health Insurance in OECD Countries*, Paris: OECD.

Palier, Bruno (2005a). *Gouverner la sécurité sociale*, 2nd ed., Paris: Presses Universitaires de France.

Palier, Bruno (2005b). "Ambiguous agreement, Cumulative Change," in Streeck, Wolfgang, and Thelen, Kathleen A. (eds.), *Beyond Continuity*, Oxford: Oxford University Press, pp. 127–145.

Palier, Bruno (2010). "The Dualizations of the French Welfare System," in Palier, Bruno (ed.), *A Long Goodbye to Bismarck?* Amsterdam: Amsterdam University Press, pp. 73–99.

Pontusson, Jonas (2005). *Inequality and Prosperity*, Ithaca, NY: Cornell University Press.

Reynaud, E. (1997). "France: A National and Contractual Second Tier," in Rein, Martin, and Wadensjö, Eskil (eds.), *Enterprise and the Welfare State*, Cheltenham, UK: Edward Elgar, pp. 65–98.

Root, Lawrence S. (1987). "Britain's Redundancy Payments for Displaced Workers," *Monthly Labor Review*, 110(6): 18–23.

Russell, Alice (1991). *The Growth of Occupational Welfare in Britain*, Aldershot, UK: Avebury.

Saunders, Adam M. (2009). "New Perspectives on the Political Economy of Social Policy Change," *Barnett Papers in Social Research*, No. 4, University of Oxford.

Schmähl, Winfried (1999). "Rentenversicherung in der Bewährung," in Kaase, Max, and Schmid, Günther (eds.), *Eine lernende Demokratie—50 Jahre Bundesrepublik Deutschland*, WZB-Jahrbuch 1999, Berlin: Edition Sigma, pp. 397–423.

Schmähl, Winfried (2007). "Dismantling an Earnings-Related Social Pension Scheme: Germany's New Pension Policy," *Journal of Social Policy*, 36(2): 319–340.

Seeleib-Kaiser, Martin (2001). *Globalisierung und Sozialpolitik*, Frankfurt/New York: Campus.

Seeleib-Kaiser, Martin (2008). "Shifting Boundaries of 'Public and Private'," in Seeleib-Kaiser, Martin (ed.), *Welfare State Transformations*, Basingstoke, UK: Palgrave Macmillan, pp. 1–13.

Seeleib-Kaiser, Martin, and Fleckenstein, Timo (2007). "Discourse, Learning and Welfare State Change," *Social Policy and Administration*, 41(5): 427–448.

Skolnik, A. (1976). "Twenty-Five Years of Employee-Benefit Plans," *Social Security Bulletin*, 39(9): 3–21.

Solis, Hilda L. (2009). "Statement of Secretary of Labor Hilda L. Solis on COBRA Subsidy," U.S. Department of Labor, March 19, 2009.

Standing, Guy (2009). *Work after Globalization*, Cheltenham, UK: Edward Elgar.

Stolberg, Sheryl Gay, and Pear, Robert (2010). "Obama Signs Health Care Overhaul Bill, with a Flourish," *New York Times*, March 23, 2010.

Titmuss, Richard (1958). "The Social Division of Welfare," in R. Titmuss, *Essays on 'The Welfare State,'* London: George Allen and Unwin, pp. 34–55.

Tussing, A. Dale (1975). *Poverty in a Dual Economy*, New York: St. Martin's Press.

Vroman, Wayne (1990). "The Aggregate Performance of Unemployment Insurance, 1980–1985," in Hansen, W. Lee, and Byers, James T. (eds.), *Unemployment Insurance: The Second Half-Century*, Madison: University of Wisconsin Press, pp. 19–46.

Ways and Means Committee (2004). *Green Book*. Washington, DC: GPO.

Weir, Margaret, Orloff, Ann Shola, and Skocpol, Theda (eds.) (1988). *The Politics of Social Policy in the United States*, Princeton, NJ: Princeton University Press.

Wilensky, Harold L. (1975). *The Welfare State and Equality*, Berkeley: University of California Press.

Williamson, John B., and Pampel, Fred C. (1993). *Old-Age Security in Comparative Perspective*, Oxford: Oxford University Press.

8

RESPONSES TO LABOR MARKET DIVIDES IN SMALL STATES SINCE THE 1990s

HERBERT OBINGER, PETER STARKE, AND ALEXANDRA KAASCH

INTRODUCTION

Since the 1980s, countries across the Organisation for Economic Co-operation and Development (OECD) were confronted with processes of deindustrialization, a massive labor market entry of women, increased levels of atypical employment, and a lower demand for low-skilled workers in the wake of technological changes and economic globalization. This has led to increasing numbers of people outside formal labor markets, as well as a new perception of insider- and outsiderness. Typically, those workers with highly protected jobs are considered to be insiders. Outsiders, by contrast, "are either unemployed or hold jobs characterized by low levels of protection and employment rights, lower salaries and precarious levels of benefits and social security regulations" (Rueda 2006: 387).

Public policies—particularly employment regulation, social protection, active and passive labor market policies, but also education and training— shape the insider-outsider divide to a significant degree, even though possibly unintentionally. In order to understand how these divides are addressed in different political settings and whether this follows a common or divergent logic, this chapter examines the response to structural changes of labor markets in three small OECD countries since the 1990s. Is there a shift from policies aimed at creating employment opportunities through benefit cutbacks and labor market deregulation toward policies designed to strike a new balance between labor market flexibility and social security? Has the divide between labor market insiders and outsiders received more attention in recent years, or have countries even adopted policies that have reinforced these divides on the labor market and in social protection?

The OECD and actors at the European Union (EU) level have devoted increasing attention to labor market inequalities in recent years. This indicates a general shift from focusing purely on overall labor market performance to also considering the *distribution* of outcomes across the population. This realignment is remarkable since the 1994 OECD *Jobs Study*, for instance, was still largely concerned with lifting the overall level of employment by means of neoliberal policy recipes. Most recommendations concerned the deregulation of the labor market by allowing more flexible working time arrangements, lower unemployment benefit levels, the deregulation of wage setting, the phasing out of favorable early retirement rules, and so on (OECD 1994). From 2003 onward, however, the OECD "updated" its earlier employment strategy in light of policy evaluations and found the problem of labor market inequalities to be of great importance. The strategy to approaching these challenges proposed by the OECD has been termed "flexicurity," that is, a policy route that combines a high level of social protection with activation policies in a flexible labor market. A similar strategy is promoted by EU.[1]

Against the backdrop of these transnationally formulated strategies to meet common structural divides, this chapter is interested in the role of national institutions and politics for explaining specific adjustment pathways. We focus on two main hypotheses. Following Esping-Andersen (1990), different welfare regimes are expected not only to shape different patterns of insider-outsider divides but also to preconfigure particular policy responses (hypothesis 1). Accordingly, national strategies will significantly diverge from those recommended by the OECD or the EU or, at the very least, will be differently translated into national reforms. Furthermore, we assume that an insider-outsider divide is most likely to be contained under leftist corporatism, that is, a situation in which a left-wing government cooperates with strong encompassing interest organizations of labor (hypothesis 2). The reason is that encompassing labor organizations transcend particular interests and thus have an incentive to speak on behalf of outsiders (e.g., to support the social protection of atypical employees). In contrast, all other actor constellations are problematic in this respect. For example, strong sectoral unions may prioritize insider interests even under a left-wing government, whereas no activities to rein in labor market inequalities can be expected under right-wing governments confronting weak unions.

In order to assess these hypotheses, we look at reform trajectories in Austria, New Zealand, and Sweden since 1990, and examine the policy changes and their outcomes looking both at welfare state institutions and on the interactions between political parties and unions. The case selection is motivated by two reasons. First, our sample covers the three worlds of welfare capitalism distinguished by Esping-Andersen (1990). At the end of the "golden age," Sweden was typically classified as a Social-democratic welfare regime, whereas Austria was across the board assigned to the Conservative regime cluster. New Zealand represents the Liberal regime, especially after the demise of the postwar "wage earner's welfare state" in the 1980s and early 1990s (Castles and Mitchell 1993; Starke 2008). Second, the three countries represent diverse cases in terms of interest mediation and power resources of labor: Austria and Sweden are classical neo-corporatist cases with highly encompassing interest organizations of labor. However, industrial relations—particularly in Sweden—were decentralized to a significant extent. New Zealand has a pluralist system of industrial relations based on small sectoral trade unions.

A TYPOLOGY OF RESPONSES TO LABOR MARKET INEQUALITIES

Even though OECD-wide structural economic changes are evident, and the OECD and the EU have proposed a standard set of recommendations on how to tackle associated problems, we assume, in line with Esping-Andersen (1990, 1999), that the three welfare regimes generate different patterns of inequalities and social divides (see also Häusermann and Schwander, Chapter 2 of this volume), which, in turn, are likely to foreshadow different national strategies for coping with labor market change.

The Liberal regime is based on the "unconstrained functioning of capitalist labour markets" (Castles 2010: 640) and "cultivates dualisms" in social protection since the good risks can be self-reliant in the market (including private forms of social provision), while the bad ones are dependent on meager public welfare benefits (Esping-Andersen 1999: 76; see also Seeleib-Kaiser et al., Chapter 7 of this volume). The Social-democratic regime, in contrast, is characterized by universalism, benefit generosity, a comprehensive socialization of risks, and a crowding-out of markets from social provision (Esping-Andersen 1999: 79). Along with comprehensive family-related social services and active labor market policies, inequalities are attenuated both in the labor market and in the realm of social protection. The opposite should apply to Conservative welfare regimes. The tight nexus between employment and social protection inherent in this model almost automatically implicates that any deviation from the standard employment contract is translated into inequalities in terms of social protection. Given the lack of comprehensive active labor market policies and traditionally high levels of employment protection for the core labor force, there is a real danger of an entrenched insider-outsider divide. Moreover, this regime type is prone to gender inequality emanating from poorly developed social services and to status segmentation in social protection along occupational lines.

In a nutshell, even in light of common structural changes, the patterns of inequality vary across different regime types. So do, arguably, the policy responses. Four ideal-typical adjustment pathways to *combat* social and labor

Table 8-1: Four possible responses to social and labor market divides

	Liberal	Conservative	Social Democratic	New Paradigm
	Flexibility	Dualization	Encompassing security	Flexicurity
Social protection	Low for all, benefit cuts	High for insiders, enhanced social protection for outsiders (e.g., atypical employees)	High for all	High for all
Activation				
– *workfare*	High	Low	Low	Low
– *human capital/ mobility oriented*	Low	High	High	High
Employment protection	Low for all	High for insiders	High for all	Low for all

market divides are conceivable (see Table 8-1). Three of them are basically path-dependent in the sense that they require the retrenchment/expansion of existing benefits in order to cope with the specific pattern of inequalities inherent to each regime type. The fourth reform pathway ("flexicurity") is the one constructed in transnational processes and recommended by the OECD and the EU. As embarking on the latter strategy would require significant policy shifts in each of the three welfare regimes, we expect that this adjustment path is rather unlikely to be used in a comprehensive sense, while the associated terms may nevertheless pop up in national policy debates.

The *flexibility* strategy expands flexibility to the realm of social protection. We would expect across-the-board welfare state cutbacks, especially in working-age benefits. In other words, this strategy means flexibility for all, and in all respects. The activating policies it entails should be more of a "workfare" kind, rather than high-investment active labor market policies (King 1995). We expect this outcome in political settings characterized by weak unions and right-wing governments.

Alternatively, policy makers can opt for a *dualization* strategy. In this case, we would expect a differential treatment of insiders and outsiders. Dualization can come in two forms. In the case of smoothed dualization, measures that support outsiders prevail. For instance, governments can promote active labor market policies, increase efforts to enhance family-related social services, and improve the social security of atypical employees, while still allowing for some liberalization at the margins, that is, in the "cheap labor" section of the labor market (King and Rueda 2008). In the case of pronounced dualization, government measures even reinforce social and labor market divides. Political actors, and unions in particular, might defend insider interests, which—according to authors such as David Rueda and Desmond King—is even rational for most established parties (including Social Democrats) if we assume that policies to assist outsiders to some extent always threaten the privileged status of insiders (King and Rueda 2008; Rueda 2006; Lindvall and Rueda, Chapter 12 of this volume). This, however, particularly holds for sectoral trade unions. Encompassing unions tend to have more members who hold atypical jobs or are threatened to become outsiders. Hence we assume that efforts to mitigate labor market inequality (smoothed dualization) are most likely in settings where interest organizations of labor are encompassing. Otherwise, pronounced dualization is the likely outcome.

Governments may also opt for a policy route that seeks to guarantee encompassing social and employment *security for all*. In stark contrast to the flexibility approach, this strategy consists in rejecting deregulation and marketization altogether. Basically, this strategy is an attempt to defend the past achievements of the social democratic model. The political constellation most likely to follow this trajectory is left corporatism.

These possible strategies to deal with social and labor market divides also illustrate that *flexicurity*, typically presented as a one-size-fits-all solution, is by no means the only conceivable response to the challenges of post-industrial labor markets.

The following sections examine which kinds of responses were chosen by policy makers in three distinct welfare regimes. This includes changes in unemployment benefits and labor law, as well as reforms in other fields of the welfare state that affect insider-outsider divides. Starting in 1990, we proceed chronologically and distinguish between different phases demarcated by changes in the partisan complexion of government.

AUSTRIA: COMBATING SOCIAL DIVIDES IN A CONSERVATIVE WELFARE STATE

Austria is not only a Bismarckian welfare regime and therefore allegedly prone to pronounced insider-outsider divides but also a prototype of corporatist interest mediation. Austrian corporatism is highly centralized and interest representation is encompassing since membership in the Chamber of Labor (employees), the Chamber of Commerce (employers), and the Chamber of Agriculture (farmers) is mandatory. In contrast, membership in the Austrian Trade Union Federation (the fourth key player of Austrian social partnership) is voluntary and has been declining over time. However, the decrease in union density is to some extent offset by compulsory membership of employees in the Chamber of Labor, which also includes atypical employees and even the registered unemployed.

While Austria was remarkably successful in weathering the economic crisis of the 1970s, labor market problems increased from the mid-1980s onward.

Rising unemployment (affecting mainly young persons, older workers, foreigners, and the low-skilled labor force) was paralleled by a growing number of atypical jobs[2] (Bock-Schappelwein 2005; Tàlos 1999, 255–263). These developments had significant consequences for the social protection of outsiders as wage-centered social security is strongly imbued with the actuarial principle, which leads to a close relationship between the contribution record and the level of cash benefits. In consequence, a perdurability of outsiderness is a real threat, as longer spells of precarious employment or unemployment are translated into lower levels of social protection, notably with regard to unemployment benefits and old age pensions.

The Grand Coalition: Balanced Reforms in the 1990s

In the 1990s, Austria was governed by a Grand Coalition formed by Social Democrats (SPÖ) and Christian Democrats (ÖVP) in 1987. While the traditional style of corporatist interest mediation was widely practiced in the early 1990s, EU accession in 1995 forced the government to adopt a tighter approach in fiscal policy in order to rein in derailing public debt. In consequence, tensions between both parties and the social partners increased. Nevertheless, the interest organizations of labor remained powerful enough to delay measures that went beyond incremental reforms. As a result, balanced reforms concerning outsiders were adopted, and the basic contours of labor market policy remained largely intact.

In 1992, a bill stipulating the non-discrimination of part-time work and marginal employment was passed, mainly in an effort to preempt European Court of Justice rulings (Tàlos 1999, 268). Temporary agency work had already been regulated by law in 1988. This bill was based on a compromise between the interest organizations of labor (calling for a ban of temporary agency), and the employers (considering this type of employment a suitable instrument to overcome labor shortage in times of excessive demand) (Wroblewski 2001: 5–6). Benefit enhancement in the area of unemployment insurance included the introduction of a uniform net replacement rate of 57.9 percent, the reduction of the qualifying period for unemployed under 25 years of age from 52 to 20 weeks and the extension of benefit duration for older unemployed with long insurance records. This was clearly a political response to the increasing unemployment among young and elderly employees. The emergency benefit (the means-tested follow-up benefit to unemployment insurance) was altered: women dependent on a full-time employed partner were no longer excluded, and the benefit was extended to particular groups of foreigners in response to a Constitutional Court ruling. However, the Grand Coalition also increased the pressure on the (long-term) unemployed. Sanctions were tightened and the emergency benefit was subject to moderate retrenchment.

While the expansion of benefits outweighed welfare cutbacks in the early 1990s, this changed in the late 1990s. The government increasingly relied on (moderate) benefit cutbacks, the activation of the unemployed, and measures for increased labor market flexibility. Fiscal issues and efforts to stabilize non-wage labor costs mainly motivated these restrictive reforms. For example, the net replacement rate of unemployment insurance was slightly lowered to 57 percent, and the two so-called austerity packages (a strategy to meet the Maastricht convergence criteria), entailed a series of benefit cuts (Tàlos and Wörister 1998: 270–273). The numerous pension reforms of that decade restricted early retirement and strengthened the actuarial principle. Finally, a bill aiming at working-time flexibilization, an area in which Austria has been an international laggard (Unger 2001), was passed by the Austrian parliament in 1997.

On the other hand, the Grand Coalition extended spending on active labor market policy and was increasingly concerned with the social protection of atypical employees. Quasi-freelancers were integrated into compulsory pension, health, and accident insurance in 1996. Two years later the marginally employed (traditionally only covered by accident insurance) were entitled to take out voluntary health and pension insurance (opting in). While Social Democrats, the unions, and the Chamber of Labor supported the extension of social protection to atypical workers, the employers rejected these demands. The extension of social protection for outsiders was also motivated by efforts to raise additional social insurance revenues in the short-run (Tàlos 1999: 272, 274).

Center-Right Coalition: Toward Supply-side Oriented Reforms

The takeover of a coalition government formed by the ÖVP and the right-wing populist Freedom Party (FPÖ) in 2000 led to a realignment of labor market policy toward an approach emphasizing flexibility, containment of non-wage labor costs, activation, and employability. The overriding goal of this government was to achieve a supply-side oriented paradigm shift in economic and social policy. With a view to bypass the informal veto powers held by the unions, the government excluded the interest organizations of labor from the decision-making process (e.g., pre-parliamentary consultation). With a few exceptions, corporatism therefore virtually came to an end.

Based on the slogan "speed kills" cutbacks of unemployment compensation were quickly imposed. Already in 2000, the family surcharge was reduced and the net replacement rate was lowered to 55 percent. Regulations concerning suitable job offers were repeatedly tightened while those concerning a reasonable time span to commute to and from work were made more flexible. In addition, the so-called job protection clause (no requirement to accept a job below one's former qualification level) was limited to 100 days and was supplemented by a system aiming to preserve previous salary levels.

With its Job Promotion Act, passed in 2005, the government made an attempt to create new jobs in the low-wage sector. The coalition introduced, for example, a so-called service check to create (legal) jobs in private households and to provide minimum social security for the home help. Moreover, the government paved the way for in-work benefits, albeit on an experimental basis only. Both the take-up and the evaluation of these programs were rather poor, however.

The Center-Right government also paved the way toward a multi-pillar pension system, which will disadvantage atypical workers in the long run due to the accentuation of the actuarial principle. Public pensions (still the most important pillar) henceforth are calculated on the basis of the average lifetime income (instead of the 15 so-called best years under the previous system). The number of years required to qualify for the maximum pension was extended from 40 to 45 years. However, there is a means-tested minimum pension (the equalization supplement), which tops up very low pensions to a certain floor (€783/€1,175 per month for singles/couples in 2010).

Severance payment (a lump-sum payment that was due in case of termination of employment) was converted into the so-called corporate staff provision with a view to establish a fully funded second pension pillar in the long run. Even though atypical employees are covered by this program, its strictly actuarial nature disadvantages outsiders. The same holds true for the third pension pillar, which is based on public subsidies paid to private forms of savings such as life insurance.

Since the Center-Right coalition has also significantly curtailed early retirement, the government enacted some measures to enhance the employment opportunities for the elderly. Besides qualification programs, the main approach has been to reduce non-wage labor costs (employees aged 57+ henceforth exempt from unemployment insurance contributions).

The ÖVP-FPÖ coalition increased expenditure devoted to active and activating labor market policies from €762 million (2000) to €1.92 million in 2006 (BMWA 2008; see also Grand 2009). Special emphasis has been put on measures to improve the skills of women and to combat rising youth unemployment.

Grand Coalition and Corporatism Reloaded

In 2007, a Grand Coalition under the auspices of the Social Democrats took power again. Once more, the change in government brought about a change in labor market policy, not least because of a recurrence of corporatism (Tàlos 2008: 115–122). The government adopted a policy route that was mainly based on two white papers issued by the Austrian Institute for Economic Research and the social partners in 2006–2007. Both the government and the social partners adhered, at least rhetorically, to the idea of "flexicurity." The actual policy route adopted included a mix of measures aimed at enhancing social protection for outsiders and increasing general labor market flexibility.

In terms of the former, the social partners agreed to establish a (gross) minimum wage of €1,000 per month for full-time employees (except quasi-freelancers) in 2007. The minimum wage for part-time workers is calculated in proportion to the respective working time. Moreover, a *means-tested* minimum income scheme (*bedarfsorientierte Mindestsicherung*) came into effect in

September 2010, and replaced the territorially fragmented social assistance benefits offered by the nine *Länder*.

Unemployment insurance was revised in two important ways. First, employees with earnings up to €1,100 are henceforth exempted from contribution payments, whereas unemployment contribution rate of employees with earnings between €1,100 and €1,350 per month was lowered. The resulting revenue shortage is covered by the federal budget. Second, quasi-freelancers were incorporated into compulsory unemployment insurance, whereas self-employed were entitled to take out voluntary unemployment insurance (opting-in). In addition, quasi-freelancers as well as various groups of the self-employed are henceforth entitled to occupational pensions, compensation in case of bankruptcy of employer, maternity cash benefits, and sick pay. Accordingly, most atypical employees are now either covered by compulsory social insurance or they gained the opportunity to take out voluntary insurance (see Table 8-2).

In contrast, employment rights stipulated by labor law (continued remuneration, five weeks of vacation) only apply if this was agreed by contract. While unions and the Chamber of Labor argued for an equal treatment, this was rejected by employers. Moreover, the interest organizations of labor criticized the stricter regulations concerning suitable job offers that were included in this reform package (Tàlos 2008: 118).

Table 8-2: Number and social protection of atypical employees in 2007/2009

Type of atypical employment	2007		Social protection in 2009				
	Number	Share of women (%)	Pension (public)	Pension (2nd pillar)	Accident	Health	Unemployment
Marginal employment	245,832	69.4	(X)	X[b]	X	(X)	None
Part-time work	779,200	85.9	X	X	X	X	X
Temporary agency work	66,688	18.7	X	X	X	X	X
Quasi-freelancer	26,077	51.9	X	X	X	X	X
New self-employed	38,147	41.1	X[a]	X[a]	(X)[a]	(X)[a]	(X)[a]
Total (active) employment	3,227,449	44.7					

Notes: X = mandatory insurance, (X) = voluntary insurance (opting-in) possible, a = mandatory insurance if annual gross income exceeds 6,453 €, b = under certain circumstances.
Source: BMWA (2008), Bock-Schappelwein and Mühlberger (2008), adjusted by the authors.

Efforts aimed at increasing flexibility mainly focused on the liberalization of working time. Moreover, the role of shop agreements in this policy area was strengthened. Compensatory measures included a new 25 percent overtime supplement for part-time workers. One motive for this measure that benefited outsiders was to lower the incentive for employers to split up full-time employment contracts.[3]

Recent reform activities were influenced by the advent of the global financial crisis. Parliament unanimously passed a reform package in July 2009 to cope with the repercussions of the economic crisis. The measures adopted were based upon an agreement negotiated by the social partners and included the extension of short-time work to a maximum of 24 months, the establishment of a foundation to combat youth unemployment, and easier access to partial retirement. In May 2010 parliament further agreed on a strict austerity policy and announced tax increases in order to rein in the increase in public debt caused by the economic crisis. The measures also include cutbacks of welfare benefits, notably family cash benefits.

Summary

Social protection of atypical workers was enhanced over the past 20 years. Moreover, employment rights were extended but there still exist some differences compared to the regular labor force (Bock-Schappelwein and Mühlberger 2008). All these measures were enacted by a Grand Coalition in close cooperation with the social partners. By contrast, retrenchment and activation prevailed under the Center-Right government, which deliberately suspended the traditional style of corporatist policy making. The pension reform passed by the ÖVP-FPÖ coalition further accentuated the actuarial principle of public pensions and strengthened private forms of provision. This will negatively affect the future social protection of a growing host of atypical workers. The number of marginal jobs, temporary agency work and part-time work peaked out in absolute terms in 2010. This involves a significant gender effect, since more than 85 percent of women work part-time.

In sum, enhanced social protection of outsiders certainly did not eliminate insider-outsider divides, but because these measures overall improved social minimum standards, Austria's adjustment path should be considered a case of smoothed dualization. Perhaps even more important is the fact that a hardening of the insider-outsider divide was prevented by a very favorable labor market performance. Even in the crisis year of 2009, the unemployment rate was less than 5 percent and income inequality is, despite an increase in the period of interest, still low by international standards. Overall, the Austrian adjustment pathway suggests that the argument that pronounced dualization is the natural policy outcome in post-industrial Continental welfare states (Palier and Thelen, Chapter 9 of this volume) is to some extent premature. This qualification is also supported by the labor market performance in other small states in Continental Europe, such as Switzerland and the Netherlands. However, it is not merely country size that matters for social outcomes but rather the institutions of corporatism and the higher political flexibility characterizing small states (Katzenstein 1985). In line with our hypothesis, it is therefore corporatism that makes a strategy of "smoothed dualization" most likely to occur in Continental welfare regimes.

NEW ZEALAND: FLEXIBILITY RULES

New Zealand has been characterized as a "wage earners' welfare state" (Castles 1985) because, traditionally, the formal system of social protection was accompanied by a system of "social protection by other means", including a highly regulated wage-setting system and trade protectionism. Nonetheless, the formal welfare state always resembled the "Liberal regime" most. Most benefits for working-age people were means-tested (unemployment benefits, sickness benefits, most family transfers) while health care and pensions largely followed the design of universal, basic provision. Despite Esping-Andersen's (1999) assumption that the specific kind of insider-outsider divides in Liberal countries stems from the fact that higher-income groups are able to privately provide for a higher level of social benefits than other groups, in New Zealand, the extent of private provision in health care and pensions was rather low in a comparative perspective (OECD 1993). Nor did New Zealand, historically, have a specifically "Liberal" pattern of inequality of wages and disposable income. The wage earners' welfare state, with its notion of an egalitarian "family wage," effectively reduced inequalities, at least during the immediate postwar decades.

Likewise, employment protection has always been relatively weak in New Zealand. Pre-1990 employment protection with regard to atypical work was not primarily based on statutory regulation but was tied to the comprehensive system of industrial conciliation and arbitration, dating back to 1894. The industry awards and collective agreements negotiated in this system regulated not only wage rates and immediate working conditions but also protected full-time work by imposing limits on the amount of casual and part-time work in an industry or by fixing pay rates for part-time and casual work *above* the full-time rate (G. Anderson et al. 1994: 495) in order to create disincentives for employers to rely excessively on atypical labor. In addition to the award wages, there was a minimum wage (Minimum Wage Act 1983) subject to an annual review. Overall, "legislation guaranteed non-standard workers similar protections to standard workers" (G. Anderson et al. 1994: 498). It is fair to say that, overall, the labor market regime in New Zealand was already flexible at the beginning of the period under review, despite the arbitration regime.

In consequence, the light but egalitarian employment protection regime prevented the insider-outsider divide seen in some of the Continental and Southern European countries. In addition, the fact that the old age pension benefit, as well as secondary health care, were fully universal[4] helped to crowd out private provision to a large extent.

As in other OECD countries, atypical employment has risen in New Zealand, especially part-time employment, which reached the threshold of 20 percent of total employment in the early 1990s (Carroll 1999). Moreover, the share of involuntary part-timers is high by OECD standards (OECD 2010). Politically, however, the issue of insider-outsider politics as it is conventionally understood has not played a very big role in New Zealand. This has to do with the fact that, as has been shown, the gap between potential insiders and outsiders in terms of protection and benefits is rather small. Of course, this is not to say that nobody is disadvantaged. This is true in at least two respects. First, one particular feature of the New Zealand labor market is its segmentation along ethnic lines. The unemployment rate of Maori and Pacific Islanders, for instance, has always been much higher than the rate for New Zealanders of European descent. At the height of the crisis, the Maori unemployment rate stood at around 30 percent, that is, almost threefold the rate for non-Maori (Chapple and Rea 1998: 132). Similar imbalances exist in terms of poverty and other social indicators. While the divergence has narrowed significantly afterward, it is still considerable. In late 2009, the unemployment rate for Maori (11.2 percent) was still more than twice the average rate for all persons (5.5 percent). The situation is very similar with respect to Pacific Islanders in New Zealand.[5] Second, the flexibility strategy is associated with a high degree of income inequality, in terms of both pre- and post-tax and transfer inequality (OECD 2008). The flexibility strategy may have prevented classical insider-outsider divides among workers and welfare state clienteles, but this does not mean that it does not produce losers.

The Early 1990s: Retrenchment and Liberalization

While, up to the 1980s, the country had a curious mix of flexible and rigid elements in the labor market, including a state-led system of wage arbitration and conciliation, the market-liberal "Rogernomics" reforms of the 1980s cleared the way for a labor market policy based on neoclassical prescriptions. Partly due to the new economic policies, the unemployment rate started to rise fast in the 1980s and peaked at 10.4 percent in 1992, at the height of the economic crisis. The economic situation eased from about 1993 onward and the better economic performance continued—only shortly interrupted by the 1997 Asian financial crisis—until about 2008, when the financial crisis began to have an impact.

In general, the state of the economy and the partisan composition of government were the strongest drivers of welfare state reform initiatives since

1990 (Starke 2008). This is also true for the realm of labor market policies. Retrenchment and deregulation were initiated by conservatives and market-liberals. Interestingly, both the slight re-regulation of employment law and the move toward work-centered transfers have been pursued most vigorously by the Labor-led government of Helen Clark (1999–2008), partly with trade union support.

Together with a range of other cash transfers, the unemployment benefit was severely cut back in 1991 by the incoming (conservative) National Party government. Against the backdrop of a serious fiscal crisis, the government implemented what probably amounts to the most radical welfare retrenchment initiative that an OECD country has seen in the last 30 years or so. In nominal terms, the unemployment benefit was cut by between 3.1 (married couple with children) and 24.7 percent (single unemployed between 20 and 24 years of age) (Bolger et al. 1990). The maximum waiting period in case of "voluntary" unemployment was extended from 6 to 26 weeks.

The most important change in the area of employment regulation during the period under review came with the 1991 Employment Contracts Act (ECA). It effectively dismantled the traditional arbitration system and replaced the existing system of "industry awards" and collective bargaining with a system that favored individual contracts. The weakening of the awards-based system also meant that the reach of clauses regulating non-standard employment contained in the awards was restricted. On the other hand, the personal grievance provisions in case of dismissal, which previously had only been available to union members, were extended to all employees.

Workfare Reforms

In the mid-1990s, the so-called "work for the dole" approach was introduced (Humpage et al. 2008). Although recipients of the unemployment benefit had always been legally required to actively look for work, there is plenty of anecdotal evidence that this obligation was only seldom enforced. It was only in the mid-1990s that this "'work test" was taken more seriously. Inspired by the U.S. experience, labor market policy moved clearly in a "workfare" direction, most clearly in relation to the unemployment and sickness benefits but also, for example, in the field of accident compensation. Some community work schemes, case management, and specialized schemes for transition into work were also set up, albeit on a small scale. In 1996, however, when the National Party formed a coalition with the New Zealand First Party, activation became a central issue. The coalition agreement included the Community Wage, a workfare scheme which replaced the unemployment, training, and sickness benefit. Beneficiaries were expected to participate in community work or training in return for their benefit. In the late 1990s, work testing was gradually extended to other categories of beneficiaries, including the sick, widows, single parents and the partners and spouses of beneficiaries.

Cautious Re-regulation since 1999

The cutbacks of 1991 were heavily criticized by beneficiary groups, trade unions, and the Labor opposition at the time. Yet, when entering office in 1999, the Labor-led government of Helen Clark did *not* repeal the 1991 cuts. Instead, the government chose to compensate selected groups, particularly so-called "working families" (Lunt et al. 2008; Lunt 2009). The most important new program in this respect was the Working for Families package, a major expansion of in-work tax credits for low-to-medium income families (St. John 2008). Some, however, have largely missed out from this new strategy of combating poverty by "making work pay." A government report shows that there are remaining "pockets of hardship" among those who, for a variety of reasons, still do not participate in the labor market (Ministry of Social Development 2007). The year 2008 saw a change in office to a conservative government, as well as the beginning of the worldwide financial crisis. As part of the emergency responses to the crisis, the new government unveiled the so-called "ReStart" package for those who are being made redundant from full-time work in the course of the economic downturn. It includes an extra payment on top of the unemployment benefit available for those who would lose entitlement for the in-work tax credit (a part of the Working for Families package) due to their being made redundant.

In social policy, there has been a slight tendency toward dualization, that is, toward favoring the full-time employed in recent years. Traditionally, the system of means-tested, flat rate benefits does not discriminate against outsiders, since benefits are usually not based on contribution records or similar conditions. However, in other areas of the welfare state, reforms since 1990 could be interpreted in line with insider-outsider dynamics. Family policy has been remodeled in New Zealand in an attempt to help "working families" in particular. Through a complex system of in-work benefits, and, since 2002, paid parental leave, families are supported by the state. Eligibility criteria, however, increasingly target labor market insiders, and exclude many casual or temporary workers. In a similar vein, there are two main types of tax credits for families, the family tax credit (FTC) and the in-work tax credit (IWTC). The former is paid regardless of the source of family income; the latter is only paid to families who work a minimum number of hours. Again, this excludes not only the unemployed but also many part-time and casual employees from supplementary family transfers. While this may still be a far cry from the dualization patterns observed in other OECD countries, it shows that New Zealand's welfare state has also moved somewhat away from its strictly egalitarian (but needs-based) tradition.[6]

The Labor-led governments after 1999 also continued along the path of activation, though with a slightly different take. The Community Wage was abolished, while the work test was scrapped or softened for beneficiaries with children and sickness beneficiaries. For the unemployed, however, the range of instruments to get them back into work was widened.

With regard to employment regulation, the pendulum swung back from the purely contractual approach enshrined in the 1991 ECA toward cautious intervention after a Labor-led government took office in 1999. The Employment Relations Act of 2000 reversed many of the deregulation measures introduced in 1991 and demanded that dismissals must have a sufficient cause, and must be carried out in a procedurally fair way. In addition, the act stipulated that employers give genuine reasons for using fixed-term employment contracts. Already in 1994, a youth minimum wage for people between 16 and 20 years of age had been introduced (60 percent of the adult minimum wage). In 2001, the age threshold was lowered to 18 years, and the level of the youth minimum wage was lifted to 80 percent of the adult rate (Hyslop and Stillman 2005).

Summary

There have been relatively few reforms in New Zealand that have had a significant direct impact on the relationship between insiders and outsiders. The most important exception is the unemployment benefit cut of 1991, a serious blow to the unemployed. Activation has been strengthened, but rather of a "workfare" type. Expenditure on active labor market policies is low. When it comes to employment regulation, New Zealand still has a very light legal regime. Although, overall, the system of employment relations was deregulated in the 1990s, regulations regarding non-standard forms of employment (particularly fixed-term contracts) were slightly strengthened post-1999.

New Zealand was and still is an almost perfect example of what we call the "flexibility" response to increasing labor market inequalities. Standard employees by and large do not benefit from enhanced protection compared to atypical workers. The consequences of this policy on overall social inequality are unclear. While, on the one hand, the lack of earnings-related welfare schemes and private provision does not reproduce market inequalities in the welfare state, on the other hand, this "hands-off egalitarianism" might be insufficient in mitigating inequalities stemming from income or labor market status. And overall inequality increased extremely fast from the late 1980s onward, even by international standards. In terms of political dynamics, the New Zealand case also supports the expectation—as implied by hypothesis 2—that left-wing partisanship alone is not enough to cope with labor market divides. Insider-outsider politics also depend on the structure of industrial relations. Trade unions in New Zealand are notoriously pluralist and far from encompassing, especially after the 1991 Employment Contracts Act. Therefore, the post-1999 Labor-led government cannot be regarded as an example of leftist corporatism. This may explain the policy of labor market re-regulation combined with in-work benefits that tend to advantage full-time workers.

SWEDEN: DEPARTING FROM THE ENCOMPASSING SECURITY MODEL?

Sweden is *the* example of the Social-democratic welfare state. The "Swedish model" stands for a welfare state that offers high social protection, and for strong corporatism. Traditionally, negotiations between social partners were centralized and involved the Swedish Employer's Confederation (SAF) and the Swedish Trade Union Confederation (LO). However, already in the early 1980s, the most important actors began to negotiate separately, starting a process of "decorporatization" (Lundqvist 2008). This was further accelerated by organizational changes that led to a more diverse picture of interest representation, both for employers' organizations and trade unions. Nevertheless, the close link between union membership and unemployment insurance gives the trade unions, which are closely linked to the Social Democratic Party (SAP), an important position in social and labor policy-making. Accordingly, the Swedish welfare state has produced a status of high equality among citizens, realized through generous universal social benefits, training-and-employment-based ALMPs (originating from the so-called Rehn-Meidner model), and high levels of public employment.

Rising unemployment in the early 1990s challenged the system significantly, and outsiderness began to matter also in Sweden (Davidsson 2009; Lindvall and Rueda, Chapter 12 of this volume). Particular problems emerged with respect to the integration of young people and immigrants into the labor market. The response came, quite in line with the traditional approach, primarily through the use of various ALMPs that became increasingly targeted at specific groups of the population. Nevertheless, unemployment could not be reduced as intended, and the unemployed faced lower unemployment benefits and more restrictive rules for benefit entitlement.

The 1990s: Benefit Cuts in a Period of Economic Crisis

Given a situation of almost full employment, the crisis of the early 1990s and the resulting dramatic increase in unemployment[7] called various governments to action, as the existing labor market policies appeared not to be sustainable for overcoming a crisis of that scale.

In order to contain public deficits, unemployment insurance (UI) was significantly restructured, with a specific focus on replacement rates, duration of benefits, and contribution rates. The politics differed from the otherwise rather consensual policy making in Sweden in that the decision-making process was characterized by antagonistic interests and a power struggle between the trade unions and the political parties (Bergh and Erlingsson 2008: 77–78). More concretely, the Center-Right government (1991–1994) lowered the replacement rate from 90 to 80 percent of previous earnings and introduced five waiting days for receiving benefits. It also attempted to impose limits on benefit duration as, in practice, the benefit could be received for an unlimited period due to a complex system of requalification through participation in ALMPs ("endless carousel") (K. M. Anderson 2001: 1080–1081). However, these limits did not come into effect; the Social Democrats, once back in government in 1994, restored the original entitlement period of 300 days (450 days for people aged 57+).

Nonetheless, the same government further reduced the maximum replacement rate to 75 percent in 1996, even though the Social Democrats had opposed the benefits cuts imposed by the former government (Björklund 2000: 157). This led to a break with the unions and, in consequence, to an alliance with the Center Party in order to realize the benefit reduction (K. M. Anderson 2001: 1082). Once the economy had recovered, though, the level was restored to 80 percent in September 1997. A proposal by the Social Democrats to impose a limit on benefit receipt was averted by fierce trade union protests (Björklund 2000: 156). Nevertheless, the left-wing government tightened eligibility rules and retained the waiting days. The reform of 1997 also linked benefit entitlement to an employment record of six months (Olsen 2008: 330).

Somewhat moderating the negative outcomes of these reforms for outsiders, ALMPs emerged to be the main policy instrument to tackle open unemployment (Calmfors et al. 2002: 4), and the Center-Right government put increasing emphasis on integrating people into employment programs. As low-skilled workers and young people were particularly hard hit by the employment crisis of the early 1990s, the response was re-orienting active labor market policy toward labor market training and further education, as well as increasing educational enrollment rates of younger people (Anxo and Niklasson 2006: 357–359). Whereas Bonoli and Emmenegger (2010: 842–843) emphasize the resemblance to the "flexicurity" strategy, this policy shift has also been interpreted as a return to the original model (Anxo and Niklasson 2006).

In addition, major discussions focused on employment protection legislation in the early 1990s. The debate was particularly connected to the so-called Lindbeck Commission, appointed by the Center-Right government, which proposed various measures to increase labor market flexibility (e.g., more temporary and flexible employment contracts). Actual changes came in 1997 under Social Democratic auspices with a reform providing employers with the opportunity to hire employees on the basis of fixed-term contracts without giving a particular reason. Fixed-term contracts are, however, still subject to restrictions regarding the number of such contracts per firm, and the possibility to renew such contracts with the same employee (Holmlund and Storrie 2002: F248). Unions strongly opposed many of these reforms. Nonetheless, the share of temporary employment increased from 14.6 percent in the 1990s to 17.5 in 2007, according to the OECD Labour Force Statistics.

The year 2001, still under Social Democratic government, brought a new package of labor market reforms. A maximum entitlement period of 60 weeks, irrespective of age, was introduced, implying a significant disadvantage for older unemployed who previously had been eligible for 90 weeks (Bennmarker et al. 2007: 91–92). In addition, participation in ALMP programs is no longer considered a qualification period. Moreover, a new ALMP scheme, the so-called "activity guarantee," was introduced, requiring participants to engage in job search, participate in labor market training or study full-time (Olsen 2008: 331). A further reform, passed in 2001, introduced sanctions in the form of lower benefit levels for those refusing suitable employment (Palme et al. 2001; Statens Offentliga Utredningar [SOU] 2000).

Reforms of the health system (sick leave), pension system, and family policy had also important distributional consequences, and thus sharpened the insider-outsider divides further. The pension reform passed in the late 1990s significantly lowered the redistributive character of the pension system. Benefits offered by ATP (the earnings-related pension) are now based on lifetime earnings rather than on the best 15 of 30 years of earnings. This results in lower pensions for those who have switched between insider and outsider statuses. With regard to family and care policies, Bennmarker et al. (2007) point out that the child care reforms enacted in 2001–2002 included a child care guarantee for unemployed people for at least 3 hours per day or 15 hours per week, and a cap on the user fee for parents using day care services. Particularly the former measure has a potentially positive effect on unemployed women with children.

In sum, the crisis that struck the country in the early 1990s considerably shook the Swedish model—unemployment soared and was not easily offset by the system's automatic stabilizers. The labor market reforms passed since the early 1990s have undercut the previously very generous and encompassing system of social protection. Outsiders were particularly affected by these measures (Davidsson 2009). Bergmark and Palme (2003), for example, argue that labor market policy rather failed to protect the most vulnerable groups (particularly young people and migrants). The adopted measures contributed to growing insider-outsider divides in several ways. Not only did the rise in unemployment generate more outsiders, but lower benefit levels also widened income differences. Combating the worst forms of outsiderness was further complicated by restrictions to requalify for UI benefits. The situation for outsiders further worsened through cutbacks in social assistance benefits in 1996, which were later, though, to some extent reversed (Brännström and Stenberg 2007) until a national minimum benefit rate was eventually introduced in 1998. Nevertheless, Nelson (2009) provides evidence that the adequacy of benefit levels has deteriorated since the mid-1990s.

The Late 2000s: Maintaining the Welfare State—But Not for Outsiders?

Since 2006, Sweden is again governed by a Center-Right coalition that has continued reforming unemployment insurance, ALMPs, and employment protection. As the number of participants in activation programs increased since

2003, the Center-Right government replaced the "activity guarantee" with a new "job and development guarantee" for those no longer covered by unemployment insurance, and a "special job guarantee" for people under 25 (Olsen 2008). In 2006, a number of new activation programs have been introduced, which are targeted at particular groups of outsiders, such as long-term unemployed, young people, and immigrants. While these schemes do not mark an improvement in terms of more economic security (the right to requalify for UI benefits by that way has not been reintroduced), these measures can nevertheless be seen as an attempt to support outsiders.

Employment protection reforms in 2007 increased the maximum duration of temporary contracts from 14 to 24 months, and made it easier for employers to dismiss temporary contract workers. Once more, flexibilization of employment protection spared insiders. In April 2008, new restrictive regulations related to the right to work part-time and the part-time unemployment benefits were enacted. Compared to the regular benefit duration of 300 days, part-time workers are only entitled to the benefit for 75 days. These measures led to lower levels of social protection for those working part-time and are therefore indicative of growing social divides. Moreover, the waiting period for cash benefits was extended from 5 to 7 days in July 2008.

Other recent social policy reforms also point to increasing insider-outsider divides. While the gender divide is less of an issue of concern in Sweden compared to other countries, the recent introduction of a home care allowance could lead to a withdrawal of women from the labor market. A similar outcome may arise from efforts to privatize elder care (Meager and Szebehely 2010). The recent changes in the Swedish health system may have further dualizing effects in the sense of better care provision for insiders (Burström 2009). Measures to tackle the persistent problem of sickness absence have included a limitation to one year of sick leave, but it cannot yet be said if this results in shorter sickness spells (which then would affect insiders) or to pushing people out of the labor market (creating outsiders) (Forslund 2009).

Summary
Over the past 20 years, significant changes have taken place in the Swedish welfare state that have provoked questions of whether or not the Swedish model still exists. The scope of social protection was somewhat reduced, even if the Swedish welfare state is still generous and encompassing in comparative perspective. Particularly the 1990s witnessed retrenchment. Reforms of the social security system and employment protection legislation have had clearly dualizing effects, even if not all of them were intended, and some of them reversed. Outsiders mainly suffer from lower benefit levels and stricter eligibility rules. In addition, the proliferation of part-time and fixed-term employment implies less security at the margins of the labor market. At the same time, reforms in

ALMPs have attempted to reintegrate outsiders through human capital oriented measures.

Both Center-Right governments and Social Democrats have contributed to these developments. While party differences alone cannot account for the erosion of the Swedish model, it is economic problem pressure and the decline of corporatism (Lindvall and Sebring 2005) that matter. In line with our second hypothesis, the weakening of leftist corporatism has had a dualizing effect. The dominance of the Social Democratic Party has vanished, tensions between the unions and the party have significantly increased in economically hard times, and industrial relations have become less centralized and more adversarial. Confronted with severe economic difficulties in the 1990s and non-cooperative employers, the political Left increasingly faced difficulties to defend the status quo in social protection. In this situation, particularly the SAP opted for reforms that protected insider interests in the first place. However, as Lindvall and Rueda (Chapter 12 of this volume) argue, the party had to pay a high price for this strategy.

CONCLUSION

This chapter was concerned with the political responses to mounting labor market inequalities in three distinct welfare regimes. We hypothesized that national adjustment pathways are preconfigured by the distinct vulnerabilities of welfare regimes vis-à-vis common structural labor market changes. Moreover, we argued that the political responses to the challenges of post-industrial labor markets vary subject to the institutional characteristics of the system of interest mediation.

In fact, we do not find a common policy route adopted by all countries. In line with hypothesis 1, the different welfare state regimes seem to generate distinctive patterns of insider-outsider divides, and the three countries developed quite different, albeit mainly path-dependent responses. With the exception of a radical reform episode in New Zealand in the early 1990s, the adjustment pathways were rather incremental. Most measures were selected from the existing policy repertoire and basically relied on traditional routines of problem solving. However, the country case studies do not perfectly match the response patterns laid out at the beginning of this chapter. While in Bismarckian Austria various measures were taken that assisted outsiders in line with the strategy of "smoothed dualization" and New Zealand by and large followed the liberal path of flexibility, Sweden encountered growing difficulties to maintain its model of "encompassing security." Thus, the case study evidence does not fully support our first hypothesis.

In contrast, the evidence corroborates the second hypothesis related to actor constellations of parties and economic interest groups. Austrian corporatism led to incremental labor market reforms that were negotiated between the Social and Christian Democrats and the affiliated peak organizations of labor and capital. On the other hand, no major initiatives in favor of outsiders were launched once the interest organizations of labor and the Social Democrats were excluded from the decision-making process under a Center-Right government. The Austrian experience thus underscores that the primary focus of the interest organizations of labor was not purely insider-oriented. The two peak associations of labor supported and pushed for the expansion of social protection and employment rights also for outsiders. This can, at least in part, be attributed to the organizational peculiarities of Austrian corporatism, notably the statutory compulsory membership of all employees and the registered unemployed in the Chamber of Labor.

New Zealand, in contrast, has a pluralist system of interest intermediation. Therefore, the actor constellation of leftist corporatism has not emerged in the 1990s and 2000s. Consequently, many of the social policy reforms have tended to prioritize labor market insiders—"working families" in particular. Following hypothesis 2, the fragmented trade union structure has probably contributed to this particular trajectory. After the Employment Contracts Act of 1991, the trade unions structure in New Zealand was significantly weakened. Membership decline was particularly pronounced in the private service sector as well as among women and less-qualified and/or atypical workers (Charlwood and Haynes 2008). In other words, the representation of outsiders was the worst affected by these changes. This probably contributed to the more pro-insider policy pattern seen in recent years.

Sweden has witnessed the decline of a traditionally strong Social Democratic Party and corporatism. This has led to the creation of some new institutional dualisms. However, there have also been several attempts to reintegrate outsiders through ALMPs, even under conditions of general benefit cutbacks in times of severe economic crisis.

These different policy responses and their relative success or failure are particularly interesting regarding the fact that none of the countries subscribed to the "flexicurity" model. While the term appeared in political debates in the 2000s, one cannot observe serious political attempts to combine high levels of social protection with activation policies in a flexible labor market. The Austrian strategy was mainly based on the idea of establishing minimum social standards for outsiders but did not include efforts to raise replacement rates. Moreover, the measures aimed at increasing labor market flexibility focused on working time legislation but spared employment protection. New Zealand has not reformed its social protection system as to guarantee higher benefits or introduce more of a human capital orientation. Expenditure on active labor market policy, for instance, remains low by international standards. Finally, employment protection remained intact for insiders in Sweden. Overall, it seems that "flexicurity" is more of a catchword used by national policy actors to signal compliance with international/European reform agendas than a model that is actually being implemented in a comprehensive way.

NOTES

1 See, for example, Communication from the Commission to the European Parliament, the Council, the European Economic and Social Committee and the Committee of the Regions - Towards Common Principles of Flexicurity: More and Better Jobs Through Flexibility and Security (COM/2007/359 final).

2 Atypical forms of employment in Austria include part-time work, marginal employment (*geringfügige Beschäftigung*, defined as a salary less than € 366 per month [2010]), temporary agency employment (*Leiharbeit*), quasi-freelancer (*freie Dienstnehmer*), and the so-called new self-employed (*Neue Selbständige*).

3 This was explicitly emphasized by the social partners in their common statement on the draft law.

4 In 1985, the government introduced the Superannuation Surcharge, a tax on additional income. This claw-back tax further increased the disincentives for private provision, even though private pension income was only partly taken into account.

5 Disadvantages due to segmentation along ethnic lines and high levels of inequality can also be the result of dualization processes (see Emmenegger and Careja, Chapter 6 of this volume). In this chapter, however, the focus is on unemployment and atypical employment relationships.

6 The difference from other Liberal welfare states might be smaller in terms of poverty dynamics, the amount of casual work, and the extent of income inequality. However, due to serious data limitations, there is very little research on income dynamics in New Zealand. Neither is there good comparative data on the casualization of work in New Zealand.

7 Unemployment levels were about 10 percent between 1993 and 1997. After 2000, the unemployment rate went down to 6 to 7 percent.

REFERENCES

Anderson, Gordon, Brosnan, Peter, and Walsh, Pat (1994). "Flexibility, Casualization and Externalization in the New Zealand Workforce," *Journal of Industrial Relations*, 36 (4): 491–518.

Anderson, Karen M. (2001). "The Politics of Retrenchment in a Social Democratic Welfare State: Reform of Swedish Pensions and Unemployment Insurance," *Comparative Political Studies*, 34 (9): 1063–1091.

Anxo, Dominique, and Niklasson, Harald (2006). "The Swedish Model in Turbulent Times: Decline or Renaissance," *International Labour Review*, 145 (4): 339–372.

Bennmarker, Helge, Carling, Kenneth, and Holmlund, Bertil (2007). "Do Benefit Hikes Damage Job Finding? Evidence from Swedish Unemployment Insurance Reforms," *Labour,* 21 (1): 85–120.

Bergh, Andreas, and Erlingsson, Gissur O. (2008). "Liberalization without Retrenchment: Understanding the Consensus on Swedish Welfare State Reforms," *Scandinavian Political Studies,* 32 (1): 71–93.

Bergmark, Ake, and Palme, Joakim (2003). "Welfare and the Unemployment Crisis: Sweden in the 1990s," *International Journal of Social Welfare,* 12(2): 108–122.

Björklund, Anders (2000). "Going Different Ways: Labour Market Policy in Denmark and Sweden," in Esping-Andersen, Gøsta, and Regini, Marino (eds.), *Why Deregulate Labour Markets?,* Oxford: Oxford University Press, pp. 148–180.

BMWA (Bundesministerium für Wirtschaft und Arbeit) (2008). *Wirtschaftsbericht Österreich 2008,* Vienna.

Bock-Schappelwein, Julia (2005). "Entwicklung und Formen der Arbeitslosigkeit in Österreich seit 1990," *WIFO Monatsberichte 7/2005,* pp. 499–510.

Bock-Schappelwein, Julia, and Mühlberger, Ulrike (2008). "Beschäftigungsformen in Österreich: Rechtliche und quantitative Aspekte," *WIFO Monatsberichte 12/2008,* pp. 941–951.

Bolger, James, Richardson, Ruth, and Birch, Willia B. (1990). *Economic and Social Initiative,* Wellington: New Zealand Government.

Bonoli, Guiliano, and Emmenegger, Patrick (2010). "State-Society Relationships, Social Trust and the Development of Labour Market Policies in Italy and Sweden," *West European Politics,* 33 (4): 830–850.

Brännström, Lars, and Stenberg, Sten-Ake (2007). "Does Social Assistance Recipiency Influence Unemployment? Macro-Level Findings from Sweden in a Period of Turbulence," *Acta Sociologica,* 50: 347–364.

Burström, Bo (2009). "Market-Oriented, Demand-Driven Health Care Reforms and Equity in Health and Health Care Utilization in Sweden," *International Journal of Health Services,* 39 (2): 271–285.

Calmfors, Lars, Forslund, Anders, and Hemström, Maria (2002). "Does Active Labour Market Policy Work? Lessons from the Swedish Experiences," *CESifo Working Paper,* 675 (4).

Carroll, Nick (1999). "Non-standard Employment: A Note on Levels, Trends, and Some Implications," *Labour Market Bulletin,* 1: 101–121.

Castles, Francis G. (1985). *The Working Class and Welfare: Reflections on the Political Development of the Welfare State in Australia and New Zealand, 1890–1980,* Sydney: Allen & Unwin.

Castles, Francis G. (2010). "The English-speaking Countries," in Castles, Francis G., Leibfried, Stephan, Lewis, Jane, Obinger, Herbert and Christopher, Pierson (eds.), *The Oxford Handbook of the Welfare State,* Oxford: Oxford University Press, pp. 630–642.

Castles, Francis G., and Mitchell, Deborah (1993). "Worlds of Welfare and Families of Nations," *Families of Nations: Patterns of Public Policy in Western Democracies,* Aldershot, UK: Dartmouth, pp. 93–128.

Chapple, Simon, and Rea, David (1998). "Time Series Analysis of Disparity Between Maori and non-Maori Labour Market Outcomes in the Household Labour Force Survey," *Labour Market Bulletin*, 1–2: 127–144.

Charlwood, Andy, and Haynes, Peter (2008). "Union Membership Decline in New Zealand, 1990–2002," *Journal of Industrial Relations*, 50 (1): 87–110.

Davidsson, Johan (2009). *Outsiders to Welfare: Dualisation in the Swedish Welfare System, Labour Market Policy after 1990*, unpublished manuscript, San Domenico di Fiesole: European University Institute, Department of Social and Political Science.

Esping-Andersen, Gosta (1990). *The Three Worlds of Welfare Capitalism*, Cambridge: Policy Press.

Esping-Andersen, Gosta (1999). *Social Foundations of Postindustrial Economies*, Oxford: Oxford University Press.

Forslund, Anders (2009). *Labour Supply Incentives, Income Support Systems and Taxes in Sweden*, IFAU - Institute for Labour Market Policy Evaluation Working Paper 2009: 30.

Grand, Peter (2009). "Wann sind 'umfassende' Reformen auch ausreichend? Die janusköpfige Entwicklung der österreichischen Arbeitsmarktpolitik 1998–2007," *Österreichische Zeitschrift für Politikwissenschaft*, 38 (2): 213–230.

Holmlund, Bertil, and Storrie, Donald (2002). "Temporary Work in Turbulent Times: The Swedish Experience," *The Economic Journal*, 112 (480 Features): F245–F269.

Humpage, Louise, Craig, David, Lunt, Neil, O'Brien, Mike, and Stephens, Robert (2008). "From Welfare to Welfare-To-Work," in Lunt, Neil, O'Brien, Mike, and Stephens, Robert (eds.), *New Welfare, New Zealand: New Developments in Welfare and Work*, South Melbourne: Cengage Learning, pp. 41–48.

Hyslop, Dean, and Stillman, Steven (2005). "Youth Minimum Wage Reform and the Labour Market in New Zealand," *Labour Economics*, 14 (2): 201–230.

Katzenstein, Peter J. (1985). *Small States in World Markets. Industrial Policy in Europe*, Ithaca: Cornell University Press.

King, Desmond (1995). *Actively Seeking Work? The Politics of Employment and Welfare Policy in the United States and Great Britain*, Chicago: University of Chicago Press.

King, Desmond, and Rueda, David (2008). "Cheap Labor: The New Politics of 'Bread and Roses' in Industrial Democracies," *Perspectives on Politics*, 6 (2): 279–297.

Lindvall, Johannes, and Sebring, Joakim (2005). "Policy Reform and the Decline of Corporatism in Sweden," *West European Politics*, 28(5): 1057–1074.

Lundqvist, Torbjörn (2008). "The Employers in the Swedish Model: The Importance of Labour Market Competition and Organisation," in Rathkolb, Oliver (ed.), *Sweden-Austria: Two Roads to Neutrality and a Modern Welfare State*, Wien, Berlin: Lit Verlag, pp. 23–49.

Lunt, Neil (2009). "The Rise of a 'Social Development' Agenda in New Zealand," *International Journal of Social Welfare*, 18 (1): 3–12.

Lunt, Neil, O'Brien, Mike, and Stephens, Robert (2008). "New Welfare, New Zealand?," in Lunt, Neil, O'Brien, Mike and Stephens, Robert (eds.),

New Welfare, New Zealand: New Developments in Welfare and Work, South Melbourne: Cengage Learning, pp. 3–9.

Meager, Gabrielle, and Szebehely, Marta (2010). *Private Financing of Elder Care in Sweden. Arguments For and Against*, Working Paper Institute for Future Studies, 1, Stockholm.

Ministry of Social Development (2007). *Pockets of Significant Hardship and Poverty*, Wellington: Ministry of Social Development, Centre for Social Research and Evaluation.

Nelson, Kenneth (2009). *Minimum Income Protection and Low-Income Standards: Is Social Assistance Enough for Poverty Alleviation?*, SOFI Working Paper 9/2009, Stockholm: University of Stockholm.

OECD (1993). *Private Pensions in OECD Countries: New Zealand*, OECD Social Policy Studies, Paris: OECD.

OECD (1994). *The OECD Jobs Study*, Paris: OECD.

OECD (2008). *Growing Unequal? Income Distribution and Poverty in OECD Countries*, Paris: OECD.

OECD (2010). *Labour Fource Survey*, Paris: OECD.

Olsen, Gregg M. (2008). "Labour Market Policy in the United States, Canada and Sweden: Addressing the Issue of Convergence," *Social Policy and Administration*, 42 (4): 323–341.

Palme, Joakim, Bergmark, Åke, Bäckman, Olof, Estrada, Felipe, Fritzell, Johan, Sjöberg, Ola, and Szebehely, Marta (2001). *Welfare in Sweden: The Balance Sheet for the 1990s*, Stockholm: Ministry for Health and Social Services.

Rueda, David (2006). "Social Democracy and Active-Labour Market Policies: Insiders, Outsiders and the Politics of Employment Promotion," *British Journal of Political Science*, 36 (3): 385–406.

St. John, Susan (2008). "Working for Families: Work, Families and Poverty," in Lunt, Neil, O'Brien, Mike, and Stephens, Robert (eds.), *New Welfare, New Zealand: New Developments in Welfare and Work*, South Melbourne: Cengage Learning, pp. 78–91.

Starke, Peter (2008). *Radical Welfare State Retrenchment: A Comparative Analysis*, Houndsmills, Basingstoke: Palgrave MacMillan.

Statens Offentliga Utredningar (SOU) (2000). *Välfärd vid Vägskäl*, Stockholm: Fritzes.

Tàlos, Emmerich (1999). "Atypische Beschäftigung in Österreich," in Tàlos, Emmerich (ed.), *Atypische Beschäftigung. Internationale Trends und sozialstaatliche Regelungen*, Vienna: Manz, pp. 252–284.

Tàlos, Emmerich (2008). *Sozialpartnerschaft. Ein zentraler politischer Gestaltungsfaktor der zweiten Republik*, Innsbruck: Studienverlag.

Tàlos, Emmerich, and Wörister, Karl (1998). "Soziale Sicherung in Österreich," in Tàlos, Emmerich (ed.), *Soziale Sicherung im Wandel*, Vienna et al.: Böhlau, pp. 209–288.

Unger, Brigitte (2001). "Österreichs Beschäftigungs- und Sozialpolitik von 1970–2000," *Zeitschrift für Sozialreform*, 47 (4): 340–361.

Wroblewski, Angela (2001). *Leiharbeit in Österreich. Übergangslösung oder Sackgasse?*, IHS Working Paper 48, Reihe Soziologie, Vienna.

9

DUALIZATION AND INSTITUTIONAL COMPLEMENTARITIES

INDUSTRIAL RELATIONS, LABOR MARKET, AND WELFARE STATE CHANGES IN FRANCE AND GERMANY

BRUNO PALIER AND KATHLEEN THELEN[1]

INTRODUCTION

In the face of significant new challenges associated with changing international markets, ever-increasing competition in manufacturing, and the rise of services, many Continental European political economies have been significantly reconfigured over the past two decades. One of the most interesting features of recent developments is that some of the most important changes have occurred under the cover of a high degree of formal institutional stability, and many have been negotiated and "sold" politically as a way of preserving, not undermining, traditional arrangements and the kind of social order that they reflect and represent.

This chapter tracks developments across three institutional arenas (industrial relations, labor markets, and social protection) in two important Continental political economies, Germany and France. While some authors see developments in each of these realms as representing liberalization and a move toward the American model (Glyn 2006; Howell 2006; Streeck 2009), we argue instead that both the politics and the outcomes are better captured in the concept of dualization that lies at the heart of this volume (see Chapter 1). In both France and Germany, actors in the "core" economy have been relatively well positioned to defend traditional institutions and practices for themselves, but they are no longer able to serve the leadership functions they once did of providing crucial collective goods for all.[2] Thus, while France and Germany have been able to resist outright liberalization, they appear at the same time and for many of the same reasons to be especially vulnerable to dualization.

Our dualization thesis draws on theories from the late 1970s and early 1980s, when a group of economists and political scientists identified trends toward labor market segmentation (Edwards et al. 1982; Berger and Piore 1980; Sengenberger 1978). However, where that previous literature focused on the micro-level of firm strategies (as employers responded to conditions of uncertainty emanating from the market or, in some cases, the upsurge in labor militancy in the 1960s), we find that current trends point to a more durable new pattern based on a stable cross-class coalition, progressively institutionalized across successive institutional domains, and increasingly underwritten by state policy.

In our view, the dualization process has been tied up in the linkages—unexplored both in the earlier literature on labor market segmentation and in the current literature on insider-outsider cleavages—between industrial relations changes, labor market policy, and welfare state reforms. Here we rely on the political economy literature that has underlined the importance of "institutional complementarities" in the functioning of economic and social models. In both France and Germany, the core industrial sectors traditionally defined the "standard employment relationship" (cf. Mückenberger 1985) that established the benchmarks for other economic sectors in terms of wages and working conditions, labor contracts, and social protection. In Germany the economic model was premised on successful export firms in manufacturing (e.g., automobiles and machine tools); in France it was rooted in state-owned *champions nationaux* such as Renault and large public enterprises like EDF (electricity) or SNCF (railways) that traditionally played the role of *vitrine sociale* ("social window," i.e., providing a model for "good" social practices within companies). In both countries, the social partners from manufacturing industry, unions from the public sector, and state policies contributed to the diffusion, generalization, and institutionalization of the standards set in these contexts to cover (almost) the entire population—directly for male wage earners, and indirectly for their wives and families.

Some authors have suggested that the connections across related institutional realms operate as a stabilizing force, since would-be reformers in one area will have to consider the costs of possible "collateral damage" to complementary institutions (Pierson 2004). In the political economy literature, for example, it has been argued that employers will be loath to undertake reforms in one arena if achieving the desired effects is contingent on adjustments in all other arenas as well (Hall and Soskice 2001: Chapter 1). But most of these accounts also acknowledge the possibility of a reverse effect, essentially an unraveling, as changes in one area destabilize relations in others. This second possibility is in fact more consistent with what we observe in Germany and France. In these cases, tight coupling among institutional realms has been an important driver of change, as responses to emerging pressures in one arena created new

problems and thus inspired or indeed required reforms in adjoining policy arenas as well (see also Streeck 2009).

In this chapter, we focus on developments in France and Germany because,
despite their differences, both countries embraced a similar economic and political strategy in response to the new globalized economic context that emerged in
the 1970s. This strategy revolved around an attempt to save their core industrial
activities by reducing the size of the manufacturing workforce and increasing
its productivity, a response which, as we argue, then set in motion parallel pressures for adaptive changes in labor market and social policies. Notwithstanding
important differences in the specific policies pursued in each country and especially in the compensatory anti-poverty programs that in France in particular
have limited the effects of these trends on poverty and inequality,[3] we observe
and document developments in both countries that follow an economic and
political logic of dualization that has been progressively institutionalized in
new labor market and social policies. By logic of dualization, we mean here a
way of negotiating and elaborating policies that treat different groups differently, maintaining wherever possible traditional protections for labor market
insiders while accepting inferior status and protections for a growing number
of labor market outsiders.

In both Germany and France, early responses to the economic crisis of the
1970s and 1980s were organized around saving the core manufacturing economy,
which was the foundation for both the economic and the social model. Many
of the initial changes occurred within firms themselves, and found expression
first in the realm of industrial relations. In both countries, the productivity of
the industrial sector was increased through gradual workforce reductions and
the introduction of measures to increase internal flexibility and enhance the
efficiency of the remaining workers through intensification of work. As employers streamlined operations and outsourced less productive activities, they negotiated new kinds of company-based deals with the core workforce that traded
job security against increased productivity.

This mode of adjustment, however, robbed the core industry of its ability
to serve as lead for the rest of the economy. A side effect of these strategies of
internal labor market closure was to promote the growth of new types of jobs on
the outside, contributing to the emergence of a secondary labor market made of
(and for) various non-standard employment relationships. State policy came to
support and indeed to solidify these developments by institutionalizing these
new types of employment that operate according to different rules: more flexibility, less security. The term "atypical jobs" itself implies that different rules
apply. To the extent that such employment is considered "exceptional," even as
it grows, it is also not allowed to compete with the core sector (i.e., putting so
much pressure on it as to compromise wages and security there).

The growth of the secondary labor market, in turn, generated financial and
political pressure for the expansion of a secondary type of welfare protection.

In systems such as the German and French that are premised on segregated risk pools, financed by social contributions paid by employees and employers (payroll and not general taxes), and where eligibility for benefits is based on past contribution, the increase in (especially long-term) unemployment and in the number of jobs that are (partially) exempted from contributions was bound to undermine the financial basis of the traditional regime. This system was by definition not designed to finance the social protection of those who did not participate in the "normal" economy and contribute to the social insurance funds. Thus, welfare reforms were developed that were premised on sharpening the line between social *insurance* (for those who had paid their social contributions), and social *assistance* and in-work benefits for the growing number of workers who were excluded from the normal labor market and for whom the state was asked to take responsibility.

Each of the next three sections sketches out the major changes in these three central areas of the German and French political economies. For each domain, we provide evidence of dualization processes, and give an account of the political-coalitional dynamics that are driving them.

INDUSTRIAL RELATIONS: LOCAL "EGOISM" AND THE EROSION OF COLLECTIVE BARGAINING

Germany and France have always diverged sharply from one another in terms of the usual measures that matter for industrial relations institutions. Among other differences, German unions traditionally organized a larger share of the country's workforce (though never a majority), and they also feature a higher level of unity and centralization than their counterparts in France. Nonetheless, in both countries mechanisms were in place for much of the postwar period that provided for very high levels of collective bargaining coverage (at around 80 percent in both countries), as well as a relatively high degree of national level harmonization of working conditions and wages.

In Germany, this effect was achieved through high levels of employer organization, combined with pattern bargaining, led informally by the powerful Metalworkers Union (IG Metall). These features allowed Germany in the 1970s and even 1980s to emulate the outcomes of the "more corporatist" countries of Scandinavia (Thelen 1991: Chapter 1). In France, on the other hand, high coverage and harmonization were traditionally achieved through the lead role played by nationalized companies as well as the *procedure d'extension*—a tool allowing the state to extend sector- or national-level agreements to all firms active within the industry or the country (Lallemand 2006).

In both Germany and France, however, the usual mechanisms for achieving harmonization/standardization have been severely compromised over the last three decades, as a result of a shrinkage in the traditional "core" and an associated "inward turn" on the part of firms and sectors that once led the economy. In Germany, the decline of manufacturing employment has been accompanied by falling organization levels (among both workers and firms) and declining collective bargaining coverage.[4] Despite the shift in jobs away from industry, membership in German unions still largely reflects employment structures of the 1960s, with strongholds in manufacturing and low representation in services (Hassel 1999: 501).[5] The picture is similar on the employer side, where association membership among firms is low outside manufacturing, so that collective bargaining coverage rates in emerging sectors are well below those in industry (Hassel 1999: 495).

Major shifts in the structure of employment have also taken their toll on French unions. Employment declined in the industrial sector (from 25 percent of jobs in 1978 to 14 percent in 2006) as a result of both industrial decline and restructuring, including outsourcing jobs to the service sector (Niel and Okham 2007). But in addition, leading public companies (another union stronghold in France) were successively privatized, beginning in the mid-1980s and increasingly after 1993. In the process, some of the key "models" of socially responsible companies, such as Renault and, later, France Telecom and Gaz de France, were progressively passed on to the private sector as the state's shares declined. Unionization in France fell from 17 percent to less than 8 percent, while (as in Germany) the composition of unions remained largely the same—with membership rates three times higher in big companies (public or private) than in small ones, and two to three times higher in industry than in the service sectors (including services to industry) (DARES 2008).

As the traditional core shrank, it also turned inward in ways that compromised the ability of leading firms and sectors to continue to play their traditional role of defining the level of wages and protection for all. Already in the first oil crisis, large industrial firms in both countries had begun pursuing more conservative hiring policies organized around protecting core skilled workers. In Germany the Revised Works Constitution Act of 1972 strengthened local bargaining rights in ways that made collective dismissals more difficult and costly, while in France a similar effect was achieved through a 1974 law that required "administrative authorization for firing" (Maurin 2009: 14). In an important sense, these and subsequent legal innovations (e.g., the Auroux laws in 1983 in France) facilitated this "inward turn" by encouraging decentralized negotiations. In both countries, these developments set the scene for local labor representatives to use their powers to participate in personnel policies organized around stabilizing employment for the current workforce while accommodating market fluctuations through the use of overtime and similar measures (Sengenberger 1978; Brandt et al. 1982; Windolf and Hohn 1984; Schultz-Wild 1978).

In Germany, the last 20 years have seen a massive growth in company-level pacts for employment and competitiveness negotiated with works councils (*betriebliche Bündnisse zur Beschäftigungs- und Wettbewerbssicherung*) (Rehder 2003). While there is nothing new in local bargaining per se, the kinds of deals that have emerged since the 1990s embody a new and clearly more segmentalist logic, involving trade-offs and compromises in which managers secure cost-saving concessions on working times and some aspects of company-level pay packages in exchange for increased job security (Hassel and Rehder 2001). Two recent examples of such deals are an agreement by Daimler to guarantee the jobs of all workers at its largest German plant until 2019 in exchange for concessions on wage and working time flexibility (ABC News Associated Press, Frankfurt, December 9, 2009) and a more open-ended promise by Siemens to preserve the jobs of all 128,000 of its Germany-based employees until 2013 (Deutsche Welle, September 23, 2010).

Alongside these changes in large manufacturing firms, a divide opened up within the labor movement between unions representing workers with different skill levels and different levels of organization. These divisions were manifest, among other issues, in debates over the introduction of a statutory minimum wage. The German Food and Restaurant Workers' Union (NGG)—representing poorly organized workers with low skills—for more than a decade now has supported the introduction of minimum wage legislation (Schulten 1999), and by 2004 Germany's new (and more encompassing) United Service Sector Union (ver.di) was also in favor. However, manufacturing unions until relatively recently were more skeptical, fearing that a minimum wage would compromise bargaining autonomy and put downward pressure on wages in their sectors (Dribbusch 2004a). While organized labor is now more unified than before, proposals to introduce a statutory minimum wage still run into strong opposition from the main employer confederations, the German Employers' Association (BDA) and the Confederation of German Industries (BDI) (Dribbusch 2004a). The result of this political stalemate (in the context of declining bargaining coverage) has been the growth of what in the meantime is a very significant low-wage sector.[6]

In France, industrial downsizing and widespread privatizations across a broader range of sectors have similarly undermined trade unions' capacity to negotiate favorable deals to cover a majority of workers. In the past, unions had relied on strikes or government action to settle conflicts at the industry level and to establish a relatively high and uniform level of wages and working conditions. Now, however, "the French model of industrial relations appears increasingly oriented to outcomes that are negotiated and debated at the level of the firm rather than the sector" (Culpepper 2006: 40). Moreover, though state enterprises used to establish a model for emulation, new privatized companies operate under a different governance structure, and are centrally preoccupied with firm profitability (Goyer 2006). Concern for "public duties," for example, with regard to "social" wages, has been removed, leading large privatized firms to increase productivity by all means. In short, with privatization, the idea of channeling state social policy through its public companies has been progressively dismantled.[7]

France continues to maintain a relatively high statutory minimum wage, and this has prevented strong wage dispersion among regular full-time employees (Salverda and Mayhew 2009), which in turn helps to explain why France is performing rather better than other countries in terms of income inequalities (OECD 2008). However, as Michel Lallemand notes, the wage range has grown since the 1980s as a result of the widespread use of bonuses added to the basic wage (Lallemand 2006: 56). The compulsory minimum wage has also not impeded the emergence of a divide between workers who remained within large firms and secured favorable deals through local bargaining, and outsourced workers in smaller firms or employed under atypical working contracts, whose protection and working conditions have deteriorated.[8]

Legislation in the 1990s on working-time reduction in France further widened the gap between firms with different organization levels and different union bargaining capacities. Each law on working-time reduction (starting in 1993 with the Robien laws and ending with the Aubry II law in 2000) called for local negotiations. In large industrial firms and the public sector—where unions maintain a presence—the typical deal was to trade working-time flexibility and increased productivity for job security, while in small firms and low-skill service sectors, working arrangements and conditions have deteriorated and external flexibility has increased (Gazier and Petit 2007). Thus, while high-skill and white-collar workers were able to translate working-time reduction into much-appreciated improvements in work and life quality, lower paid and less skilled workers suffered income losses, more variable schedules, and intensified work (Hayden 2006; Méda and Orain 2002). All these trends toward decentralized bargaining were then "capped by a 2004 law on social dialogue which reinforced the autonomy of firm-level bargainers in almost every domain save wages" (Culpepper 2006: 37).

In short, in both Germany and France, industrial restructuring in the 1980s and 1990s mainly involved shoring up the competitiveness of core sectors by reducing the size of the workforce and increasing the productivity of the remaining workers. Massive use in both countries of early retirement allowed for a relatively orderly retreat, even if the departure of older workers did not—as advertised—make room for younger workers so much as it stabilized the remaining jobs, whose inhabitants were also then expected to work harder and more flexibly than before. Clearly, these trends reflect conflicts between labor and capital, but some of them have also, paradoxically, involved an intensification of cooperation between managers and workers in leading firms (in Germany especially in large manufacturing companies and in France in large enterprises, both privatized companies and also those in the remaining state sector), which, however, complicated rather than reinforced coordination at higher levels (Thelen and Kume 2006).

LABOR MARKET REFORMS: THE INSTITUTIONALIZATION OF A SECONDARY LABOR MARKET

Achieving competitiveness through increased productivity and internal flexibility made it difficult to continue to align working standards for the less skilled with those of more productive workers in the core. Government policy responded to but also solidified the new and increasing divide that was emerging in the labor market between different types of jobs. Reforms did not impose a unified flexibilization for all, and most of them did not seriously compromise the status of core workers in either country.

In Germany the safeguards protecting those in standard employment relationships include various legal stipulations and strong works council rights, as well as provisions in collective contracts that protect, especially, older workers and employees with long tenure (Ebbinghaus and Eichhorst 2007: 26). Moreover, state policy supports stable employment in the industrial core through government subsidies for short-time work (*Kurzarbeit*), which have been much more widely used in manufacturing than in other sectors.[9] Short-time work allows firms to reduce employees' working hours on a temporary basis as an alternative to layoffs. A part of the resulting lost wages is paid by the government,[10] and frequently the firm also tops this up (*Aufstockung*) (see, e.g., Vogel 2009b; Vogel 2009a; IG Metall, Baden-Württemberg 2009). The program allows employers to hold on to their most valuable skilled workers through cyclical downturns; and, for their part, labor representatives of course always prefer short-time work to the alternative of dismissals.

In France, as well, those in standard employment relationships enjoy strong protections. The Rocard government in 1988 reinstated previously long-standing protections for regular workers that had been cut two years earlier by Chirac by introducing a new requirement, the "social plan," which again extended the role of the public administration and then courts of justice in controlling economic dismissals. In 1993, this requirement was reinforced by a further law that required social plans to contain detailed provisions concerning the workers to be dismissed (Malo et al. 2000).

However, one of the consequences of the stabilization of employment in this shrinking core was to drive a general outsourcing of certain functions that were formerly performed within large companies to smaller firms that could make use of cheaper and more flexible forms of employment (see Eichhorst and Marx, Chapter 4 of this volume). These trends, along with the progressive expansion of the service sector, fueled the rise of a secondary labor market, characterized by "non-standard" work contracts and lower standards (for pay, working conditions, and social protection). Thus, alongside stable and still well-protected jobs, various forms of "atypical" employment have been on the rise in both countries. While the trade unions have been able to resist major changes in employment protection for core workers, they have experienced growing pressure to accept flexibility for other types of jobs.

In Germany, the increase in these "atypical" jobs dates back to the 1970s, but their numbers have increased steadily over the past two decades, even as their pay and benefits have declined relative to "regular" employees.[11] Reforms in the 1980s and 1990s relaxed restrictions on the use of agency workers, whose maximum terms were successively extended from three months in 1972 to 12 months by 1997 before the limit was abolished altogether in 2003. In Germany, the use of temporary workers (negotiated with works councils) now provides flexibility in key industries. Of the workforce at the Mercedes-Benz factory in Wörth, for example, almost 10 percent consists of temps; at another auto plant, the proportion is nearly one-third (29 percent) (*Der Spiegel*, December 30, 2006: 60; also Mitlacher 2007: 591–592).[12] Restrictions on fixed-term contracts were likewise eased in reforms in 1985 and 1996, so that employers can now offer contracts for up to 24 months without special justification (Ebbinghaus and Eichhorst 2007: 19–21; Dekker and Kaiser 2000: 5; Mitlacher 2007: 584–585).

However, as Eichhorst and Marx (in Chapter 4 of this volume) point out, perhaps a more important source of dualization in Germany is defection from full-time jobs, and especially an increase in so-called "mini-jobs" that have flourished in the less unionized service sector and at the service of the core sectors. Mini-jobs refer to low-level, part-time work that is not fully covered by social insurance contributions. These jobs have been around for a long time. In the past, they were occupied by students and housewives. Because the holders of these jobs enjoyed benefits through their connection to full-time male breadwinners, this type of employment was traditionally exempt from all contributions up to a threshold of earnings (in 1998 the limit was 630DM) (Silvia 2002: 14). Employees paid no payroll taxes at all, and for their part employers paid a lump-sum tax amounting to 20 percent of the worker's earnings. As non-wage labor costs grew in the 1980s and 1990s, employers found this arrangement increasingly attractive, and as a result the number of such jobs increased well beyond the originally intended clientele (Silvia 2002: 14).

Over the course of two reforms (1999 and 2002), the Red-Green government under Gerhard Schröder addressed the issue of these mini-jobs. Unions worried—with justification—that the increase in mini-jobs, deliberately chosen by employers in order to avoid social contributions, would undermine the financial stability of the insurance funds. The 1999 reform thus replaced the lump-sum tax with employer contributions into the social insurance funds, amounting to 22 percent of gross earnings (without, however, requiring matching contributions on the part of the worker).[13] A subsequent 2002 law followed the same formula of unmatched employer contributions, while promoting the growth of this type of employment by raising the threshold of earnings for mini-jobs (to a maximum €400 per month) and eliminating a previous limit of 15 hours per month. The new law also allowed mini-jobs as second jobs, something that had not been possible under the 1999 legislation.[14] While employers had criticized the 1999 reform (the switch to contributions) as overly bureaucratic, they welcomed the later changes that lifted the earnings threshold and eased other restrictions (Funk 2003). Eichhorst and Kaiser document a steady rise in the number of mini-jobs between 1999 and 2003, followed by a more rapid increase after the 2002 legislation went into effect (a rise that was particularly dramatic in the case of mini-jobs as second jobs) (Eichhorst and Kaiser 2006: 33).

The politics on the labor side were complex. Service sector unions are most directly affected by the growth of mini-jobs, since fully two-thirds of these jobs are in services, concentrated especially at the low-skill end (Eichhorst and Kaiser 2006: 17). Service sector unions therefore had sought to limit mini-jobs altogether and instead to promote regular part-time work (with full benefits, and subject to the usual matched employer-worker contributions). Manufacturing unions also feared that the use of mini-jobs would undermine standard employment contracts, but their core constituencies (skilled or semi-skilled male workers) do not typically find themselves in direct competition with mini-jobbers; core workers were therefore overall more concerned about the stability of the social insurance funds.

These concerns, as we have seen, were addressed in the 1999 reform. In the debate over this legislation, SPD spokesman Dessler argued that the shift from a tax on mini-jobs to employer contributions would bring 10 billion desperately needed DM into the strapped insurance funds. These additional resources, he noted, were "urgently needed" in order to avert another increase in social contributions on standard, full-time jobs (which otherwise would be "nearly unavoidable"); they would also be necessary to avoid a "zero round for retirees" (*Handelsblatt*, August 11, 1998). In contrast, neither the 1999 nor the 2002 reform did much to improve the situation for mini-jobbers themselves with respect to benefits. While mini-jobbers carry health insurance coverage through the public system, they are not entitled to unemployment insurance, and their pension entitlements are trivial, being tied to income on what are by definition very low earnings.[15]

In general, government policies facilitating the expansion of benefit-poor mini-jobs in services stands in rather stark contrast to other policies, like that on short-time work, that protect jobs, benefits, and skills in manufacturing.[16] The short-time work program has been (justifiably) praised (e.g., Krugman 2010), but as we have seen, it redounds largely to the benefit of the core industrial workers. Meanwhile, and as many authors have noted, Germany's efforts in the area of active labor market policies for low-skill, hard-to-employ workers have over the years been far more uneven and lackluster (e.g., Bleses and Seeleib-Kaiser 2004: Chapter 4).

The growth of mini-job employment has been substantial, increasing from about 2 million in the early 1990s to 4.7 million in 2005, and this does not include another 1.7 million mini-jobs as secondary employment (the increase in the latter coming strongly after the 2002 legislation) (Ebbinghaus and Eichhorst 2007: 22; see also Bäcker 2006; Mitlacher 2007: 585). By 2009, the number of mini-jobs had reached 7.3 million (Bosch and Weinkopf 2010: 8). Currently almost 20 percent of low-skill service sector jobs are mini-jobs (Eichhorst and Marx, Chapter 4 of this volume). As this form of employment has grown most rapidly in the service sector, there is a strong gender component to these developments. [17] And while some research has shown that certain forms of atypical employment (e.g., fixed-term contracts) can serve as a bridge to permanent jobs in Germany (Gash 2008), this is not true for mini-jobs.[18]

In France as well, the number of what became to be known as "atypical"[19] working contracts and jobs has expanded massively over the past three decades. In 1970, a-typical jobs (including fixed term, part time and agency jobs) represented just 3 percent of all employment, but by 2007 this figure had jumped to more than 25 percent. Most strikingly, perhaps, 70 percent of the new job contracts are currently "atypical" (Castel 2009: 165). Even as developments in the late 1980s and early 1990s reinforced protections for those in standard employment relationships, other reforms promoted the use of new fixed-term, temporary or agency work, and part-time contracts.

As a result of such policies, atypical work of all varieties has been on the rise. The share of agency workers in the total workforce increased from 0.6 percent in 1982 to 2.5 percent in 2001 and 2.2 percent in 2005, which translates into 585,700 such jobs (full time equivalent) (Niel and Okham 2007). On average, during the 2000s, about 10 percent of the French car industry's workforce was temporary workers (Erhel et al. 2009). Fixed-term contracts have also risen from 4.7 percent of total employment in 1985 to reach a peak of 12.5 percent in 1996 (Malo et al. 2000: 268). In 2007, such contracts represented 8.5 percent of total employment (11.1 percent for women and 6.3 percent for men) (INSEE 2008). Part-time work has also grown, from 10.9 percent of total employment in 1985, to 11.9 percent in 1990, 15.5 percent in 1995, and 16.6 percent in 1997 (Malo et al. 2000: 268). By 2007, 17.2 percent of the employed were working part-time (30.2 percent of women, and 5.7 percent of men) (INSEE 2008).[20]

In France another important source of atypical employment growth has taken place through an increase in state-subsidized jobs since the early 1980s. Starting in 1982 with *Travaux d'utilité collective,* and then *Contrats emplois solidarités,* followed in the late 1990s by the *emplois jeunes,* and then CIVIS in the early 2000s, there have been around 30 different types of these subsidized jobs (called *contrats aidés* in French). The number of subsidized fixed-term, low-paid jobs for low-skilled workers peaked in 2005 at around 500,000.

Increases in all these new forms of employment stand against virtually stagnant "standard" employment. Looking across a range of different types of atypical work, Lallemand observes:

> Between 1990 and 2000, people employed with a short-term contract grew by 60 percent, those who benefited from a training period or special contracts with public financing, by 65 percent, and temporary workers by 130 percent. During the same period, employment in "regular" jobs increased by only 2 percent. The victims of the kind of flexibility [represented by new forms of atypical work in France] are mainly found among youth, women, and groups with lower skill populations. (Lallemand 2006: 57)

As in Germany, we see in France strong resistance by unions to allow for a general flexibilization of the labor market, especially with respect to regulations governing hiring and firing, but weak defenses against the development of cheaper and more flexible jobs on the periphery through the relaxation of conditions for the use of fixed-term contracts, part-time and agency work. In a detailed analysis of what he calls "dual reforms," Davidsson analyzes the position of French employers and unions. He shows that, since the early 1980s, employers pushed for more flexibility on the French labor market, and unions resisted this general trend, while, however, accepting in "pre-negotiations" legislation that allowed more flexibility on the margins of the labor market (Davidsson 2009). For example, in negotiations over fixed-term contracts, it was "clear that the unions did not regard a softening of the regulations surrounding temporary work as a threat to the *droits acquis*" (Davidsson 2009: 6).

In 1985, when the socialist government passed two pieces of legislation on flexibility (softening the regulation on temporary work and allowing companies more flexibility on working time),[21] it secured the implicit consent of the unions for these measures in exchange for further working time reduction. In general, and as later examples analyzed by Davidsson also show, each time that flexibility and employment protection were discussed: "When the unions have had the possibility to influence reforms they have prioritized to defend the employment protection legislation for regular workers and have instead agreed on the introduction of flexibility at the margins, in the form of easing the regulations concerning temporary employment, and thereby creating a *dual reform*" (Davidsson 2009: 15).

One could argue that the increase in contingency is beneficial if it enhances mobility in the labor market and if people who start in temporary jobs end up with full-time employment. Gazier and Petit review several panel surveys to test this hypothesis and find that in France, workers in short-term work contracts actually are trapped in this situation (Gazier and Petit 2007). Meanwhile, and by way of contrast, average job tenure in the core economy has been rising slowly in France since the 1980s, reaching levels (11–12 years) similar to Germany and Sweden. "This stability suggests that more and more well protected workers stay longer in their enterprise (possibly fearing the consequences of a mobility decision), while another group of less favoured workers is trapped into a circuit and alternate unstable jobs and spells of unemployment" (Gazier and Petit 2007: 1048).

Even the policies providing for state-subsidized jobs and associated with government "insertion" efforts are seen to have contributed to reinforcing dualism on the labor market rather than reducing it (Gazier and Petit 2007: 1048). In this way, the multiplication of subsidized (but poorly paid) jobs for a specific (low-skilled) population—while clearly generating employment for significant numbers of French outsiders (mainly women and young workers of foreign origins)—has also contributed to increased segmentation of the labor market.

In sum, Ebbinghaus and Eichhorst's conclusions with respect to recent developments in German labor market policy echo French experts' conclusions on the French situation: "labour market institutions foster a *dual* labour market with high security and stability at the core and higher turnover and instability at the margin. In order to enhance labour market flexibility without threatening the stability of regular employment, gradual reforms fostered atypical employment" (Ebbinghaus and Eichhorst 2007: 11–12; Malo et al. 2000: 252). This pattern—division of labor markets (internal flexibility and work intensity but job security for the insiders, labor market flexibility and lower standards for the others)—has had important implications for welfare policy, to which we now turn.

THE DUALIZING DYNAMIC OF WELFARE REFORMS IN FRANCE AND GERMANY

In both France and Germany, responses to the economic crisis of the 1970s and 1980s created a vicious cycle in which increasing numbers of inactive workers had to be supported by fewer active workers, driving up non-wage labor costs (in both cases to over 40 percent of gross wages) and dampening job creation (Streeck and Trampusch 2005: 176; Palier 2005: 209). In this context, the social partners increasingly criticized the fact that social insurances had to pay for people who did not contribute enough (or at all) to the insurance funds (Palier 2010).

In this context, the search for solutions to stabilize the Bismarckian insurance-based model came increasingly to focus on "clarifying" the line between occupational insurance/contributory benefits and non-occupational/non-contributory benefits—with the idea that the state should take more responsibility for the latter. The result has been to increase the role of residual, income-tested, and in-work benefits for some, with continued contributory benefits (albeit lower) for insiders that can be supplemented through collective bargaining or firm-level deals (Trampusch 2007; Palier 2010). Thus, while those with full-time permanent jobs continue to be insured, more people must now rely on other types of social protection than typical social insurance. These flat-rate assistance benefits, usually financed by taxation and run by the state, are targeted to the excluded. We deal first with the changes in France, since that is where developments in this field started earliest.

The period between winter 1982 and spring 1984 was one of intense public conflict over unemployment insurance in France. But it was also a period during which an implicit compromise was being negotiated between the unions, employers, and the government over a way of adapting policy to an emergent preoccupation with fiscal austerity. This compromise respected the Bismarckian heritage of UNEDIC (unemployment insurance managed by the social partners), but reinterpreted it in a manner compatible with cost containment, if not—initially—retrenchment. The idea was to better distinguish between the sphere of insurance (benefits financed through social contributions and managed by UNEDIC) and the sphere of "solidarity" (benefits financed through taxes and managed by the state). An agreement signed by the social partners on February 24, 1984, excluded those with the shortest contribution records from any entitlement to unemployment insurance benefits.

The restriction, and then retrenchment, of unemployment insurance was negotiated in exchange for the state taking over responsibility for benefits that had previously been financed out of social contributions and managed by UNEDIC. The creation of state-managed, tax-financed unemployment assistance benefits—the *allocation spécifique de solidarité* (ASS) for the long-term unemployed, and the *allocation d'insertion* (AI) for labor-market entrants—was the explicit compensatory measure agreed by the then socialist Minister of Finance Pierre Bérégovoy in the protocol agreement of January 1984, a concession that allowed the social partners to arrive, one month later, at an acceptable compromise over the reform of unemployment insurance (Clegg and Palier 2007).

Due in part to these reforms, the proportion of "excluded people" increased, becoming one of the most pressing social issues of the late 1980s. In order to cope with new social problems that social insurance was unwilling and unable to deal with, governments have been developing new policies named "insertion policies" (Palier 2005: Chapter 6), the most important of which is the RMI (*revenu minimum d'insertion*). This non-contributory scheme, meant for persons with no or very low income (in some cases having exhausted their right to unemployment insurance) guarantees a minimum level of income-tested differential benefits to anyone aged 25 or over. Recipients must, in exchange, commit to participate in some "reinsertion" program, which can involve intensified searching for employment, undertaking vocational training, or participating in activities designed to enhance the recipient's social autonomy.

When it was created, this new benefit was supposed to be delivered to 300,000–400,000 people. However, by March 2009, 1.13 million persons were receiving RMI (with a peak in 2006 at 1.3 million—i.e., fully 3 percent of the French active population) (DREES 2009: 1). Besides RMI, France now has eight other social minimum income benefit programs. More than 10 percent of the French population is currently receiving one of these (Palier 2005: Chapter 6). Thus, through the development of new social policies and minimum income benefits, part of the French social protection system is now targeting specific populations and using new instruments (income-tested benefits delivered according to need, financed through state taxation and managed by national and local public authorities), and relying on a new logic (to combat social exclusion instead of guarantee income and status maintenance).

The creation of these assistance schemes eased cuts in the unemployment insurance system itself. Each time retrenchments in unemployment insurance were introduced, more people were shifted from insurance benefits to social assistance. Exemplary of this trend is the 1992 unemployment insurance reform, which was accomplished through an agreement between one trade union (CFDT) and the employers' association. The reform replaced all previous unemployment insurance benefits with a new one, the *allocation unique dégressive* (AUD), with benefits paid only for a limited duration and with support levels declining over time according to a mechanism called "degressivity."[22] Once an unemployed person's insurance benefits expire entirely (after 30 months), he or she must rely on tax-financed income-tested benefits. As AUD was delivering smaller benefits for a shorter period, the minimum income benefits increasingly functioned as a safety net for the long-term unemployed.

Overall, this whole "clarification" process has reinforced the distinction between workers who are still linked to the core labor market (even if temporarily unemployed) and those who are moving away from it, for whom assistance and in-work benefits have been created. In order to improve the incentives to go back to the labor market, the Jospin government in 2001 created a tax credit, called *prime à l'emploi*, which is a negative income tax for low-paid jobs (in-work benefits). With that, a totally new rhetoric (unemployment trap, work disincentive) and a new type of social policy instrument (working family tax credit) have been imported into the world of poverty alleviation in France. In the same vein, in 2003, the Raffarin government wanted to increase incentives to work by transforming the RMI into RMA (*revenu minimum d'activité*) for those having benefited from RMI for two years.[23] Since June 2009, a new scheme, called *revenu de solidarité active* (which combines a social minimum and a supplementary income given to those entering subsidized low-skill, low-paid jobs), is replacing RMI.

The development of the many French social minima guarantees that nobody can be left without any support. The new *revenu de solidarité active* (RSA) is even promising a better situation for those who accept some activity, providing social contribution exemptions to employers hiring RSA beneficiaries or long-term unemployed, and guaranteeing a negative income tax to the new low-wage workers so that they get at least €200 more than what the RMI would have provided. The expansion of the basic safety net has provided some check on the growth of poverty in France, but this did not prevent the increasing bifurcation in the logic of the old and new systems of social protection. The fight against poverty has been devoted to specific social benefits, different from the typical social insurance ones, and in this sense is consistent with the overall trend toward the dualization of the French welfare system.[24]

As in France, expanding social expenditure appeared increasingly untenable in Germany in the 1990s, due in large part to the staggering costs of supporting the early retired and the unemployed (particularly in the East). The Red-Green government's solutions to these problems mirrored those adopted in France, redrawing and sharpening the line between those who will be supported by insurance funds and on a contributory basis, and the growing number of citizens who slip outside this system and into state-financed, income-tested assistance. As the head of the Federal Chancellery (and Minister in Charge of Special Tasks) under the first Schröder government put it, "social assistance should be concentrated on the neediest, and the line between contribution- and tax-based benefits should be drawn more sharply" (*Frankfurter Allgemeine Zeitung*, November 9, 1998).

The most comprehensive measures in this direction were undertaken in the so-called Hartz reforms, of which Hartz IV is the most directly relevant in this context. Before Hartz IV, there were three levels of assistance: unemployment insurance (benefits related to earnings), unemployment assistance (lower benefits but still earnings-related) and social assistance (means-tested). The Hartz reforms brought two important changes: one was to reduce the duration of unemployment insurance (for older workers, from previous 32 months to 18 months,[25] for other workers down to 12 months); the second was to do away with the middle tier of unemployment assistance altogether and instead merge this with social assistance (geared not toward status/income maintenance but basic poverty alleviation). The merging of unemployment assistance and social assistance produced a new benefit type—the so-called unemployment benefit II, *Arbeitslosengeld* II (ALG II), which is designed for those of employable age who are "able to work" (and therefore also obliged to seek employment). The logic of ALG II is distinct from the system of unemployment insurance (ALG I) that continues to cover workers with sufficient contributions, at least through shorter bouts of unemployment.[26]

The politics surrounding Hartz IV were complicated, and they played into the divisions that previous developments in industrial relations and labor market policy had generated. The strong employment protections for core workers cited above meant that workers in large firms (typically with strong works councils) were less likely to become unemployed in the first place, and skilled workers (particularly in the West) are highly unlikely to stay unemployed for more than a year. While manufacturing unions like the metalworkers took a vocal position against the Hartz legislation as it worked its way through the parliamentary committees, some evidence suggests that they were motivated to maintain unemployment support of long duration in large part because this had traditionally provided the "bridge" to full pensions on which early retirement agreements with employers rested.[27] In fact, the union confederation representative who was directly involved in a government reform commission at this time was herself "publicly critical of the tendency of the manufacturing unions to protect insiders" (Hassel and Schiller 2009: 19).[28] Low-skill workers and service sector unions like ver.di, by contrast, were justifiably concerned both about the activation rules and associated wage effects, since ALG II recipients have to accept any legal job they are offered, whether or not it is covered by a collective bargain (Dribbusch 2004b).

There is also a strong regional dimension to the impact of Hartz IV, since the hardships it imposed were far more likely to be borne by workers in the East, where long-term unemployment is a much bigger problem than in the West. Before the law took effect, there had been some protest in the West, but once the cuts to long-term unemployment assistance were being implemented, the demonstrations were almost exclusively concentrated in the East. When letters went out in July 2004 to all unemployment assistance recipients, to assess their eligibility for benefits under Hartz IV, this triggered weekly protests that ran through August. But the vast majority of these "Monday demonstrations" (harking back to the Monday demonstrations that had precipitated the fall of the communist regime) took place in the East.[29]

Moreover, on the financing side, Hartz IV shores up the traditional model by preserving a social insurance logic for core constituencies, while for others less tightly linked to the labor market "social benefits break with the principle of status-protection and turn more and more into a basic protection regime" (Eichhorst and Kaiser 2006: 22). Summarizing the overall trend since the 1970s, Bleses and Seeleib-Kaiser note that changes to unemployment benefits "primarily affected those workers with relatively short contributory periods and the long term unemployed" (Bleses and Seeleib-Kaiser 2004: 66–67). The Hartz reforms represent a culmination of these developments, moving Germany toward a system organized more around poverty reduction (with activation) rather than income/status maintenance for labor-market "outsiders." The new model features financing that shifts the unemployed (especially those with shorter and/or spottier contribution records) more quickly into the category of social assistance and that relies on taxation to support the (non-contributing) working poor. Such changes helped to make it possible to reduce contributions for regular workers (and their employers) from 6.5 percent to 4.2 percent in 2007 and further, to 3.3 percent by 2008 (Hinrichs 2010: 63).

As in France, then, recent reforms in Germany preserve a social insurance logic for core constituencies even as they recognize that the days are over when benefits to male breadwinners in manufacturing will suffice to cover all. Subsequent proposals to revise Hartz IV do not attack the core logic that separates contributory social insurance from income-tested social assistance. They focus, rather, on (re-)extending insurance coverage to reincorporate long-time contributing "standard" workers. Thus, in December 2007, the Grand Coalition government amended the unemployment rules to allow unemployed persons over the age of 50 to draw regular unemployment benefits for 15 (rather than 12) months, for 55+ year olds, for 18 months, and for 58+ for two years (Dribbusch 2008).

In sum, recent developments in both France and Germany have increased the "contributivity" of the benefits, that is, they have strengthened the link between the amount of contribution and the volume of the benefits (through a change in the calculation formula and/or stricter entitlement rules). In both cases, these changes have been framed as part of a *quid pro quo* (Bonoli 1997)—one that is based on the distinction between what should remain in the world of occupational social protection (and be financed through contributions) and what should be distinguished as a new world of social protection, aimed at those with an atypical employment situations (and financed through taxation). Retrenchment in social insurance programs thus reinforces dualization to the extent that it is accompanied by a clarification of responsibility and a shift in funding as part of the welfare system has come to rely more heavily on taxation to support the (non-contributing) working poor.

CONCLUSION

By tracing the interrelated changes in industrial relations, labor market policy, and welfare reforms in Germany and France, we have documented a process of dualization. Both countries appear to have progressively built a new (less egalitarian but possibly quite robust) equilibrium in order to adapt their political economies to the rise of the service sector and a new, more competitive, international economic context. Recent developments and reforms across all three arenas have mostly spared the core workforce in the ways we have described above, even as they have involved some redistribution among the lowest income groups—redounding to the disadvantage of low-wage workers but in some respects also benefiting some of the most marginal segments of society.

In each of the realms we have analyzed—industrial relations, labor market policy, social protection—the changes we observe have mostly been gradual and were often undertaken in the name of stability, billed as necessary adjustments to preserve core economic activities and the existing institutions around them. What has disappeared, though, is the capacity of the model to be encompassing and to cover all citizens under one type of work contract and social protection. In both countries, the industrial relations system has seen a gradual erosion that has proceeded not so much through rupture or even a full frontal attack by employers, but, in fact, partly through the effects on the periphery of cooperation between labor and management in a still-solid core with its center, in Germany, in large manufacturing companies, and in France, in large manufacturing and large high-skill service sector firms. Related to this, labor market reforms have generally promoted developments in which the status and privileges of labor market insiders remain relatively well protected, with the flexibility necessary to stabilize the core being achieved at the expense of a growing number of workers in "atypical" or "non-standard" employment relationships. Welfare reforms are also characterized by a gradual dualization, with a sharper line being drawn between occupational insurance/contributory benefits for core workers and a world of assistance and in-work/non-contributory benefits for a growing number of labor market outsiders.

NOTES

1 This chapter is a revised and abridged version of a longer article that appeared in *Politics & Society*, volume 38, number 1 (March 2010), 119–148. We thank the journal for permission to reprint it here. Thanks also go to Martin Seeleib-Kaiser, Patrick Emmenegger, Werner Eichhorst, and Paul Marx for their very helpful comments.

2 The previous apparent universalism of continental CMEs—it now seems clear—was premised on the now-absent capacities of the system to generate full employment (Palier and Martin 2007; Martin and Thelen 2007).

3 On the role of the French minimum wage, see Salverda and Mayhew 2009. On the difference in inequalities between France and Germany, see, in this volume, Chapter 2 by Häusermann and Schwander, Chapter 4 by Eichhorst and Marx, and Chapter 5 by Kroos and Gottschall.

4 According to the OECD, union density rates (once as high as 35 percent) have fallen steadily, from 25.3 percent in 1999 to 19.1 percent by 2008 (OECD Statistical Extracts, December 2010). These are national level figures; union organization is considerably weaker in the East than in the West.

5 In 1981, 58 percent of union members were blue-collar workers, and in 2002 the percentage was still over half (51.1 percent). The share of white-collar members has been rising (from 24.2 percent in 1981 to 32.5 percent by 2002), but this lags behind employment growth in those sectors (Addison et al. 2007: 9).

6 In 2007 the Grand Coalition government did create two mechanisms for implementing *industry-specific* minimum wages, but these options have not been taken up on a broad scale, so the number of workers affected remains rather small (Bosch and Weinkopf 2010).

7 The text presenting the law of July 2, 1986, explicitly freed the privatized companies to adapt to the new competitive environment as they saw fit (including, of course, through job reductions and outsourcing) (*Loi 86–793 du 02 Juillet 1986, autorisant le Gouvernement à prendre diverses mesures d'ordre économique et social.* 1986).

8 Much of this occurs through outsourcing. As INSEE shows, the share of services bought by firms multiplied by 2.5 between 1959 and 2006, to become the fourth largest category of intermediary expenditure (Niel and Okham 2007).

9 The top five industries making use of short-time work in the last recession were all in metalworking broadly defined (Bundesagentur für Arbeit 2009: 12).

10 The government reimburses 60 percent of the lost wages (net of taxes), 67 percent for employees with children.

11 Eichhorst and Marx (this volume) provide a breakdown of the relative magnitude of different types of atypical jobs in both Germany and France. For Germany specifically, Peter Bleses and Martin Seeleib-Kaiser note that "in the early 1970s the relationship between regular employment and atypical work was 5:1, by the mid-1980s the relationship had dropped to 3:1, and by the mid-1990s it had reached a level of 2:1" (Bleses and Seeleib-Kaiser 2004: 33).

12 Temporary agency workers are more concentrated in manufacturing than in services in Germany (34.8 percent of temps work in manufacturing, as against 15.5 percent in services) (Mitlacher 2007: 582).

13 In the meantime, employers pay a lump sum of 30 percent of gross wages (up from 25 percent since 2006) that goes to health insurance contributions and pension contributions (Ebbinghaus and Eichhorst 2007: 21). The lack of employee contributions and favorable tax treatment, however, keeps the overall costs of these jobs for employers low compared to regular part-time employment (Neubäumer 2007: 6).

14 Earnings between €400–800 are subject to reduced contributions on a progressive scale rising to regular levels (Neubäumer and Tretter 2008).

15 Mini-jobbers can supplement this with individual pension contributions but of course, given the low wages, few are actually in a position to do this.

16 Indeed, new and more generous regulations on Kurzarbeit were put in place to cope with the recent economic recession (Vogel, June 15, 2009).

17 About two-thirds of mini-jobs (64 percent) are held by women (Eichhorst and Kaiser 2006: 17).

18 Bäcker's analysis suggests that women in mini-jobs are mostly "shunted into the traditional role of supplementing family income" (Bäcker 2006: 259).

19 The term "atypical working contract" refers to working contracts different from full-time open-ended working contracts.

20 See Eichhorst and Marx (Chapter 4 of this volume) for a breakdown and comparison to Germany on the relative proportion of workers in each category of atypical employment. In general, they argue that in France fixed-term employment is a bigger part of the "dualization" story, while in Germany the key issue is the mini-jobs, as discussed above.

21 On temporary work: the duration of fixed-term contracts was extended from 6 or 12 months to 24 months for the long-term unemployed; on working time: the new provisions allowed working times to be averaged on a yearly rather than a weekly basis for companies that adopted a 38-hour work week.

22 The AUD increased the minimum contribution period required for access to any unemployment insurance benefit from 3 to 4 months in the last 8 months. It also sharply reduced the duration of benefit entitlements for those with only 6 months of contributions in the last year, from 15 months of benefits for persons under 50 years old (21 months for those over 50) to only 7 months (for unemployed of all ages) (Clegg and Palier 2007).

23 This would have provided social contribution exemptions to employers who hired people under RMA and also guaranteed state income supplements to the RMA employee. However, this did not work, since firms by and large declined to hire people under RMA.

24 For the dualization of health care and pension systems, see Seeleib-Kaiser et al., Chapter 7 of this volume.

25 Since 2007, back up to 24 months; see below.

26 ALG II allows other types of in-work benefits (e.g., the mini-jobs discussed above), so that already by October 2006, about 1.2 million persons combined ALG II with income from waged work—an increase of 500,000 compared to early 2005.

27 Hassel and Schiller note that extended periods of unemployment based on earnings-related benefits were centrally important to early retirement strategies, with long benefits (often topped up by employers) carrying them to retirement (Hassel and Schiller 2009: 15–16, 18). And Hinrichs notes that, despite measures in the late 1990s discouraging the use of early retirement, the reversal in this practice did not really set in until 2000 (Hinrichs 2010), largely as a result of the pension reforms in the 1990s. In fact, some unions were still calling for retirement at 60 as late as 1999 (Streeck and Trampusch 2005: 181).

28 Hassel and Schiller argue, however, that the weight of the fiscal crisis pushed the government to undertake reforms that went well beyond what these unions would have preferred, cutting also into the interests of their core constituencies by in fact drastically limiting the duration of earnings-related unemployment benefits.

29 Compare the numbers: 20,000–30,000 showed up in Leipzig, 15,000 in Magdeburg, 5,000 in Rostock, and only 1,200 in Dortmund. On the demonstrations, see Dribbusch 2004b: 51–54 and Rucht and Yang 2004.

REFERENCES

Addison, John T., Schnabel, Claus, and Wagner, Joachim (2007). "The (Parlous) State of German Unions," *Journal of Labor Research*, XXVIII(1), Winter 2007: 3–18.

Bäcker, Gerhard (2006). "Was heisst hier geringfügig? Minijobs als wachsendes Segment prekärer Beschäftigung," *WSI Mitteilungen*. 56(5): 255–261.

Berger, Suzanne, and Piore, Michael (1980). *Dualism and Discontinuity*, Cambridge: Cambridge University Press.

Bleses, Peter, and Seeleib-Kaiser, Martin (2004). *The Dual Transformation of the German Welfare State*, New York: Palgrave.

Bonoli, Giuliano (1997). "Pension Politics in France: Patterns of Co-operation and Conflict in Two Recent Reforms," *West European Politics* 20, 4: 160–181.

Bosch, Gerhard, and Weinkopf, Claudia (2010). "National Report Germany," in *EC Project: Minimum Wage Systems and Changing Industrial Relations in Europe*, Duisburg-Essen: University Duisburg-Essen, pp. 1–44.

Brandt, Gerhard, Jacobi, Otto, and Müller-Jentsch, Walther (1982). *Anpassung an der Krise: Gewerkschaften in den siebziger Jahren*, Frankfurt: Campus.

Bundesagentur für Arbeit (2009). "Arbeitsmarktberichterstattung. Der Arbeitsmarkt in Deutschland, Kurzarbeit," Bundesagentur für Arbeit (ed.) Nürnberg: Bundesagentur für Arbeit.

Castel, Robert (2009). *La montée des incertitudes,* Paris: Seuil.

Clegg, Daniel, and Palier, Bruno (2007). "From Labour Shedding to Labour Mobilisation: The Staggered Transformation of French Labour Market Policy,'paper presented at the *Annual Meeting of the American Political Science Association*. Chicago, Illinois, August 30 to September 2, 2007.

Culpepper, Pepper (2006). "Capitalism, Coordination and Economic Change," in Culpepper, Pepper, Hall, Peter, and Palier, Bruno (eds.), *Changing France: The Politics That Markets Make*, London: Palgrave, pp. 29–49.

DARES (2008). "Le paradoxe du syndicalisme français," in *Premières syntheses*, Paris: Ministère des Affaires sociales.

Davidsson, Johan Bo (2009). "The Politics of Employment Policy in Europe: Two Patterns of Reform," in *ECPR Conference*, April 14–19, 2009: Lisbon.

Dekker, Ronald, and Kaiser, Lutz C. (2000). "Atypical or Flexible: How to Define Non-Standard Employment Patterns: The Cases of Germany, the Netherlands, and the United Kingdom," Tilburg, The Netherlands: Tilburg Institute for Social Security Research and German Institute for Economic Research.

DREES (2009). "Le nombre d'allocataires du RMI." *Etudes et Résultats*, N° 693, June. Paris: Ministry of Social Affairs.

Dribbusch, Heiner (2004a). "Debate on Introduction of Statutory Minimum Wage." Online. *EIROnline*, 2004/09 (accessed September 22, 2004).

Dribbusch, Heiner (2004b). "Major Protests Against Cuts in Unemployment Assistance." Online. *EIROnline*, 2004/09 (accessed September 6, 2004).

Dribbusch, Heiner (2008). "Germany: Industrial Relations Developments in Europe 2007." Online. *EIROnline* (accessed September 23, 2008).

Ebbinghaus, Bernhard, and Eichhorst, Werner (2007). "Distribution of Responsibility for Social Security and Labour Market Policy, Country Report: Germany," in *Amsterdam Institute for Advanced Labour Studies Working Paper*, University of Amsterdam, 07/52.

Edwards, Richard, Reich, Michael, and Gordon, David M. (1982). *Segmented Work, Divided Workers*, New York: Cambridge University Press.

Eichhorst, Werner, and Kaiser, Lutz C. (2006). "The German Labor Market: Still Adjusting Badly?" in IZA Discussion Paper No. 2215, *Forschungsinstitut zur Zukunft der Arbeit*.

Erhel, Christine, Lefevre, Gilbert, and Michon, François (2009). "L'intérim: Un secteur dual, entre protection et précarité," in Caroli, Eve, and Gautié, Jérôme (eds.) *Bas salaires et qualité de l'emploi: l'Exception Française?*, Paris: CEPREMAP, Editions Rue D'Ulm, pp. 455–506.

Funk, Lothar (2003). "New Legislation Promotes 'Minor Jobs: *EIROnline*, March 6, 2003.

Gash, Vanessa (2008). "Bridge or Trap? Temporary Workers' Transitions to Unemployment and to the Standard Employment Contract," *European Sociological Review* 24(5): 651–668.

Gazier, Bernard, and Petit, Héloïse (2007). "French Labour Market Segmentation and French Labour Market Policies since the Seventies: Connecting Changes," *Socio-Économie du travail, Économies et Sociétés AB* 28: 1027–1055.

Glyn, Andrew (2006). *Capitalism Unleashed: Finance Globalization and Welfare*, Oxford: Oxford University Press.

Goyer, Michel (2006). "The Transformation of Corporate Governance in France," in Culpepper, Pepper, Hall, Peter, and Palier, Bruno (eds.), *Changing France, The Politics That Markets Make*, London: Palgrave, pp. 80–104.

Hall, Peter A., and Soskice, David (eds.) (2001). *Varieties of Capitalism: The Institutional Foundations of Comparative Advantage*, New York: Oxford University Press.

Hassel, Anke (1999). "The Erosion of the German System of Industrial Relations," *British Journal of Industrial Relations* 37(3): 484–505.

Hassel, Anke, and Rehder, Britta (2001). "Institutional Change in the German Wage Bargaining System: The Role of Big Companies," in *MPIfG Working Paper*, December 2001 01/9.

Hassel, Anke, and Schiller, Christof (2009). "Bringing the State Back In: The Role of Fiscal Federalism for Welfare Restructuring," in *Society for the Advancement of Socio-Economics Conference*, July 16–18, 2009, Paris.

Hayden, Anders (2006). "France's 35-hour Week: Attack on Business? Win-Win Reform? Or Betrayal of Disadvantaged Workers?" *Politics & Society* 34(4): 503–542.

Hinrichs, Karl (2010). "A Social Insurance State Withers Away. Welfare State Reforms in Germany—or: Attempts to Turn Around in a Cul de sac," in Palier, Bruno (ed.), *A Long Goodbye to Bismarck?* Amsterdam: Amsterdam University Press, pp. 45–72.

Howell, Chris (2006). "Varieties of Capitalism: And Then There Was One?" *Comparative Politics* 36(1): 103–124.

IG Metall, Baden-Württemberg (2009). "IG Metall Pressedienst 11/09," Stuttgart: Pressestelle der IG Metall Baden-Württemberg.

INSEE (2008). "Une photographie du marché du travail en 2007, résultats de l'enquête emploi' Institut national de la statistique et des etudes économiques," *INSEE première*, 1206.

Krugman, Paul (2010). "The Conscience of a Liberal," *New York Times*, September 2, 2010.

Lallemand, Michel (2006). "New Patterns of Industrial Relations and Political Action since the 1980s," in Culpepper, Pepper, Hall, Peter, and Palier, Bruno (eds) *Changing France, The Politics That Markets Make*, London: Palgrave, pp. 50–79.

Loi 86–793 du 02 Juillet 1986, autorisant le Gouvernement à prendre diverses mesures d'ordre économique et social, 02 Juillet 1986.

Malo, Miguel, Toharia, Luis and J. Gautié (2000). "France: The Deregulation That Never Existed," in Esping-Andersen, Gøsta, and Regini, Marino (eds.), *Why Deregulate Labour Markets?* Oxford: Oxford University Press, pp. 245–270.

Martin, Cathie Jo, and Thelen, Kathleen (2007). "The State and Coordinated Capitalism: Contributions of the Public Sector to Social Solidarity in Post-Industrial Societies," *World Politics*, 60, October 2007: 1–36.

Maurin, Eric (2009). *La peur du déclassement*, Paris: Seuil.

Méda, Dominique, and Orain, Renaud (2002). "Transformation du travail et du hors-travail: le jugement des salariés sur la réduction du temps de travail," *Travail et emploi* N° 90, April, pp. 23–38.

Mitlacher, Lars W. (2007). "The Role of Temporary Agency Work in Different Industrial Relations Systems," *British Journal of Industrial Relations* 45(3) September 2007: 581–606.

Mückenberger, Ulrich (1985). "Die Krise des Normalarbeitsverhältnisses: Hat das Arbeitsrecht noch eine Zukunft?" *Zeitschrift für Sozialreform*. 415–434; 457–475.

Neubäumer, Renate (2007). "Mehr Beschäftigung durch weniger Kündigungs-schutz?" *Wirtschaftsdienst* 3: 1–8.

Neubäumer, Renate, and Tretter, Dominik (2008). "Mehr atypische Beschäftigung aus Theoretischer Sicht," *Industrielle Beziehungen* 15 (3): 256–278.

Niel, Xavier, and Mustapha Okham (2007). "Les ressorts de l'économie des ser-vices: dynamique propre et externalisation," *INSEE Premières* 1163, November 2007.

OECD (2008) *Growing Unequal? Income Distribution and Poverty in OECD Countries*, Paris: OECD.

Palier, Bruno (2005). *Gouverner la Sécurité sociale*, Paris: PUF.

Palier, Bruno (2010). *A Long Goodbye to Bismarck? The Politics of Welfare Reforms in Continental Europe*, Amsterdam: Amsterdam University Press.

Palier, Bruno, and Martin, Claude (2007). "Reforming the Bismarckian Welfare Systems," *Social Policy and Administration* 41 (6 Special Issue).

Pierson, Paul (2004). *Politics in Time: History, Institutions, and Political Analysis*, Princeton, NJ: Princeton University Press.

Rehder, Britta (2003). *Betriebliche Bündnisse für Arbeit in Deutschland. Mitbestimmung und Flächentarif im Wandel*, Frankfurt am Main: Campus.

Rucht, Dieter, and Mundo Yang (2004). "Wer demonstrierte gegen Hartz IV?" *WZB-Mitteilungen* 106 (December 2004): 51–54.

Salverda, Wiemer, and Mayhew, Ken (2009). "Capitalist Economies and Wage Inequality," *Oxford Review of Economic Policy* 25(1): 126–154.

Schulten, Torsten (1999). "Union Demands Statutory Minimum Wage," Online. *EIROnline (1999/11) (accessed November 28, 1999)*.

Schultz-Wild, Rainer (1978). *Betriebliche Beschäftigungspolitik in der Krise*, Frankfurt: Campus.

Sengenberger, Werner (1978). *Der gespaltene Arbeitsmarkt Probleme der Arbeitsmarktsegmentation*, Frankfurt: Campus.

Silvia, Stephen (2002). "The Rise and Fall of Unemployment in Germany," *German Politics* 11(1): 14.

Streeck, Wolfgang (2009). *Re-Forming Capitalism*, Oxford: Oxford University Press.

Streeck, Wolfgang, and Christine Trampusch (2005). "Economic Reform and the Political Economy of the German Welfare State," *German Politics* 14(2): 174–195.

Thelen, Kathleen (1991). *Union of Parts: Labor Politics in Postwar Germany*. Ithaca, NY: Cornell University Press.

Thelen, Kathleen, and Ikuo Kume (2006). "Coordination as a Political Problem in Coordinated Market Economies," *Governance* 19(1): 11–42.

Trampusch, Christine (2007). "Industrial Relations as a Source of Social Policy: A Typology of the Institutional Conditions for Industrial Agreements on Social Benefits," *Social Policy and Administration* 41(3): 251–270.

Vogel, Sandra (2009a). "New Collective Agreement in Metalworking Sector,' *EIROnline*, June 15, 2009.

Vogel, Sandra (2009b). "New Allowances for Short-Time Work in Bid to Offset Economic Crisis,"*EIROnline,*June 15, 2009.

Windolf, Paul, and Hohn, Hans-Willy. 1984. *Arbeitsmarktchancen in der Krise*, Frankfurt: Campus.

10

ECONOMIC DUALIZATION IN JAPAN AND SOUTH KOREA

ITO PENG

INTRODUCTION

After World War II, the two East Asian developmental states of Japan and South Korea (hereafter Korea) shared similar economic development strategies based on state-led industrial development and the investment of political and fiscal capital in core export industries.[1] This privileged a core group of workers, mainly male industrial workers in large companies. These employees enjoyed employment security, high wages, and generous company welfare, making them the first workers to receive health, pension, and other occupationally based social insurance coverage in the fledgling Japanese and Korean welfare states. Even though social insurance systems in both countries were eventually expanded to cover the main social risks in the population at large, the social insurance coverage of this core group of industrial workers is still more generous and comprehensive than that of workers in peripheral sectors, those working in small and medium size enterprises (SMEs), or non-standard employees.

From the beginning, the postwar labor markets in Japan and Korea were fundamentally dualistic. Nevertheless, until the 1990s, the two countries were able to—at least partially—shield their populations from the economic inequalities that derive from labor market dualization. For one thing, both were able to sustain high levels of economic growth, with near full male employment, largely due to their demographically young populations and their successful export-led industrial strategies. In addition, wage differentials between managers and blue-collar industrial workers were relatively low compared to Europe and North America, thus minimizing income disparity. This scenario began to change in the mid- to late 1980s; like some countries in Continental Europe, in Japan and Korea, the labor market dualization deepened as a result of changes in the global economic structure. Since then, gaps between the core and the periphery have become more evident, and this has proceeded alongside partial economic liberalization. The shrinking of the core and the expansion of the periphery are illustrated by the decline of standard employment and the expansion of non-standard employment,[2] as well as the weakening of labor unions' position in relation to wage setting and employment protection. The results are increased labor market insecurity and compensatory state responses in the form of welfare state expansion. These changes were mediated by corresponding changes in industrial relations, and labor market and welfare state reforms.

Of course, Japan and Korea are valuable cases for study in and of themselves, but an examination of their situation stands to further our understanding of labor market dualization in Europe. First, despite their different histories of development, Japan and Korea's experiences of labor market dualization processes are very similar to those of their European counterparts, such as Germany and France. Second, in Japan and Korea, as in Germany and France, the pattern of industrial relations, based on interactions between the state, the employers, and labor, has precluded wholesale economic liberalization, despite significant pressure from countries like the United States in the form of bilateral and multilateral trade negotiations. Rather, like their Continental European counterparts, both countries have opted to maintain their national competitiveness by saving large firms by, on the one hand, reducing the size of the core workforce and raising worker productivity, and on the other, increasing the hiring of non-standard workers (see Palier and Thelen, Chapter 9 of this volume, for discussions on Germany and France). As a result, they have witnessed the contraction and consolidation of the core, and the expansion of the peripheral labor market—in other words, the intensification of the preexisting labor market divide between insiders and outsiders. These similarities provide important evidence that the process of labor market dualization is not confined to Europe but is a pervasive global phenomenon.

However, it is also important to point out that the underlying institutional structures and contexts of Japan and Korea are significantly different from many of their Continental European counterparts. Japan and Korea share similar familialistic and developmental state underpinnings, in which the state plays a dominant role in coordinating economic and industrial development, and a negligible role in social welfare (Japan's social spending to GDP in 2008 is only about 19 percent whereas Korea spends about 7.5 percent) (Goodman and Peng 1996; Holiday 2000). This means that in both countries, the basic form of social security protection has been employment and familial mutual support. As such, until recently, industrial relations took on a paternalistic form, with tendencies toward strong employment and wage protection for male breadwinners, enterprise-based unions, and a strong bias against women. The state-led economic development model was also premised on a highly familial care regime that relied on women to provide almost all care and welfare within the household in an uncommodified form (Esping-Andersen 1999; Peng 2009). Ironically, this latter institutional underpinning is contributing to the process of fertility decline and rapid population aging, thus exerting huge pressure on the state to expand social welfare (Peng 2004, 2009).

Nor are the two countries totally alike. First, Japan has a comparatively longer modernization and industrialization history compared to Korea. Having started its modernization process in the late 1900s, Japan was already well industrialized by the 1970s, when Korea's industrialization began to accelerate. By the end of the 1980s, the Japanese economy had moved beyond the industrialization phase and had moved into a low-growth period, whereas Korea's economic growth peaked in the 1980s and the 1990s. By the early 1990s, the Japanese economy had begun to stagnate, while the Korean economy continued to grow. Similarly, while Japan democratized immediately after the end of World War II, Korea's democratic political history has been much shorter, starting in 1987. Having played a central role in the democratization movement, labor in Korea is significantly more militant politically than in Japan. These time lag in Japan and South Korea's developmental trajectories have, in turn, contributed to different political economic processes above and beyond the differences resulting from social and cultural factors.

Moreover, although both are relatively small welfare states, suggesting that they have more fiscal and policy spaces for enlargement than many European welfare states, Korea's relatively later economic development and its noticeably smaller welfare state (even compared to Japan) means that Korea is, arguably, more able to engage in welfare state expansion. Indeed, what is interesting about the Japanese and Korean cases is that, as in many European countries, the reorganization of the labor market since the 1990s has entailed a significant rearticulation of the state's role vis-à-vis social policy; but, unlike most European welfare states, this has resulted in net welfare state expansion, particularly in the areas of unemployment insurance and social care, with the Korean welfare state expanding at a strikingly rapid pace. Simply stated, these divergent outcomes are the result of different political choices made in different structural contexts. More importantly, they underscore distinct dualization trajectories that derive from differences in contexts and policy responses.

This chapter will examine the processes of labor market dualization in Japan and Korea by tracing the political economic dimensions of the three subsystems—industrial relations, the labor market, and the welfare state—and their interaction. I argue that the deepening labor market dualization in Japan and Korea proceeded as follows. To begin, the two countries were able to successfully ride out the economic crisis of the 1970s because of their developmental state strategies of focusing on "the winners" (i.e., large export-oriented industrial enterprises) and maintaining high productivity by redeploying redundant workers to subsidiary companies. Then, sustained economic growth until the 1990s effectively shielded people from the adverse effects of the existing labor market dualization. Social and economic contexts, however, changed significantly in the 1990s. Faced with increased global economic competition, the two countries were forced to re-articulate their political economies. This time, a radical reduction in the size of core workers in the industrial sector was required, while imperatives to raise productivity remained constant. Rather than mass layoffs, employers opted to reduce the intake of new core workers, and to expand the hiring of atypical or non-standard workers. This pushed a growing number of labor market entrants, the vast majority of whom were recent college graduates, into the secondary labor market. The level of labor market flexibilization was, in both cases, much more significant for small and medium-size enterprises (SMEs), which were not as well protected by the state as larger enterprises; nor did they have the capacity to protect their core workers.

Although this process was aimed to protect existing core workers, it eroded the core industry and deprived unions of their economic leadership role, including wage setting, further widening the gap between the core and the periphery. In response, the Japanese and Korean governments expanded welfare state policies in a bid to compensate for the growing disparity. In both cases, the increased social welfare demands of an aging population became a growing imperative for the state to expand social care. This, in light of the changing labor market structure, provided a useful vehicle to simultaneously address the issues of care services and job creation. In the case of Korea, the Asian economic crisis of 1997 and the political regime shift further enabled the government to implement a radical welfare state expansion.

In summary, the dualization processes in Japan and Korea are not only intensifying the existing labor market divides along the lines of gender and establishment size, but are adding a new demographic dimension between generations, with the overall effects of increased income inequality and disrupted individual life course patterns. The states have taken a more active role in social welfare: in the case of Japan, through gradual policy changes, and in Korea, through a more radical resetting of economic and social policies. In both countries, politics and political processes have helped to determine state responses to socio-economic changes.

INDUSTRIAL RELATIONS: PROTECTING THE CORE UNDER DURESS

In Japan and Korea, the core industry's economic leadership began to flounder in the 1990s, partly as a result of a gradual weakening of labor union effectiveness and partly because of changes in business environment after the 1997 economic crisis.

In Japan, the unionization rate fell from 35.4 percent in 1970 to 18.5 percent in 2009, and the total number of union members began to drop after 1994 (JIL 2010; Nakamura 2007). The decline of union membership coincided with the collapse of the so-called "spring wage offensive," *Shunto*, in the late-1990s. As an established form of collective wage-setting mechanism, *Shunto* has been an important basis for socially acceptable wage standards in Japan. Its decline marks the end of the nationwide and broad-based wage-setting system and the commitment of key unions (e.g., steelworkers) to serve as the wage-setting leaders for smaller enterprises and to ensure general wage standards. In other words, it indicates the acceptance of disparities in wage standards among companies, particularly between the large enterprises and SMEs. Indeed, the average wage of standard employees in firms with 10–99 employees relative to that of employees in firms with 1,000 or more workers dropped from 91.4 percent to 84.9 percent between 1990 and 2004. At the same time, the corporate welfare benefit differential began to rise. By 2006, corporate welfare benefits of standard employees in firms with fewer than 100 employees amounted to 41.7 percent of that of their counterparts in firms with 1,000 or more employees (Japan—Statistics Bureau 2010). In effect, with the decline of *Shunto*, labor unions focused on wage negotiations at the company level, not at shared nationwide wage levels.

In addition, Japanese labor's policy-making power also weakened in the 1990s. Political support for Japan's Socialist Party declined after 1994, and the role of the umbrella national labor union, Rengo, diminished as a result of legislative changes in the policy-making processes. Rengo had been an active participant in the Ministry of Labor's deliberation council and thus had input into the content of reform legislation. But with the establishment of the Deregulation Subcommittee in 1995 (later renamed the Council for Regulatory Reform from 2001 to 2004), the deliberation council lost its policy review and debate functions, along with its power to revise reform legislation before it reached the Diet. The 1998 Labor Standard Law reform (introducing discretionary work system),[3] the 1999 Worker Dispatching Law reform (deregulating dispatch work),[4] and 2003 revisions to the Labor Standard Law (relaxing regulations on dismissal) and the Worker Dispatching Law (extending dispatch work) underscore the deliberation council's (and hence Rengo's) diminished influence on policy making.

In Korea, labor had a significant presence in industrial relations after the 1987 political democratization and continued to wield political and policy-making power for most of the 1990s. But even here, labor unions' positions vis-à-vis industrial relations became increasingly defensive after the middle of the decade. As the main oppositional force against the authoritarian regime, Korean labor not only turned the previous employer-centered workplace into a more corporatist one, but also gained a more equal share in the government's tripartite policy-making processes. Building on the momentum of the democratization movement, Korean workers, particularly in large enterprises (e.g., Chaebol workers), quickly organized into powerful company unions after 1988, demanding wage hikes, job security, and more welfare benefits. Not surprisingly, both the number of labor unions and the number of industrial disputes rose immediately after democratization, from 2,765 in 1986 to 7,883 in 1989, and 276 in 1986 to 3,749 in 1987, respectively (KOILAF 2009). The labor disputes during the early democratic years proved highly profitable for industrial workers, especially those in large enterprises: their nominal wage growth rate rose from 15.5 percent in 1988 to 21.1 percent in 1989 and remained in the double digits until the mid-1990s.

The success of the large enterprise unions in Korea was, however, a loss for workers in the SMEs, and the wage gap between the two began to widen after 1990. Average wages of workers in firms with 30 to 99 workers as a percentage of those in firms with over 500 workers declined from approximately 99 percent in 1980 to 60 percent by 2008. In a similar vein, disparities in company welfare benefits grew between workers in large enterprises and SMEs, with the differentials between firms with 30 to 99 employees and those with over 1,000 employees dropping from 80 percent in 1984 to 43.0 percent in 2003. Korea's powerful national labor movement, dominated by large enterprise unions, further contributed to the widening gap between the large enterprises and SMEs by rejecting government attempts to reign in wage escalation in the early years of democracy. Between 1987 and 2001, corporate labor cost quintupled, while corporate welfare cost expanded eleven-fold, further widening the divide between workers in large enterprises and those in SMEs (Kim 2002).

As in Japan, union density in Korea also began to decline in the 1990s, and the role of unions in setting wage standards for workers in SMEs in Korea began to decline as well. After peaking at 19.8 percent in 1989, union density fell to 10.5 percent in 2008 (KOILAF 2009).

In both Japan and Korea, the decline in unionization rates and the weakening of the unions' wage-setting role result from structural changes. In both countries, the share of employment in the manufacturing sector has been generally declining since the 1980s (the 1990s in Korea), while that in service sector has grown at the expense of a sharp decline in agricultural employment. In Japan, the total share of employment in the industrial/manufacturing sector dropped from 33.6 percent in 1980 to 26.1 percent in 2005, while service sector employment expanded from to 55.4 percent to 67.2 percent. In Korea, the proportion of employees in the industrial/manufacturing sector rose from 22.5 percent in 1980 to 32.6 percent in 1990, before falling to 26.3 percent in 2006, while the service sector rose from 43.5 percent to 56.2 percent and then to 66.0 percent, respectively. In both countries, the rapid expansion of the service sector industry has eroded the traditional labor union base— the industrial workers. While the labor movement has been slow to organize workers in non-traditional employment (service sector and atypical workers), these workers are admittedly difficult to organize. In Japan, the unionization rate of part-time workers, who represent 23 percent of all employees, was 7.0 percent in 2009, as compared to 18.5 percent for all employees (JIL 2010); in Korea, the unionization rate of non-standard workers (most are contract workers) was 2.9 percent, as compared to 15.6 percent for standard workers in 2008 (KOILAF 2009).

The two countries' enterprise-based union system also contributed to increased labor market dualization after the 1990s. First, not only are many labor negotiations in Japan and Korea conducted at the enterprise level, but workers' fortunes, and hence, those of their unions, are closely tied to the success of their companies. On the one hand, this creates a strong sense of enterprise consciousness, which ensures a high level of labor-management cooperation. On the other hand, this may pit one enterprise's union against another, particularly in competitive industries or during difficult economic times. Indeed, in hard economic times, unions often concede to management demands for wage restraints to maintain competitiveness (Weathers 2003); in return, during good economic times, workers are rewarded with wage and benefit increases.

Second, large enterprise unions have little incentive to form nationwide or sector-wide industrial unions with small enterprise unions. This is particularly evident in economically hard times: for example, in Korea during the 1990s, large enterprise unions became increasingly focused on protecting the benefits of their own members. In Korea, the unionization rate of workers in enterprises with 300+ employees was 45.4 percent in 2008; the rate for enterprises with 100–299 employees was 13.6 percent; and for those enterprises with less than 30 workers, the rate was 0.2 percent (KOILAF 2009). In Japan, the unionization rate of workers in companies with 1,000+ employees was 46.2 percent in 2009, as compared to 1.1 percent for companies with fewer than 99 employees (JIL 2010). In sum, enterprise unionism discourages the formation of broad-based labor solidarity, and during economically hard times, it reinforces the existing labor market divide between insiders and outsiders based on firm size.

Briefly stated, the various forms of internal fragmentation within Japanese and Korean labor contribute to divisions not only between unionized and non-unionized workers, but between unionized workers in large enterprises and those in SMEs, and between those in unions representing standard and non-standard workers within the same enterprise. As illustrated above, in both countries, the basic structure of enterprise unionism means that large corporate unions are more able to negotiate a strategy to protect core industrial workers, while leaving behind labor market outsiders. Indeed, as illustrated below, this happened after the 1990s, when the two East Asian countries faced significant global economic competition and pressure to liberalize the labor market.

CHANGING CONTEXTS: MARKET LIBERALIZATION PRESSURES AND INDUSTRIAL RELATIONS CHANGES

The economic contexts in Japan and Korea changed markedly in the 1990s. Japan's economic fortunes turned sour in the early 1990s, and for the rest of the decade, the economy languished with little hope of recovery (Hutchinson and Westermann 2006; Ikawa 2005; Kojima 2009). In Korea, more than a decade of sustained high economic growth came to an abrupt end in 1997 with the Asian economic crisis. With the country's economy on the brink of bankruptcy, the government implemented radical corporate, governance, and welfare restructuring (Kwon 2009; Peng 2004; Song 2003). In both cases, the imperatives to maintain national competitiveness in the face of growing competition from other parts of East Asia, particularly China, dictated much of the political economic reconfiguration. Both countries adopted a partial rather than a full market liberalization strategy. Rather than mass layoffs, employers opted to protect core workers by reducing entry-level standard hires and flexibilizing the labor market by increasing the number of non-standard workers. Labor in both countries initially opposed the change, but eventually consented to the flexibilization in exchange for the protection of core workers. The state also stepped in with economic liberalization policies and welfare state expansion.

Japan: Steady and Gradual Transformation

Changing Employment System

In Japan, employers cut labor costs by dispatching their older standard workers to regional offices and subsidiary companies and reducing the number of new hires. For its part, labor tried to protect jobs by accepting low wage increases; since the start of the 1990s, unions have pulled back from demanding large wage increases. An important breakthrough came in 1995, with the National Telephone and Telegraph (NTT) union's unexpectedly large wage concession in negotiations. This was soon followed by the Private Railway Workers Union Federation and the Federation of Steelworkers Union, both settling for a minimal wage increase. The Federation of Steelworkers Union had hitherto been the industry union leader in *Shunto* (Weathers 2003), but the steel industry was particularly hard hit by competition from China. Given the poor economic growth over the previous years, it was difficult for labor to push for wage increases. Therefore, unions agreed to cut back on their demands to protect national competitiveness. Profitability returned in 1996, but this proved short-lived as the nascent economic growth in 1996 was set back by the Asian economic crisis in 1997.

The post-economic crisis period led to further efforts by Japanese employers to reduce labor costs. Beginning in 1997, some companies began to put more emphasis on bonuses in the total wage settlement, while gradually cutting down their size. Other companies, such as Matsushita, introduced an area-specific employment system, which set wages according to local rather than national wage and cost-of-living indexes (Weathers 2003). There was also discussion of the ending of Japan's lifetime employment system and a shift to "diversified" employment, thus warning workers not to expect long-term continuous employment. Much of this was targeted to new labor market entrants in a bid to prepare them for future changes.

In reality, institutional change was gradual, and companies tried to resist imposing a radical restructuring of the employment system on core workers. A 1997 EPA survey of corporate hiring policies found that although more than half of the corporations surveyed (53.7 percent) claimed that at the time of the survey, they were hiring workers based on the idea of long-term continuous employment (another 41 percent *preferred* to hire on the basis of long-term continuous employment, and only 4.4 percent specifically did *not* hire on the basis of long-term continuous employment), only 9.3 percent thought that they would continue to have such hiring policies in five years. Instead, 38.8 percent expected their companies would *not be* hiring on the basis of long-term continuous employment, and another 46.9 percent believed that their hiring policies would shift to *preferring* to hire for long-term continuous employment (EPA 1997). A subsequent survey in 2004 found that 40.0 percent of corporate employers believed the lifetime employment system had to be reformed; another 15.3 percent thought it should be drastically revised; and only about a third (36.1 percent) believed that they would retain the lifetime employment system (MHLW 2005).

Many employers also began to introduce a performance-related wage system after 1997. In a 1998 survey, approximately 80 percent of listed corporations were actively planning to adopt performance related pay. By 2004, not only had most companies (approximately 70 percent) adopted performance-related pay, but they had also increased the proportion of performance-related wages in their total wage calculations (Rodoseisaku Kenkyu Kenshu Kikan (RKKK) 2004; MHLW 2005).

Studies show that changes in employment and wage systems have not been uniformly implemented. Whereas SMEs and new industries implemented them quickly, large industrial enterprises phased them in more gradually. Indeed, as Thelen and Kume (2006) point out, despite the discussions of employment reforms, large successful firms have basically maintained their commitment to protect core workers.

Employment Policy Reforms

At the state policy level, the Japanese government worked in conjunction with employers to facilitate the process of partial market liberalization. The Third Administrative Reform Promotion Council (ARPC) established in 1990 and led by Suzuki Eichi, a prominent businessman and director of the Japan Employers' Federation (*Nikkeiren*), set the agenda for major administrative and policy reforms. The ARPC's final report in 1993 supported market liberalization and an overhaul of the Japanese employment system. The report of the Deregulation Subcommittee of the ARPC in 1995 was even more direct. It urged the government to accelerate economic deregulation, including labor market liberalization

(Weathers 2004). At the same time, the Ministry of Labor became increasingly convinced of the need to deregulate the Japanese labor market. Following the ARPC's policy direction, the Ministry of Labor began to undertake systematic reforms of employment legislations.

The Ministry of Labor sought to reform the Labor Standard Law and the Worker Dispatching Law to activate the secondary labor market. In both cases, the Ministry played a central role by guiding the reform proposal through delib-eration councils and to the Diet (Weathers 2004). In the case of the Dispatching Workers Law reform, the Ministry created the Central Employment Security Council made up of 21 members, chaired by Suwa Yasuo, an academic and a supporter of liberalization. From this group, a subcommittee of 12 members[5] took on the main deliberation work. The representatives from labor and busi-ness were selected, not for their expertise or knowledge of the issue, but by virtue of their positions as representatives of key institutions within Rengo and Nikkeiren. Labor members opposed issues of time limits, disclosure of temporary workers' personal information, and the use of temporary workers in manufacturing. Rengo mobilized the opposition DPJ and Komeito par-ties to pressure the Diet to pass the bill in 1999 with many of labor's demands included. However, when the Dispatching Workers Law was revised in 2003, earlier reforms were rescinded; this led to significant deregulation, including a longer list of occupational groups included in dispatch work, and changes in the operations of worker dispatching agencies.

Despite labor's initial protests, both the Labor Standard Law and the Worker Dispatching Law reforms passed reasonably quickly. First, government and business agreed on the issue of employment deregulation. Both actors wanted to see the expansion of non-standard workers and the deregulation of restric-tions on worker layoffs and dispatch agencies. Second, although Rengo's for-mal position was against the reform measures, it was not able to override the positions of its member labor unions. The mainstream labor movement was, in fact, divided and ambivalent over the issue. While some labor unions were clearly against the reforms, others regarded the expansion of non-standard employment as undesirable but necessary to protect industrial competitive-ness (Weathers 2004: 429). Third, labor unions' ambivalence about and com-placency toward these two employment legislation reforms also stemmed from the fact that they neither understood nor were seriously interested in the issue of non-standard workers. Most mainstream labor unions represented the interests of standard full-time male workers in large enterprises, thus tac-itly supporting labor market dualism—the discrimination against women and workers in SMEs, and the dual-track system within the labor market. The mainstream labor unions lacked both the motive and the incentive to fight for non-standard workers who were primarily women and non-unionized, nor did they fully understand the issues at hand. In many ways, the Dispatching Workers Law reforms simply reinforced what Gottfried (2008) refers to as the "supporting pillars of the Japanese employment system"—namely, labor market dualization.

Korea: Contested Labor Market Transformation
Changing Employment System

In Korea, the politics of labor market restructuring was more contentious, but the outcomes were not unlike Japan: the Asian economic crisis facilitated a shift toward partial labor market flexibilization. But here too, efforts were made to protect core industrial workers while employers relied increasingly on non-standard employment to reduce labor cost. Although employers had been lobbying for labor market deregulation since the beginning of the 1990s, they were not always successful in changing employment policies until 1997, even with government support. For example, Korea's first civilian president, Kim Young-Sam, tried to reform employment legislation in 1996, but his attempt backfired when he tried to hasten the process. Kim Young-Sam came to power with a mandate to fight corruption and to bring Korea into the global economy. Significant strides were made on the economic front: Korea joined the World Trade Organization (WTO) in 1995 and ascended to the Organisation for Economic Co-operation and Development (OECD) in 1996. Korea's new international position, however, came with significant international pressure for market liberalization, particularly from the United States.

To move forward with an employment flexibilization plan, the president created a Tripartite Committee in 1996 to formulate employment legislation reform, the main point of which was to relax the rule against worker layoffs and expand the hiring of non-standard workers, something for which employers had been lobbying for some time. Labor vehemently opposed the reforms. When employers and labor failed to reach consensus, the president took a political gamble by railroading the reform legislation at a special session of the parliament in the absence of the opposition parties. This resulted in opposition parties and labor calling for a nationwide strike, forcing the Kim Young-Sam government to rescind the law (Lee 2000; Lee and Lee 2004; Jung and Cheon 2006).

But Korea's economic situation changed almost overnight with the 1997 Asian economic crisis. Faced with the IMF bailout conditions, incoming president Kim Dae-Jung brought back the three actors—state, labor, and employers—in a new Tripartite Commission in 1998. The labor market restructuring plan included the same set of items as had Kim Young-Sam's 1996 plan: employment flexibility by relaxing restrictions on worker layoffs and increased non-standard employment, including temporary and dispatch workers. This time, labor was significantly more compromised. With 8 of 16 Chaebols bankrupt and the country near economic collapse, labor had little to fight with. Additionally, given that it had backed Kim Dae-Jung's presidency and fearing that the alternative would be worse, labor conceded to the employment legislation reform in *quid pro quo* for welfare state expansion. The tripartite consensus gave employers the right to dismiss workers on the grounds of economic difficulty and allowed them more leeway to hire non-standard workers. The government was given a green light for radical corporate governance reform, and labor was promised a significant welfare state expansion.

As in Japan, Korean employers increased the use of non-standard workers once the employment policy reforms passed, but at the same time, they sought to protect core workers from radical employment restructuring, opting for more gradual change when it came to labor market insiders. True, many workers were laid off in the immediate aftermath of the economic crisis, but most layoffs were due to corporate and business bankruptcies. Once the crisis was over, employers, particularly the large enterprises, resumed their practice of protecting core employment.

Employment Reforms

The Labor Standard Law reforms have gradually replaced Korea's de facto lifetime employment system and seniority wage system with a more flexible employment system. The flexible labor market policy introduced in 1998 has made it easier to lay off employees and has legalized temporary work. The unemployment rate in Korea rose from 2.5 percent in 1997 to 6.8 percent in 1998, but with the return of economic growth (albeit at a much lower rate than in the pre-1997 period), it gradually leveled down to 4.0 percent in 2001, and thereafter remained between 3 and 4 percent. The unemployment rate at the end of 2010 stood at 3.0 percent (KSIS 2011).

As in Japan, Korean employers responded to the new economic conditions by gradually paring down the core workforce through a combination of regular and early retirements, and by increasing non-standard workers to cut labor costs. This was partly because of the tacit employer-labor agreement to protect core employment. As in Japan, the brunt of the employment restructuring was taken by labor market entrants, the youth entering into the labor market for the first time. In both countries, the shrinking in entry-level standard employment left new graduates with less prospect of secure future employment. In Japan, unemployment rates among males aged 25 to 34 rose from 1.8 percent to 5.0 percent between 1990 and 2000, and remained at that level until 2009. For women, the figure increased from 3.4 percent to 6.4 percent, respectively, and stayed around 5–6 percent until 2009 (JIL 2010). In Korea, the rate of youth (15–29 years old) unemployment rose from 4.5 percent to 12.2 percent between 1996 and 1998, before stabilizing at 9–10 percent until 2009. This was more than double the rate of total unemployment, at 2.0 percent in 1996, 7.0 percent in 1998, and around 3–4 percent from 2000 to 2009 (KNSO 2008; KSIS 2011).

Employment deregulation in Korea is much more politically contentious than in Japan, with labor and business often clashing, but in the end, labor agreed to the reforms, partly because labor was divided and ambivalent, and partly because there was a general consensus among all actors that some form of market liberalization was unavoidable. During the negotiation process, the Korean Confederation of Trade Unions (KCTU), the more radical of the two peak unions in Korea, walked out of the Tripartite Commission several times, leaving the Federation of Korean Trade Unions (FKTU), the more moderate union, to work with business and government, though it returned to the table at the last minute. Business was also in disarray, as the government vowed not to rescue failing enterprises, resulting in eight Chaebol bankruptcies within a year. Not only the hiring of non-standard workers, but the ability to lay off standard workers—the main source of contention with labor—was imperative for business survival. The Kim Dae-Jung government, supported by labor and civil society groups, was in a precarious situation, as it wanted to use this opportunity to crack down on the historical problem of Chaebol-government collusions while dealing with the immediate issue of economic rescue and the International Monetary Fund (IMF) bailout conditions, which included market liberalization (Lee 2000; Lee and Lee 2004).

In the final round of the Tripartite Agreement, labor accepted deregulation, understanding that this was the only way to protect their membership. In exchange, the government conceded to labor a significant social security expansion, starting with the overhaul of employment insurance.

Consequences of Labor Market and Industrial Relations Changes

In Korea, the proportion of temporary and daily workers as the percentage of total salaried workers increased from 41.9 percent in 1995 to 52.9 percent in 2000, and then gradually declined to 42.9 percent in 2009 (see Table 10-1). The reasons for the gradual decline are, first, that the Korean economy rebounded between 5 and 9 percent per annum after corporate and labor market restructuring between 1998 and 2000. This enabled employers to hire more standard workers. Second, in the 1990s, Korea was still emerging as a newly industrialized economy. As such, the proportions of non-standard and informal employment (which had been accounted for under the same heading until the 1990s) had been declining since the 1980s. Therefore, the Asian economic crisis reversed the trend toward increased formalization and standardization of employment that had been steadily taking place over the previous decade. The proportion of non-standard employment in 2009 was higher than in 1995, suggesting that the trajectory of labor market formalization stalled if not reversed.

In Japan, the proportion of non-standard employees among total employees increased from 23.8 percent in 1990 to 34.1 percent in 2008. What is unique in Japan, even compared to Korea, is that the majority of non-standard workers are part-time workers, most of whom are employed for a long period of time and work hours similar to those of standard employees, but without employment security and with few social security benefits.[6] The proportion

Table 10-1: Proportion of non-standard workers to salaried employees in Japan and Korea, 1990–2009

Country	Year	% Part-time workers*	% Contract/temp/and daily workers
Japan	1990	Total: 19.2 Male: 9.5 Female: 33.4	Total: 3.6
	2004	Total (2001): 24.9 Male: 13.7 Female: 41.0	Total (2004): 8.9
	2008	Total: 22.3 Male: 8.5 Female: 40.3	Total: 11.8 Male: 10.7 Female: 13.3
Korea	1995	Total: 4.4 Male: 2.9 Female: 6.7	Total: 41.9 Male: 32.3 Female: 57.2
	2001	Total (2001): 7.5 Male: 5.3 Female: 10.5	Total: 52.9 Male: 40.8 Female: 68.9
	2009	n.a.	Total: 42.9 Male: 33.2 Female: 56.1

* Part-time workers are normally considered those who work fewer than 30 hours per week. In the case of Japan, it refers to those who work fewer than 35 hours per week.
Sources: Figures on part-time workers: JIL, 2005, and 2010; figures on contract/temp/and other workers in Japan: MHLW (2005); figures on contract/temp/and other workers in Korea: Lee and Lee (2004); KOILAF (2009).

of part-time workers to total employees in Japan rose from 19.2 percent to 24.9 percent between 1990 and 2001(JIL, 2004). As shown in Table 10-1, the proportion of women in nonstandard employment far surpasses that of men in both countries. Furthermore, the gender gap in employment status opened up significantly in the 1990s.

The main consequences of labor market and industrial relations changes for the two countries since the 1990s, and particularly after 1997, are, therefore, partial liberalization, and the intensification of the labor market divides, as illustrated in the widening of the income gap between workers in the core (primarily standard, full-time, male workers) and those in the periphery (primarily women and youth). In Korea, not only did the wage gap between standard and nonstandard workers widen after 1998, but the gap between production and managerial/white-collar employees also increased as production workers took greater pay cuts than non-production workers in the aftermath of the economic crisis (Lee 2000; Lee and Lee 2004). This reversed the trend of a narrowing wage gap between production and managerial/white-collar workers that had been taking place in Korea since the 1980s. Japanese studies also show a similarly widening gap in the wages of standard and nonstandard workers (JIL 2004, 2010).

THE COMPENSATORY STATE RESPONSES: SOCIAL WELFARE POLICY REFORMS

It is widely acknowledged that the lack of state welfare support in Japan and Korea prior to the 1990s could be explained by their employment regime that provided job protection for many workers in the less productive sectors of the economy. Indeed, in both countries until the recent reforms, employment legislations made worker layoffs difficult and non-standard forms of employment tightly regulated and limited. In other words, these employment legislations and practices served as functional equivalents of welfare state support (Estevez-Abe 2008; Gao 2001; Kasza 2006; Peng 2009; Seeleib-Kaiser 2001). It is therefore not difficult to consider, in light of the labor market liberalization process, that this will lead to welfare state reconfiguration in order to address the issue of increasing outsiders (Estevez-Abe 2008; Seeleib-Kaiser 2001).

Indeed, welfare policies in both countries have been reformed in conjunction with labor market policy reforms to compensate for increased labor market dualization. Both have expanded employment insurance and social welfare, particularly social care. In concert with labor market policy reforms, the social security system in Japan and Korea has been expanded to address the fallout from the partial liberalization of the labor market and declining employment security. Although labor market insiders did benefit from welfare expansion, the main beneficiaries were the outsiders. For example, the expansion of old age insurance, increased work-family reconciliation policies such as parental leave, and universal long-term care for the elderly benefited both insiders and outsiders, but in many cases, insiders already had generous pension and family support through their company welfare. It was the outsiders who stood to gain more from these programs. Moreover, the expansion of other welfare programs, such as the expansion of employment insurance coverage and employment support and skills-training programs, were clearly directed to labor market outsiders. Finally, social care programs such as child care and elder care benefited mainly women, who were more likely to be the outsiders, as these programs provided support for them, and, as well, created new jobs in care services that would likely employ women.

In Korea, the employment and workers' compensation insurances expanded in 1998 and 2000 to cover a much broader population, while the pension reform of 1998 widened the safety net for population coverage. The latter was finalized in the universalization of the National Pension in 1999.

A variety of social policy measures were adopted after 1998 in direct response to the economic crisis and as compensation for the partial labor market liberalization. For example, a number of macro- and micro-economic measures were introduced to support SMEs and to develop venture capital and new businesses. Workers' Compensation Insurance was expanded to cover all workplaces, including self-employed and unpaid family workers in 2000, with income replacement at 70 percent of the average wage. Unemployment insurance at the income replacement rate of 50 percent of the average wage was expanded to cover all workers, including daily and temporary workers in 1998. As well, the coverage was increased from 90 days to eight months, with further extension if re-employment was difficult. The National Basic Livelihood Security Law (basic public assistance) was restructured in 2000, changing the criterion of receiving public assistance from the individual's labor market attachment to household income level.

In total, the government expenditure for employment insurance increased from 4.7 million won in 1996 to 306,172 million won in 1999; the budget for child care rose from 41,876 million won to 436,903 million won between 1991 and 2002, and elderly welfare increased from 37,861 million won in 1990 to 407,767 million won in 2003 (Lee and Park 2003). Korean social expenditure as a proportion of GDP rose from 3.9 percent in 1990 to 10.8 percent in 1998, and thereafter maintained at approximately 7.5 percent (Korea Institute for Health and Social Affairs 1998; OECD 2008). The scale of Korean welfare state expansion speaks of the extent of economic devastation caused by the economic crisis. But it also indicates its low starting point before 1997.

The Korean government also shifted the focus of welfare state expansion from the immediate economic rescue of crisis victims to family and labor market oriented welfare support after 2002. Expenditures on child and elder care rose sharply under the Roh Moo-hyun government's social investment policy reforms. The government focused on social care as a policy tool to promote pro-natalism and, at the same time, to stimulate job creation and economic development (Peng 2009). The national government budget for early childhood education increased from 356 billion won in 2002 to 886 billion won in 2006, with child care nearly quintupling from 435 billion to 2,038 billion, in 2002 and 2006, respectively. The total national budget for Early Child Education and Care (ECEC) to GDP rose from 0.12 percent to 0.35 percent during this same period (Rhee 2007). The Long-term Care Insurance Scheme (LTCI) was introduced and implemented in 2008, universalizing care of the elderly. Within the first year of its implementation, the LTCI provided care to 230,000 elderly (5.3 percent of the 65+ population), amounting to a total expenditure of 1.4 trillion won, far exceeding the initial expectation of servicing 158,000 elderly. A revised government budget estimates the number of LTCI recipients to rise to 276,000 (and 1.7 trillion won) in 2010, and 320,000 recipients (2.2 trillion won) by 2013 (MOHWFA 2009). Far from being deterred, the current conservative Lee Myung-bak government has further bolstered the government support for social care, thus building on the left-of-center Roh Moo-hyun government's legacy of social care expansion, and realigning it more closely to the idea of creating an economic growth engine through social service expansion (Peng 2009, 2011).

In Japan, the government's initial attempts to combat the economic recession through expansionary fiscal policy (e.g., emergency spending packages focused on public works and special loan guarantees to rescue businesses from corporate bankruptcy) eventually gave way to the idea that an "inactive external market was [in fact] impeding the flow of workers from declining industries to emerging new businesses and slowing restructuring of the economy" (Araki 1999: 1). The government policies thus shifted to highlighting activation of the external labor market through deregulation in the mid-1990s (Ministry of Labor, Japan, 1999). Because of the increased early retirements and layoffs among older workers, and the anticipated rise in pension age starting in 2001, a series of compensatory employment and social policy reforms were introduced to support older workers who fall out of the core labor market.[7] The revised Worker Dispatching Law of 1998 expanded the category of dispatch work to include more younger and older workers. A new employment income allowance was introduced for pension recipients between the ages of 60 and 65 to earn income up to 250,000 yen per month without penalty. Employment insurance legislation was also amended to provide employees between the ages of 60 and 65 with compensation allowances up to 25 percent of their salary, if their total income declined by more than 15 percent as a result of job restructuring.

Reforms of the Employment Security and Worker Dispatching Laws thus accomplished the aims of deregulation and the activation of the external labor market, but not unlike the case of flexible labor market policies introduced by the Korean government in 1998, these reforms combined both deregulation of the labor market *and* extension of social protections for labor market outsiders. For example, under the revised Worker Dispatching Law, the dispatching agencies are obliged to inform the companies whether the dispatched worker is enrolled in social and labor insurance or not, and the company must ensure a proper working environment and facilities for dispatched workers, something usually accorded only to standard employees. Dispute resolution processes also have been improved,[8] and provisions for sexual harassment, as well as special work arrangements and working hours for pregnant women, have been included in the reforms.

To address the high unemployment and underemployment of youth, Japan and Korea have introduced job training and skills development programs. For example, the Japanese government has implemented a "Plan for Regularising 250,000 Nonstandard Workers" (*Freetah 25-man'nin Joyokoyoka Plan*) in 2006 to help unemployed youth acquire standard employment through career counseling, job searches, and retraining. In 2008, the target was increased to 326,000 jobs (MHLW 2009).

As in Korea, the Japanese government expenditure on unemployment insurance rose from 1.18 trillion yen (2.3 percent of total social security budget) in 1991 to 2.67 trillion yen (3.4 percent) in 2000; the compensation allowance for older workers (implemented in 1995) increased from 1.17 billion yen in 1995 to 10.86 billion yen in 2000 (NIPSSR 2002). On a wider social policy front, the broadening of social welfare in Japan is also evident in the expansion of social care provisions throughout the 1990s (see, for example, the Gold Plan in 1989, the Angel Plan in 1994, and finally, the Long-term Care Insurance in 1997). By 2007, social expenditures as a proportion of GDP in Japan had grown to 19 percent, up from 10 percent in 1990, with the *social welfare* portion of expenditure rising from 4.8 trillion yen (10 percent of total social security expenditure) in 1990 to 10.9 trillion yen (15.5 percent) in 2007 (NIPSSR 2008). The number of children enrolled in licensed child care centers jumped from 1.8 million to 2.02 million between 1990 and 2008. Total social expenditure on children and family increased from 1.6 trillion yen in 1990 to 3.6 trillion yen in 2007. Similarly, the number of LTIC recipients in Japan more than doubled from 1.49 million in 2000 to 3.29 million in 2005, while its expenditures increased from 3.25 trillion yen to 6.3 trillion yen between 2000 and 2007 (NIPSSR, 2008). Additionally, the Hatoyama government passed a 93 trillion yen budget in March 2010, much of which focused on expanding support for the family, including further increase in public child care spaces, implementation of universal child allowance, free tuition for public high schools, and tax exemptions for private high school tuition. It is important to point out that, like Korea, social care expansion in Japan has been employed instrumentally to incentivize fertility increase, enhance women's employment rate, and create new service sector employment. As in Korea, there has been a significant expansion of child and elder care jobs since 2000. Much of this, however, is in the form of non-standard employment for women, contributing to the deepening of the labor market divide between insiders and outsiders.

Even with these significant social policy expansion, Japan and Korea have yet to fully compensate for the loss of employment and income security of workers on the outside. Although welfare state expansion has helped mitigate income inequality and social polarization, it is unlikely that it will stem the increasing labor market dualization. In some cases—for example, the focus on expansion of social care jobs—it may exacerbate and further entrench the labor market divide between insiders and outsiders.

First, despite policies protecting non-standard employees and expanded social insurance and social welfare coverage, a significant proportion of non-standard workers are still not adequately covered. For example, in Japan, whereas coverage for employee pension, health insurance, and employment insurance are 99.3 percent, 99.6 percent, and 99.4 percent, respectively for standard employees, the figures are 47.1 percent, 49.3 percent, and 63.0 percent for non-standard workers (Jones 2008). In Korea, enrollment rates for national pension, national health insurance, and employment insurance programs in 2008 for standard employees were 94.9 percent, 95.1 percent, and 94.0 percent, respectively, and 47.2 percent, 49.1 percent, and 51.3 percent, respectively for non-standard (KOILAF 2009).

Second, as gaps in the wages *and* company welfare (e.g., bonuses) between workers in large enterprises and SMEs, and between those in standard and non-standard employment continue to widen, we will see increasing disparities between the smaller number of workers in core employment and the growing number in peripheral employment. These suggest an ongoing distance between formal welfare state policies and labor market realities.

CONCLUSION

As the above discussion of industrial relations and labor market and welfare policy in Japan and Korea makes clear, the two countries have undergone significant system changes since the 1990s in response to the evolving global economic context.

First, in both cases, the governments actively pursued labor market reforms, including partial flexibilization and employment deregulation to maintain national competitiveness, often in alignment with business and with the tacit consent of labor. Labor movements in Japan and Korea were, in fact, ambivalent over labor market reforms, particularly the issue of non-standard employment; many mainstream labor unions thought that its development was an unavoidable option to protect competitiveness. Nor did they fully understand the situation of non-standard workers; they lacked the incentive to fight for the rights of non-standard workers, as they were primarily women and the non-unionized. More to the point, most mainstream labor unions represented full-time standard male employees and were more concerned about protecting core workers; hence, they saw the expansion of non-standard employment as an inevitable (albeit undesirable) trade-off for core employment protection. This widened the existing labor market divide between insiders and outsiders, who included women, youth, and atypical workers. Another reason for the unclear labor responses, and hence tacit consent, to government and business was its belief in and commitment to work with the management, a natural condition of the enterprise union system. In sum, labor in Japan and Korea was in a relatively weak position vis-à-vis labor market policy reforms. Simply stated, the post-1990s labor market reforms have continued to widen and deepen labor market divides along gender and generational lines, by consigning more people to the outside, and allowing the wage and benefit disparities between insiders and outsiders to grow.

Second, it is also important to point out, however, that in both countries, the process of labor market dualization has been a gradual one, beginning in the 1990s and picking up speed over the decade. While it is often thought that the 1997 Asian Economic Crisis was the trigger for the two economies to switch to a neoliberal model, in reality, the process of market liberalization, albeit gradual, was well underway when the crisis hit. The crisis merely hastened the process by making the issue politically imperative. This is particularly evident in Korea, where an attempt by Kim Young-Sam's government to reform the Labor Standard Law was defeated in 1996, only to be resurrected in 1998 under the Kim Dae-Jung administration. The point is that labor market dualization in Japan and Korea has been a continuous process, not a sudden shift in direction.

Third, despite the nearly two decades of shifting toward labor market liberalization, one would be hard pressed to claim that Japan and Korea have become Liberal market economies. In fact, like German and France, labor market liberalization in Japan and Korea has been a partial one, through employment deregulation. The triumvirate of labor, business, and the state selected this route because they believed it was the best way to protect core workers and maintain national competitiveness. In addition, the nature of developmental state and enterprise-based unionism helped shape a more coordinated policy approach and conciliatory labor-management relationship. However, the outcome of this cooperation is increased labor market dualization, reflected in increased wage and income inequalities, along with inequalities in social insurance and company welfare coverage between workers in large enterprises and SMEs, between men and women, and between standard and non-standard workers in the same enterprise.

Fourth, unlike the case of many Continental European countries, the partial labor market liberalization process since the 1990s in Japan and Korea has also spurred the respective governments to expand the welfare state to compensate for the increased economic insecurity. The reasons for welfare state expansion in these countries are partly fiscal and policy spaces, and partly policy instrumentalism. Both Japan and Korea have comparatively larger fiscal space to expand social welfare owing to their traditionally low level of social expenditure. This, combined with social welfare imperatives arising from low fertility and an aging society, afford both countries a significant political justification for welfare state expansion. However, in addition to that, the new social policies have been explicitly instrumental. In both cases, social policy expansion has been employed to support victims of economic restructuring, to provide incentives for women's employment, to trigger an increase in the fertility rate, and to ignite the engine of economic development. The combination of fiscal and policy spaces and policy instrumentalism thus serve as powerful bases for both the Japanese and Korean governments to use welfare state expansion to coordinate and compensate for labor market restructuring.

Fifth and finally, the recent process of labor market dualization in Japan and Korea has increased the division between labor market insiders and outsiders. In addition to traditional divisions based on gender and firm size, the expansion of non-standard employment has created an ever-growing group of labor market outsiders made up of young people. This situation is particularly serious in Japan, where youth unemployment has been a social problem since the mid-1990s. Indeed, a key policy agenda for the two countries, particularly Japan, in the future would be intergenerational contract. This would involve finding ways to ensure continuing support for social welfare for older generation in exchange for employment and income security for younger generation.

NOTES

1   Japanese and Korean states are often considered exemplary cases of developmental states because of their states' active role in economic development. Latecomers to industrialization, the states took on developmental functions, pushing for industrialization and leading the industrialization processes.

2   I use the term "non-standard employment" here to mean temporary, part-time, short-term contract and daily employment. Some authors may refer to these as "atypical employment."

3   Discretionary work system refers to a new management system emphasizing job performance rather than hours worked. The new law thus enabled employers to flexibilize employees' working hours, presumably to allow employees to plan their own work schedules, particularly in relation to helping workers reconcile family responsibilities.

4   Dispatch work is a form of temporary contract employment brokered through dispatching agencies. In Japan, dispatching agencies are regulated by the Ministry of Health, Labor, and Welfare. Japanese labor law also stipulates that dispatch work must be limited to 26 listed special skills.

5   Perhaps not surprisingly, given the previous discussion of gender divisions, only two of the 12 members were women (Weathers 2004).

6   Some attempts are being made to address the social security benefits of non-standard workers, for example, the extension of employment insurance and occupational accident insurance to non-standard workers.

7   The 1994 Pension Reform, among other things, resulted in an incremental raise of the pension age from 60 to 65, to be implemented between 2001 and 2013 for men and between 2006 and 2018 for women. The majority of employers, however, did not heed the government's recommendation to raise the retirement age to match the new pension conditions. Even now, most companies continue to retire workers at 60 or less, leaving a huge gap in income security for these workers.

8   Under the revised Worker Dispatching Law, workers can report company violations directly to the Ministry of Health, Welfare, and Labor.

REFERENCES

Araki, Takashi (1999). "1999 Revision of Employment Security Law and Worker Dispatch Law: Drastic Reforms of Japanese Labor Market Regulation," *Japan Labor Bulletin*, 38(9). September. (http://www.jil.go.jp/bulletin/year/1999/vol.38–09/06.htm) (accessed October 06, 2009).

Economic Planning Agency—Japan (EPA) (1997). *Heisei-9-nendo Kigyog Kodo ni Kansuru Anketochosa (1997 Questionnaire Survey of Business Behavior)*, Tokyo: EPA.

Esping-Andersen, Gosta (1999). *Social Foundation of Post-industrial Economie,,* Oxford: Oxford University Press.

Estevez-Abe, Margarita (2008) *Welfare Capitalism in Postwar Japan*, New York: Cambridge University Press.

Gao, Bai (2001). *Japan's Economic Dilemma: The Institutional Origins of Prosperity and Stagnation*, Cambridge MA: Cambridge University Press.

Goodman, Roger, and Peng, Ito (1996). "East Asian Welfare States," in Gosta Esping-Andersen (ed.), *Welfare States in Transition*, London: Sage, pp. 192–224.

Gottfried, Heidi (2008). "Pathway to Economic Security: Gender and Nonstandard Employment in Contemporary Japan," *Social Indicator Research*, 88(1): 176–196.

Holiday, Ian (2000). "Productivist Welfare Capitalism: Social Policy in East Asia," *Political Studies*, 48(4): 708–723.

Hutchinson, Michael M., and Westermann, Frank (eds.) (2006). *Japan's Great Stagnation: Financial and Monetary Policy Lessons for Advanced Economies*, Cambridge, MA: MIT Press.

Ikawa, Motomichi (2005). "Where Is the Japanese Economy Headed?," *Pacific Economic Review*, 10(4): 493–514.

Japan Institute of Labor (JIL) (2004). *Labor Situation in Japan - 2004*, Tokyo: JIL.

Japan Institute of Labor (JIL) (2010). *Labor Situation in Japan - 2008/09*, Tokyo: JIL.

Japan Statistics Bureau. 2010. *Historical Statistics of Japan–2010*, http://www.stat.go.jp/english/data/chouki/index.htm (accessed September 12, 2010).

Jones, Randall S. (2008). "Reforming the Labor Market in Japan to Cope with Increasing Dualism and Population Ageing," *OECD Economics Department Working Papers* No. 652, Paris: OECD.

Jung, EeHwan, and Cheon, Byung-Yon (2006). "Economic Crisis and Changes in Employment Relations in Japan and Korea," *Asian Survey*, 46 (Supplement-May/June): 457–476.

Kasza, Gregory J. (2006). *One World of Welfare: Japan in Comparative Perspective*, Ithaca, NY: Cornell University Press.

Kim, Won-Bae (2002). "Industrial Relations Policies," in Lee Wonduck (ed.), *Labor in Korea: 1978–2002*, Seoul: KLI, pp. 204–242.

Kojima, Akira (2009). "Japan's Economy and the Global Finanical Crisis," *Asia-Pacific Review*, 16(2): 15–25.

Korea Institute for Health and Social Affairs (1998). *Health and Welfare Indicators in Korea*, Seoul: Korea Institute for Health and Social Affairs.

Korea International Labor Foundation (KOILAF) (2009). *Statistics on Industrial Relations*, (http://www.koilaf.org/KFeng/engStatistics/bbs.php?code1=8) (accessed December 12, 2009).

Korea National Statistics Office (KNSO) (2008). *Statistical Yearbook 2008*, Seoul: KNSO.

Korea Statistical Information Services (KSIS) (2011). *Statistical Data*, http://www.kosis.kr/eng/index/index.jsp (accessed January 04, 2011).

Kwon, Huck-ju (2009). "The Reform of the Developmental Welfare State in East Asia," *International Journal of Social Welfare*, 18(1): S12-S21.

Lee, Hey-Kyung, and Park, Yeong-Ran (2003). "Families in Transition and the Family Welfare Policies in Korea," presented at the Canada-Korea Social Policy Research Symposium, Seoul National University, Seoul, November 22–23, 2003.

Lee, Joohee (2000). "Protecting Worker Welfare in the Age of Flexibility: Employment Adjustment and the Trade Union Movement in South Korea," presented at *International Conference of ASEM/World Bank/KSSA - Flexibility vs. Security? Social Policy and the Labor Market in Europe and Asia*, Seoul, South Korea, November 30–December 1, 2000.

Lee, Wonduck, and Lee, Joohee (2004). "Will the Model of Uncoordinated Decentralization Persist? Changes in Korean Industrial Relations after the Financial Crisis," in Katz, R., et. al. (eds.), *The New Structure of Labor Relations*, Ithaca, NY: Cornell University Press, pp. 143–165.

Ministry of Health Labor and Welfare—Japan (MHLW) (2005). *Heisei-17 Rodokeizai Hakusho (2005 White Paper on Labor and Economy)*, Tokyo: MHLW.

Ministry of Health Labor and Welfare—Japan (MHLW) (2009). *Heisei-21 Rodokeizai Hakusho (2009 White Paper on Labor and Economy)*, Tokyo: MHLW.

Ministry of Health, Welfare and Family Affairs—Korea (MOHWFA) (2009). http://english.mw.go.kr/front_eng/main.jsp (accessed December 12, 2009).

Ministry of Labor—Japan (MOL) (1999). *Heisei-11 Rodokeizai Hakusho (1999 White Paper on Labor Economy)*, Tokyo: MOL.

Nakamura, Keisuke (2007). "Decline or Revival?: Japanese Labor Unions," *Japan Labor Review*, 4(1): 7–22.

National Institute for Population and Social Security Research (NIPSSR) (2002). *The Cost of Social Security in Japan—Fiscal Year 2001*, Tokyo: NIPSSR.

National Institute for Population and Social Security Research (NIPSSR) (2008). *The Cost of Social Security in Japan—Fiscal Year 2007*, Tokyo: NIPSSR.

OECD (2008). *OECD Family Database*. http://www.oecd.org/document/4/0,3343,en_2649_34819_37836996_1_1_1_1,00.html (accessed December 12, 2009).

OECD (2004). *OECD Employment Outlook: Statistical Annex*. Paris: OECD.

Peng, Ito (2004) "Postindustrial Pressures, Political Regime Shifts, and Social Policy Reforms in Japan and South Korea," *Journal of East Asian Studies*, 4(3): 389–425.

Peng, Ito (2009). *Political and Social Economy of Care in South Korea*, Research Report #3, UNRISD Research Project on Social and Political Economy of Care. (http://www.unrisd.org/unrisd/website/document.nsf/(httpPublications)/2B5879FBCD1DBD3FC12576A200470FA3?OpenDocument) (accessed December 12, 2009).

Peng, Ito (2011). "Social Investment Policies in South Korea," in Rianne Mahon and Fiona Robinson (eds.), *The Global Political Economy of Care: Integrating Ethics and Social Politics*, Vancouver: UBC Press, pp. 94–110.

Rhee, Ock (2007). "Childcare Policy in Korea: Current Status and Major Issues," *International Journal of Child Care and Education Policy*, 1(1): 59–72.

Rodoseisaku Kenkyu Kenshu Kikan (2004). *Jinkogensho Shakai ni okeru Jinjisenryaku to Shokugyoishiki ni kansuru Chosa (Survey on Management Strategies and Employee Consciousness in Context of Population Decline)*, Tokyo: RKKK.

Seeleib-Kaiser, Martin (2001). *Globalization and Social Politics: A comparison of the Discourses and Welfare Systems in Germany, Japan, and the USA*, Frankfurt/Main Saliz, Germany: Campus Verlag GmbH.

Song, Ho Keun (2003). "The Birth of a Welfare State in Korea: The Unfinished Symphony of Democratization and Globalization," *Journal of East Asian Studies*, 3(3): 405–432.

Thelen, Kathleen and Kume, Ikuo (2006). "Coordination as a Political Problem in Coordinated Market Economies," *Governance*, 19(1): 11–42.

Weathers, Charles (2003). "The Decentralization of Japan's Wage Setting System in Comparative Perspective," *Industrial Relations Journal*, 34(2): 119–134.

Weathers, Charles (2004). "Temporary Workers, Women and Labor Policy-making in Japan," *Japan Forum*, 16(3): 423–447.

PART IV

THE POLITICS OF DUALIZATION

11

SOLIDARITY OR DUALIZATION?

SOCIAL GOVERNANCE, UNION PREFERENCES, AND UNEMPLOYMENT BENEFIT ADJUSTMENT IN BELGIUM AND FRANCE

DANIEL CLEGG

In accounts of European nations' adjustment trajectories over the last quarter-century, Belgium and France are usually considered analogous cases. Both countries are members of the Bismarckian family of social protection, with production regimes that are underpinned by real, if imperfectly operating, mechanisms of coordination, via the involvement of the "social partners" (trade unions and employers' associations) in national-level social and economic policy making (see Eichhorst and Marx, Chapter 4 of this volume). Partly because of these macro-institutional characteristics, both are understood to be experiencing difficult transitions to a post-industrial economic structure, with low levels of service-sector employment growth and stubbornly high rates of structural inactivity. Though in both cases the adjustment trajectory followed since the late 1970s has created problems for social cohesion and long-term economic sustainability, in neither have overt structural reforms proved easy to implement.

Given these parallels, it is striking that in one key institutional field, patterns of policy development have actually followed markedly *divergent* tracks in Belgium and France in recent decades. In 1980, the Belgian and French unemployment insurance regimes both combined income maintenance and anti-poverty functions within a single benefit scheme. Since then, however, very different parametric choices have been made in each country to attempt to adapt these systems to persistently high levels of unemployment. In France, insurance-based support and assistance-based support for the unemployed were explicitly separated in the early 1980s, an institutional dualization that has subsequently stabilized and served as an adjustment model for other branches of the French income maintenance system (Palier 2005). In Belgium, by contrast, unemployment protection instead "evolved from a social insurance system fairly much in the classic Bismarckian mould into what effectively amounts to a minimum income protection system" (Marx 2007: 122).

This chapter explores the political dynamics behind the contrasting institutional and distributive choices in the unemployment benefit reforms of these two otherwise similar countries, in the process shedding light on the politics of welfare state dualization more generally. In particular, it suggests that rather fine-grained differences in social governance—the way that social policy space is shared between the state and social actors (Ebbinghaus 2010)—have had a crucial impact on processes of unemployment policy preference formation in Belgian and French trade unions, whose influence has driven policy down distinctive paths. While it has long been recognized that the administrative structures of the welfare state can impact the power resources of unions (Rothstein 1992; Scruggs 2002), this chapter shows how they can also shape their organizational interests in ways that are consequential for patterns of policy choice. More generally, the impact of such proximate institutional environments on preference formation implies that common structural tendencies toward a post-industrial employment structure can be expected to elicit diverse social policy responses in different countries, even within the same welfare-production regime.

The chapter is organized in three sections. Section one summarizes some key features of the economic and regulatory context in which Belgian and French unemployment policies have evolved since the early 1980s, elaborating more fully on the similarities in the overall socioeconomic adjustment trajectories of the two cases. A second section then examines the divergent development of income protection policies for the unemployed since 1980 in more detail, focusing on both the institutional structures of protection and the social rights that different groups of the unemployed enjoy within these. Section three discusses the limitations of a range of alternative explanations for the cross-case variation, before demonstrating how the structure of social governance institutions has shaped unions' organizational preferences and has encouraged them to champion very different parametric reform options in the unemployment protection sphere. The chapter concludes by drawing out some of the implications of the comparison for our understanding of the politics of welfare state dualization as well as—somewhat more speculatively—for our appreciation of its impact on social cohesion.

DOWN THE SAME PATH: BELGIAN AND FRENCH LABOR MARKETS AFTER THE "GOLDEN AGE"

In France and Belgium, as everywhere in the developed world, unemployment increased sharply in the wake of the oil shocks of the mid-1970s. Unlike in some other European countries, though, they remained stubbornly high for much of the next quarter-century. In this respect, the Belgian performance has been marginally better than the French, but arguably only because a greater share of the non-employed have been encouraged out of the labor market altogether. In the mid 2000s, the inactivity rate in Belgium was the highest in Western Europe, some 5 percent above the EU average level. Rates of inactivity are particularly high among older citizens in both countries, more than 10 percent above the EU average in France and nearly 15 percent in Belgium. Furthermore, Belgium has long had rates of long-term unemployment that are above the European average, and has been joined in this by France since the turn of the millennium (Eurostat 2010a).

Belgium and France thus represent two clear examples of the "welfare without work" syndrome that has plagued many Continental European countries since the late 1970s. Responsibility for this problem is seen to reside with institutional features of Continental European labor markets and social protection systems, in particular a tradition of strict employment protection and high non-wage labor costs at the bottom end of the labor market, as a result of the contribution-based financing structure of social protection (Eichhorst and Hemerijck 2010; Esping-Andersen and Regini 2000; Scharpf 1997).

There have, however, been only timid attempts to make labor markets more generally flexible in either country. In Belgium, while there were some reforms to the regulation of collective dismissals, attempts to reduce levels of individual employment protection "have remained gridlocked because of a fundamental disagreement between the social partners" (De Deken 2009: 189). Likewise in France, collective dismissals have seen rounds of de- and re-regulation, but the protection of individual employees under regular employment contracts has remained unchanged, and generally off-limits politically (Cahuc and Zylberberg 2009). There has been rather more activity around the regulation of temporary employment contracts in both countries; this has been relaxed in Belgium, and tightened in France. Despite the differing directions of regulatory change in this area, each country has nonetheless witnessed an expansion of temporary employment, though interestingly by rather less in Belgium (from 5.4 percent of all employment in 1983 to a peak of 10.3 percent in 1999) than in France (from 3.3 percent of all employment in 1983 to a peak of 15.5 percent in 2000) (OECD 2010a). In a comparable way but to differing degrees, temporary employment has been used by employers to circumvent the strict regulation of regular employment, in line with the "dual path" to labor market reform common to Continental welfare-production regimes (see Eichhorst and Marx, Chapter 4 of this volume; Iversen 2005: 257–268).

A similar dynamic can be seen at work in employment policy measures, which in both countries have been heavily focused on the problem of non-wage labor costs. These were initially addressed through targeted subsidies to employers taking on certain categories of workers (young people, the long-term unemployed, trainees), but have tended to gradually expand to cover all employment up to a certain wage level (Clegg 2011; De Deken 2011). Along with extensive creation of temporary and part-time jobs in the public and para-public sectors, again targeted on specific groups of the unemployed, such measures have contributed to the flexibilization of the lower reaches of the labor market in both countries, and have provided an employment foothold for low-skilled workers who would otherwise be priced out of jobs. But they have also served to increase the social acceptability and politically legitimacy of an adjustment strategy that remains fundamentally characterized by a de facto acceptance of high unemployment or non-employment.

The political context of the two countries differs significantly, but in neither has it been conducive to encouraging a more decisive break with the regulatory status quo. Due to the politicization and division of organized labor and the often execrable relations between the social partners and the state, the negotiation of explicit and encompassing "social pacts" has remained a vain hope in France (Ebbinghaus and Hassel 2000). Belgium, too, has been characterized by "troubled and conflictual" relationships between the social partners (Hemerijck et al. 2000: 193), though this has not prevented many attempts to negotiate a new policy direction. However "there is no country where governments designed so many pacts, plans and proposals...with so little success" (Hemerijck and Visser 2000: 253). Belgian governments have, furthermore, been poorly positioned to drive through unilateral reforms; weak and often short-lived coalition governments operating in a context of deepening federalism and growing linguistic conflict have struggled to exert authority (Hemerijck and Marx 2010; Kuipers 2006). In France, executives face fewer obvious institutional barriers, but elites from across the political spectrum have been accused of lacking the courage and imagination to exploit their room for maneuver (Smith 2004; Cahuc and Zylberberg 2009). Though institutional change has been in many respects profound, it has been incremental and lacking in obvious strategic direction (Hall 2006).

In sum, there are many parallels in the post-industrial adjustment trajectories of Belgium and France. Adaptations to the changing economic structure have been hesitant and marginal, with the employment conditions of the lowest skilled and least well-integrated workers most often the privileged adjustment variable. In both countries, there has been an apparent desire to preserve—or at least unwillingness to challenge—the protections enjoyed by more stably integrated labor market "insiders." Similar institutional decisions and non-decisions, with similar distributional implications, have thus characterized much Belgian and French labor market policy making over the past quarter-century. It is against this backdrop that the divergent development in Belgian and French unemployment protection policies over the same period is particularly striking.

SOLIDARITY VERSUS DUALIZATION: UNEMPLOYMENT BENEFIT POLICIES IN BELGIUM AND FRANCE SINCE 1980

Looking only at expenditure figures, the story of unemployment benefit policies in Belgium and France since the mid-1980s would at first glance appear to be one of convergence (see Figure 11-1). Belgium has traditionally spent more than France on unemployment benefits, and while this remains true today, the gap between the two countries on this indicator has narrowed somewhat in the last two-to-three decades.

This dynamic of increasingly similar expenditure levels has, however, been driven by very different institutional developments and distributive logics. While in 1980 unemployment protection in both countries essentially comprised one encompassing benefit tier covering all unemployed claimants, this integrated benefit structure was an early victim of economic pressures in France, giving way to a dualized approach to unemployment protection organized around a distinction between "insurance" and "solidarity" in which the quality of benefit entitlement became more dependent on prior work and contribution. But no parallel institutional evolution occurred in Belgium, where unemployment benefit entitlements have actually tended to become less, rather than more, status dependent. While Belgium and France invest increasingly similar sums in unemployment protection, the recent period has in fact seen them diverge in how they target these collective resources on, and deliver them to, different parts of the unemployed population.

Figure 11-1: Unemployment protection effort

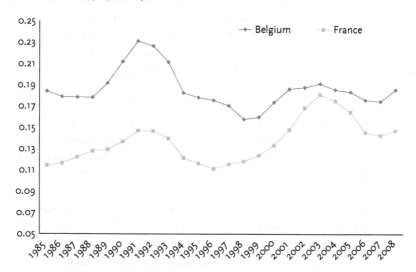

Source: Own calculations from OECD 2010b and Eurostat 2010a: calculated as expenditure on unemployment benefits as percent GDP/unemployment as percent labor force.

France: Stripping the Solidarity Out of Insurance

An encompassing benefit system was only introduced in France in 1979, when the tax-financed unemployment assistance system was absorbed by the contribution-financed unemployment insurance system, the culmination of a "logic of integration" that had been underway since the establishment the latter in 1958 (Daniel 2000). Under the 1979 agreement reached between the Barre government and the social partners—who manage unemployment insurance through periodically renegotiated national-level collective agreements, extended after agreement by the state—the newly integrated system was jointly financed from contributions and a state subsidy, with management control remaining formally with the social partners.

In a context of fast-rising unemployment, the new system soon ran into serious financial difficulties, compounded by the use of unemployment insurance funds to finance a vast expansion of early retirement pensions under the first Mitterrand administration. The employers in particular protested about this "improper" usage of unemployment benefits, and refused to agree to the contribution increases necessary to restore the financial equilibrium of the unemployment insurance fund, UNEDIC.[1] The government, however, conditioned any increase in the level of state subsidy on an enhancement of its managerial oversight of the system, something the social partners refused to countenance (Clegg 2005). The resultant deadlock was confirmed by the employers formally suspending their participation in UNEDIC in November 1982.

Their return in 1984 resulted from an implicit tripartite agreement on a new division of labor between the social partners and the state in French unemployment protection policy, premised on a more actuarial conception of unemployment insurance. The president at the time of the main French employers' confederation provided the clearest statement of this in a newspaper article published in the wake of the employer walk-out in 1982. He argued that a "new bipartite unemployment insurance, and not an unemployment assistance, must be put in place. The former can be for a large part financed by the contributions of workers and firms. The latter is entirely an issue of national solidarity."[2] The idea was to better distinguish between the sphere of insurance (benefits financed through social contributions and managed by the social partners) and the sphere of so-called "national solidarity" (benefits financed by taxes, often means-tested, and managed by the state); an institutional dualization of unemployment protection based on a "clarification" between the functions of income maintenance and protection against poverty.

The clarification mechanism was the contribution principle—the relationship between the amounts of contributions paid in work and the level and duration of entitlements in unemployment—which was now applied with a rigor never before seen in French unemployment insurance. A 1982 government decree first introduced distinct benefit streams in which rights to unemployment insurance

benefits no longer varied just on the basis of age, but also on the basis of contribution history. The 1984 unemployment insurance agreement between the
social partners then excluded those with the shortest contribution records from
any eligibility, and shortened the duration of entitlement for others, on the basis
that first-time job seekers and the longer-term unemployed would, if needy,
receive benefits under the new "solidarity" system (see below). The new organizing principles generated winners as well as losers, though: the calculation formula for the basic unemployment insurance benefit introduced in 1984 meant
that replacement rate and duration of benefits for those with longer contribution histories actually improved slightly (Daniel and Tuchszirer 1999: 290).

The eligibility and entitlement rules for unemployment insurance have been
recalibrated on numerous occasions subsequently, with the economic context at the time of renegotiation of collective agreements largely determining
whether changes are expansionary or restrictive overall. Due to the continuing
centrality of the contribution principle, though, the distribution among different groups in the unemployed population of cuts in the bad times and benefits
in the good has been far from even. During the 1990s and most of the 2000s,
negotiated cuts to unemployment insurance always fell most heavily on those
with weak labor market attachment, while benefits have been directed to those
with longer work records (Daniel 2000; Tuchszirer 2008). The 1992 reform of
unemployment benefits, negotiated in a context of rapidly rising unemployment and concerns about public deficits in the run up to the European single-
currency, offers perhaps the clearest example. Aside from the introduction of a
so-called "degressivity" mechanism, under which benefit levels were reduced as
unemployment duration lengthened, the reform levered most savings through
increases in minimum contribution periods and reductions in benefit durations
for those with the shortest contribution records. Those who found themselves
excluded from access to insurance benefits as a result—the beneficiary rate fell
from 52.5 percent in 1992 to 45.3 percent in 1994—were thus disproportionately
young, long-term unemployed, or those entering unemployment at the end of a
fixed-term contract (Daniel and Tuchszirer 1999: 307). When, as a result of this
reform, the unemployment insurance system returned to a healthy surplus by
the middle of the decade, these cuts were not simply repaired, however. Instead,
in 1995 a new early retirement benefit was introduced in the unemployment
insurance scheme, and the following year the application of the degressivity
mechanism was slowed down—changes that both benefited those who already
had entitlement to unemployment insurance.

Allied to the rapid expansion of temporary employment, the effect of these
parametric reform choices was that the percentage of unemployed people not
entitled to insurance benefits continued to fall over the remainder of the 1990s,
reaching nearly 60 percent late in 1999 (UNIstatis, 2010). Even when needy, only
a small proportion of this group could fall back on unemployment assistance

benefits, moreover. From its introduction in the 1984 reform, the main French unemployment assistance scheme combined means-testing with contribution conditions—5 years of employment in the last 10—that were stricter than in unemployment insurance. And while a flat-rate unemployment assistance scheme for those seeking stable labor market integration had also been introduced in 1984, eligibility for its main group of potential beneficiaries—young people—was limited by a requirement of holding certain kinds of technical or professional diplomas. This benefit was also very low relative to the minimum wage, which possibly explains why there was almost no protest when eligibility for it was removed from young people entirely in the 1992 budget, causing the stock of beneficiaries to fall from 110,000 in December 1991 to 29,000 one year later, and 17,000 by December 1995 (ibid.). In 1999, unemployment assistance only increased the beneficiary rate of all French unemployment protection by around 10 percent.

In this context, an important share of the burden of supporting parts of the unemployed population has fallen on France's general minimum income program. When a national minimum income was created in France in 1988 it had 400,000 beneficiaries, but by 1995 its caseload had swelled to just under 1 million. The year 1993—following the major unemployment insurance reform—witnessed the biggest single year-on-year caseload increase (DREES 2010). Though until the late 2000s it was not formally part of labor market policy, fluctuations in French social assistance caseloads owe most to the lagged effect of changes in the employment context, and the adjustments of the unemployment insurance system that followed. It is thus general social assistance that is today the main pillar of the "national solidarity" tier of France's dualized system of unemployment protection (Audier et al. 1998). Due notably to the fact that under-25-year-olds are not entitled to social assistance in France, however, it represents only a partial safety net stretched under the unemployment insurance system.

During the 2000s, the proportion of unemployed receiving insurance benefits in France has increased somewhat from its historic lows of the late 1990s (Seeleib-Kaiser et al., Chapter 7 of this volume). In a reform that introduced new activation requirements for recipients of insurance benefits, in 2000 the social partners negotiated a relaxation of contribution conditions. The 2009 unemployment insurance agreement then traded some reduction in benefit levels and durations for better contributors against some limited benefit rights for those with the shortest work records (Clegg 2011). But even though a 2008 reform harmonized the "responsibilities"—such as the job-search requirements and suitable work conditions—of all job-seekers, the rights-provision for different categories of French job-seekers retains a marked institutional duality, and an individuals' prior labor market attachment continues to be a strong determinant of the level and the type of benefit they will receive if unemployed.

Belgium: Preserving Inclusiveness Through Residualization

Unlike France, in the early 1980s Belgium had a long history of institutionally integrated provision for all the unemployed. From its inception, the unemployment benefit system was in principle open to everyone who was unable to find a job (De Lathouwer 1997). Though some contributory requirements were introduced in 1951, they remained very loose, intended essentially to avoid certain kinds of abuse (Palsterman 2005: 156). The 1951 regulations also extended eligibility for unemployment insurance to young people with no professional experience who had recently finished their studies. The functional need for supplementary systems of provision was further diminished by the fact that, uniquely among developed countries, entitlement to unemployment benefit has always been unlimited in time in Belgium. Though a national Minimum Income Scheme was introduced in 1974, there were, for the above reasons, very few unemployed people among its beneficiaries.

Originally, Belgian unemployment benefits were also entirely flat rate, though with levels differentiated between rural and urban areas, on the one hand, and men and women, on the other. A more Bismarckian earnings-related benefit structure was adopted in 1971, with benefits henceforth paying 60 percent of the previous salary for the first year of unemployment, and 40 percent thereafter to all the unemployed who were not heads of households (for whom benefit levels were maintained). However, the application of a strict insurance principle was limited not only by the continuing reference to heads of households, but also by the ceiling for the salary on which benefits were calculated being rather low. The system was financed from contributions by employers and employees, the rates of which were fixed by law. A state subsidy had, however, always covered any difference between contributory receipts and expenditures, and by 1981—after the explosion of unemployment in the 1970s—this subsidy represented just under 80 percent of total funds (De Deken, 2011).

With Belgium's exceptionally high indebtedness becoming a major concern, efforts were intensified in the early 1980s to reduce government contributions to unemployment insurance. Contribution ceilings that had been relaxed in the 1970s were scrapped altogether in 1982, and by 1993 the government subsidy represented only 7 percent of unemployment insurance finance (De Lathouwer 1997). During the same period, though, an increasing share of unemployment insurance funds was simultaneously being devoted to early retirement measures, mainly providing unemployment benefit "top-ups" to older unemployed workers who did not have access to collectively negotiated arrangements of the same kind introduced in the 1970s (De Deken 2011). These classic "labor shedding" measures have remained important up to the present day, and go a long way in explaining Belgium's very low activity rates among over 55-year-olds in particular. Although there is growing recognition that such measures are unsustainable, efforts to scale them back substantially have always foundered

(De Deken 2009). Given this, cost-cutting pressures resulting from growing concerns about levels of non-wage costs were very quickly instead focused on the structure of unemployment benefits for young and prime-age workers.

While cost-containment initiatives were indeed introduced in this area from the early 1980s in Belgium, they were, however, far more concentrated on reducing benefit levels than on reducing the scope or coverage of the unemployment benefit system by tightening contribution requirements or limiting the duration of payments. Benefit reductions were not necessarily universal, though. In 1980, the group of "non-heads of households" was further subdivided for the purposes of calculating benefit rights into "singles" and "cohabitees." Benefits for the latter—a group comprised essentially of school-leavers living with parents and married women with partners in work—became degressive in time, falling to an eventually flat-rate allowance that took no account of prior earnings. In 1982 benefits for young unemployed graduates—again, unless they were heads of households—were then disconnected from the minimum wage and replaced with a low flat-rate allowance, called the bridging allowance. The principle for reigning in the cost of benefits in Belgian unemployment protection was thus a kind of need-testing under which need was inferred from age and household status (De Deken 2009, 2011; Hemerijck and Marx 2010), rather than a stricter application of the contribution principle as had been seen in France.

Subsequent parametric reforms to the benefit system have generally further confirmed this strengthening of a basic protection orientation (Palsterman 2005). Having been decoupled from wages in the late 1970s, benefits were soon totally disconnected from consumer price developments and their level regulated on a discretionary basis. In practice, the relative value of maximum benefits was allowed to stagnate, not being increased even in line with inflation in 1984, 1985, or 1986, while minimum benefits were increased more rapidly, albeit somewhat selectively, in function of perceived household needs; "heads of households" did best, the "cohabitee" group created by the 1981 reforms worst. As a result, the gap between maximum and minimum benefits for a head of household fell from around 25 percent in the late 1970s to just over 10 percent in the mid-1990s (Marx 2007: 132). In the process, the insurance function of Belgian unemployment benefits has been increasingly abandoned; average benefit rates fell from a little more than 40 percent of the average gross wage in the private sector in 1980 to around 27 percent by 2004 (Faniel 2008: 55).

There have been very few efforts, in contrast, to limit entrance or continuing entitlement to unemployment benefit receipt, and time-unlimited unemployment benefit has been a "sacred cow" in Belgian social policy debates (Kuipers 2006: 82–83). The one major attempt to limit entitlement is noteworthy mainly for the controversy it caused, despite its rather limited scope. In 1987 the so-called "Suspension Article 80" was introduced, under which individuals from the "cohabitee" group could—provided household income exceeded a relatively high threshold—be disqualified from benefit receipt if their unemployment spell was deemed "abnormally long." In 1987 this was considered to be twice the regional average duration, controlling for age and gender of the benefit claimant, and in 1993 was shortened to 1.5 times the regional average—which still meant that termination proceedings would not be initiated before at least three years of benefit receipt, and in some regions not until around seven or eight years (Marx 2007: 129). When in the 1990s the Ministry of Labor stepped up efforts to actually enforce this rule—which had previously been implemented with a discretion that shaded into deliberate laxity—there was still a major public outcry, and a strong mobilization led by movements of the unemployed and supported by the trade unions eventually forced the government to limit the powers of the agents of the Public Employment Office to pursue cases of suspected abuse (Faniel 2005).

The upshot of this pattern of adjustment is that, although unemployment benefits have lost value for all groups—and for some groups rather more so than for others—Belgian unemployment protection remains an institutionally integrated system, with a beneficiary rate consistently estimated at over 80 percent of the unemployed (De Lathouwer 1997; De Deken 2011; Schömann et al 2000). Unlike in many developed countries, there is furthermore no notable difference between men and women in the proportion of unemployed people in receipt of unemployment benefits in Belgium (De Deken 2011). Following from this, social assistance has traditionally played only a very marginal role in the social protection of the unemployed. While total minimum income recipiency rates increased somewhat in the 1990s, towards the end of the decade the total numbers of social assistance recipients were still less than a tenth of the number of people in receipt of unemployment benefits (De Lathouwer 1997). Today social assistance remains a "truly residual system only providing means-tested benefits to those who are not part of the wage earning population, and a small minority of former wage earners who fail to meet the eligibility requirements of an otherwise very inclusive unemployment insurance scheme" (De Deken 2011: 118).

SOLIDARITY INCENTIVES: EXPLAINING POLICY CHOICE IN UNEMPLOYMENT PROTECTION

The Belgian and French unemployment protection systems have thus both undergone considerable parametric reform in recent decades. In certain respects, the winners and losers in this adjustment process have been similar in both countries; being young or being a woman makes it more likely to have lower levels of unemployment benefit entitlement in Belgium, just as it makes it less likely to receive an insurance benefit when unemployed in France. But the fact that Belgian and French policy makers have pulled on different reform levers—mainly benefit levels in the former case, mainly contribution conditions and benefit duration in the latter—has had important consequences. In Belgium, an accessible and encompassing unemployment benefit system was maintained, but at the cost of a progressive leveling down of benefits to a basic protection level, with a concomitant abandonment of any real insurance role of unemployment benefit for higher earners. In France, by contrast, preserving better rates of income replacement for many groups has meant accepting an increasingly exclusive "top tier" unemployment benefit system, with the implication that other risk profiles would be provided for—if at all—through subsidiary arrangements, on an explicitly means-tested basis. Accordingly, most recent data shows that while unemployed people in France are less likely than their Belgian counterparts to have less than 70 percent of the equivalized median income, they are rather more likely to have less than 40 percent or 50 percent (Eurostat 2010b).

Although levels of overall expenditure on unemployment benefits have converged in the two countries over the last quarter-century, the institutional and distributive logics at play have therefore been different. While in the French case we can witness an explicit dualization of unemployment protection into overlapping but discrete arrangements of distinctly different quality for "insiders" and "outsiders," in Belgium there has been an apparently more "solidaristic" sharing of the burdens of adjustment in this policy sector among different risk groups in the labor market. Given that the policy logic and distributive thrust of the broader socioeconomic adjustment trajectories in both countries are otherwise so similar, the intriguing question is why unemployment insurance has not followed suit.

In the existing literature on the dualization of regulatory and institutional arrangements in Continental welfare-production regimes, the reform of unemployment protection arrangements has largely been understood as a spillover from the labor market adjustment strategies of powerful insider interests represented in coordinative institutions. In their analysis of France and Germany, Palier and Thelen (2010 and Chapter 9 of this volume) thus argue that the dualization of unemployment protection in the two cases followed from the political and financial pressures generated by labor shedding strategies and the gradual development of a secondary labor market that resulted from the negotiated closure of internal labor markets by insiders. The logic is thus one of complementarities between welfare state reforms and broader labor market adjustment strategies, with the latter driving the former. As discussed above, however, labor shedding has been if anything more prevalent and consensual in Belgium than in France since the 1980s, and atypical employment has also expanded, albeit by less than in the French case. There is thus little reason to think that the less dualistic reform pattern in Belgian unemployment protection results from markedly different adjustment strategies and coalitional dynamics in the industrial relations sphere, and the functional pressures for change that these generate.

An alternative explanation for Franco-Belgian divergence could potentially reside in the party political sphere. It is widely argued that social democratic governments may have a significant impact on the extent to which dualizing labor market and social policy reforms will be pursued, though controversy remains over the nature of the relationship (Palier and Thelen 2010; Rueda 2007). But over the period from 1980 to 2007 as a whole, the left-wing share of cabinet seats in Belgium and France is very similar, averaging 40 percent and 48 percent (own calculations from Armingeon 2007). While the nature of the countries' electoral systems means left-wing party participation in governments has been more intermittent in France than Belgium, there appears to be no clear link between the partisan composition of government and the reform choices made. Strongly dualizing reforms in French unemployment protection were enacted under governments of both the Left (1982–1984) and the Right (1993), while the "basic protection turn" in Belgian unemployment protection began when the Left was out of government and has been continued since their return. In reality, governments of all partisan stripes find it difficult to exert influence over the direction of unemployment benefit reforms in both countries. Parametric adjustments in France are, as mentioned, formally based on autonomous collective agreements between the social partners, which are usually directly translated into law. In Belgium, unemployment insurance legislation is mainly based on royal decrees that are not subject to parliamentary debate, and the content of which is strongly influenced by a process of upstream negotiation with the social actors (Kuipers 2006: 84).

When examining the Belgian case, it is of course important to consider the possible impact of the federal political system and the underlying linguistic cleavages, which have become considerably more salient in the period since 1980. This is undoubtedly important in understanding aspects of social policy (non-)reform in the Belgian case, particularly as the linguistic cleavage coincides with sharp differences in the social and labor market situations of Flanders and Wallonia (Poirier and Vansteenkiste 2000). This incendiary nature of the "regional question" perhaps can help to explain why governments and/or social actors have been reticent to push for tighter eligibility conditions for, or more limited entitlement to, unemployment benefit payments that might drive some of the unemployed onto the social assistance scheme. Given that the latter is partly financed by local government, such a change would lead to a damaging and highly controversial alteration in the flow of resources within the country (OECD 1998: 102–103). More generally, distinguishing "professional solidarity" from "national solidarity" is undoubtedly more problematic when the latter is now so difficult and contested. But as discussed below, the other policy preferences of social actors appear to systematically trump their regional identities, and thus moderate the influence of sub-state nationalism on policy decisions and non-decisions (see also Béland and Lecours 2005).

It might be also argued, finally, that different historical and ideational legacies can help to explain why processes of post-industrialization in the labor
market have produced such different unemployment policy responses in the
two cases. In part, the story told in the previous section is less one of divergence from a truly common starting point as it is of a reversion to first principles. As noted, the Belgian unemployment benefit system was always more
oriented to basic protection, and had only really taken on a stronger insurance
character in the 1970s; inversely, in France the original vocation of UNEDIC
was to provide replacement incomes to the normally securely employed, and
it had only integrated more basic protection functions over time. Despite the
institutional convergence at the end of the "golden age," it could be argued that
certain policy principles—such as time-unlimited unemployment benefits in
Belgium, or their "professional" character in France—had endured, and served
as "cognitive locks" (cf. Blyth 2001) that shaped the attitude and preferences of
all actors when later faced with intensified cost pressures. Such an argument
would, however, overstate the degree of consensus over the parametric reform
options available, and downplay the role of agency and choice in the privileg-
ing of one over others. For example, in their contribution to debates on the
modernization of social security in the mid-1990s, the Belgian employers' confederation argued that in each sector of social protection it was necessary to distinguish "that which is concerned with general solidarity—and must therefore
be covered by general means—and that which is concerned with professional
solidarity—and must be covered by contributions" (cited in Arcq and Reman
1996: 27). A dualistic policy response to structural change was, then, on the table
in Belgium as well as France. To explain why it was less influential in unemployment protection reforms in one case than the other, we need to understand how
different reform options intersect with the interests and preferences of other
influential actors.

It is argued here that the divergence between Belgian and French unemployment protection policies is best understood in relation to the preferences and
strategies of trade unions in the two countries. Palier and Thelen (2010; and
Chapter 9 of this volume) also focus on (some) unions, emphasizing how the
compromises they reach with the representatives of (some) employers when
faced with the challenges of structural change encourage the adoption of dualistic policies across interrelated sub-spheres of coordinated market economies.
With respect to unemployment protection issues, however, it is suggested here
that the most important influence on the preferences of the unions is not the
interests of their (insider) members, but rather their interests as organizations
participating in the governance of unemployment insurance arrangements.
While these organizational interests generate preferences for dualistic policies
in the French case, the difference in the way that social governance functions
means that this is not the case in Belgium.

French and Belgian trade unions are very different.[3] While France has the lowest rates of union density of any developed country, trade unions in Belgium are not only relatively strong in membership terms, but have also bucked a widespread trend by avoiding membership decline since the early 1980s. Between 1980 and 2007, union density fell from just under 20 percent to around 9 percent in France, while in Belgium it remained stable at around 55 percent (Visser 2009). Some of the explanation for both the different levels of union density and, even more so, for the divergent trends since the 1980s, is commonly argued to be found in the specific role of Belgian trade unions in the unemployment benefit system (Vandaele 2006). Belgium is characterized by a "pseudo-Ghent" unemployment benefit system, with unions acting as the "cash desks" of the public unemployment insurance system, paying out benefits to the unemployed on behalf of the Public Employment Office. Though, unlike in true Ghent systems, unemployment insurance is compulsory and it is not necessary to join a union to be able claim benefits, 85 percent of the unemployed choose to do exactly that, because of the denser network of union payment offices, the better legal support services they provide, and the fact that the union funds often pay benefits more rapidly (Faniel 2008: 54). As a result, "the prospect of becoming unemployed...drives employees into the unions" (Vandaele 2006: 652).

Is it simply the greater overall strength of the Belgian unions, or the related fact that unemployed "outsiders" are thus a significant minority of their members, that explains the divergence in Belgian and French unemployment policy (cf. De Deken 2011; Eichhorst and Marx, Chapter 4 of this volume)? If this were the case, then we would surely anticipate the divergence between the Belgian and French cases to be even more wide-ranging and clear-cut than it is. In the field of unemployment benefit policy, we would expect cost-containment pressures to have been headed off in Belgium altogether, rather than simply channeled in particular ways. We would furthermore not expect Belgian divergence to be contained to the sphere of unemployment, but also to impact the broader socioeconomic adjustment trajectory discussed in the section one. In particular, if the important variable were the greater representation of "outsiders" in Belgian unions, we would anticipate that labor market adjustment strategies as a whole, and not just in unemployment protection, should be more "outsider friendly." The reality is that, despite their membership profile, Belgian unions do in fact generally privilege the interests of insiders, notably as a result of the limited mobilization of unemployed members inside them and the role of the unions' leaders—always drawn from the core "rank and file" of employed members—in setting policy strategies (Faniel 2006, 2009).

If the Belgian unions have resisted the dualization of unemployment protection specifically, it is rather because of the way their organizational interests have shaped their policy preferences in this field. The unions' governance role in unemployment benefit impacts not only their inherited membership profile, but also their forward-looking strategic preoccupations. As mentioned, participation in unemployment benefit administration acts as a "recruiting sergeant" for Belgian trade unions, but it does so all the more effectively if employees know that they will be able to continue to receive benefits from the union funds irrespective of their contribution history or unemployment duration. Furthermore, in addition to the cost of the benefits they pay out, the unions additionally receive a set administration fee—covering both operating and personnel costs—from ONEM for every unemployed person to whom they pay benefits. The resources flowing from this fee alone is estimated to represent around 25 percent of all union funds in Belgium (IGAS 2004: 25), an income stream that would diminish if some of the unemployed were to receive benefits elsewhere, either from the public payment desk or in an alternative benefit system. Both recruitment and financial considerations can explain why the unions have long tried to limit the attractiveness of competing cash desks in the public system (Faniel 2007: 19), but also why they are so eager to maintain the integrated structure of benefit provision. It thus helps us to understand why they fought much harder against attempts to limit the duration of benefits than they have against declines in the insurance function (Kuipers 2006: 82–83; Marx 2007: 155), despite the fact that this in principle benefits outsiders more than insiders.

The force of these organizational interests is underscored by the way that they appease the potential tensions and policy dissensions the might result from sub-national and linguistic cleavages that cut across organized labor in Belgium. Though the Catholic ACV/CSC has a clear majority of Flemish members, unlike the Flemish political parties it has never shown much enthusiasm for the regionalization of the social protection system (Béland and Lecours 2005: 279; Palsterman 2007: 21). There is far less disagreement on the importance of maintaining a federal social protection system among the various unions than between Belgian political parties, who compete for voters—many of whom are union members—on fiercely regionalist platforms (Palsterman 2007).

The historical legitimacy of the governance arrangements in unemployment insurance, rooted in history of Belgian unemployment protection and symbolically related to the "social pact" of 1944 (Pasture 1993), plays an important role, too. Due to this "organic" legitimacy, there is no perception that union administration is any less justified in the context of heavy state subsidization of unemployment insurance. As noted above, the state subsidy to the unemployment insurance fund was as high as 80 percent around 1980, without this ever seriously calling into question the legitimacy of the unions' governance role. This also allows the unions to press for the policies they prefer without their core membership necessarily having to bear a disproportionate cost through social contributions.

Though the French trade unions also participate in the governance of unemployment benefits, they face a very different set of institutional incentives. As noted, French unemployment benefits are managed through periodic collective agreements between the social partners, subject only to *erga omnes* extension by the state, a system known as *paritarisme*. Unique for any public unemployment insurance in the developed world, this governance structure is an artifact of the origins of UNEDIC, which was initially established as a complementary system of benefit provision through which the social partners could manage their labor market needs. Though it does not bring any membership benefits to the French unions, it does give them access to precious financial resources, including a share of a public subsidy for "the functioning of *paritarisme*." While it is notoriously difficult to establish their magnitude exactly (Hadas-Lebel 2006: 60), these resources—as well as the political status *paritarisme* affords—appear particularly crucial to the organizational viability of French unions, given their very low membership rates. For this reason, their interests in the unemployment protection sphere have always been about preserving the viability of *paritarisme*, as well as defending the rights of employees (Clegg 2005).

As in Belgium, though, the unions' organizational interests within a given institutional configuration help to shape their unemployment policy preferences. As the missions of UNEDIC have expanded, its *paritaire* functioning has become increasingly vulnerable to questions and criticisms regarding its appropriateness. Lacking any organic justification for their governance role in the context of a fundamentally statist political culture, the autonomous contributory financing structure of the institution is the social partners' main argument against these criticisms; unemployment insurance is funded entirely out of contributions paid by firms and workers, and it is therefore still appropriate that their representatives should be charged with its co-management. When in 1982 the employers refused to countenance further contribution increases, and the state refused to extend its recently instituted subsidy without taking on an explicit managerial role, the unions were faced with a choice: risk the demise of the *paritaire* system or negotiate selective reductions in benefits.

It would have been conceivable to maintain a relatively integrated benefit system within stable financial parameters by reducing the replacement rate at the higher end, or by restricting benefit entitlement for those with longer work- and contribution-records. Instead, the union preference was for the adjustment pattern outlined above: the maintenance of generous replacement rates for good contributors, and the acceptance that others would need to rely on tax-financed national solidarity provisions. Partly, this can be explained by their representational bias toward a core membership of older, securely employed workers. But the defense of *paritarisme* also played a role in union preference formation that was independent of any "logic of membership." On the one hand, by tightening the link between contributions and entitlements, the reform choices have reaffirmed the insurance character of unemployment insurance, and—in addition to the autonomous financing structure—helped bolster legitimacy for the system's management by the social partners. On the other, the survival of *paritarisme* required that common ground be found between the unions and the employers, which meant that the former were obliged to take on board the preferences of the latter in a way that Belgian unions were not.

As Palier and Thelen (2010; and Chapter 9 of this volume) have argued, then, the dualization of French unemployment insurance resulted from a compromise between unions and employers structuring policy development in this field. What the preceding discussion has shown, however, is that the reason the French unions sought to reach such a compromise, and accepted the parametric reform choices on which it could be built, is intimately related to their organizational interest in preserving their role in unemployment insurance governance. As the Belgian case illustrates, under a different governance arrangement the maximization of organizational benefits to unions can be much less dependent on the formation of cross-class compromises, and may encourage the adoption of a very different set of unemployment policy of preferences. Even in similar welfare-production regimes, the adoption of dualistic welfare policy responses to the post-industrialization of labor markets is therefore far from inevitable.

CONCLUSION: THE IMPORTANCE OF MINOR DIFFERENCES

The rise of the industrial working class was one of the key sociological developments of the early part of the twentieth century, and a crucial driver of social policy development. It now appears clear that post-industrialization of labor markets has been a key feature of the *fin de siècle* and is structuring social policy development into the new century. But just as the rise of labor power, along with its political and policy impact, was shaped by variations in often apparently rather technical features of existing policy institutions across countries (Rothstein 1992), so institutional variations in established public policies are mediating the impact of structural labor market change on the preferences of organized interests and on its implications for social policy development.

The analysis of the recent development of unemployment protection policies in Belgium and France in this chapter provides one example of this. Despite similar macro-institutional settings, unemployment protection policies evolved very differently in the two cases, leading to a progressive shift to a minimum protection model for all the unemployed in the Belgian case, and to the adoption and maintenance of a dualized unemployment protection structure in the French. This divergence can be explained, it has been argued, by the way that the link between union strategies to maximize organizational rents and benefits, on the one hand, and their policy preferences, on the other, is mediated by the structure and operation of social governance institutions in the sector. Even though they are generally "insider" membership organizations, unions' policy preferences will not necessarily manifest an insider bias, as these actors also—and perhaps even mainly—pursue organizational goals. How these goals translate into policy preferences, though, depends on the structure and operation of social governance arrangements, which can vary considerably between countries in the same welfare-production regime, and even from policy sector to policy sector in the same country (Ebbinghaus 2010). While unemployment protection in Belgium and France illustrates this phenomenon well, the argument also has broader relevance, as suggested by the importance of unions' organizational interests in specific governance arrangements in shaping their labor market and unemployment protection reform preferences in countries such as the Netherlands (Clegg et al. 2010) and Sweden (Anderson 2001).

What broader conclusions can we draw regarding the politics of dualization in social protection? The argument suggests, first, that even in relatively similar macro-institutional settings and faced with similar functional pressures, a dualizing dynamic will not necessarily "cascade down" into social protection reform from developments in the productive sphere. Social policies such as unemployment insurance are core societal institutions, too important in their own right to the interests and strategies of collective actors to simply reflect or react to change in the labor market. This is, of course, not to deny the existence of linkages between the productive sphere and the realm of social protection. It is to suggest, however, that—especially in the short term—coherence or complementarity between the two is not inevitable, and that the causal arrow between developments in the two spheres runs in both directions. With regard to the latter point, the cases analyzed here perhaps provide some good examples of this. If temporary employment has grown only moderately in Belgium since the 1980s despite high labor costs and relatively rigid protection of standard employment (Eichhorst and Marx, Chapter 4 of this volume), this may be in part because an encompassing unemployment insurance system has given potential cheap labor an "exit option" that they do not have elsewhere. Inversely, the fast expansion of atypical employment statuses in France was probably as much a result of the dualization of unemployment protection—which left many people without any benefit-based income protection at all—as it was a driver of it. In both cases, it can be argued that social protection reforms have their own autonomous political logic and dynamic, which shape as much as they are shaped by developments in the labor market.

A second implication of the analysis is that if the policy preferences of collective actors such as trade unions are as much institutionally as sociologically generated, then they can in principle be shaped through institutional and governance reform. Though institutional reform is never easy, governments operating in policy environments characterized by traditions of social partner influence may under certain circumstances therefore be able to alter the course of policy development and impact on distributive outcomes not only through monetary side-payments, but also through "meta-reforms" (cf. Clegg 2007) that change the incentives of social actors. This seems to be exactly what

French governments belatedly realized with respect to unemployment protection. In the process of a 2008 reform that merged the unemployment insurance system and the public employment service at delivery level in France, it was made very clear to the French unions that the preservation of *paritarisme* in unemployment insurance would depend on their negotiating policies that were a better fit with (the current government's interpretation of) the general interest (Willmann 2009). It was in this context that the 2009 unemployment insurance agreement innovated with a parametric reform that reduced the maximum duration of benefit payment for some better contributors while relaxing the minimum contribution conditions considerably. This reform seems set to enlarge access to first-tier unemployment insurance, and possibly represents a first step toward a more institutionally integrated system of post-industrial unemployment protection.

Would such a change help to combat inequalities in the French labor market and society? This brings forth a final consideration, of a more speculative nature, regarding the effect of the different reform trajectories discussed in this chapter. While it may be tempting to read social and distributional outcomes from institutional structures, it is probably a temptation that should be resisted. Though Belgian unions' organizational interests led them to support what appears *prima facie* to be a more "solidaristic" unemployment benefit reform strategy than their French homologues, it was noted above that Belgium has some of the highest rates of long- and very long-term unemployment in the developed world. Furthermore, while the Belgian adjustment trajectory appears to date to have limited the extent of severe poverty among the unemployed, the decline of the insurance function may actually undercut political support for such solidarity in the longer term (Marx 2007). This chapter has focused on the political drivers of reforms that tend to dualize, or otherwise, social protection structures and arrangements. How far these alternative reform paths reinforce or mitigate different kinds of social inequalities over the long term is a related but separate question, important enough to merit explicit investigation in its own right.

NOTES

1 *Union nationale interprofessionelle pour l'emploi dans l'industrie et le commerce.*
2 Interview with Yvon Gattaz in *Le Monde*, November 23, 1982.
3 This chapter discusses unions in an undifferentiated way, despite the existence of three representative national confederations in Belgium and five in France. While internal decision-making within confederations and competition between them obviously impacts union preference formation in both countries, exploration of this is beyond the scope

of this chapter and is not necessary to understand the comparative argument developed here.

REFERENCES

Anderson, Karen (2001). "The Politics of Retrenchment in a Social Democratic Welfare State: Reform of Swedish Pensions and Unemployment Insurance," *Comparative Political Studies*, 34(9): 1063–1091.

Arcq, Etienne, and Reman, Pierre (1996). Les interlocuteurs sociaux et la modernisation de la sécurité sociale, *Courrier Hebdomadaire du CRISP*, no. 1508–1509.

Armingeon, Klaus, Marlène Gerber, Philipp Leimgruber, and Michelle Beyeler (2009). *Comparative Political Data Set 1960–2007*. Institute of Political Science, University of Berne.

Armingeon, Klaus, et al. (2007). *Comparative Political Dataset*. Available from http://www.ipw.unibe.ch/content/team/klaus_armingeon/comparative_political_data_sets/index_ger.html (accessed October 19, 2010).

Audier, Florence, Dang, Ai-Thu, and Outin, Jean-Luc (1998). « Le RMI comme mode particulier d'indemnisation du chômage, » in Méhaut, Philippe, and Mossé, Philippe (eds.), *Les politiques sociales catégorielles: Fondements, portée et limites*, Paris: L'Harmattan, pp. 124–143.

Béland, Daniel, and Lecours, André (2005). "Nationalism, Public Policy and Institutional Development: Social Security in Belgium," *Journal of Public Policy*, 25(2): 265–285.

Blyth, Mark (2001). "The Transformation of the Swedish Model: Economic Ideas, Distributional Conflict and Institutional Change," *World Politics*, 54(1): 1–26.

Cahuc, Pierre, and Kramarz, Francis (2004). *De la Précarité à la Mobilité*, Paris: La Documentation Française.

Cahuc, Pierre, and Zylberberg, André (2009). *Les réformes ratées du Président Sarkozy*, Paris: Flammarion.

Clegg, Daniel (2005). *Activating the Multi-Tiered Welfare State: Governance, Welfare Politics and Unemployment Policies in France and the United Kingdom*, Florence: European University Institute.

Clegg, Daniel (2007). "Continental Drift: On Unemployment Policy Change in Bismarckian Welfare States," *Social Policy and Administration*, 41(6): 597–617.

Clegg, Daniel (2011). "France: Integration versus dualization," in Clasen, Jochen, and Clegg, Daniel (eds.), *Regulating the Risk of Unemployment*, Oxford: Oxford University Press, pp. 34–54.

Clegg, Daniel, Graziano, Paolo, and van Wijnbergen, Christa (2010). "Between Sectionalism and Revitalisation: Trade Unions and Activation in Europe," RECWOWE working paper no. 07/10.

Daniel, Christine (2000). « L'indemnisation du chômage depuis 1974: d'une logique d'intégration à une logique de segmentation, » *Revue française des affaires sociales*, 54(3–4): 29–46.

Daniel, Christine, and Tuchszirer, Carole (1999). *L'Etat face aux chômeurs: L'indemnisation du chômage de 1884 à nos jours,* Paris: Flammarion.

De Deken, Johan (2009). "Belgium," in De Beer, Paul, and Schills, Trudie (eds.), *The Labour Market Triangle: Employment Protection, Unemployment Compensation and Activation in Europe,* Cheltenham: Edward Elgar, pp. 145–173.

De Deken, Johan (2011). "Belgium: A Precursor or Muddling Through," in Clasen, Jochen, and Clegg, Daniel (eds.), *Regulating the Risk of Unemployment,* Oxford: Oxford University Press, pp. 100–120.

De Lathouwer, Lieve (1997). « Vingt années d'évolution de la politique menée en Belgique dans la domaine de l'assurance chômage » *Revue Belge de Sécurité Sociale,* 1997(4–3): 793–858.

DREES (2010). *Les minima sociaux et le RSA.* Available from http://www.sante-sports.gouv.fr/minima-sociaux,5910.html (accessed October 19, 2010).

Ebbinghaus, Bernhard (2010). "Union and Employers," in Castles, Francis, Leibfried, Stephan, Lewis, Jane, Obinger, Herbert, and Pierson, Christopher (eds.), *The Oxford Handbook of the Welfare State,* Oxford: Oxford University Press, pp. 196–210.

Ebbinghaus, Bernhard, and Hassel, Anke (2000). "Striking Deals: Concertation in the Reform of Continental European Welfare States," *Journal of European Public Policy,* 7(1): 44–62.

Eichhorst, Werner, and Hemerijck, Anton (2010). "Whatever Happened to the Bismarckian Welfare State? From Labor Shedding to Employment Friendly Reforms," in Palier, Bruno (ed.), *A Long Goodbye to Bismarck? The Politics of Welfare Reform in Continental Europe,* Amsterdam: Amsterdam University Press, pp. 301–332.

Esping-Andersen, Gøsta, and Regini, Marino (eds.) (2000). *Why Deregulate Labour Markets?* Oxford: Oxford University Press.

Eurostat (2010a). *Employment and Unemployment (LFS).* Available from http://epp.eurostat.ec.europa.eu/portal/page/portal/employment_unemployment_lfs/data/main_tables (accessed October 18, 2010).

Eurostat (2010b). *At-risk-of-poverty Rate by Poverty Threshold and Most Frequent Activity in the Previous Year (Source: SILC).* Available from http://epp.eurostat.ec.europa.eu/portal/page/portal/income_social_inclusion_living_conditions/data/database (accessed October 19, 2010).

Faniel, Jean (2009). "Belgian Trade Unions, the Unemployed and the Growth of Unemployment," in Guigni, Marco (ed.), *The Politics of Unemployment in Europe,* Aldershot: Ashgate, pp. 101–116.

Faniel, Jean (2008). "Belgique: L'assurance chômage entre pressions européennes et polémiques régionales," *Chronique Internationale de l'IRES,* no. 115, 52–63.

Faniel, Jean (2007) "Belgique: Le système d'assurance chômage: Un particularisme en sursis ?," *Chronique Internationale de l'IRES,* no. 108, 15–24.

Faniel, Jean (2006). "L'organisation des chômeurs dans les syndicats," *Courrier Hebdomadaire du CRISP,* no. 1929–1930.

Faniel, Jean (2005). "Le contrôle des chômeurs en Belgique: Objectifs et résistances," *Informations Sociales,* no. 126, 84–91.

Hadas-Lebel, Raphäel (2006). *Pour un dialogue social efficace et légitime: représentativité et financement des organisations professionnelles et syndicales*, Paris: La Documentation Française.

Hall, Peter (2006). "Introduction: The Politics of Social Change in France," in Culpepper, Pepper D., Hall, Peter A., and Palier, Bruno (eds.), *Changing France: The Politics that Markets Make*, Basingstoke: Palgrave, pp. 1–28.

Hemerijck, Anton, and Marx, Ive (2010). "Continental Welfare at a Crossroads: The Choice Between Activation and Minimum Income Protection in Belgium and the Netherlands," in Palier, Bruno (ed.), *A Long Goodbye to Bismarck? The Politics of Reforms in Continental Europe*, Amsterdam: Amsterdam University Press, pp. 129–156.

Hemerijck, Anton, Unger, Brigitte, and Visser, Jelle (2000). "How Small Countries Negotiate Change: Twenty Years of Policy Adjustment In Austria, Belgium and the Netherlands," in Scharpf, Fritz W., and Schmidt, Vivien A. (eds.), *Welfare and Work in the Open Economy: Volume II, Diverse Responses to Common Challenges*, Oxford: Oxford University Press, pp. 175–263.

Hemerijck, Anton, and Visser, Jelle (2000). "Change and Immobility: Three Decades of Policy Adjustment in Belgium and the Netherlands," in Ferrera, Maurizio, and Rhodes, Martin (eds.), *Recasting European Welfare States*, London: Frank Cass, pp. 229–256.

IGAS (2004). *Le financement des syndicats, étude d'administration comparée: Le cas de la Belgique*, Paris: La Documentation Française.

Iversen, Torben (2005). *Capitalism, Democracy and Welfare*, Cambridge: Cambridge University Press.

Kuipers, Saneke (2006). *The Crisis Imperative: Crisis Rhetoric and Welfare State Reform in Belgium and the Netherlands in the Early 1990s*, Amsterdam: Amsterdam University Press.

Marx, Ive (2007). *A New Social Question? On Minimum Income Protection in the Postindustrial Era*, Amsterdam: Amsterdam University Press.

OECD (1998). *The Battle Against Social Exclusion: Volume 2*, Paris: OECD.

OECD (2010a). *Employment by Permanency of the Job*. Available from http://stats.oecd.org/Index.aspx (accessed October 18, 2010).

OECD (2010b). *Public Expenditure and Participant Stocks on LMP*. Available from http://stats.oecd.org/Index.aspx (accessed October 19, 2010).

Palier, Bruno (2005). *Gouverner la sécurité sociale: les réformes du système français de protection sociale depuis 1945*, 2nd ed., Paris: Presses Universitaires de France.

Palier, Bruno, and Thelen, Kathleen (2010). "Institutionalizing Dualism: Complementarities and Change in France and Germany," *Politics and Society*, 38(1): 119–148.

Palsterman, Paul (2007). "Régionaliser la politique de l'emploi?," *Courrier Hebdomadaire du CRISP*, no. 1958–1959.

Palsterman, Paul (2005). "Evolution de la notion de chômage involontaire dans l'assurance chômage belge (1945–2004)," in Vielle, Pascale, Pochet, Philippe, and Cassiers, Isabelle (eds.), *L'Etat social actif: vers un changement de paradigme?*, Brussels, P.I.E-Peter Lang, pp. 151–178.

Pasture, Patrick (1993). "The April 1944 'Social Pact' in Belgium and Its Significance for the Post-war Welfare State," *Journal of Contemporary History*, 28(4): 695–714.

Poirier, Johann, and Vansteenkiste, Steven (2000). "Le débat sur le fédéralisation de la sécurité sociale en Belgique," *Revue belge de sécurité sociale*, 2: 331–379.

Rueda, David (2007). *Social Democracy Inside-Out*, Oxford: Oxford University Press.

Rothstein, Bo (1992). "Labor Market Institutions and Working Class Strength," in Steinmo, Sven, Thelen, Kathleen, and Longstreth, Frank (eds.), *Structuring Politics: Historical Institutionalism in Comparative Analysis*, Cambridge: Cambridge University Press, pp. 33–56.

Scharpf, Fritz W. (1997). "Employment and the Welfare State: A Continental Dilemma," MPIfG Working Paper 97/7.

Schömann, Klaus, Flechtner, Stefanie, Mytzek, Ralf, and Schömann, Isabelle (2000). "Moving Toward Employment Insurance: Unemployment Insurance and Employment Protection in the OECD," WZB Discussion Paper FSI 00–201.

Scruggs, Lyle (2002). "The Ghent System and Union Membership in Europe, 1970–2006," *Political Research Quarterly*, 55(2): 275–297.

Smith, Timothy (2004). *France in Crisis: Welfare, Inequality and Globalization since 1980*, Cambridge: Cambridge University Press.

Tuchszirer, Carole (2008). "France: Un dispositif indemnitaire devenu insensible aux évolutions du marché du travail," *Chronique Internationale de l'IRES*, no. 115, 100–111.

UNIstatis (2010). *Demandeurs d'emploi indemnisés et non indemnisés*. Available from http://info.assedic.fr/unistatis/(accessed October 19, 2010).

Vandaele, Kurt (2006). "A Report from the Homeland of the Ghent System: The Relationship Between Unemployment and Unions Membership in Belgium," *Transfer* 4(06): 647–657.

Visser, Jelle (2009). *ICTWSS Data base*. Available from http://www.uva-aias.net/207 (accessed October 19, 2010).

Willmann, Christophe (2009). "L'autonomie des partenaires sociaux en débat: Pôle emploi et la convention d'assurance chômage du 19 février 2009," *Droit Social*, no. 7–8, 830–841.

12

INSIDER-OUTSIDER POLITICS

*PARTY STRATEGIES AND POLITICAL
BEHAVIOR IN SWEDEN*

JOHANNES LINDVALL AND **DAVID RUEDA**

INTRODUCTION

The dualization of labor markets is becoming a topic of great importance to students of the advanced capitalist countries: recent work in comparative political economy emphasizes the political and economic relevance of the distinction between workers who enjoy stable and protected employment (insiders) and those who do not (outsiders).[1] Contrary to most of the other chapters in this volume, our contribution does not investigate dualization as such, but its political consequences. This chapter is concerned with the relationship between party strategies and the political behavior of insiders and outsiders in the labor market, concentrating on the risk that outsiders may become politically alienated and marginalized. Taking the case of Sweden as our guide, we argue that labor market outsiders who perceive that they are being ignored by Social Democratic parties become more likely to exit politics or to support more radical political alternatives. We combine an analysis of election campaigns in the 1990s and 2000s with an analysis of survey data from the Swedish National Election Studies.

Until recently, the distinction between insiders and outsiders was not salient in Sweden, as a result of propitious macroeconomic circumstances, a political commitment to full employment, and an encompassing labor union movement that helped to resolve latent conflicts between different categories of wage earners.[2] However, in the early 1990s, Sweden experienced a sudden and rapid increase in unemployment, from less than 2 percent in 1990 to almost 10 percent in 1993 (see Figure 12-1), placing the Swedish labor market model under great strain. A case study of Sweden therefore enables us to make

Figure 12-1: Open unemployment in Sweden

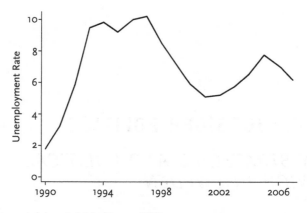

Source: Armingeon et al. (2009). Original Source: OECD.

a detailed investigation of political competition and mass political behavior in a country that has recently experienced a sudden increase in the number of outsiders. We concentrate on the four elections that have been held since mass unemployment emerged in the Swedish economy: the elections in 1994, 1998, 2002, and 2006.

PARTY POLITICS AND THE POLITICAL BEHAVIOR OF INSIDERS AND OUTSIDERS

Like Rueda (2007), we argue that the distinction between insiders and outsiders is essential to understanding politics in the industrialized democracies since the 1970s. However, whereas Rueda's work concentrates on the relationship between government partisanship and economic policy, we emphasize another matter of central importance that has not received enough attention: the interaction of party strategies and the political preferences of voters. We seek to answer a simple question: if, as Rueda argues, Social Democratic parties have incentives to promote the interests of insiders, how do outsiders respond? Our answer, in brief, is that outsiders tend to abandon the political process or vote for more radical political parties when they perceive that Social Democratic parties or other mainstream left parties are not defending their interests.

Our argument relies on the disaggregation of the working class, broadly defined, into insiders and outsiders. Theoretically, we define insiders as wage-earners with protected jobs and outsiders as individuals who are either unemployed or hold jobs with low levels of protection and employment rights.[3] The potential for conflicting interests between insiders and outsiders is related to their vulnerability to unemployment. Insiders are less affected by unemployment and are therefore less likely to support parties that dedicate substantial resources to employment promotion or cash benefits for the unemployed. Outsiders are more vulnerable to unemployment, since they are either unemployed already or enjoy little employment protection. They are therefore more concerned with the employment strategies of political parties, and favor generous benefits for the unemployed.

Of course, insiders always face *some* probability of losing their jobs (if the companies they work for go out of business, for example), but since insiders have less reason to believe that unemployment will affect them personally, we expect that they will find parties that emphasize employment policy less appealing. An increase in the resources dedicated to active labor market policies and benefits for the unemployed represents a higher tax burden for insiders, and a diversion of resources that could have been spent on public services from which insiders would benefit.

As we will demonstrate, Swedish political developments in the 1990s and 2000s provide evidence that when Social Democratic parties fail to emphasize the need to deal with unemployment, they push outsiders either to abstain from voting or to consider other options. In the last section of this chapter, we also argue that evidence from the 2006 election suggests that mainstream left parties face a dilemma: by being seen to side with outsiders, the Swedish Social Democrats appear to have antagonized some insiders, allowing the Center-Right parties to (successfully) target these insider groups.

Like studies of economic voting (Duch and Stevenson 2008), our argument assumes that there is a relationship between an individual's economic interests and her likelihood to reward a party with her vote. Our argument is also strongly related to the literature on class voting (see, for example, Evans 1999), which emphasizes the effects of other socioeconomic cleavages on political preferences. Moreover, our approach is related to the recent literature on risks and skills as determinants of political preferences, but whereas this literature associates unemployment vulnerability with particular skill profiles (Cusack, Iversen, and Rehm 2006), we highlight the importance of the more general divide between insiders and outsiders (regardless of their skills). Finally, we are indebted to an important tradition of scholarship concerning the relationship between economic and political marginalization, including landmark studies such as Schlozman and Verba (1979) and Bartels (2008). However, in contrast to most of the authors mentioned here—who are interested in individual preferences and voting choices as such—our goal is to explain how individual-level preferences are influenced by (and influence) party strategies.[4]

SWEDEN AS A HARD CASE

The main reason why we have chosen to focus on the Swedish case is that Sweden is a hard case for theories of insiders and outsiders. A number of authors have argued that whereas insider-outsider politics has emerged in Continental Europe (see, for example, Palier and Thelen 2010, and several of the chapters in this volume), it has not emerged in the Nordic countries (Iversen 2009). In the words of Jonas Pontusson, "the growing gap between labor-market 'insiders' and 'outsiders' is first and foremost a continental phenomenon" (2011: 91).

Two arguments can be made for the claim that conflicts between insiders and outsiders are likely to be less intense in Sweden than in other European democracies. The first argument emphasizes Sweden's encompassing and centralized trade unions and employer organizations. As Mancur Olson (1965) has argued, encompassing interest organizations are more likely to take general goals into consideration than organizations representing more narrowly defined groups. Swedish labor market institutions can be expected to promote solidaristic policies that bring together insiders and outsiders. The second argument emphasizes the difference between Christian Democracy and Social Democracy. Iversen and Stephens (2008, 605), for example, see insider-outsider conflicts as the outcome of Christian Democratic rather than Social Democratic politics, arguing that Social Democratic governments have "shored up employment while preventing the development of either deep insider-outsider divisions (as in the Continental European countries) or stark wage inequality as in the liberal countries" (2008: 609). For Iversen and Soskice (2009), the reason for this difference between the Continental and Nordic cases is that in countries like Sweden, the party system allows Social Democratic parties to protect low-wage workers; in countries with strong Christian Democratic parties, Social Democratic parties have to become more centrist, abandoning outsiders.

These arguments clearly demonstrate the importance of Sweden as a hard case. The scholars whom we have just cited would not expect the distinction between insiders and outsiders to have any effect on party politics and political behavior in Sweden. In other words, our hypothesis is relatively unlikely to be confirmed, given the weak divide between insiders and outsiders in Sweden, as compared to Liberal or Continental countries. If we find an effect in Sweden, we will make a general point about the importance of this divide that is not limited to an explanation of Swedish politics. It is possible that insider-outsider divides are weaker in countries with encompassing unions and proportional representation systems without strong Christian Democratic parties. Yet, the distinction between insiders and outsiders may still matter. As Iversen and Stephens would expect, our analysis shows that after the election in 1998, when their support among outsiders declined, the Swedish Social Democrats made significant attempts to recover outsider support (unlike mainstream left parties in Continental Europe). But our analysis also suggests that they paid a high price for this political choice.

There is an additional reason to concentrate on the Swedish case. Since the transition from near-full employment to mass unemployment was exceptionally sudden in early 1990s Sweden, a close examination of the four elections that have been held since then—in 1994, 1998, 2002, and 2006—allows us to examine how parties adjust to new social and economic circumstances. The Swedish model of the 1950s and 1960s ensured that most Swedes were, for all practical purposes, guaranteed a job. High economic growth and employment-oriented economic and social policies ensured reasonable chances for all those who wished to find employment. The active labor market programs that were introduced from the 1950s onward were meant to assist workers who were stranded on "islands of unemployment" in the economy (Lindvall 2004: 160). Meanwhile, employment protection was relatively weak. Ever since the so-called December Compromise between the union confederation LO and the employer confederation SAF in 1906, employers could "hire and fire workers freely." The political objective was not to guarantee employment within the same firm, but to make sure that everyone could find a job even if they were to lose their present employment.

In the mid-1970s, new labor market legislation was introduced. Most importantly, employers could no longer choose which workers to lay off (although they had, and have, a right to reduce the overall size of their workforce). The so-called "LAS-rules" (after *Lagen om anställningsskydd,* the "employment protection act") require of employers to lay off workers in reverse order of employment. The Center-Right government in 1991–1994 relaxed some of this legislation, but in all essentials, the 1970s legislation still stands. The introduction of employment protection legislation in the 1970s is an important cause of the emergence of insider-outsider cleavages across Europe (Rueda 2007), but during the 1970s and 1980s, employment protection legislation in Sweden did not appear to have created any strong political tensions between insiders and outsiders. A vast majority of wage-earners were employed on regular contracts, the trade unions were encompassing and inclusive, and, most importantly, the economic policies of both Social Democratic and Center-Right governments provided for full employment (Lindvall 2006).

However, since about 1990, outsiders have lost ground. Real incomes have increased for people with good jobs while the number of outsiders has increased dramatically. In many cases, outsiderness does not only matter to a person's income, but also to his or her social security rights: Sweden's core social insurance programs are based on income replacement, so citizens only become eligible for generous benefits once they have worked for a certain period of time. Consequently, during and after the deep economic crisis of the early 1990s, much larger groups in the labor market than before—particularly among immigrants and young people—fell outside the scope of important social insurance programs, such as unemployment insurance. For these reasons, we have chosen to make the appearance of mass unemployment in the Swedish economy in the 1990s the starting point for our analysis of employment policies, party politics, and the political behavior of insiders and outsiders.

DATA AND METHODS

The empirical sections present an analysis of election campaigns and voting behavior in the Swedish parliamentary elections in 1994, 1998, 2002, and 2006. Our theoretical claims concern the interaction of party strategies and voter responses. It is therefore essential to consider both levels in the empirical analysis.

Our description of party positions in the election campaigns relies on three sources. First, we use Esaiasson and Håkansson's POP dataset (*Partiernas opinionspåverkan*; see Brandorf et al. 1996) on the content of Swedish election campaigns, from which we use data on the saliency of various political issues in the final, televised party leader debates.[5] Second, we draw on election reports in *Electoral Studies, European Journal of Political Research* and *Scandinavian Political Studies* (and on books by the principal investigators of the Swedish National Election Study) in order to provide more detail on the content of the election campaigns (specific references are given throughout the text). Third, we provide our own analysis of survey data from the National Election Studies in order to examine voter perceptions and evaluations of election campaigns and party messages. The quantitative data on election campaigns only allow us to identify the proportion of party leader statements that were concerned with "employment" in general—the data do not provide any more detailed information about the *kinds* of employment policies that different parties favored. However, as we explain in the empirical sections, the qualitative sources that we use show that at least when it comes to the Social Democrats, the pattern that we observe in the quantitative data reflects important differences in the attention that the party paid to issues that mattered to outsiders.

Our individual-level analysis of voting choices relies on data from the Swedish National Election Studies. Sweden's election studies program is one of the oldest in the world—second only to the United States—and the data benefit from very high response rates (in our case, the response rate varied between 82 percent in 1998 and 70 percent in 2002). Our dependent variable, party choice, is based on a survey item that asked voters to name the party they actually voted for.[6] The dependent variable has nine categories: (1) Left Party, (2) Social Democrats, (3) Green Party, (4) Centre Party, (5) Liberals, (6) Moderate Party, (7) Christian Democrats, (8) another party, and (9) did not vote (or left an empty ballot).[7] Since electoral participation is a matter of public record in Sweden, we have objective information on non-voting. Respondents who claim to have voted are coded as non-voters if their survey answers are contradicted by official data.

Table 12-1 summarizes the distribution of the dependent variable. We will look at these numbers in more detail later. For now, we will only mention the variation that exists in our sample both across parties and over time. We believe that differences in the behavior of insiders and outsiders across elections explain

Table 12-1: The distribution of the dependent variable (percent of sample)

	1994	1998	2002	2006
Left Party	6.0	10.3	7.8	5.2
Social Democratic Party	41.4	31.7	33.9	29.7
Green Party	4.7	3.8	5.8	5.8
Center Party	7.6	4.3	5.2	7.5
Liberal Party	7.2	4.5	13.8	7.2
Christian Democrats	3.7	9.7	8.2	6.4
Moderate Party	18.5	20.2	10.9	22.9
Other party	1.3	1.9	1.3	4.6
No vote	9.7	13.5	13.1	10.8
Sum	100.0	100.0	100.0	100.0
N	2,472	2,073	2,260	2,306

Table 12-2: Swedish election results, 1994–2006 (percent of the vote)

Party	1994	1998	2002	2006
Left Party	6.2	12.0	8.4	5.9
Green Party	5.0	4.5	4.6	5.2
Social Democratic Party	45.2	36.4	39.9	35.0
Center Party	7.7	5.1	6.2	7.9
Liberal Party	7.2	4.7	13.4	7.6
Christian Democrats	4.1	11.8	9.1	6.6
Moderate Party	22.4	22.9	15.3	26.2
Other parties (below threshold)	2.2	2.6	3.1	5.7
Sum	100.0	100.0	100.0	100.0
Total left-wing bloc	56.4	52.9	52.9	46.1
Total right-wing bloc	41.4	44.5	44.0	48.3
Turnout	86.8	81.4	80.1	82.0

some of this variation. The variation in our sample is very similar to the actual election results, which increases our confidence in the reliability of the data (see Table 12-2).

Our main explanatory variables are insider and outsider status. The unemployed and those respondents who were enrolled in active labor market programs such as training or subsidized employment count as outsiders in all our models. Two categories of wage-earners are usually considered as having precarious employment: fixed-term and involuntary part-time workers. A number of analysts have found that such "atypical" jobs increase job insecurity (see, for example, Näswall and De Witte 2003 and Burgoon and Dekker 2010). Regrettably, we do not have data on fixed-term employment for the 1994 and 1998 elections, nor do we have data on involuntary part-time employment for the 2002 and 2006 elections. In our models for 1994 and 1998, we therefore count respondents who were employed in full-time jobs or worked part-time voluntarily as insiders (excluding managers, businessmen, and farmers), whereas we count the unemployed, respondents enrolled in active labor market programs, and involuntary part-time employees as outsiders. In our models for 2002 and 2006, on the other hand, insiders are gainfully employed with permanent contracts (excluding managers, businessmen, and farmers), whereas outsiders are unemployed, enrolled in active labor market programs, or fixed-term employees. The fact that our results are based on two different definitions of outsiderness complicates intertemporal comparisons, but almost all of the results that we report here hold if we re-run our analyses on the basis of a "narrow" definition of outsiderness (counting only the unemployed and participants in active labor market programs). The only exception is the effect of outsiderness on voting for the Social Democrats in the 2006 election (which diminishes and is no longer statistically significant at the 95 percent level). Individuals who are neither insiders nor outsiders are either students, farmers, managers, business owners, self-employed, or retired.

We include a number of control variables that have been shown to influence party choices and electoral participation in the comparative literature, the literature on the Swedish case, or both.[8] First of all, we control for a set of demographic variables: age, gender, education, and immigrant status. These variables are almost always used as control variables in studies of public opinion and political behavior, but there are also substantive reasons why they should be included in our analysis. In industrialized democracies, new social risks have become increasingly important when analyzing policy preferences and political behavior. As Bonoli (2005) explains, the new social risks that are generated by post-industrial labor markets and family structures tend to concentrate among women, the young, and the low-skilled. We attempt to control for the effect of these new social risks by including variables that capture age, gender, and education. Controlling for these variables is particularly important since women, the young, the less educated, and immigrants are overrepresented in the outsider group, and we want to distinguish between the effects of insider-outsider status and the other factors just mentioned. Moreover, age, education, and immigrant status are known to be powerful predictors of electoral participation.

A large literature has emphasized the connection between union membership and left party strength. At the aggregate level, the idea of such a relationship is supported by power-resource theories in comparative political economy (Stephens 1979; Korpi 1983; Huber and Stephens 2001). At the individual level, union members have consistently been found to be more likely to support left parties. This may be because of the role of unions as a channel of communication for shared problems—as in the pioneering work of Lipset (1960)—or as an intermediary organization for specific classes (see, for example, Kumlin and Svallfors 2007). Union membership is also likely to be a predictor of participation, since it integrates the individual in a social network and makes her a likely target of mobilization efforts (as Allern et al. 2007 document, Sweden's largest union, LO, is affiliated with the Social Democrats and supports them in elections). For all these reasons, we include union membership in the statistical analysis.

We also include social class, religiosity, and public sector employment.[9] A vast literature has developed about the influence of class on voting (see for example, Lipset 1960; Evans 1999; Svallfors 2006; Brooks and Manza 1997; and, on the Swedish case, Oskarson 1994). We use a set of dummies that corresponds roughly to the most widely used conceptualization of class in the contemporary literature: the Erikson-Goldthorpe schema (Holmberg and Oscarsson 2004: 56).[10]

Religion has been recognized as an influence on voting behavior for a long time (see, for example, Lipset 1960). We control for religiosity by including a variable that picks up respondents who say that they attend a religious service at least once a month. Our final variable in the third model is public sector employment. A number of authors have noted that public sector workers are more likely to support left parties since left parties tend to promote large public budgets and a generous welfare state (Kitschelt 1994; Blais et al. 1997; Knutsen 2001).

Since our dependent variable is a (nominal) choice among parties—plus the option of not voting or leaving an empty ballot—we estimate a multinomial logit model.[11] The reference category is voting for the Social Democrats. Because we run our model on four datasets (one dataset per election), our main results consist of 32 sets of estimates of the effects of all the independent variables on the likelihood of choosing a certain category (the Left Party, the Green Party, etc.) rather than the reference category (the Social Democrats).

The raw estimates are complex and—more importantly—do not directly reflect the relationships of interest, so we do not present them in the chapter.[12] Instead, we concentrate on the marginal effects of insider and outsider status on the probability of choosing a certain party (or not voting) in each of the four elections. Using the estimated coefficients, we calculate the probability that an individual with a particular set of values on the independent variables would vote for a particular party (or not vote). In order to get point estimates for the predicted probabilities and to test whether the differences between insiders and outsiders are significant, we use a procedure proposed by Long and Freese (2006: 249), and which is based on the SPost package for Stata. When we calculate the predicted probabilities, we concentrate on the effect of a change from "insider" to "outsider" for a typical member of the broad working class that we concentrate on. In other words, we vary the outsider and insider variables, but assign the modes or means for all individuals that are *either insiders or outsiders* to all other variables in our model. A typical member of this group, in our sample, is a 40-year-old man who was born in Sweden and has three years of secondary-school education.[13] He is a mid-level white-collar worker and a union member, and does not work in the public sector.[14] He does not go to church regularly.

PARTY POLITICS AND VOTE CHOICE IN SWEDEN, 1994–2006

The 1994 Election

The parliamentary election in 1994 was the first to follow the large increase in unemployment in the early 1990s. However, it resembled past elections, held in the era of full employment, in the sense that the Social Democrats were able to benefit from their traditionally strong profile in the area of employment policy (Martinsson 2009): unemployment had begun to increase before the Social Democrats lost power in September 1991, but most of the blame for the emergence of mass unemployment fell on the Center-Right parties that were in power in 1991–1994.

For much of 1994, a Social Democratic victory was seen as a foregone conclusion. Before the summer, some opinion polls even suggested that the Social Democrats would win more than 50 percent of the vote (Widfeldt 1995: 209). As the election drew nearer, the Social Democrats tried to lower expectations. The budget deficit had increased greatly during the deep economic crisis in the early 1990s, and there was broad political agreement that spending cuts and tax increases would become necessary in the 1994–1998 parliament (Gilljam and Holmberg 1995: 21). For this reason, the Social Democrats presented a harsh election manifesto in August, proposing some drastic cuts in the welfare state, as a "precaution against a future opinion backlash" (Widfeldt and Pierre 1995: 481).

When it comes to employment, however, there is no doubt that the Social Democrats kept a high profile in 1994.[15] They emphasized employment in the campaign, and in the final televised debate between the party leaders, almost 19 percent of the Social Democratic Party leader Ingvar Carlsson's statements concerned employment or unemployment (see Figure 12-2). National Election Study data also reveal that in the minds of the voters, the issue of employment was strongly associated with the Social Democrats—70 percent of the respondents said that the Social Democrats had emphasized this issue during the campaign. This is an unusually large number. No other party scored higher than 26 percent (Gilljam and Holmberg 1995: 52). Moreover, voters approved of Social Democratic employment policies. As Figure 12-3a shows, the difference between those who believed the Social Democrats had good employment policies and those who believed that they had bad policies was large, both among outsiders and insiders. Figure 12-3b, on the other hand, reveals that many voters were critical of the employment policies of the Moderates (the prime minister's party in 1991–1994).

The 1994 election was a big success for the Social Democrats, who won 45.2 percent of the vote. It was also a success for other left parties. With 6.2 percent, the Left Party had its best result since the 1940s, and the Greens, who had lost all

Figure 12-2: **The salience of employment in election campaigns**

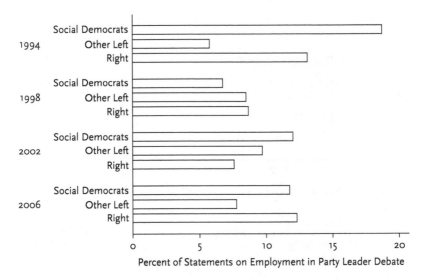

Percent of Statements on Employment in Party Leader Debate

Note: The bars represent the percentage of statements in the final, televised election debates between party leaders that were mainly concerned with the issue of employment (including unemployment).
Source: POP data set (Brandorf et al. 1996).

Figure 12-3: **Attitudes toward employment policies**

(a)   Attitudes toward Social Democratic employment policies

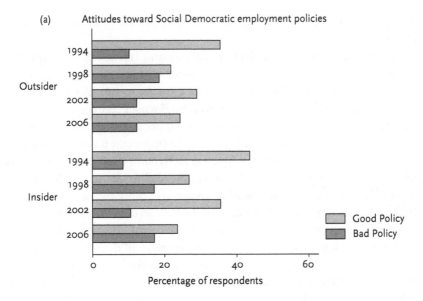

Percentage of respondents

Figure 12-3: (Contd.)

(b) Attitudes toward the Moderate Party's employment policies

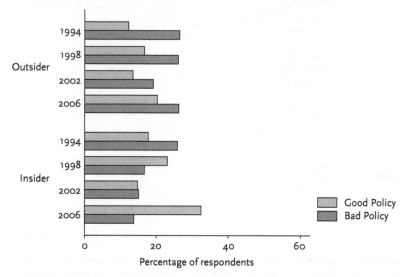

Note: Lighter bars represent the percentage of respondents (within each of the two labor market groups) who believed that the Social Democratic Party (panel 3a) or the Moderate Party (panel 3b) had a good policy on employment. The darker bars represent the number of respondents who believed that the party had a bad policy on employment.
Source: Swedish National Election Studies.

their seats in 1991, passed the 4 percent electoral threshold, winning 5 percent of the vote.

In their book on the 1994 election, Gilljam and Holmberg wrote that the Social Democrats won because of a widespread belief that the previous government had failed to deal with the economic crisis (1995: 188). Voters had more confidence in Social Democratic policies on employment, the economy, and the welfare state. The data we have presented so far are consistent with this interpretation, but add important details. The most important features of the 1994 campaign, for our purposes, were: (1) it was an election where employment was salient; (2) voters perceived that they were offered clear alternatives in employment policy; and (3) *all* labor market groups had more confidence in Social Democratic employment policies than in the policies of other parties.

In 1994, then, the Social Democrats were perceived as a party interested in promoting the interests of wage-earners in general, and therefore as an attractive alternative for both insiders and outsiders. On the basis of the theoretical ideas that we presented in the section Party Politics and the Political Behavior of Insiders and Outsiders, we expect that this should lead to relatively small differences between insiders and outsiders when it comes to non-voting. If there are any differences in party choice, we would expect outsiders to vote for Left-of-Center parties, since the Left was identified with employment promotion.

Table 12-3: Predicted probabilities

	1994			1998			2002			2006		
	Outsiders	Insiders	Diff.	Outsiders	Insiders	Diff.	Outsiders	Insiders	Diff.	Outsiders	Insiders	Diff.
Left Party	4.4	3.1	1.3	10.7	5.9	4.9**	7.0	6.5	0.6	7.3	5.4	1.9
Social Democrats	52.5	45.9	6.6	34.2	37.4	-3.2	38.0	38.1	0.0	39.7	32.3	7.5**
Green Party	3.0	2.7	0.3	3.2	2.8	0.3	8.3	4.9	3.4	4.5	5.4	-1.0
Center Party	2.3	4.7	-3.4**	1.0	2.4	-1.4	2.7	4.4	-1.7	3.6	5.0	-1.4
Liberal Party	8.2	7.1	1.1	6.2	5.4	0.8	11.7	14.4	-2.7	7.0	9.3	-2.3
Christian Democrats	1.0	1.1	-0.1	8.0	6.3	1.7	7.2	7.2	0.1	3.0	4.2	-1.2
Moderate Party	18.6	29.3	-10.7**	19.5	30.6	-11.1**	13.6	12.7	0.9	18.2	25.6	-7.4**
Other Party	3.0	1.7	1.3	1.3	0.6	0.7	1.3	0.9	0.3	5.2	3.2	2.0
No vote	7.2	4.4	2.8	16.0	8.7	7.3**	10.2	10.9	-0.7	11.5	9.6	1.9

A detailed analysis of individual-level data shows that these expectations are largely met. Table 12-3, which is based on our full model of voting behavior, presents the predicted probabilities for the nine voting choices that we consider for both insiders and outsiders (holding all other variables constant). The main result is that outsiders were less likely than insiders to vote for two of the Center-Right parties, the Center Party and the Moderate Party. Overall, the results confirm our expectations for an election in which the Social Democrats manage to appeal to both insiders and outsiders: outsiders were less likely than insiders to vote Center-Right, and more likely to vote Center-Left. This is also how outsiders behave in existing studies of pre-1990s elections (Holmberg 2000: 99), before the distinction between insiders and outsiders became politically salient in Sweden.

The 1998 Election

Circumstances in 1998 were very different from 1994. For four years, a Social Democratic government had administered a high unemployment economy. In some respects, economic prospects had improved since the first half of the 1990s, but unemployment remained high. The Social Democrats had also made large cuts in welfare programs, including unemployment benefits, and they had cooperated with the Center Party, traditionally regarded as a member of the right-wing bloc. All this is likely to have led to disaffection and disappointment among many leftist voters, particularly among outsiders.

Because of the focus on core left-right issues such as the choice between public spending and tax cuts, the 1998 election campaign is often described as "traditional" (Pierre and Widfeldt 1999: 514). It is true that voters chose between Social Democratic policies based on investments in the welfare state and Center-Right policies based on tax cuts. However, there are strong indications that the Social Democrats were unable to reconcile the demands of labor market outsiders, who were more concerned with the problem of unemployment, and labor market insiders, who were more concerned with public services. Faced with these competing demands, the Social Democrats concentrated on winning over middle class voters.[16] One of the main events of the election campaign was a late Social Democratic promise to cap public child care user-fees (Elinder, Jordahl, and Poutvaara 2009). This policy (*maxtaxan*) benefited medium- and high-income earners with children, who are more likely to be insiders than outsiders.

For many voters, however, employment remained an important concern. According to National Election Study data, 34 percent of the voters mentioned employment when they were asked which issues mattered to their party choice. This was lower than the exceptionally high 1994 figure of 41 percent, but it was very high compared to most other issues. In the Social Democratic campaign, however, the employment issue was much less prominent in 1998 than it had been in 1994. As Figure 12-2 shows, only 6.8 percent of Prime Minister Göran Persson's statements in the final election debate dealt with employment or unemployment, *less* than the average figures for the Center-Right parties and for the other left-wing parties (the Greens and the Left Party). Unemployment, as well as the fact that the government "was not able to do much about it," as Pierre and Widfeldt wrote at the time (1999: 513), was not something that the Social Democrats were eager to discuss.

Both insiders and outsiders looked less favorably on Social Democratic employment policies in 1998 than they had in 1994, but the shift is especially noteworthy among outsiders (see Figure 12-3a). Many outsiders found the Left Party's employment policies more appealing. The number of outsiders believing the Left Party to have good policies on employment significantly outnumbered those who thought that it had bad policies. In the other three elections included in our analysis, no group was ever this supportive of the Left Party's policies on employment.[17]

The 1998 election was a disaster for the Social Democrats, who won only 36.4 percent of the vote, almost 9 percentage points less than in 1994. This was the party's worst result since the introduction of general suffrage in the early 1920s. The big winner among the left-wing parties in 1998 was the Left Party, and there was a big flow of voters from the Social Democrats to the left.[18] It also seems clear that many Social Democratic voters chose to abstain, accounting for some of the big drop in turnout, which reached the lowest level since the 1950s. In spite of the election result, however, the Social Democratic government stayed in power, since most party changes between 1994 and 1998 occurred within the two main ideological blocs.

Several scholars have tried to explain the decline in Social Democratic support and the fall in electoral participation in the 1998 election. Regarding the Social Democratic vote, most authors attribute the reduced support to the cuts in welfare spending that occurred in the mid-1990s (Arter 1999: 298; Möller 1999: 263), but the role of employment has also been noted. For example, Arter's election report claimed that "[t]here was clearly discontent among rank-and-file members over the fact that unemployment had been given insufficient prominence in the campaign" (1999: 298). In fact, the Social Democratic Party's own evaluation of the election said that one of the main problems had been that voters had higher confidence in other parties when it came to employment. The report argued that one explanation for the election result was that large groups had failed to find jobs under the Social Democrats (Socialdemokraterna 1999). Several previous studies have also noted the decline of voting among socially marginalized groups, such as the unemployed. For example, Bennulf and Hedberg (1999) have shown that the effect of unemployment (and other socioeconomic variables) on electoral participation increased sharply between 1994 and 1998 (see also Hedberg et al. 2001), and Adman (2004) has documented, on the basis of late 1990s data, that unemployment decreased political participation in general and voting in particular (see also Martinsson 2009: 170).

In our view, what happened in 1998 was that the Social Democrats were unable to reconcile the competing claims of two groups that had traditionally supported them. Their failure to address the employment problem when they were in power in 1994–1998, combined with their emphasis on issues with middle-class appeal (such as child care user-fees), led to disapproval among outsider groups. This means that the 1998 election offers us an excellent opportunity for evaluating our hypothesis. Do outsiders abandon the political process or vote for more radical political parties when they perceive that mainstream left parties are not promoting their interests? We turn again to a detailed analysis of individual-level data.

As before, Table 12-3 presents the predicted probabilities for insiders and outsiders (holding all other variables constant, as explained above). This time, we also discuss some differences between the 1998 election and the results for 1994. In 1998, outsiders were still much less likely than insiders to vote for the Moderate Party. The two most important findings, however, relate to non-voting and support for the Left Party. In 1998, outsiders were much more likely than insiders not to vote. The difference in predicted probabilities is much larger than it was in 1994, and moreover, it is now statistically significant. Among insiders in our samples, the probability of not voting increased from 4.4 to 8.7 percent, but among outsiders, it increased from 7.2 to 16.0 percent. The difference between insiders and outsiders, therefore, almost tripled (from 2.8 to 7.3 percentage points). Support for the Left Party also increased dramatically among outsiders. In 1994 the difference in predicted probabilities between insiders and outsiders was small and statistically insignificant; in 1998 it was significant and substantial: the predicted probability of voting for the Left Party for outsiders (10.7 percent) is almost twice as large as that for insiders (5.9 percent).

The 2002 Election

In contrast to 1998, voters in 2002 looked back on four years of *declining* unemployment under a Social Democratic government. Most voters in 2002 placed the quality and provision of public services on top of the agenda—not economic policy and employment, which traditionally score highly. In fact, compared to the other three elections considered in this chapter, employment mattered very little to voters in 2002: only 7 percent of survey respondents mentioned employment when they were asked if there were any issues that mattered to their party choice (Holmberg and Oscarsson 2004: 123). This is probably a result of the decline in unemployment after the deep economic crisis of the 1990s. After a decade when macroeconomic problems had dominated the political agenda, other issues became more salient.

Still, the Social Democrats paid more attention to employment than they had in 1998, at least judging from the final party leader debate (Figure 12-2). More than 12 percent of Göran Persson's statements dealt with this issue, more than other party leader. As in previous elections, this influenced the perceptions of the voters. According to National Election Study data, the issue of employment was identified more strongly with the Social Democrats than with any other party: 11 percent of respondents said that the Social Democrats had emphasized employment in the campaign, whereas no other party scored more than 2 percent (Holmberg and Oscarsson 2004: 128). As Figure 12-3a shows, both insiders and outsiders tended to think highly of Social Democratic employment policies.

The Social Democrats increased their vote share in 2002, winning 39.9 percent of the vote. However, in terms of the competition between Left and Right, there was almost no change compared to 1998. Within the left-wing bloc, the Left Party lost many of the votes they had won from the Social Democrats in 1998 (Widfeldt 2003: 1095). Within the right-wing bloc, the Moderate Party lost almost a third of its vote share, whereas the Liberal Party increased its vote share from 4.7 to 13.4 percent.

Most scholars and political commentators have concentrated on the ability of the Social Democrats to press home their message of spending on public services in the 2002 election campaign. In addition to this, we would argue that an important difference between 1998 and 2002 was economic performance. Sweden's growth, the relatively favorable development of employment and unemployment rates, and the low salience of employment made it possible for the Social Democrats to appeal to a broader range of voters than in the previous election: the Social Democrats attracted both outsiders (by emphasizing employment more than other parties) and the middle class (by suggesting that Center-Right tax policies would lead to a deterioration of public services). It is true that the support of insiders and outsiders did not return to the high numbers seen in the 1994 election. Nevertheless, propitious macroeconomic circumstances allowed the Social Democrats to minimize the influence of insider-outsider differences.

The points made in the previous paragraph are confirmed by the detailed analysis of the individual data in Table 12-3. Probably because employment issues had such low salience, 2002 was different from the two previous elections (and the election in 2006): there were few significant differences between insiders and outsiders, either substantively or statistically. Neither the difference in the probability of non-voting nor the difference in the probability of voting for the Left Party was particularly large in 2002, nor were these differences statistically significant.

The 2006 Election

At the time of the 2006 election, voters looked back on four years of slightly increasing unemployment. The Swedish economy was doing well compared with other European countries, but for the Social Democrats, who had been in government since 1994, it was problematic that "the strong economy was not sufficiently translated into jobs," as Anders Widfeldt put it in his election report

(2007a: 1118). Employment was a salient issue in the campaign, even if the prime minister, Göran Persson, famously said that it would not be (Oscarsson and Holmberg 2008: 182). As many as 35 percent of the voters in our sample claimed that employment was important for their party choice, which was approximately the same level as 1998. Once more, employment was more salient than any other political issue.

The Social Democrats did not ignore unemployment: 11.8 percent of Göran Persson's statements in the final televised party leader debate dealt with this issue (Figure 12-2). But unlike in 2002, the Center-Right opposition also paid a great deal of attention to it. As in previous years, the campaign content data are remarkably highly correlated with voter perceptions of the campaign: the Social Democrats, the Center Party, and the Moderate Party were all associated with the issue of employment by more than 15 percent of survey respondents (Oscarsson and Holmberg 2008: 52).

As several Swedish scholars have pointed out (notably Martinsson 2009: Chapter 8), the Social Democrats lost issue ownership in the area of employment policy for the first time ever, since the Moderate Party's employment policies were more popular than the policies of the Social Democrats. While 35 percent of survey respondents believed that the Moderate Party had good employment policies, only 21 percent thought the same of the Social Democrats. This was the lowest score for Social Democratic employment policies since measurements began in 1979 (Oscarsson and Holmberg 2008: 182).

However, when we consider the attitudes of different labor market groups (Figures 12-3a and 12-3b), we find that the decline in the support for Social Democratic employment policies was larger among insiders than among outsiders. More importantly, whereas many insiders were enthusiastic about the Moderate Party's employment policies, outsiders were more likely to say that the Moderate Party's employment policies were bad, just as in previous elections. In other words, while the Social Democrats became associated with outsiders, the Moderate Party and its partners in the Center-Right coalition successfully targeted insiders. The Center-Right did not win the support of all social groups with their approach to employment and unemployment. This is not surprising, for their labor market policies were designed to cut benefits to the unemployed while cutting taxes on incomes from paid employment. In his election report, Widfeldt noted that the policy of the Center-Right parties "was criticized by SAP as punishing the weakest in society," yet this "attempt to introduce traditional left-right rhetoric into the campaign had little apparent effect" (Widfeldt 2007b: 821). The data we have presented suggest that this rhetoric *did* have an effect, but only on the party's popularity among outsiders. The price the party paid for emphasizing generous transfers to the unemployed and the inactive population was lower support among insiders.

The Social Democrats had their worst election outcome since pre-democratic times, winning only 35.0 percent of the vote. Unlike in 1998, the voters did not go to the Left Party or the Green Party. Instead, many previous Social Democratic voters (remarkably) supported the main ideological opponent of the Social Democrats: the Moderate Party. Unlike in the 1998 and 2002 elections, the Center-Right parties were able to generate a net flow of voters from left to right.

Our interpretation of the 2006 election is similar to those of earlier studies in the sense that we believe that the Social Democrats lost the 2006 election since they "were no longer regarded as the party that offered the best solutions for employment and the economy" (Oscarsson and Holmberg 2008: 184) and were "on the defensive regarding jobs" (Widfeldt 2007a: 1122). However, the successful Center-Right message on employment was targeted at insiders, not outsiders (and it attracted insiders, as we will show below). The political problem for the Social Democrats in 2006 was that—just as in 1998—they faced competing claims from outsiders (who wanted to preserve their level of benefits) and the insiders (who were attracted by the Center-Right message of lower taxes for people in work, paid for by reducing benefits for the unemployed). In 1998, the Social Democrats chose the insiders, which led to a marginalization of outsiders and increased support for the Left Party. In 2006, the Social Democrats were seen to support outsiders by preserving generous transfers for the unemployed and the inactive, allowing the Center-Right to target insider groups that had previously voted for the Social Democrats.

The estimates in Table 12-3 clearly demonstrate the effects of the Moderate Party's appeal to insider voters. There are only two statistically significant differences between the predicted probabilities for insiders and outsiders: outsiders were more likely to vote for the Social Democrats and less likely to vote for the Moderate Party. Remarkably, these two differences are of almost identical size, but with opposite signs. Judging from our data, the Social Democrats were in fact slightly *more* popular among outsiders than they had been in 2002, but they lost a great deal of their support among insiders. Our interpretation is that by being seen to defend the interests of outsiders, the Social Democrats avoided the effects that we observed in 1998, but they appear to have paid a political price, becoming vulnerable to a targeted attack from the Center-Right opposition.

CONCLUSIONS

In this chapter, we have shown that the strategies of political parties influence the electoral behavior of insiders and outsiders. An analysis of the Swedish case—a hard case for our hypotheses—leads to the following two conclusions.

First, the 1998 election was the only election of the four that we have studied in which the Social Democrats clearly paid less attention to employment issues than other parties, and instead concentrated on winning the votes of middle-class insiders. As a result, 1998 stands out as the election in which labor market outsiders were politically alienated, as shown by the large effects of outsiderness on non-voting and voting for the Left Party. In other words, the Swedish experience suggests that when mainstream left parties choose to focus on issues that are primarily relevant to insiders, they are punished by outsiders.

Second, a comparison between the 1998 election and the 2006 election suggests that Social Democratic parties—and other mainstream left parties—may face an "insider-outsider dilemma": tailoring their message to one group may alienate the other. After the 1998 election, the Social Democrats appear to have made new efforts to reconcile insider and outsider interests. In 2002, this strategy worked, since the macroeconomic circumstances were propitious and unemployment was relatively low. However, in 2006, the risks of the strategy became clear: since economic circumstances were no longer beneficial to such "inclusive" strategies, the Swedish Center-Right parties were able to win over insider voters. Our results suggest that what happened in 2006 was not that the Social Democrats failed to recognize that voters cared about employment; what happened was that the Social Democrats failed to reconcile the interests of insiders and outsiders when they were faced with a Center-Right opposition that tailored their message to attract labor market insiders.

The main implication of our results is that the strategies of political parties matter greatly to whether the economic marginalization of vulnerable groups in the labor market also leads to their political marginalization.

APPENDIX 1: VARIABLES

The data sources for all National Election Studies data used in the paper are Holmberg and Gilljam (1997), Holmberg (2002), Holmberg and Oscarsson (2006), and Holmberg and Oscarsson (2008).

Party Choice
Party choice, with non-voting and empty ballots included in the choice set, can take the following values: (1) Left Party, (2) Social Democrats, (3) Green Party, (4) Center Party, (5) Liberals, (6) Moderate Party, (7) Christian Democrats, (8) another party, and (9) did not vote (or left an empty ballot).

Insiders and Outsiders
"Insider" status is a dummy variable. Those gainfully employed are insiders (unless they are managers, businessmen, or farmers). "Outsider" status, also a dummy variable, codes the openly unemployed as outsiders, along with

respondents who are enrolled in active labor market training programs or subsidized employment programs. We also count involuntary part-time employees
(1994 and 1998) and fixed-term workers (2002 and 2006) as outsiders.

Gender and Age
Gender is a dummy variable (coded 1 for women, 0 for men). Age is given in
years. The coding of these two variables is based on public records.

Education
The education variables we use are dummy variables based on an ordinal-
scale categorization of the highest level of education attended by the respondents. The dummies are "Vocational School," "Secondary 1," Secondary 2," and
"University" ("Primary School Only" is the reference category).

Immigration Status
"Immigrant" is a dummy variable (coded 1 for immigrants, 0 for non-immi-
grants). In 1994 and 1998, we code respondents who have become Swedish
citizens sometime after birth as immigrants. In 2002 and 2006, we code respondents who were born outside Sweden as immigrants. The coding of this variable
is based on public records.

Union Membership
Union membership is a dummy variable (coded 1 for union members, 0 for others). The coding is based on a survey question asking whether respondents are
members of a trade union, professional association, or an organization for the
self-employed.

Class
We use a set of dummy variables that identify members of the following eight
groups: industrial workers, other workers, lower-level white-collar workers,
mid-level white-collar workers, senior white-collar workers and businessmen,
self-employed, and farmers (the reference category is students). The coding of
this variable is based on an analysis of answers to an open-ended question about
which job respondents have (or used to have).

Religiosity
This is a dummy variable (coded 1 for respondents who say that they attend a
religious service at least once a month, 0 for others).

Sector
Sector is a dummy variable (coded 1 for respondents who work in the public
sector, 0 for others).

NOTES

1 See, for example, Mares (2006), Martin and Thelen (2007), Rueda (2007), Iversen and Stephens (2008), Swank, Martin, and Thelen (2008), Palier and Thelen (2010), and Iversen (2009).

2 Some types of precarious employment, such as fixed-term employment, are still relatively rare in Sweden and the other Nordic countries (Pontusson 2011).

3 There are different ways of conceptualizing insider-outsider differences, emphasizing employment status, access to benefits and protection, political representation, and citizenship (see, in this volume, Chapter 7 by Seeleib-Kaiser et al. and Chapter 2 by Häusermann and Schwander for more detailed analyses). We are agnostic about the costs and benefits of these definitions and defend a more practical approach: in this chapter, we are interested in the interaction between individual political preferences and party strategies, and we consider unemployment and precarious employment to be the politically salient issues, so we regard unemployment vulnerability as the defining characteristic that divides outsiders from insiders.

4 See Evans and Tilley (2009) for a similar approach.

5 The final party leader debate is one of the last events of the election campaign and usually sums up the campaign as a whole. It is also one of the most widely watched programs on Swedish television. According to data from the National Election Studies, a remarkably high number of voters claim to have seen at least parts of the final party leader debates: from 65 percent of the respondents in 1994 to 57 percent in 2006 (Oscarsson and Holmberg 2008: 75).

6 Our sample contains respondents whose main interview took place before the election, but these respondents received a brief questionnaire after the election where they were asked for this information.

7 Sweden has a largely bipolar party system. (1)–(3) are normally included in the left-wing bloc whereas (4)–(7) are included in the right-wing bloc. Ever since 1957 (with the exception of a Liberal single-party minority government in 1978–1979), governments in Sweden have alternated between Social Democratic single-party minority governments and Center-Right coalition governments including some combination of parties (4)–(7). The most prominent parties in category (8) are New Democracy (*Ny Demokrati*), a right-wing populist party that was represented in the Swedish parliament in 1991–1994, and—more recently—the anti-immigrant Sweden Democrats (*Sverigedemokraterna*).

8 Details about the operationalization of all variables can be found in Appendix 1. For detailed information about the empirical relationships between the control variables in our model and the party choices of Swedish voters, we refer to the four books on the 1994–2006 elections that have been produced within the Swedish National Election Studies program: Gilljam and Holmberg (1995), Holmberg (2000), Holmberg and Oscarsson (2004), and Oscarsson and Holmberg (2008).

9   We do not add income since it is highly correlated with the class variables in model 3. Furthermore, the Swedish literature has shown that the relationship between income and party choice in Sweden is weak (see Martinsson 2009, Chapter 3, for a literature review).

10 It should be noted that since some classes are more vulnerable to unemployment than others, controlling for class is a tough test for our theory.

11 The main limitation of the multinomial logistic model is that it assumes the independence of irrelevant alternatives (IIA). We perform a Hausman test for the IIA assumption. Our tests do not provide any evidence against the assumption that the odds between any two categories of the dependent variable are independent. The results are available from the authors.

12 All results are available from the authors.

13 Average education levels have increased over time, which complicates matters somewhat. We have chosen to calculate predicted probabilities for respondents who have completed three years of secondary school (and have no university education), since this is the median level of education in the later elections, and we wish to make the predicted probabilities comparable between elections.

14 In 1994, "other worker" is the modal class category, closely followed by mid-level white-collars. In all other years, medium-level white-collars are most common, so we stick to that.

15 When the National Election Study respondents in 1994 were asked an open-ended question about which issues mattered most for their party choice, 41 percent of respondents declared that employment was important—the second highest number for any issue in any election since this question was first asked in 1979 (Gilljam and Holmberg 1995: 23–26).

16 In an interview conducted in May 1997 but published only in 2007, the Social Democratic Prime Minister Göran Persson said that he expected the macroeconomic situation to improve before the 1998 election and that this would reduce the salience of employment issues (Fichtelius 2007: 208).

17 Figure for the Left Party not shown, available from the authors.

18 Of those who voted for the Social Democrats in 1994, 10 percent voted for the Left Party in 1998 (Holmberg 2000: 20). Considering the fact that the Social Democrats won more than 40 percent of the vote in 1994, this is a very large number.

REFERENCES

Adman, Per (2004). *Arbetslöshet, arbetsplatsdemokrati och politiskt deltagande*, Uppsala: Acta Universitatis Upsaliensis.

Allern, Elin H., Aylott, Nicholas, and Christiansen, Flemming J. (2007). "Social Democrats and Trade Unions in Scandinavia: The Decline and Persistence of Institutional Relationships," *European Journal of Political Research*, 46 (5): 607–635.

Armingeon, Klaus, Marlène Gerber, Philipp Leimgruber, and Michelle Beyeler (2009). *Comparative Political Data Set 1960–2007*. Institute of Political Science, University of Berne.

Arter, David (1999). "The Swedish General Election of 20th September 1998: A Victory for Values over Policies?" *Electoral Studies*, 18 (2): 296–300.

Bartels, Larry (2008). *Unequal Democracy*, Princeton: Princeton University Press.

Bennulf, Martin, and Hedberg, Per (1999). "Utanför demokratin," In *Valdeltagande i förändring*, Stockholm: Justitiedepartementet, pp. 75–135.

Blais, André, Blake, Donald, and Dion, Stephane (1997). *Governments, Parties, and Public Sector Employees*, Pittsburgh: University of Pittsburgh Press.

Bonoli, Giuliano (2005). "The Politics of the New Social Policies: Providing Coverage against New Social Risks in Mature Welfare States," *Policy & Politics*, 33 (3): 431–449.

Brandorf, Martin, Esaiasson, Peter, and Håkansson, Nicklas (1996). "Svenska valfrågor. Partiernas valdebatt 1902–1994," *Statsvetenskaplig tidskrift*, 98 (4): 1–36.

Brooks, Clem, and Manza, Jeff (1997). "Class Politics and Political Change in the United States," *American Sociological Review*, 76 (2): 379–408.

Burgoon, Brian and Dekker, Fabian (2010). "Flexible Employment and Social Policy Preferences in Europe," *Journal of European Social Policy*, 20 (2): 126–141.

Cusack, Thomas, Iversen, Torben, and Rehm, Philipp (2006). "Risks at Work: The Demand and Supply Sides of Redistribution," *Oxford Review of Economic Policy*, 22 (3): 365–389.

Dahlström, Carl, and Möller, Ulrika (2004). "Statens väljarskola. Strategin för att öka valdeltagandet bland utländska medborgare bosatta i Sverige, 1976–2000," in Borevi, Karin, and Strömblad, Per (eds.), *Engagemang, mångfald och integration*, Stockholm: Fritzes.

Duch, Raymond, and Stevenson, Randolph (2008), *The Economic Vote: How Political and Economic Institutions Condition Election Results*, New York: Cambridge University Press.

Elinder, Mikael, Jordahl, Henrik, and Poutvaara, Panu (2009). "Själviska och framåtblickande väljare – Hur många röster köpte maxtaxan i barnomsorgen?" *Ekonomisk Debatt*, 37(2): 6–12.

Evans, Geoffrey (ed.) (1999). *The End of Class Politics? Class Voting in Comparative Context*, Oxford: Oxford University Press.

Evans, Geoffrey, and Tilley, James (2009). "How Parties Shape Class Politics: Structural Transformation, Ideological Convergence and the Decline of Class Voting in Britain," Unpublished manuscript. Department of Politics and IR, Oxford University.

Fichtelius, Erik (2007). *Aldrig ensam, alltid ensam. Samtalen med Göran Persson 1996–2006*, Stockholm: Norstedts.

Gilljam, Mikael, and Holmberg, Sören (1995). *Väljarnas val*, Stockholm: Fritzes.

Hedberg, Per, Oscarsson, Henrik, and Bennulf, Martin (2001). "Lågt valdeltagande," in Sören Holmberg, Hedberg, Per, Oscarsson, Henrik, Bennulf,

Martin, Kumlin, Staffan, Oskarson, Maria, Lindahl, Rutger, and Brothén, Martin (eds.), *Europaopinionen*, Göteborg: Department of Political Science.

Holmberg, Sören (2000). *Välja parti*, Stockholm: Norstedts juridik.

Holmberg, Sören (2002). "Swedish Election Study 1998" [Computer file]. Department of Political Science, Göteborg University and Statistics Sweden (SCB) [producers], 2001. Göteborg, Sweden: Swedish Social Science Data Service (SSD) [distributor].

Holmberg, Sören, and Gilljam, Mikael (1997). "Swedish Election Study 1994" [Computer file]. Department of Political Science, Göteborg University and Statistics Sweden (SCB) [producers], Göteborg, Sweden: Swedish Social Science Data Service (SSD) [distributor].

Holmberg, Sören, and Oscarsson, Henrik (2004). *Väljare*, Stockholm: Norstedts Juridik.

Holmberg, Sören and Oscarsson, Henrik (2006). "Swedish Election Study 2002" [Computer file]. Department of Political Science, Göteborg University and Statistics Sweden (SCB) [producers], 2004. Göteborg, Sweden: Swedish Social Science Data Service (SSD) [distributor].

Holmberg, Sören, and Oscarsson, Henrik (2008.) "Swedish Election Study 2006" [Computer file]. Department of Political Science, Göteborg University and Statistics Sweden (SCB) [producers]. Göteborg, Sweden: Swedish Social Science Data Service (SSD) [distributor].

Huber, Evelyne, and Stephens, John (2001). *Development and Crisis of the Welfare State*, Chicago, IL: University of Chicago Press.

Iversen, Torben and Soskice, David (2009). "Dualism and Political Coalitions: Inclusionary versus Exclusionary Reforms in an Age of Rising Inequality," paper presented at the Annual Meeting of the American Political Science Association, September, 2009. Toronto, Canada.

Iversen, Torben, and Stephens, John (2008). "Partisan Politics, the Welfare State and Three Worlds of Human Capital Formation," *Comparative Political Studies*, 41 (4/5): 600–637.

Kitschelt, Herbert (1994). *The Transformation of European Social Democracy*, New York: Cambridge University Press.

Knutsen, Oddbjørn (2001). "Social Class, Sector Employment, and Gender as Party Cleavages in the Scandinavian Countries," *Scandinavian Political Studies*, 24 (4): 311–350.

Korpi, Walter (1983). *The Democratic Class Struggle*, Boston, MA: Routledge and Kegan Paul.

Kumlin, Staffan and Svallfors, Stefan (2007). "Social Stratification and Political Articulation," in Mau, Steffen, and Veghte, Benjamin (eds.), *The Welfare State, Legitimacy, and Social Justice*, Aldershot: Ashgate, pp. 19–46.

Lindvall, Johannes (2004). *The Politics of Purpose: Macroeconomic Policy in Sweden after the Golden Age*. PhD thesis, Department of Political Science, University of Gothenburg.

Lindvall, Johannes (2006). "The Politics of Purpose," *Comparative Politics*, 38(3): 253–272.

Lipset, Seymour Martin (1960). *Political Man: The Social Bases of Politics*, New York: Doubleday.

Long, J. Scott, and Freese, Jeremy (2006). *Regression Models for Categorical Dependent Variables Using Stata*, College Station, TX: Stata Press.

Mares, Isabela (2006). *Taxation, Wage Bargaining and Unemployment*, New York: Cambridge University.

Martin, Cathie Jo, and Thelen, Kathleen (2007). "The State and Coordinated Capitalism: Contributions of the Public Sector to Social Solidarity in Postindustrial Societies," *World Politics*, 60 (1): 1–36.

Martinsson, Johan (2009). *Economic Voting and Issue Ownership*, PhD thesis, Department of Political Science, University of Gothenburg.

Möller, Tommy (1999). "The Swedish Election 1998: A Protest Vote and the Birth of a New Political Landscape?," *Scandinavian Political Studies*, 22(3): 261–276.

Näswall, Katharina, and De Witte, Hans (2003). "Who Feels Insecure in Europe? Predicting Job Insecurity from Background Variables," *Economic and Industrial Democracy*, 24 (2): 189–215.

Olson, Mancur (1965). *The Logic of Collective Action: Public Goods and the Theory of Groups*, Cambridge, MA: Harvard University Press.

Oscarsson, Henrik, and Holmberg, Sören (2008). *Regeringsskifte*, Stockholm: Norstedts Juridik.

Oskarson, Maria (1994). *Klassröstning i Sverige*, Stockholm: Nerenius & Santérus.

Palier, Bruno, and Thelen, Kathleen (2010). "Institutionalizing Dualism: Complementarities and Change in France and Germany," *Politics and Society*, 38(1): 119–148.

Pierre, Jon, and Widfeldt, Anders (1999). "Sweden," *European Journal of Political Research*, 36(3–4): 511–518.

Pontusson, Jonas (2011). "Once Again a Model: Nordic Social Democracy in a Globalized World," in Cronin, James, Ross, George, and Shoch, James (eds.), *What's Left of the Left: Democrats and Social Democrats in Challenging Times*, Durham, NC: Duke University Press, pp 89–115.

Rueda, David (2007). *Social Democracy Inside Out: Partisanship and Labor Market Policy in Industrialized Democracies*, Oxford: Oxford University Press.

Schlozman, Kay, and Verba, Sidney (1979). *Injury to Insult*, Cambridge, MA: Harvard University Press.

Socialdemokraterna (1999). *Analys av valet 1998*, Stockholm: Socialdemokraterna.

Stephens, John (1979). *The Transition from Capitalism to Socialism*, London: Macmillan.

Svallfors, Stefan (2006). *The Moral Economy of Class: Class and Attitudes in Comparative Perspective*, Stanford, CA: Stanford University Press.

Swank, Duane, Martin, Cathie Jo, and Thelen, Kathleen (2008). "Institutional Change and the Politics of Social Solidarity in Advanced Industrial Democracies," paper presented at the annual meeting of the American Political Science Association, Boston (August 28–31, 2008).

Widfeldt, Anders (1995). "The Swedish Parliamentary Election of 1994," *Electoral Studies*, 15(2): 206–212.

Widfeldt, Anders (2003). "Sweden," *European Journal of Political Research*, 42(7–8): 1091–1101.

Widfeldt, Anders (2007a). "Sweden," *European Journal of Political Research*, 46(7–8): 1118–1126.

Widfeldt, Anders (2007b). "The Swedish Parliamentary Election of 2006," *Electoral Studies*, 26(4): 820–823.

Widfeldt, Anders, and Pierre, Jon (1995). "Sweden," *European Journal of Political Research*, 28(3–4): 477–485.

13

HOW RICH COUNTRIES COPE WITH DEINDUSTRIALIZATION

PATRICK EMMENEGGER, SILJA HÄUSERMANN, BRUNO PALIER, AND MARTIN SEELEIB-KAISER

R ising inequality throughout the Organisation for Economic Co-operation and Development (OECD) countries has been the starting point of this book. Throughout the different chapters in this volume, we have explored to what extent growing inequality is related to processes of dualization, that is, a widening, deepening, or the creation of new insider-outsider divides. This book provides evidence that growing inequalities between insiders and outsiders in deindustrializing labor markets are shaped—sometimes even exacerbated—by public policies, leading to social divides that change the distributional profile of these societies. In light of these findings, we argue that the past two or three decades can be characterized in many countries as "the age of dualization." The sweeping development of different forms of dualization and insider-outsider divides also shows how strongly the processes of division in the realms of labor markets, social policy, and political representation are linked. Dualization is certainly not the only driver of increasing inequality, but because of this encompassing development evidenced in this book, we consider dualization one of the most important current trends affecting developed societies.

However, the extent and forms of dualization that we observe vary greatly across countries. Our comparative perspective provides insights into why some countries witness lower levels of insider-outsider divides, whereas for others, they have become a core characteristic. Most importantly, the comparisons presented in this book point to the crucial importance of politics and political choice in driving and shaping the social outcomes of deindustrialization. Governments "cope" in different ways with deindustrialization. Hence, while increased structural labor market divides can be found across all countries, governments have a strong responsibility in shaping the distributive consequences of these labor market changes. Insider-outsider divides are not a straightforward consequence of deindustrialization, but rather the result of policy, that is, of political choice. This is the main finding of the analyses presented in this book, and it has important political implications.

In this final chapter, we provide a transversal reading of the insights we have gained in this volume in order to answer the key questions we set out in the introduction to this book. They can be summarized into four sets of questions that we will discuss sequentially: (1) Who are the outsiders? What divides do we observe cross-nationally and to what extent are they new or different from the ones that have characterized our societies throughout the postwar era? (2) What is driving dualization and insider-outsider divides? What are the mechanisms behind new and/or growing insider-outsider inequalities? (3) What is specific to our approach and to our understanding of the "age of dualization"? And finally (4), based on the findings of the chapters, we speculate about the future development of dualized societies: Are they on road to ever more inequality, marginalization, and social exclusion, or can we expect new equilibria to form and to last?

WHO ARE THE OUTSIDERS? DUALIZATION AND INSIDER-OUTSIDER DIVIDES ACROSS COUNTRIES

Dualization is a process that is characterized by the differential treatment of insiders and outsiders. Hence, the definition of who we consider to be insiders and outsiders affects our analysis of the spread and extent of dualization a great deal. On a general level, and in line with the political science literature on insider-outsider divides (Rueda 2005; King and Rueda 2008; Emmenegger 2009; Häusermann and Schwander 2009), we have defined insiders and outsiders on the basis of their labor market position. While insiders typically benefit from standard employment relations, outsiders are often either unemployed or in employment relationships typically characterized by low levels of pay, social benefits, and employment protection. Outsiders are thus those individuals who incur a particularly high risk of being in atypical employment or unemployment. Seeleib-Kaiser et al. (in Chapter 7 of this volume) use a somewhat different conceptualization because of their focus on social protection dualisms. They define social protection insiders as individuals covered either through comprehensive public/statutory social protection or those whose public/statutory entitlements are complemented or supplemented by private/occupational social protection to a level that maintains living standards. In contrast, outsiders are defined as those that would have to rely on modest (largely means-tested) public provision, primarily intended to ameliorate poverty.

One may argue that dualization is nothing new, since people in non-standard employment or unemployment have always been less protected, less paid, and less valued than the core workforce. In this sense, there have always been insiders and outsiders, and institutional dualism was always a source of inequality and social divides. This is certainly true, but we maintain that the recent decades differ from previous periods in at least four respects that are distinctive to the context of deindustrialization: the extent of people affected, the composition of outsiders, the saliency or visibility of dualization, and the political sources of dualization.

First, atypical employment and (long-term) unemployment have become much more widespread in deindustrializing societies. Throughout the OECD, average unemployment levels have increased since the early 1970s by 5 to 10 percentage points and have more or less stabilized between 5 and 15 percent since the 1980s. Similarly, the share of atypical employment in the overall OECD workforce (part-time and fixed-term combined) has grown from an average of around 10 percent to country-specific levels of 25 to 35 percent.[1] This increase is a consequence of both structural job growth in the service sector and political choice (cf. labor market flexibilization, as illustrated by Eichhorst and Marx in Chapter 4 of this volume).

The second specific aspect about the group of outsiders we are dealing with in the "age of dualization" is its socio-structural composition, especially with regard to women and young people. Due to societal change and changing family patterns, women have entered the labor market in increasing numbers, struggling to reconcile work and family life. Throughout the OECD, women cluster in sectors and occupations that are particularly strongly affected by atypical employment. Also, labor market entrants experience particular difficulties entering stable, standard employment, especially in Southern Europe. One may argue that women and young workers have always been more loosely integrated into labor markets than older men, but the decisive difference between the industrial age and the present is that especially women are less and less protected through their families and derived benefits, which have been particular important in corporatist conservative welfare systems.

This point relates to the third argument why we think that the "age of dualization" is new and specific, that is, its visibility and saliency. Until the 1970s, many outsiders were "invisible" to the political arena, since marriage and family arrangements provided protection. Their labor market situation was simply not politicized. And while this non-politicization to some extent still holds for the large share of immigrant workers among outsiders (see Emmenegger and Careja in Chapter 6 of this volume), welfare risks of female workers have become a salient issue on the political agenda, especially in the wake of growing family instability (on this topic, see the new social risk literature, e.g., Armingeon and Bonoli 2006).

The saliency of dualization and insider–outsider divides is also related to the fourth aspect that makes them specific: their political origins. Not only do low levels of economic growth make it more difficult for governments to compensate labor market inequalities, but the development of non-standard labor contracts has been actively facilitated by government policies, as activation measures often define any job as suitable, irrespective of its terms and conditions, and employment policies create new, more flexible types of work contracts.

In sum, outsiderness in the "age of dualization" differs from previous periods because it affects a larger portion of the workforce, as well as different groups of people in more precarious social situations than in the past; additionally, the deepening, widening, and creation of new divides between insiders and outsiders have been the result of deliberate deregulation of labor markets. Hence, while divides between insiders and outsiders have always been part of industrial labor markets, they now have risen in salience and constitute a core element of labor markets in deindustrializing economies.

Who are these outsiders and what do they have in common? Some societal groups are overrepresented among outsiders in all countries studied: women, young labor market participants, low-skilled workers, especially in the service sector, immigrants and workers of migrant origin. These groups are more likely to be unemployed or atypically employed, and they are more likely to be poor and to suffer from insufficient social rights. The available evidence suggests that their inferior status is persistent over time. Indeed, if people were continuously shifting back and forth between insider and outsider status, the disadvantages of outsiders in the social and political realm would not necessarily present a social problem. However, this is not the case. As Tomlinson and Walker (in Chapter 3 of this volume) show, those prone to poverty in the present are much more likely to experience or remain in poverty in future periods. The lasting structural disadvantages are what outsiders have in common. And they imply that policies dealing with insiders and outsiders must be adapted. Either they need to target these groups specifically, or they need to develop a new universalism that is able to cover both types of labor market situation.

However, even though similar societal groups are affected by the risk of being outsiders across all countries studied in this volume, we observe important variations along at least three dimensions. First, as shown by Häusermann and Schwander (in Chapter 2 of this volume), the composition and extent of insiders and outsiders differs across welfare regimes: in the Nordic and Continental countries, gender is the most important dimension, while in Southern Europe outsiderness concerns mostly young labor market participants, and in the Anglo-Saxon countries, outsiders are predominantly found among the low-skilled. Only immigrants seem to be an important source of cheap labor in all countries (Emmenegger and Careja, Chapter 6 of this volume). Also, some countries are more affected by dualization than others: Häusermann and Schwander (Chapter 2 of this volume) as well as Seeleib-Kaiser et al. (Chapter 7 of this volume) demonstrate that Liberal welfare regimes account for the highest share of labor market and social protection outsiders in Western democracies. However, in all Western European countries, between 40 and 53 percent of workers are employed in occupations that are strongly affected by unemployment and/or atypical employment.

Second, the actual forms of atypical employment that characterize the country-specific insider-outsider divide differ, since countries have used different pathways to circumvent the existing rules and costs associated with standard work contracts. For instance, Eichhorst and Marx (in Chapter 4 of this volume) document five different paths taken by Continental European countries in the realm of the private service sector: (1) defection from permanent contracts plays a particular role in labor market dualization in France and the Netherlands; (2) defection from full-time jobs is particularly pronounced in the Netherlands, but also Austria and Germany; (3) defection from dependent employment in the form of precarious self-employment is widespread in Belgium and France; (4) increasing levels of wage dispersion to integrate low-skilled workers into the labor market are used in Austria and Germany; and (5) large government-sponsored labor-cheapening schemes have been developed in Belgium and France. In a similar vein, Kroos and Gottschall (in Chapter 5 of this volume) document the changing employment structures in the public social services in France and Germany. They contrast the "high road" of social service provision and employment in France with the more semi-professional "low road" in Germany. Given these different paths toward labor cost reduction, the "typical" outsider actually looks quite different, depending on the importance of fixed- and part-time work, precarious self-employment, and low-wage work in a particular country. This heterogeneity of the composition of insiders and outsiders accounts for the fact that both inequalities and possible policy strategies against insider-outsider divides are largely country-specific. Nevertheless, the different manifestations of the insider-outsider divide are part of the same dualization trend, because the social and political disadvantages that outsiders encounter are similar across countries.

Third, countries differ in the extent to which labor market segmentation between insiders and outsiders actually translates into social divides. Indeed, welfare states can either compensate inequalities between insiders and outsiders, or they can reproduce or even reinforce them. In this sense, dualization does not necessarily lead to inequality, if outsiders are entitled to generous welfare rights (whether they are specifically targeted at them, or whether they are the same as for insiders). In this respect, Häusermann and Schwander (Chapter 2 of this volume) document that the welfare and tax systems of France, Germany, and Spain not only reproduce, but even exacerbate insider-outsider divides: while France and Sweden, for example, have very similar average income differences between insiders and outsiders before taxes and transfers, the French welfare system contributes to an increase of these differences by 7.9 percentage points (up to 40.4 percent), while the Swedish welfare system diminishes these differences by 7.1 percentage points (down to 24.9 percent). This shows how tremendously important policies are in shaping insider-outsider divides; however, it does not imply that outsiders are worst off in absolute terms in those countries that exacerbate these divides. For example, while the German welfare system accentuates income-differences between insiders and outsiders, it is nonetheless more successful in preventing the onset of poverty than the British welfare system (Tomlinson and Walker, Chapter 3 of this volume). This can be explained by the fact that, despite its conservative-corporatist character, the German welfare system has a considerably higher social wage than the British welfare system.

Despite the country variations that we have evidenced throughout this book, it is clear that dualization and insider-outsider divides have amplified throughout the OECD. Today's outsiders differ from labor market outsiders in past periods in terms of numbers, socio-structural characteristics, and political visibility. In addition, they, more so than in the past, share an additional characteristic, that is, participation in the labor market. Indeed, in Continental Europe specifically, outsiders were traditionally kept outside the labor market, which caused the syndrome of "welfare without work" that dominated the discourse of the 1990s. In the "age of dualization," outsiders are participating in the labor market, as they have been in the past in the Anglo-Saxon and Nordic countries. However, they do so in inferior jobs deviating from the standard employment relationship that has dominated much of the post–World War II era. Thereby, the divide of the workforce into insiders and outsiders has become a common phenomenon throughout the developed world. The break with the past is strongest in the Continental world, which relied most heavily on standard employment relationships in the past (hence the emphasis within this book on these countries). However, the chapters in this book demonstrate that the processes and outcomes that characterize the "age of dualization" transcend Continental Europe and apply to all deindustrializing countries.

CREATING NEW DIVIDES: DUALIZATION AND POLITICAL CHOICE

What are the drivers of dualization? Why do we see new and increasing insider-outsider divides in most countries? And why are these divides deeper in some countries than in others? Which political actors are deepening and widening institutional dualisms, and which actors are trying to prevent dualization or to smoothen its distributional consequences? Surely, the processes of deindustrialization as well as globalization are common structural trends that have unsettled previous arrangements. However, the resulting insider-outsider divides differ across regimes (see Häusermann and Schwander, Chapter 2 of this volume); and even similar countries have various options as to how they deal with these challenges (Eichhorst and Marx, Chapter 4 of this volume; Seeleib-Kaiser et al., Chapter 7 of this volume). This variation points to the importance of the politics of dualization, that is, the actors and coalitions driving institutional change. While the chapters in this book shed some light on the common political patterns underlying dualization, they also reveal a complex picture. Dualization is often facilitated by complex cross-class coalitions, which may both exacerbate or smoothen social divides resulting from dualization. In the following, we review the role of the key actors in the politics of dualization: employers, trade unions, and political parties.

Throughout the chapters of this book, we have identified how important the role of employers and trade unions has been in shaping the specific dualization trajectories. Employers as protagonists for cost containment, labor market flexibilization, and limiting social protection have been politically crucial for dualization processes (cf. Seeleib-Kaiser et al. 2011). However, it should not be neglected that policy makers often prefer packages that do not directly challenge the institutional core, as pointed out by Eichhorst and Marx (Chapter 4 of this volume). Whether or not and in what ways employers are successful with their demands for labor market flexibilization largely depends on prior institutional arrangements, governance structures and power resources, as well as the specific economic circumstances.

While employers are consistently pro-dualization, the role of trade unions is not only more complex, but probably even more important, as their support can be pivotal for the formation of a political coalition facilitating dualization. The ambiguity of trade unions' position toward dualization must first be linked to the overall context of deindustrialization: the expansion of private service sector employment as well as atypical employment has had an overall negative effect on union density, as it has contributed to the erosion of the traditional base of unions in the manufacturing sector, putting unions in a largely defensive position. In a number of countries, labor unions have thus agreed to various labor market and social policy reforms negatively affecting outsiders through concession bargaining, while maintaining the level of protection for insiders (either through the defense of preexisting social insurance arrangements, or through the introduction of new [semi-]private insurance complements). In other words, unions, especially traditional unions in the manufacturing sector (Palier and Thelen, Chapter 9 of this volume), as well as corporate unions in East-Asian economies (Peng, Chapter 10 of this volume) have acted as consenters, facilitating dualization (for the differentiation between protagonists and consenters cf. Korpi 2006). These cross-class alliances, primarily within the manufacturing sector and with the support of the state, have in various countries contributed to "saving" the manufacturing base of the economy at the expense of outsiders, primarily employed in the service sectors.

However, as Obinger et al. (Chapter 8 of this volume) demonstrate, it would be wrong to simply characterize trade unions as "dualizers." Leftist corporatism, that is, a corporate arrangement between a leftist government with strong and encompassing interest organizations, can also mitigate processes of dualization. Particularly encompassing labor unions can to some extent overcome the core organizational dilemma faced by many unions, whereby member-ship interests of more narrow unions in the short term cannot be reconciled with their long-term organizational interests.[2] Consequently, encompassing unions may also represent the interests of outsiders (for a similar argument, see Anderson 2001). As Clegg (Chapter 11 of this volume) clearly demonstrates in his comparison of Belgian and French unemployment protection, the participa-tion of unions in the unemployment benefit administration acts as a "recruiting sergeant" for Belgian trade unions. Thereby, Belgian unions acquired a very encompassing membership and were thus interested in a more universalistic and encompassing organization of unemployment benefits. In contrast, French unions only represent about 10 percent of the workforce, but play a very strong role in the administration of unemployment benefits. As a consequence, Belgian unions have advocated more "solidaristic" reforms of unemployment policies than the French unions. Consequently, where unions are narrow and weak, they are more likely to play a dualizing role, defending the interests of insiders at the expense of outsiders. Similarly, as Kroos and Gottschall (Chapter 5 of this volume) show, union weakness in the social services combined with a declin-ing financial commitment by the state has strongly sharpened dualization of employment relationships in the German third sector.

Finally, the role of political parties is equally complex as the role of trade unions. Overall, the chapters in this book do not report strong differences between left- and right-wing governments with regard to dualization. Palier and Thelen observe similar developments in Germany and France, while the former was governed by a Left-Green coalition during much of the discussed reforms and the latter by a Center-Right government. Similarly, Peng ana-lyzes politics in Japan and Korea quasi-independently of the composition of government, and Obinger et al. are unable to identify a common pattern of party differences regarding dualization in Austria, Sweden, and New Zealand. Their results seem to suggest that the role of particular governments is much more situational and context-driven: favorable economic conditions prevented a hardening of insider-outsider divides in the case of the Austrian adjustment pathway, whereas in Sweden economic problem pressure and the decline of cor-poratism have provided the backdrop for the Swedish Social Democrats to opt for reforms that primarily protected insider interests (Obinger et al., Chapter 8 of this volume). Hence, this book shows that trade unions or left-wing par-ties cannot generally be characterized as "pro-insider" or "pro-outsider." Their stance on dualization depends on the context, their political coalition partners, and their electoral and strategic calculations. In this respect, it is crucial to point to the dilemma that dualization can create for Social Democratic parties. When the Swedish Social Democrats, for instance, chose to advocate insider interests at the expense of outsiders, this had significant electoral ramifications. Lindvall and Rueda (Chapter 12 of this volume) suggest that when mainstream left-wing parties choose to focus on issues that are primarily relevant to insiders (as the Swedish Social Democrats did in the election of 1998), they are punished by outsiders; however, a strategy reconciling the interests of insiders and outsiders is not necessarily the best option for Social Democrats either, as it may lead to the defection of labor market insiders to Center-Right parties in unfavorable economic times. In this sense, the authors argue, Social Democratic parties face a new electoral dilemma: whether they prevent or advocate dualization, they alienate one part of their (potential) electorate. This electoral dilemma may explain why the partisan politics of dualization are hard to grasp: party strategies can go either way and they can shift over time.

A MULTIDIMENSIONAL APPROACH TO DUALIZATION

The previous section has argued that dualization is not just a structural development, but rather a consequence of politics and policies, which affect different social groups in very distinct ways. This is a crucial insight because it sets our qualification of growing job insecurity, welfare restructuring, and income inequalities in developed societies apart from other characterizations of these trends.

Many of the terms and concepts that have been used to characterize the past 30 years—such as "post-industrialism" (Esping-Andersen 1999), deregulation of labor markets, retrenchment of the welfare state (Pierson 2001), or the "silver age of the welfare state" (Taylor-Gooby 2002)—use the "golden era" of exceptional economic growth, characterized by full employment and expansion of the welfare state, as their reference point. In addition to providing an all too "rosy" characterization of the "Trente Glorieuses," especially when taking into account the living standards and poverty rates in the 1950s or even 1960s, or the dependent condition of most women, these concepts are quite limited in contributing to a better understanding of our recent past and present.

In this book, we characterize the new economic and social realities not only in relation to the past, but as driven by a specific dynamic and logic. Based on an analysis of income inequalities, labor market developments, social rights, and political representations, as well as labor market policies, welfare state reforms, and their linkages, we conceptualize the past three decades as "the age of dualization," which is characterized by a widening, deepening, and creation of institutional dualisms and social divides. This book combines the analyses of structure, policies, and politics to achieve an encompassing understanding of dualization in developed countries. The chapters in the first part of this book have combined analyses of income distribution and their dynamics with analyses of the development of labor market structures, and with an analysis of social rights development. As a result, we know who the losers of recent developments are, where they work, what type of jobs and social protection they receive. In the second part of the book, we introduced public policies into the analyses, demonstrating that the witnessed socioeconomic developments do not solely reflect "automatic" market adjustments, but have been actively facilitated and shaped by public policies. Whether these policies have reinforced or mitigated the dualization trend differs across countries, depending on what could be called "the politics of dualization."

Our multidimensional approach allows us to overcome the limits of analyses with a narrower focus that have dominated much of the recent political and academic debates. Focusing solely on income distribution (as the OECD "growing unequal" study [2008] does, for instance) an increase in inequalities can be ascertained. Analyzing labor market developments (as do Goos et al. 2009), one may come to the conclusion of polarizing labor markets. Scrutinizing social rights and social policies, observers often identify a general "crisis" of the welfare state (Huber and Stephens 2001), retrenchment, and potentially a recalibration of social policies (Pierson 2001), without sufficiently acknowledging the interactions of social policies with labor market developments. In other words, social policies can echo and reinforce developments on the labor market or on the contrary counterbalance the consequences of deteriorating labor market conditions. Our comprehensive analysis of structural trends, policies, and politics shows clearly that recent trends do not affect all social groups in a similar way. Of course, we do not claim to be the first ones to highlight increasing divides in society, as our review of the literature in the introduction emphasizes. As shown in the first part of this conclusion, we however claim to have been able to provide a clearer view of the "losers" of recent socioeconomic developments and a better understanding of the insider-outsider divides. Moreover, we claim that part of the originality in our approach is to highlight the role of policies and politics in shaping the dualization processes.

By emphasizing the role of politics we stress the importance of political responsibility and choice. Indeed, a striking characteristic of recent accounts of increased inequalities or social divides is that they are often perceived as an "unavoidable" mechanism. The OECD's (2008) report on increasing inequalities does not aim to explain why inequalities have grown over the past decades. Goos et al.'s (2009) hypotheses for explaining job polarization are based on mere market mechanisms (routinization, off-shoring, or growing income inequalities). They eventually understand job polarization as a correlate to technological progress that is progressively (and apparently mechanically) "replacing 'routine' labor which tends to be clerical and craft jobs in the middle of the wage distribution" (Goos et al. 2009: 58).

Even prominent political economy scholars seem to have lost confidence in the impact and effectiveness of policies. Many of those who have pointed to increased insider-outsider divides as a likely feature of socioeconomic development in Continental Europe have done so not necessarily by referring to market mechanisms, but to institutional path dependency. Esping-Andersen (1996) as well as Iversen and Wren (1998) assume that insider-outsider divides will increase in Continental welfare systems in face of deindustrialization, mainly because of their traditional institutional settings. Their prediction that labor would continue to be shed because of the logic of the corporatist conservative welfare model has, however, proven to be wrong. What our chapters show is that, starting in the early 1990s (and in some countries even sooner), new employment policies, accompanied by important welfare reforms (especially in unemployment and old age insurance), have diverted the Continental European (as well as East Asian) models from their traditional routes. As shown by Eichhorst and Marx, Kroos and Gottschall, Seeleib-Kaiser et al., Palier and Thelen (all in this volume), corporatist conservative systems were able to overcome the "welfare without work" problem of the 1990s, by creating many non-standards jobs and new types of social beneficiaries. As Eichhorst and Marx put it, "we can speak of a common trend in Continental Europe to redefine labor market outsiders: while they were typically kept outside the labor market in the 1990s (as expressed in high shares of long-term unemployment and inactivity), they now increasingly participate in the labor market, but in inferior jobs that deviate from the rule of the standard employment relationship." The social partners and the political actors have played an important role in this process. "Policy makers and—even more importantly—economic actors created different types of non-standard employment, thereby effectively circumventing or converting existing regulations, without dismantling the institutional core. These new divides between different types of jobs and workers also produced new inequalities in terms of remuneration, job stability and social security coverage" (Eichhorst and Marx, Chapter 4 of in this volume).

Common to all policies that have facilitated and reinforced dualization processes is that they have been inspired by a "neoliberal" agenda, which was only partially implemented, that is, only for some parts of the workforce, but not for others. The chapters analyzing employment policies show that the job strategy advocated by the OECD in the beginning of the 1990s[3] has been implemented primarily for the secondary labor market, while job protection was largely maintained or even increased in some countries for those working in the (shrinking) core sectors and benefiting from typical employment contracts (see Eichhorst and Marx, Palier and Thelen, and Peng in this volume). In a similar vein, retrenchment and privatization of social policies have primarily affected particularly vulnerable segments of the workforce in corporatist conservative welfare systems, as, for example, Seeleib-Kaiser et al. and Palier and Thelen (both in this volume) demonstrate.

This is probably where we differ from a view that identifies recent developments as a general trend toward liberalization (such as in Streeck's [2009] account of the transformation of German capitalism). Whereas these accounts identify a general transformation of capitalism, eventually eroding security and benefits for all members of the workforce, we argue that liberalization was partial, as it has been primarily applied to "new" jobs in the tertiary sector, while an ever-shrinking core of insiders continues to enjoy relatively generous employment and social protection. In some countries, it can be argued that this strategy of partial flexibilization and liberalization is (explicitly) aimed at preserving the logic of economic and social systems relying on manufacturing/production industry even in an era of deindustrialization. This strategy of "saving the industry" is clearly at work in the cases of Germany and France (Palier and Thelen, Chapter 9 of this volume) and in the case of Japan and South Korea (Peng, Chapter 10 of this volume).

WILL DUALIZATION LAST?

It remains, of course, an open question whether this type of dualistic structure of labor market and social protection policies will be sustained in the future. Regardless of its future, though, a first point to be made here is that it has characterized the socioeconomic developments of the largest Continental European countries as well as Japan and South Korea for the last two to three decades. But in the longer run, one may ask if dualization is only a transitory stage toward liberalization. Streeck relevantly asks "why the fringe should not continue to eat into the core until nothing much remains of it?" (Streeck 2010: 512). In other words: Why should the extension and marginalization of outsiders not continue until no insiders are left? If that was happening, dualization would merely be a transitory phenomenon in a much more general trend toward liberalization. Even if we cannot directly answer this question on the future of developed capitalist economies, we can ponder the various arguments for and against stability of dualized policies and labor markets. Two main dimensions—one political and one economic—should be looked at here.

Politically, two arguments suggest that dualization and insider-outsider divides may last: a clear segmentation of insiders and outsiders in the labor market and institutional feedback effects. First, one may argue that the fringe is not really eating the core, since the outsiders are not competing directly with the insiders for jobs, income, and social rights: as shown in particular by Häusermann and Schwander, Eichhorst and Marx, Emmenegger and Careja, as well as Kroos and Gottschall (all in this volume), outsiders do not have the same occupations, usually do not work in the same economic sectors (male blue-collar workers, e.g., are not outsiders in Continental Europe), they do not have the same skills, and they sometimes lack citizenship. Because of this rather clear occupational segmentation of the labor force into insiders and outsiders, outsiders do not directly increase the cost of the insider workforce: this means that outsiders do not work in the same jobs for less money, they work in different jobs. Hence, two different "labor market regimes" may coexist alongside each other, one for the insiders and one for the outsiders, as is reflected in the idea of primary and secondary labor markets that are not necessarily merging.

A second mechanism that may stabilize dualistic patterns is institutional. As we argue, liberalization and flexibilization have been targeted at atypical workers, while the shrinking core has remained largely protected. In addition, outsiders are clearly less active politically. As demonstrated by Häusermann and Schwander (Chapter 2 of this volume), in Continental and Southern Europe "outsiders are clearly, strongly and significantly less represented in organized labor" than insiders. "The labor market segmentation thus translates into clear differences in terms of power resources." At least for corporatist conservative countries, one can then hypothesize a self-reinforcement effect again related to power asymmetries between insiders and outsiders: the worse the conditions of outsiders, the less they will mobilize and organize. The greater the difference in social and political resources between insiders and outsiders, the more able the insiders will be to secure political power and to secure their status.

However, one could in principle imagine a tipping point, at which outsiders outnumber insiders, develop a collective identity, and are strong enough politically to effectively mobilize and demand policy changes. Although theoretically an option, this does not seem to be very realistic. The *Linkspartei* in Germany, or forms of working class authoritarianism in France, Switzerland, Austria, and so on (in the form of right-wing populist parties) seem to be mobilizations of insiders protecting their privileges from the industrial age, rather than outsider mobilization (Kriesi et al. 2008). Moreover, outsiders are a very heterogeneous group socio-structurally, which makes their mobilization difficult and more unlikely (Kitschelt and Rehm 2006), despite their persistently disadvantaged status.

Undeniably though, some of the current dualization policies are undermining the privileged status of insiders in the future. In many European countries, future pensions will be much lower for most of the pensioners (see Seeleib-Kaiser et al., Chapter 7 of this volume, and Palier 2010 for pension reforms in the other Bismarckian welfare states). Also, as we have shown, in many cases such as Germany, France, Sweden, Japan, or South Korea, new entrants in the labor market, even in core sector industries, are—upon entering the labor market—usually offered much less protected conditions than the older generations in the same occupations. In the long run, once the older insiders will have left the labor market, the new ones will experience new, more flexible, and more precarious employment systems. In that sense, part of the insiders will disappear through generational transformations, thereby possibly lowering the dualistic structure of current labor markets. But it will take another 30 years or so to see this demographic transition unfold.

Economically, business may have an interest in stabilizing dualistic structures. As we have shown, employers are important actors of the dualization processes (see also Seeleib-Kaiser et al. 2011). Employers will continue to forge alliances with insiders as long as they depend on their skill sets and high levels of productivity. The German export-oriented strategy of wage moderation and diversified quality production (Streeck 1991), coupled with an increasingly dualized workforce, seems to suggest that dualization can contribute to an economic success story. As long as this strategy is politically and economically viable in the domestic and international contexts, employers will have an interest in protecting a core of highly productive and skilled workers, as these constitute a main element of their comparative advantage vis-à-vis competitors in low-wage economies.

Although the future is uncertain, the responses to the financial, economic, and social crisis seem to suggest further dualization (at least in some countries). Although the unemployment rate among OECD countries has risen to an average of 8.7 percent in early 2010, the development has been very uneven. Increases in unemployment have been particularly high in Ireland, Spain, and the United States and comparatively limited in the Netherlands, Japan, and the United Kingdom. In Germany the unemployment rate has even been declining more recently and is at its lowest level since the early 1990s. What has been unusual in this crisis is that on average within the OECD "employment has fallen significantly more for men than for women, probably due to the sectoral profile of the recession (i.e. especially large employment losses in mining, manufacturing, and construction)" (OECD 2010: 18). This seems to indicate that the Great Recession of 2008–2009 has had a negative impact on insider employment. However, the OECD also reports that in a number of countries short-time work schemes have played a crucial role in largely preserving insider jobs during the crisis. As highlighted in the OECD report, "the positive impact of Short-Time Work was limited to workers with permanent contracts, further increasing labor market segmentation between workers in regular jobs and workers in part-time jobs" (OECD 2010: 19). In that sense, the crisis seems to have strengthened the dualization processes even further in a number of countries.

However, dualization is not a functional necessity. As several chapters in this volume show, governments have room for political maneuver. Even within the most corporatist conservative systems, some countries have been able to implement policies designed to smoothen the effects of dualization. As Peng (Chapter 10 of this volume) shows, Japan and South Korea have enacted new social policies to offset some of the negative effects of the partial liberalization and flexibilization of the labor market. Similarly, several contributions show that, despite similar economic and political dynamics, France is still less dualized than Germany, but more dualized compared to Belgium in the realm of unemployment protection. However, the most interesting cases of "smoothened dualization" in Europe are probably Austria, the Netherlands, and Switzerland, providing effective minimum social standards for outsiders.

More egalitarian policies are complicated by the difficulties to form sustainable political coalitions between insiders and outsiders on the various issues encapsulated within the dualization processes in rich democracies. A possible solution could be a social investment strategy (Morel, Palier, and Palme 2011). Investments in child-care, human capital, education, and lifelong learning could benefit both insiders and outsiders and might provide the glue for a new universalistic policy orientation. Not only could such a strategy bridge the differences between insiders and outsiders, but also, if successfully implemented, it could potentially contribute to socially sustainable economic growth.

NOTES

1   Numbers are based on OECD Employment and Labour Market Statistics, Labour Force Statistics, http://new.sourceoecd.org/
2   E.g., unions in declining sectors face the dilemma of presenting their members' immediate interest, while potentially sacrificing their long-term organizational interest of organizing new members. More encompassing unions representing a broader base do not face this dilemma.
3   Obinger et al. (Chapter 8 of this volume) describe the OECD job strategy as follows: "The 1994 OECD *Jobs Study*, for instance, was still largely concerned with lifting the overall level of employment by means of neo-liberal policy recipes. Most recommendations concerned the deregulation of the labor market by allowing more flexible working time arrangements, lower unemployment benefit levels, the deregulation of wage setting, the phasing-out of favorable early retirement rules and so on (OECD 1994)."

REFERENCES

Anderson, Karen M. (2001). "The Politics of Retrenchment in a Social Democratic Welfare State: Reform of Swedish Pensions and Unemployment Insurance," *Comparative Political Studies*, 34(9): 1063–1091.

Armingeon, Klaus, and Bonoli, Giuliano (2006). *The Politics of Post-Industrial Welfare States: Adapting Post-War Policies to New Social Risks*, London: Routledge.

Emmenegger, Patrick (2009). "Barriers to Entry: Insider/Outsider Politics and the Political Determinants of Job Security Regulations," *Journal of European Social Policy*, 19(2): 131–146.

Esping-Andersen, Gøsta (1996). "Welfare States without Work: The Impasse of Labour Shedding and Familialism in Continental European Social Policy," in Esping-Andersen, Gøsta (ed.), *Welfare States in Transition: National Adaptations in Global Economies*, London: Sage, pp. 66–87.

Esping-Andersen, Gøsta (1999). *Social Foundations of Postindustrial Economies*, Oxford: Oxford University Press.

Goos, Maarten, Manning, Alan, and Salomons, Anna (2009). "Job Polarization in Europe," *American Economic Review*, 99(2): 58–63.

Häusermann, Silja, and Schwander, Hanna (2009). "Identifying Outsiders Across Countries: Similarities and Differences in the Patterns of Dualization," RECWOWE *Working Paper* 09/2009.

Huber, Evelyn, and Stephens, John D. (2001). *Development and Crisis of the Welfare State. Parties and Policies in Global Markets*, Chicago, IL, and London: University of Chicago Press.

Iversen, Torben, and Wren, Anne (1998). "Equality, Employment, and Budgetary Restraint: The Trilemma of the Service Economy," *World Politics*, 50(4): 507–546.

King, Desmond, and Rueda, David (2008). "Cheap Labor: The New Politics of 'Bread and Roses' in Industrial Democracies," *Perspectives on Politics*, 6(2): 279–297.

Kitschelt, Herbert, and Rehm, Philipp (2006). "New Social Risk and Political Preferences," in Armingeon, Klaus, and Bonoli, Giuliano (eds.), *The Politics of Post-Industrial Welfare States: Adapting Postwar Policies to New Social Risks*, London: Routledge, pp. 52–82.

Korpi, Walter (2006). "Power Resources and Employer-Centered Approaches in Explanations of Welfare States and Varieties of Capitalism," *World Politics*, 58(2): 167–206.

Kriesi, Hanspeter, Grande, Edgar, Lachat, Romain, Dolezal, Martin, Bornschier, Simon, and Frey, Timotheus (2008). *West European Politics in the Age of Globalization: Six Countries Compared*, New York: Cambridge University Press.

Morel, Nathalie, Palier, Bruno, and Palme, Joakim (2011). *Towards a Social Investment Welfare State? Ideas, Policies and Challenges*, Bristol: Policy Press.

OECD (1994). *The OECD Jobs Study*, Paris: OECD.

OECD (2008). *Growing Unequal? Income Distribution and Poverty in OECD Countries*, Paris: OECD.

OECD (2010). *Employment Outlook 2010*, Paris: OECD.

Palier, Bruno (2010). *A Long Good Bye to Bismarck? The Politics of Welfare Reforms in Continental Europe*, Amsterdam: Amsterdam University Press.

Pierson, Paul (2001). *The New Politics of the Welfare State*, New York: Oxford University Press.

Rueda, David (2005). "Insider-Outsider Politics in Industrialized Democracies: The Challenge to Social Democratic Parties," *American Political Science Review*, 99(1): 61–74.

Seeleib-Kaiser, Martin, Saunders, Adam, and Naczyk, Marek (2011). "Social Protection Dualism, Deindustrialization and Cost Containment," in Brady, David (ed.), *Comparing European Workers Part B: Policies and Institutions. Research in the Sociology of Work* Volume 22, Bingley: Emerald, pp. 83–118.

Streeck, Wolfgang (1991). "On the Institutional Conditions of Diversified Quality Production," in Matzner, Egon and Streeck, Wolfgang (eds.), *Beyond*

Keynesianism: The Socio-Economics of Production and Full Employment, London: Edward Elgar, pp. 21–61.

Streeck, Wolfgang (2009). *Re-Forming Capitalism: Institutional Change in the German Political Economy,* Oxford: Oxford University Press.

Streeck, Wolfgang (2010). "The Fiscal Crisis Continues: From Liberalization to Consolidation," *Comparative European Politics,* 8(4): 505–514.

Taylor-Gooby, Peter (2002). "The *Silver Age of the Welfare State:* Perspectives on Resilience," *Journal of Social Policy,* 31(4): 597–621.

INDEX

321